Canning & Preserving

ALL-IN-ONE

FOR DUMMIES®

by Eve Adamson, Traci Cumbay, Karan Davis Cutler,
Suzanne DeJohn, Kathleen Fisher,
Theresa A. Husarik, Amy Jeanroy, Rob Ludlow,
Bryan Miller, Marty Nachel,
The National Gardening Association (NGA),
M. Brittain Phillips, Marie Rama, Tom Schneider,
Cheryl K. Smith, Karen Ward, Kimberly Willis,
Gerald D. Wootan, DO, M.Ed.

WILEY

John Wiley & Sons, Inc.

Canning & Preserving All-in-One For Dummies®

Published by
John Wiley & Sons, Inc.
111 River St.
Hoboken, NJ 07030-5774
www.wiley.com

WILEY

About the Authors

Eve Adamson is a *New York Times* best-selling author who has written or coauthored more than 50 books on food, cooking, dieting, and lifestyle subjects, including several other *For Dummies* guides, several books on the Mediterranean diet, and a book on craft beer. Eve is a member of the International Association of Culinary Professionals and a self-taught home cook who loves to travel and sample the cuisines of different regions and cultures. She lives in Iowa City with her family. To find out more about Eve, visit her website at www.eveadamson.com.

Traci Cumbay cooks and eats quite a bit and then writes about the experiences for publications in Indianapolis, Indiana, where she lives with her husband and son.

Karan Davis Cutler, a former magazine editor and newspaper columnist, is the author of seven other garden books. She publishes regularly in horticultural magazines and is an eight-time winner of the Quill & Trowel Award from the Garden Writers Association of America.

Suzanne DeJohn, a writer and horticulturist at the National Gardening Association for 14 years, now writes, gardens, and runs a pet-friendly B&B in northern Vermont.

Kathleen Fisher was an editor of *The American Gardener,* published by the American Horticultural Society, and a longtime newspaper reporter and magazine editor. The author of several books and many articles, she died in May 2005.

Theresa A. Husarik is a writer, photographer, crafter, fiber person, and animal lover who lives on a small plot far away from the heart of the city. When she is not tending to her brood (which includes llamas, alpacas, angora goats, cats, dogs, peacocks, and chickens), Theresa can usually be found either behind the computer writing something or in the craft room making something.

Amy Jeanroy has been canning and preserving foods for 20 years. She is passionate about filling the pantry with useful, delicious foods and creating healthy meals from her own small farm. Amy is a Master Gardener, Food writer for Foodista.com as well as an Herb Garden writer for About.com.

Rob Ludlow, his wife Emily, and their two beautiful daughters, Alana and April, are the perfect example of the suburban family with a small flock of backyard chickens. Like countless others, what started out as a fun hobby raising a few egg-laying hens has almost turned into an addiction. Rob owns and manages www.backyardchickens.com (BYC), the largest and fastest-growing community of chicken enthusiasts in the world.

Bryan Miller is a food and wine writer and a former restaurant critic for *The New York Times.* He has written and cowritten 11 books. In the past 25 years, he has received numerous awards, including three writing awards from the James Beard Foundation and the organization's prestigious Lifetime Achievement Award.

Marty Nachel is a freelance writer on beer and brewing. A former president of the Chicago Beer Society and founding member of the Brewers Of South Suburbia (B.O.S.S.) homebrew and beer appreciation club, Marty has been brewing his own award-winning beers since 1985. His articles have appeared in *All About Beer* magazine, *Brew Magazine, Brew Your Own* magazine, *Celebrator Beer News, Drink* magazine, and Epicurious.com. His first book on the microbrewing industry, *Beer Across America* (Storey Communications), was published in July 1995. Marty's second book, *Beer For Dummies* (IDG Books Worldwide, Inc.), followed in 1996.

The National Gardening Association (NGA) is committed to sustaining and renewing the fundamental links between people, plants, and the Earth. Founded in 1972 (as "Gardens for All") to spearhead the community garden movement, today's NGA promotes environmental responsibility, advances multidisciplinary learning and scientific literacy, and creates partnerships that restore and enhance communities. For more information about the National Gardening Association, write to 1100 Dorset St., South Burlington, VT 05403, or visit its website at www.garden.org or www.kidsgardening.org.

M. Brittain Phillips didn't used to think much about toxins, but after working with Dr. Wootan, he's not putting anything in his shopping cart without checking the label for high fructose corn syrup. (It's everywhere!) He studied biology and English at DePauw University, and he's happy to report that he finally found a way to combine the disciplines. He works and writes in Charleston, South Carolina.

Marie Rama grew up in the restaurant business surrounded by a large Italian family of food professionals and entrepreneurs. She has worked as a pastry chef, a recipe tester, and an account executive and spokesperson for national companies and associations, such as Tabasco Sauce, Korbel Champagne, and Sunkist Growers. In addition to *Cooking For Dummies,* Marie also wrote *Grilling For Dummies* (with John Mariani) and is working on a cookbook that celebrates the many uses and irresistible enticement of bacon. Marie has two sons, Nicholas and William, and lives in Yonkers, New York, with her husband and literary agent Mark Reiter.

Tom Schneider's passion for authentic barbecue arose during his high school days in Oklahoma and burgeoned over 20 years of uncovering traditional barbecue joints while traveling the United States. Tom is primarily a self-taught cook who, for the past decade, has leveraged his commitment to barbecue into award-winning barbecue recipes while competing in sanctioned barbecue competitions and formal barbecue judging. Tom is owner and pit master for Poppi-Q Bar-B-Que, a specialty catering business in the Indianapolis market.

Cheryl K. Smith has raised goats since 1998 when she got two Nigerian Dwarves. She published *Ruminations, the Nigerian Dwarf and Mini Dairy Goat Magazine* from 2001 through 2007 and published the book *Goat Health Care* (Karmadillo Press) in 2009. She has written for *Dairy Goat Journal, Countryside,* and other magazines. Cheryl served as legal counsel for the American Goat Society (AGS) from 2003 to 2005 and was on their board of directors from 2005 to 2009. She volunteers as a goat expert on allexperts. com. Cheryl lives in the community of Low Pass, located in the coast range of Oregon, with her herd of experimental miniature dairy goats, Mystic Acres Oberians.

Karen Ward, the author of *Pickles, Peaches, and Chocolate,* is a life-long home canner, home economist, and recipe developer. In addition to judging pre-served food at the San Diego County Fair each year, Karen teaches canning and preserving to men and women of all ages. Karen has been a featured guest on many television shows, including QVC and HGTV's *Smart Solutions.* She is a founding member of the San Diego Chapter of Les Dames d'Escoffier International, a nonprofit organization mentoring women and providing scholarships in the culinary arts. Karen makes her home in San Diego with her husband, Chris.

Kimberly Willis lives with her husband, Steve, on a small farm in the thumb area of Michigan. When not writing, she works at the MSU Extension office in Lapeer County, Michigan, as a horticulturist and doubles as the resident chicken expert. Kim has raised a number of breeds of chickens and other types of poultry for over 30 years. Kim is also a garden writer and has numerous articles in print and online. You can read her work at www. life123.com or www.squidoo.com/gardeninggranny or her blog at www.gardeninggranny.blogspot.com.

Gerald D. Wootan, DO, M.Ed. is an osteopathic physician board-certified in family practice and geriatrics. He holds bachelor's degrees in biology, psychology, and medicine, a master's degree in counseling psychology, and a doctorate in osteopathic medicine with board certification in family practice and geriatrics. He is the medical director of Jenks Health Team in Jenks, Oklahoma, a medical practice that specializes in integrative medicine with a strong emphasis on natural detoxification and nutritional supplementation. Dr. Wootan is trained in and utilizes the Defeat Autism Now! protocol for treating children on the autism spectrum and is an active member of the American College for the Advancement of Medicine.

Publisher's Acknowledgments

We're proud of this book; please send us your comments at http://dummies.custhelp.com. For other comments, please contact our Customer Care Department within the U.S. at 877-762-2974, outside the U.S. at 317-572-3993, or fax 317-572-4002.

Some of the people who helped bring this book to market include the following:

Acquisitions, Editorial, and Vertical Websites

Project Editor: Kelly Ewing

Acquisitions Editor: Stacy Kennedy

Copy Editor: Sarah Faulkner, Christine Pingleton

Assistant Editor: David Lutton

Editorial Program Coordinator: Joe Niesen

General Reviewer and Recipe Tester: Emily Nolan

Nutritionist: Patricia Santelli

Senior Editorial Manager: Jennifer Ehrlich

Editorial Supervisor and Reprint Editor: Carmen Krikorian

Editorial Assistant: Rachelle S. Amick, Alexa Koschier

Art Coordinator: Alicia B. South

Cover Photos: ©iStockphoto.com/ Elzbieta Sekowska

Cartoons: Rich Tennant (www.the5thwave.com)

Composition Services

Project Coordinator: Nikki Gee

Layout and Graphics: Timothy C. Detrick, Joyce Haughey, Christin Swinford

Proofreaders: Melissa Cossell, Shannon Ramsey

Indexer: BIM Indexing & Proofreading Services

Illustrator: Elizabeth Kurtzman

Publishing and Editorial for Consumer Dummies

Kathleen Nebenhaus, Vice President and Executive Publisher

David Palmer, Associate Publisher

Kristin Ferguson-Wagstaffe, Product Development Director

Publishing for Technology Dummies

Andy Cummings, Vice President and Publisher

Composition Services

Debbie Stailey, Director of Composition Services

Contents at a Glance

Table of Contents

Introduction

*Y*ou're not alone if you've thought about canning and preserving your own food but haven't tried it because you're afraid it's too involved. Well, it's time to set aside your hesitation. Today's methods and procedures for methods such as pickling, freezing, smoking, and drying food are simple and easy. Many of the techniques may be similar to those your grandmother used, but you'll find they've been perfected. In *Canning & Preserving All-in-One For Dummies*, you get all the information you need to can and preserve food safely.

About This Book

This book presents eight preserving methods — water-bath canning, pickling, fermenting and brewing, pressure canning, freezing, drying, smoking, and juicing — in an easy-to-understand format and walks you step by step through each technique. You don't need any previous canning or preserving experience in order to start, or continue, your endeavor to become a first-class food preserver. Within these pages, you'll find information like the following:

- ✔ What to look for to ensure that you're preserving the best, freshest fruits and veggies.

- ✔ A list of supplies and equipment (complete with illustrations), as well as instructions on how to ensure that your equipment is in good working order.

- ✔ What techniques help you preserve the best flavor in your foods and how to avoid spoilage and recognize it if it does occur.

- ✔ Illustrations of different techniques and equipment, along with tips for making your food preserving journey fun and rewarding.

- ✔ A whole host of favorite recipes for your enjoyment.

Consider this book your guide to discovering simple ways to preserve all the foods your family loves, without any mystery or confusion along the way.

Conventions Used in This Book

The recipes in this book include preparation times, cooking times, processing times, and the yield you should expect from your efforts. Here are some details that apply to all the recipes but aren't repeated each time:

- Use a vinegar with 5 percent acidity.
- Use pure salt with no additives. (Canning or pickling salt is best.)
- Flour refers to all-purpose flour unless otherwise noted.
- Cook all food in heavy-bottomed pots and pans.
- Use nonreactive equipment and utensils (items made from glass, stainless steel, or enamel-coated steel or iron).
- Use glass jars and two-piece caps approved for home-canning.
- Always use new lids for canning.
- Start counting your water-bath processing time when the water reaches a full, rolling boil.
- Begin counting your pressure-canner processing time after releasing air in the canner and achieving the required pressure.

Also, all temperatures are Fahrenheit. All recipes and processing times are developed for altitudes at sea level to 1,000 feet above sea level. (For higher altitudes, refer to the altitude adjustment charts for water-bath canning in Book II, Chapter 1 and for pressure canning in Book V, Chapter 1.)

Foolish Assumptions

In writing this book, we made some assumptions about you, the reader:

- You know your way around a kitchen. You're familiar with basic cooking techniques and food preparation methods.
- You've never canned or preserved food or have relatively little experience with food preservation methods and want basic, easy-to-understand-and-follow instructions.
- If you've canned and preserved food, it was long enough ago that you want to find out more about the newer, safer, and easier techniques that are recommended today.
- Perhaps most importantly, you want to stock your kitchen with more natural, healthier, homemade alternatives to standard supermarket fare.

How This Book Is Organized

This book is organized into parts, called *books*. Each part includes tried-and-true, tested recipes and preserving tips that offer you a lot of practice for each technique.

Book I: Getting Started with Canning and Preserving

With so many misconceptions about canning and preserving, Book I offers an explanation of each food preservation method and dispels any fears you may have about each technique. Book I is a good starting point if you're new to canning and preserving or if you've been away from any of these techniques for a while. You can find information on specialty equipment and utensils for each method.

Don't overlook the information on food safety. It's important to know what dangers may occur — and how to recognize them — if you skip any processing step, make adjustments to your recipe or change a processing method and time.

Book II: Water-Bath Canning with Fruits

If you like sweet spreads, relishes, or pickled food, start with Book II. Water-bath canning is the most popular food-preserving method and the easier of the two approved canning methods. Book II leads you step by step through the process while explaining what foods are suitable for this preserving method. You can try dozens of recipes, from jam and jelly to chutney and relish.

Book III: Mastering the Art of Pickling

There aren't many people who don't enjoy the crunchy taste of a flavorful pickle. Bringing that flavor to a wide variety of foods is both fun and useful. You can then have an assortment of bright tastes in your pantry all year round. After you discover the art of pickling, you can spend a lifetime trying out new recipes and unique flavors all your own.

Book IV: Fermenting and Brewing

Add fermenting and brewing to your list of culinary hobbies, and a whole new world of taste awaits. Both are age-old ways to preserve and create new foods from the ordinary. Try some of the recipes in Book IV and bring your pantry foods to a new level of taste!

Book V: Pressure Canning

Pressure canning is the approved method for processing food that's naturally low in acid — vegetables, meat, poultry, and seafood, for example. These foods contain more heat-resistant and hard-to-destroy bacteria than food that's safely water-bath processed. Book V carefully describes the procedure and steps for canning these foods, whether vegetables or meals of convenience.

Book VI: Freezing

In this book, you discover that your freezer is more than a place for leftovers and ice cream. Utilize this cold area for planning and preparing your meals with a minimum of time and effort. After reading Book VI, you see why the proper freezer containers and packaging methods, combined with correct thawing practices, prevent damage to your food while preserving its quality, flavor, and color.

Book VII: Drying and Root Cellaring

Drying, which preserves food by removing moisture, is the oldest and slowest method for preserving food. Book VII explains how to dry a variety of fruits, vegetables, and herbs for future enjoyment.

You also won't want to miss the instructions for making fruit leathers. Who doesn't like to unroll the dried sheets of pureed fruit? This is one time your kids can play with their food and get away with it.

Book VIII: Smoking, Salting, and Curing

After you've tasted a well-cured piece of meat, you'll be hooked. In Book VIII, you find out the multitude of ways to coax delicious flavors from some of your regular foods. You discover the mystery behind the cured meat selection and master the fine art of smoking your bounty.

Book IX: Juicing

More than a smoothie, juicing is a way to bring big nutrition to a small glass. In Book IX, you find out how to choose the right ingredients and the best machine for the job. You also try out a wide range of recipes that are both sweet and savory. The perfect meal in a glass awaits!

Icons Used in This Book

The following icons appear throughout this book and point out specific points or remind you of items you'll want to be sure not to miss:

This icon directs you to tips or shortcuts we've picked up over the years. The information here makes your work easier and hassle-free.

This icon marks important information you'll want to remember.

When you see this icon, pay special attention. The information tells you about a potential problem and how to overcome or avoid it.

These bits of technical information are interesting, but you can skip them, if you want to. That said, the info contained in these paragraphs makes you seem like you've been canning and preserving since you've been walking.

Where to Go from Here

Although you can start in any portion of this book, don't skip Chapter 1 of Book I. It describes safe processing methods and tells you how to identify spoiled food. If you have any doubts about canning and preserving safety, this chapter puts your fears at ease.

If you want to know about a particular food-preservation method, go to the book devoted to that method. Each book begins with a chapter that explains the technique. Review these initial chapters before selecting a recipe to make sure that you have a decent idea of what that particular food preservation method requires.

If you still can't decide where to start, review the recipes and start with one that sounds good to you! Then just back-track to the general techniques chapter as you need to.

Book I
Getting Started with Canning and Preserving

The 5th Wave   By Rich Tennant

"The kids mixed up the canning labels with the photo album labels. Just hand me a jar of Aunt Thelma, so I can finish this pie before Peaches and Pickles get here."

In this book . . .

1n Book I, you discover the benefits canning and preserving your own food can bring to your life. You see what tools and supplies make the food preservation process run smoothly and safely. You also find out whether what you've heard about canning are myths or truths. The chapters here introduce you to the language of canning and preserving, as well as outline the ingredients and equipment you need to begin filling your pantry with delicious and healthy fare.

Chapter 1

The Art and Science of Canning and Preserving

In This Chapter

▶ Preparing yourself for safely preserving your foods

▶ Becoming a successful food canner and preserver

▶ Putting your fears of home-preserved food to rest

▶ Determining your processing method

▶ Making the acquaintance of food-spoiling microorganisms and enzymes

Over the years, because of our busy lifestyles and the convenience of refrigeration and supermarkets, the art of canning and preserving has declined. Other than jams and jellies, many people started thinking of canning as sort of a novelty hobby. But today, many people have a renewed interest in learning this art. With the decline in the economy, more people are finding that canning and preserving foods is an inexpensive and easy way to have a full pantry.

This chapter gives you an overview of the canning and preserving techniques presented in this book and explains the benefits, both practical and emotional, that canning and preserving your own foods can provide.

If you're new to home food preservation, don't be overwhelmed or scared off by the rules. After you understand the basic procedures for a method, like water-bath canning, it's just a matter of concentrating on preparing your recipe.

Reaping the Benefits

Canning and *preserving* are ways to protect food from spoilage so that you can use the food at a later time. Some preserving methods, like drying and smoking, date back to ancient times; others, like canning, are a little more recent. There's no doubt that being able to offer fresh-tasting, home-canned or preserved foods to your family and friends throughout the year is definitely one of life's luxuries.

Whatever preservation method you choose, your efforts will benefit you in many ways:

- ✔ **A pantry full of fresh, homegrown foods:** Having a stocked pantry offers a cushion against the fluctuating cost of healthy foods. If you enjoy specialty foods from gourmet stores but dislike the high prices, the methods outlined in this book are safe and economical ways to preserve large or small quantities of high-quality food.

- ✔ **Convenience:** You can build a pantry of convenience foods that fit into your busy lifestyle and that your family will enjoy.

- ✔ **Protection against rising food costs:** The whole idea of canning and preserving is to take advantage of fresh food when it's abundant. And abundant food generally means lower cost.

- ✔ **A sense of relaxation and accomplishment:** For many people, working in the kitchen and handling food provides a sense of relaxation, and watching family and friends enjoy the products of your efforts gives you a great sense of accomplishment. Taking the time to select your recipe, choosing and preparing your food, and packaging and processing it for safety is fulfilling and a source of pride for you, the home-canner.

- ✔ **Confidence in the ingredients that go into your food:** If you love fresh ingredients and like to know what goes into your food, doing your own canning and preserving is the answer.

- ✔ **A good time:** Producing canned and preserved food in your kitchen is fun and easy — and who doesn't like fun?

The price of food has skyrocketed in the last few years. Food safety has become a concern for everyone. Canning is the answer to both the price dilemma and the desire to offer nutritious foods throughout the year. In addition, the preservation methods covered in this book instantly reward your efforts when you follow the proper steps for handling and processing your food.

Who's Canning and Preserving?

Although home-canning and preserving has skipped one or two generations, one thing is certain: It's on the rise. Men and women of all ages practice the art of food preservation. It no longer matters whether you live in the country or in the city or whether you grow your own food. Fresh ingredients are available just about everywhere. Farmers' markets are commonplace in many cities and towns, making it easy to find the perfect foods to preserve for an affordable price.

Book I

Getting
Started
with
Canning
and
Preserving

Exact statistics regarding home-preserving vary, but according to the largest manufacturer of home-canning products, Alltrista, approximately one out of four households in the United States cans food. Today, most home-canned products are used in the home where they're produced. In addition, a rising number of people are committed to eating locally, and these folks want to know what is in the foods they eat. By preserving their own foods, they can find the freshest products available and control what goes in their food.

Of course, you can easily become overwhelmed when you consider all the ways you can preserve foods. Along with the choices, everyone has heard stories about food-borne illness and danger. The truth is, if you start with simple techniques, using equipment that you can afford, your foods will not only be safe to eat, they will taste better and give you more satisfaction than anything you can buy in the store.

There is no one right way to preserve foods. The trick is to find out which technique works best with the foods you like to eat. Be realistic about what you'll have time to preserve. Know how much space you have to fill with preserved foods, and your efforts will all be worthwhile.

Meeting the Methods

The techniques discussed in this book are safe for home use and produce superior results when you follow all the steps for each method. You compromise the quality and safety of your food if you make your own rules. An example is when you shorten your processing period to try to cut corners and substitute important parts of recipes. It's always best to start following directions to the letter, until you become fluent in the process.

Review the basic techniques for your type of food preserving before you begin — and if you're already familiar with the techniques, review them annually just to refresh your memory. You'll experience fewer interruptions in your food-preserving process. Always do a trial walkthrough before you begin canning, to ensure that you have all the supplies you'll need and that you know the order of the steps you'll follow so that you can work quickly and efficiently.

You'll have no doubts about preparing safe home-canned and preserved food after you discover what each method does, which method is best for different foods, the rules for the technique you choose, and safe food-handling techniques. The following sections introduce you to the ancient and modern-day techniques that will help you can and preserve with ease.

Put by or *putting up* are terms that describe canning years ago, before there was refrigeration. They meant, "Save something perishable for use later when you'll need it."

Canning food

Canning is the most popular preserving method used today. Canning is the process of applying heat to food that's sealed in a jar in order to destroy any microorganisms that can cause food spoilage. All foods contain these microorganisms. Proper canning techniques stop this spoilage by heating the food for a specific period of time and killing these unwanted microorganisms. Also, during the canning process, air is driven from the jar, and a vacuum is formed as the jar cools and seals. This vacuum prevents microorganisms from entering and recontaminating the food.

Don't let anyone tell you that home-canning is complicated and unsafe. It's simply not true.

Although you may hear of many canning methods, only two are approved by the United States Department of Agriculture (USDA):

✔ **Water-bath canning:** This method, sometimes referred to as *hot water canning,* uses a large kettle of boiling water. Filled jars are submerged in the water and heated to an internal temperature of 212° for a specific period of time. Use this method for processing high-acid foods, such as tomatoes, fruit and items made from it, pickles, and pickled food. Book II explains this method in detail. Refer to Book III for all things pickled.

✔ **Pressure canning:** Pressure canning uses a large kettle that produces steam in a locked compartment. The filled jars in the kettle reach an internal temperature of 240° under a specific pressure (stated in pounds) that's measured with a dial gauge or weighted gauge on the pressure-canner cover. Use a pressure canner for processing vegetables and other low-acid foods, such as meat, poultry, and fish. For more information about pressure canning, see Book V.

Don't confuse a pressure canner with a pressure cooker, which is used to cook food quickly. A pressure cooker does not have adequate room for both the canning jars and the water needed to create the right amount of pressure to preserve foods.

In both water-bath canning and pressure canning, you heat your filled jars of food to a high temperature in order to destroy microorganisms and produce an airtight, vacuum seal. The only way to reliably produce a safe canned product is to use the correct method for your type of food, follow your recipe instructions to the letter, and complete each processing step. For all the details you need about canning and a plethora of recipes, head to Books II and V.

Book I

Getting
Started
with
Canning
and
Preserving

Freezing food

Freezing food is the art of preparing and packaging foods at their peak of freshness and plopping them into the freezer to preserve all that seasonal goodness. Freezing is a great way to preserve foods that can't withstand the high temperatures and long cooking of conventional canning methods.

The keys to freezing food are to make sure that the food you're freezing is absolutely fresh, that you freeze it as quickly as possible, and that you keep it at a proper frozen temperature (0°).

The quality of the food won't get better just because you throw it in the freezer.

Properly packaging food in freezer paper or freezer containers prevents any deterioration in its quality. Damage occurs when your food comes in contact with the dry air of a freezer. Although freezer-damaged food won't hurt you, it does make the food taste bad. Here are three tips to help you avoid freezer burn:

- ✔ **Reduce exposure to air:** Wrap food tightly.
- ✔ **Avoid fluctuating temperatures:** Keep the freezer closed as much as possible. Know what you want to remove before opening the door.
- ✔ **Don't overfill your freezer:** An overly full freezer reduces air circulation and speeds freezer damage.

For information and instructions on freezing a variety of foods, go to Book VI.

Drying food

Drying is the oldest method known for preserving food. When you dry food, you expose the food to a temperature that's high enough to remove the moisture but low enough that it doesn't cook. Good air circulation assists in evenly drying the food.

An electric dehydrator is the best and most efficient unit for drying, or dehydrating, food. Today's units include a thermostat and fan to help regulate temperatures much better. You can also dry food in your oven or by using the heat of the sun, but the process will take longer and produce inferior results to food dried in a dehydrator. Go to Book VII for drying instructions for fruits, vegetables, herbs, and meats.

Smoking, salting, and curing food

Smoking foods, especially meats, adds a new dimension of flavor to your diet. *Smoking* is a simple process that infuses smoky flavors into ordinary cuts of meat. Applying rubs and curing in brine, in addition to smoking, increases the number of ways that your ho-hum meats can become spectacular. Refer to Book VIII for all you need to know about smoking, salting, and curing.

Fermenting foods and drinks

Fermented foods have been an important part of the diet in many countries all over the world. *Fermenting* is the process of introducing good bacteria into foods, in a safe way. Much more than beer-making, fermenting is the technique behind the sour tang of sauerkraut, vinegar, and yogurts.

Fermenting is also the perfect beginner's preserving technique because it takes very little time and requires a short list of ingredients. Check out Book IV for more on fermenting foods and drinks.

Juicing

Juices were once thought of as fuel for athletes and health-food extremists. No longer. Juicing is a wonderful way to introduce healthy eating in a playful (and delicious) way to anyone who eyes a salad with suspicion.

Juicing includes fruits, greens, and vegetables in combinations that may surprise you. Full-bodied and filling, juicing is a great way to bring tasty foods that might otherwise be overlooked to the table. Portable and full of nutrition, juicing is for everyone! Book IX has the scoop on juicing.

Taking on Technical Matters

Canning and preserving methods are simple and safe, and they produce food that's nutritious, delicious, and just plain satisfying to your taste buds. Becoming a successful food preserver takes time, effort, and knowledge of the rules.

Follow these tips for achieving success as a home canner and preserver:

> ✔ **Always use the correct processing method for your food.** Process all high-acid and pickled food in a water-bath canner. Process all low-acid food in a pressure canner. To find out how to determine whether a food has a low or high acidity level, head to the next section. (You can find

out about the different canning methods in Chapter 1 of Book II and Chapter 1 of Book V.)

✔ **Preserve meats, a more fragile food, quickly and accurately.** Meats are very useful in the pantry, but they do require careful attention to proven recipes and prompt storage. For the most effective meat preservation, start small and simple. Grow your recipe lists as you learn and keep your family safe from food-borne illness.

✔ **Juicing is great for those times of year when you are overwhelmed with produce.** This simple technique results in a flavorful food your whole family will love. Perfect for picky eaters, a glass of fresh-juiced vegetables and fruits tastes like a treat, without the stigma of a vegetable stick.

Know the acidity level of your food

When canning, the acidity level of the food you're processing is important because the *pH,* the measure of acidity, determines which canning method you use: water-bath or pressure canning.

The *pH,* or potential of hydrogen, is the measure of acidity or alkalinity in food. The values range from 1 to 14. Neutral is 7. Lower values are more acidic, while higher values are more alkaline. The lower the pH value in your food, the more acidic it is.

For canning purposes, food is divided into two categories based on the amount of acid the food registers:

✔ **High-acid** foods include fruits and pickled foods. (For detailed information on identifying and processing high-acid food, refer to Chapter 2 of Book II.) Foods in this group have a pH of 4.6 or lower. Processing them in a water-bath canner destroys harmful microorganisms.

Tomatoes are considered a low-high acid food. With all the new varieties of tomatoes, home canners are now advised to add an acid to the canning process, to ensure that the proper acidity is reached every time.

✔ **Low-acid** foods, primarily vegetables, meat, poultry, and fish, contain little natural acid. Their pH level is higher than 4.6. (Check out Chapter 1 of Book V for detailed information on identifying and processing low-acid food.) Process these foods in a pressure canner, which superheats your food and destroys the more heat-resistant bacteria, like botulism.

If you want to feel like you're back in science class all over again, you can buy litmus paper at teacher- or scientific-supply stores and test the acidity level of your food yourself. Also referred to as pH paper, litmus paper is an acid-sensitive paper that measures the acid in food. When you insert a strip of pH paper into your prepared food, the paper changes color. You then compare the wet strip to the pH chart of colors that accompanies the litmus paper.

Follow the rules

The following sections offer some tips for handling, preparing, and processing your food:

- ✔ **Start with the freshest, best products available.** Preserving doesn't improve food quality. If you put garbage in, you get garbage out.

- ✔ **Know the rules and techniques for your canning or preserving method before you start your work.** Don't try to learn a technique after you've started your processing.

- ✔ **Work in short sessions to prevent fatigue and potential mistakes.** Process no more than two items in one day and work with only one canning method at a time.

- ✔ **Stay up-to-date on new or revised guidelines for your preserving method.** This book is a great start. You can also go to websites like www.freshpreserving.com, created by the makers of Ball canning supplies. Here you can find tips and directions for canning just about anything.

- ✔ **When canning, use the correct processing method and processing time to destroy microorganisms.** The recipe will tell you what method to use, but it helps if you understand the difference between high- and low-acid foods and how the canning methods for each differ.

- ✔ **Know the elevation you're working at.** Adjust your processing time or pressure when you're at an altitude over 1,000 feet above sea level. For accurate information on how to adjust for your altitude, refer to Chapter 1 of Book II for water-bath canning conversions and Chapter 1 of Book V for pressure canning conversions.

- ✔ **Put together a plan before you start your preserving session.** Read your recipe (more than once). Have the proper equipment and correct ingredients on hand to prevent last-minute shortages and inconvenient breaks. (Make a list of what you need and check off items as you gather them.)

- ✔ **Test your equipment.** If you're using an electric dehydrator or pressure canner, test out the equipment to ensure that everything's working properly. And always check the seals on your jars. When in doubt, check with your county extension office. It can provide expert, free information about any technique you're undertaking.

- ✔ **Use recipes from reliable sources or ones that you've already made successfully.** Follow your recipe to the letter. Don't substitute ingredients, adjust quantities, or make up your own food combinations. Improvisation and safe food preservation aren't compatible. This approach also means you can't double your recipe. If you require more than what the recipe yields, make another batch.

After careful preparation and wrapping, you are ready to take your food to its final destination in the preservation process. Whether you choose canning, freezing, drying, smoking, fermenting, or juicing, proceed down your canning and preserving road with confidence.

Avoiding and Detecting Spoilage

Preventing food spoilage is the key to safe canning and preserving. Over the years, home-canning has become safer and better. Scientists have standardized processing methods, and home-canners and preservers know more about using these methods. When you follow up-to-date guidelines exactly, you'll experience little concern about the quality and safety of your home-canned and preserved foods.

Before you begin your canning and preserving journey, take a stroll through the following section, which introduces you to microorganisms, enzymes, and other potentially dangerous situations that cause food spoilage. You can also read the upcoming section "Steering clear of spoilage" to find info on how to prevent and identify food spoilage. This technical section shouldn't deter you from taking on food preservation. Rest assured, after reading this information, you'll have no fear about preparing and serving your home-canned and preserved food.

Meeting the spoilers

Food spoilage is the unwanted deterioration in canned or preserved food that makes your food unsafe for eating. Ingesting spoiled food causes a wide range of ailments, depending on the type of spoilage and the amount of food consumed. Symptoms vary from mild, flulike aches and pains to more serious illnesses or even death. However, when you understand the workings of these microscopic organisms and enzymes, you'll know why using the correct processing method for the correct amount of time destroys these potentially dangerous food spoilers.

Mold, yeast, bacteria, and enzymes are the four spoilers. *Microorganisms* (mold, yeast, and bacteria) are independent organisms of microscopic size. *Enzymes* are proteins that exist in plants and animals. When any one or more of the spoilers have a suitable environment, they grow rapidly and divide or reproduce every 10 to 30 minutes! With this high-speed development, it's obvious how quickly food can spoil. Some types of spoilage can't be seen with the naked eye (like botulism), while others (like mold) make their presence known visually.

Living microorganisms are all around — in your home, in the soil, and even in the air you breathe. Sometimes microorganisms are added to food to achieve a fermented product, like beer or bread (for leavening). They're also important for making antibiotics. The point? Not all microorganisms are bad, just the ones that cause disease and food spoilage.

Mold

Mold is a fungus with dry spores. Poorly sealed jars of high-acid or pickled foods are perfect locations for these spores to set up housekeeping. After the spores float through the air and settle on one of their favorite foods, they start growing. At first, you see what looks like silken threads, then streaks of color, and finally fuzz, which covers the food. Processing high-acid and pickled food in a water-bath canner destroys mold spores.

Don't eat food that's had fuzz scraped off of it. This was thought safe at one time but not anymore. Mold contains carcinogens that filter into the remaining food. Although the food appears to be noninfected, ingesting this food can cause illness.

Yeast

Yeast spores grow on food like mold spores. They're particularly fond of high-acid food that contains lots of sugar, like jam or jelly. They grow as a dry film on the surface of your food. Prevent yeast spores from fermenting in your food by destroying them in a water-bath canner.

Bacteria

Bacteria are a large group of single-celled microorganisms. Common bacteria are staphylococcus and salmonella. Botulism, the one to be most concerned with in canning, is the most dangerous form of bacteria and can be deadly. It's almost undetectable because it's odorless and colorless. Botulism spores are stubborn and difficult to destroy.

Because botulism is undetectable without laboratory testing, handling and preparing canned food according to the most updated guidelines available is essential.

Botulism spores hate high-acid and pickled foods, but they love low-acid foods. When you provide these spores with an airless environment containing low-acid food, like a jar of green beans, the spores produce a toxin in the food that can kill anyone who eats it. The only way to destroy these spores in low-acid food is by pressure canning.

For safety's sake, before eating any home-canned, low-acid food, boil it for 15 minutes from the point of boiling at altitudes of 1,000 feet or lower. For altitudes above 1,000 feet, add 1 minute for each 1,000 feet of elevation.

Boiling does *not* kill the botulism bacteria. Symptoms from ingesting botulism-infected food occur within 12 to 36 hours after eating it. Symptoms include double vision; difficulty swallowing, breathing, and speaking; and even death. Seek medical attention immediately if you believe you've eaten infected food. Antitoxins are available to treat this poisoning, but the sooner you take them, the better off you are.

Enzymes

Enzymes are proteins that occur naturally in plants and animals. They encourage growth and ripening in food, which affects the flavor, color, texture, and nutritional value. Enzymes are more active in temperatures of 85 to 120° than they are at colder temperatures. Enzymes aren't harmful, but they can make your food overripe and unattractive while opening the door for other microorganisms or bacteria.

An example of enzymes in action occurs when you cut or peel an apple. After a few minutes, the apple starts to brown. You can stop this browning by treating the cut apple with a dipping solution (see Chapter 2 of Book II). Other methods for halting the enzymatic action in your food are blanching and hot packing.

Steering clear of spoilage

In addition to choosing the right preservation method, follow these steps to guard against food spoilage:

- **Don't experiment or take shortcuts.** Use only tested, approved methods.

- **Never use an outdated recipe.** Look for a newer version. Don't update the directions yourself. Check the publishing date at the beginning of the recipe book. If it's more than 5 years old, find a newer version.

- **Use the best ingredients and follow recipes to the letter.** Because botulism and other food-borne bacteria can be tasteless and odorless, this advice is your best defense.

- **When curing meats, always use the proper amount of cure, which includes nitrates/nitrites (pink salt).** These ingredients have gotten a bad rap in the media, but the truth is, without them, your preserved meat can be silently dangerous.

- **When smoking, don't rely solely on the dial that came with your unit.** Use a calibrated thermometer to test the internal temperature of meats.

  To quickly calibrate a thermometer, place it in a glass of ice water. It should reach 32°. Then place the thermometer in boiling water; it should reach 212°. If it doesn't, adjust it if possible.

✔ **Keep in mind that smoking is no replacement for proper handling of meats.** Always cook cold smoked meats before eating and keep them in the refrigerator or freezer, unless they're going to be eaten immediately.

✔ **Check your pressure canning equipment every year before you need it.** This service is offered free at your county extension office.

✔ **Pay particular attention to the basic rules of canning, which are covered in more detail in the appropriate books on those techniques:**

- If you're pressure canning, allow your pressure canner to depressurize to 0 pounds pressure naturally; don't take the lid off to accelerate the process.

- Allow your processed jars to cool undisturbed at room temperature.

- Process your filled jars for the correct amount of time and, if you're pressure canning, at the correct pressure. (Both will be stated in your recipe.) Make adjustments to your processing time and pressure for altitudes over 1,000 feet above sea level.

- Test each jar's seal and remove the screw band before storing your food.

Detecting spoiled foods

No one can promise you that your home-canned foods will always be free from spoilage, but you can rest assured that your chances for spoiled food are greatly reduced when you follow the precise guidelines for each preserving method. If you suspect, for any reason, that your food is spoiled or just isn't right, don't taste it. Also, just because your food doesn't look spoiled, doesn't mean that it's not. Signs of spoilage are

✔ Bulging or loosened lids on canned jars

✔ Weeping or leakage from under a previously sealed jar

✔ Bubbly or foamy contents of canned food

✔ Visible mold or mildew on the lid, inside the jar, or on the food itself.

Chapter 2

Gathering Your Ingredients

*B*efore canning a single thing, you have to gather the right ingredients. The planning and organizing you do before the produce arrives will save you time and money in the long run. Gathering ingredients isn't just about buying fruits and vegetables. You need to take into account even the most basic ingredients of salt, sugar, and water. As always, having a plan means you'll be ready when the fruits and vegetables are ready.

The Product: Fresh Is Best

Across the board, using fresh foods for preserving is always the best choice. No matter what type of food you're referring to, after it's picked, it starts the process of decaying. You may not be able to actually see this process, but on a molecular level, the decay is happening. By canning, you're actually stopping the decaying process and holding the food in a suspended animation of sorts, until you cook and eat it. Canning retains the vitamins and micronutrients that the fresh food offers. Canning really is a healthy way to keep the foods that you love, outside of their harvest time.

Buying local

You may think of this term as simply a sales pitch, but *buying local* is essential to finding the freshest foods possible.

Studies have shown that the average American's meal has traveled about 1,500 miles from farm to plate. Even if you buy the food as soon as it arrives in the supermarket, it has been picked long ago and from quite a distance away from where you live.

Skip the middle man and go to the source for your food. Get to know where your local farmers and farmers' markets are and shop there for foods to preserve.

Look into these suppliers of fresh, local produce:

- **Farm stands:** Go right to the source!
- **Farmers' markets:** Found in cities and towns, farmers' markets are a great resource for those digging into the world of food preservation.
- **Neighbors with large gardens:** Novice gardeners, especially, are known for growing more produce than they can handle (think: zucchinis).
- **Community-supported agriculture (CSA):** These are programs in which interested consumers purchase a share (kind of like a subscription) and in return receive a box of seasonal produce each week throughout the farming season.

Choosing the best varieties

Not all fruits and vegetables are the same. Some varieties are created to withstand shipping long distances and still remain unblemished. These varieties have tougher skins and are picked while still ripening. They don't make good candidates for preserving.

Types of produce that do take to canning well are usually labeled as canners or keepers. Ask your local sellers what varieties they have and ask whether any are better than others for putting up. Many times, heirloom varieties remain unhybridized (*hybridizing* is combining two or more varieties in order to get a new variety), simply because they're grown for good keeping. Look for these varieties with a long history of tasting delicious long after their season has ended.

Picking perfect produce

Getting the perfect produce means finding fresh, unblemished items. Any dents, marking, and nicks in the skin may have allowed bacteria into the flesh that will speed up decay. Many fruits and vegetables, especially berries, have a very short time after picking before they become mashed up and actually grow visible mold. Even if you remove the visible decay, you don't know whether invisible bacteria remain.

Supermarket produce for canning

The fruits and vegetables found at a super-market are not suitable for canning because they're created to withstand long-distance travel and handling by shoppers before purchase. Their skins are tougher, and they are gas-ripened (forced to change to a ripe color when still unripe). These factors all result in a flavorless, less than desirable product for canning.

To choose the perfect produce, look for these clues:

- **Firm, but slightly yielding flesh:** Ripe fruits and vegetables that are supposed to be juicy will yield slightly under the pressure of a finger, but won't feel mushy.

- **Firm and not floppy:** Fruits and vegetables that are hard and not juicy when ripe won't give way when pressed upon. Any remaining leaf or stem will also be fresh looking and not wilted.

- **Unbroken skin:** No matter how firm an item, the flesh shouldn't be broken at all. Even a small knick can be harboring a large, unseen bruise under the skin. This entire area is not suitable for canning, and it is recommended that the entire piece of fruit or vegetable be discarded or used for an alternative meal.

- **Fresh aroma:** You should smell the ripened fruit or vegetable. The smell of fresh dirt is also acceptable, but mold or mildew scents can mean trouble.

- **Background info:** Always ask the grower where the produce came from and when it was picked. Growers commonly pack their cooler the evening before, but the fresher the produce, the better. Some unscrupulous vendors have purchased fruits and vegetables from a wholesaler and haven't even grown it themselves. Always check!

What You Need to Know about Water

Water plays a special place in your canning process. Water is the basis for sweet syrups that coat your fruits, the broth in your canned meats, and the flavorful fluid that keeps your vegetables looking and tasting great. Because of the important role that water plays in everything you can, it's imperative that it taste the best it can.

Examining your water source

You may believe that you're fine using water from the tap. Although you may be right, take a minute to consider your local water supply.

No matter whether you have a private well or are on municipal water, your water should have

- ✔ **A clean taste:** Any taste that your water carries will be brought to the canned foods. Although you may have become used to a sulphur or high mineral taste over time, these tastes don't taste so good in canned goods.

- ✔ **Low mineral content:** Do you have *hard water* — water with a high mineral content? Hard water can cause your contents to discolor when canned. It can also turn your canned goods an off color as they sit on the shelf in the pantry. If your hard water touches only the outside of the jars, it may leave a milky film. You can prevent this film by adding a dollop of vinegar to the water in the canner. Your jars will come out crystal clear.

- ✔ **No chlorination:** Chlorine has no place in canned goods. If your water is municipal and has a noticeable smell of chlorine, your jars of food will definitely suffer.

  Allow your water to sit overnight for the chlorine to dissipate before using.

- ✔ **Neutral pH:** The perfect (neutral) pH of water is 7. Not everyone has that pH, however. Having water that is slightly acidic or alkaline can affect the outcome of canned produce. If you have higher acidity in your water, your canned goods will keep a firmer texture on the shelf. Alkalinity has the opposite effect.

  The colors of some foods may be affected by pH in an unappealing, but not dangerous, way. Onions canned in alkaline water tend to be a yellowish color, whereas red-colored fruits and vegetables will turn a strange green/blue hue. This color is strange, but the food is still safe to eat. With acidic water, foods that are red in color fade to shades of pink. Again, this color looks odd, but it doesn't affect taste or safety.

Understanding water impurities

Water impurities can mean fairly benign things like the presence of minerals to bigger issues like the presence of chlorine and other additives. No matter what these impurities are, knowing what they are and what they cause is important.

Book I

Getting
Started
with
Canning
and
Preserving

The following impurities are commonly found in water. Here's what happens when they're present:

- ✔ **Iron:** Water high in iron will cause some canned goods to darken and look unappetizing.

- ✔ **Copper:** Water high in copper can cause assorted colors, such as brown, gray, and even black.

- ✔ **Hard water:** Hard water is sometimes the culprit for cloudy liquid in the jars. If you see cloudy liquid, it could be a sign of bacterial growth, and it's a good idea *not* to taste the food but to simply discard it. The food may not be dangerous to eat, but it's not worth the chance. Hard water also can pull out the color in some foods. Colorless foods look unappetizing, and if your family won't eat it, the time and effort you spend putting the food into jars is wasted.

If you're unsure of your water quality, you can use a faucet filter or bottled water.

Sourcing Your Salt

We're all concerned about the overuse of salt in our diet, but salt adds an undeniable flavor that makes food just snap. The trick to having your salt and eating it, too, is to add just the right amount and find full-flavored salts that bring their own life to the food.

When you can foods, you always lose a little flavor. Losing flavor can't be helped, but you can minimize it by the addition of the right amount and type of salt.

Choosing the right salt

Salt is used as a preservative, and it adds flavor and crispness to your food, especially pickles. Use a pure, additive-free, granulated salt. Acceptable salts are *pickling and canning salt* (a fine-grained salt containing no additives), most kosher salt (any that doesn't contain iodine), and *sea salt,* salt produced from evaporated seawater.

Additives in salt cause cloudy liquid. Always read the ingredient label on your salt container to ensure that it's additive-free.

Salts *not* suitable for brining and pickling solutions are

- ✔ **Table salt and iodized salt:** These contain *anticaking agents,* additives that keep the salt from sticking together. Such additives cloud your liquid. Iodine darkens food.

- ✔ **Rock salt:** Rock salt keeps roads free of ice and isn't made for use with food. It's okay in an ice-cream freezer because it never touches the food.

- ✔ **Salt substitutes:** These products contain little or no sodium.

 A wide variety of new salts are on the market, including sea salts from around the world and smoked salt, which has its own unique flavor. These new salts are safe to use in canning, but may cause discoloration in the final product. Try a small batch or a couple of jars before committing to dozens of jars that may turn out an unwanted color.

Avoiding salty problems

Recipes that end up too salty are the single thing that plagues all canners. When following recipes exactly, one person thinks the results taste fabulous, while the next thinks the recipe tastes too salty to even eat. This difference reflects the wonders of how we taste foods.

 Pickled items in particular may initially taste very salty, yet mellow as they age on the shelf. This eventual mellowing is true for most canned goods. Before saying that a recipe is a loss due to too much salt, allow it to sit on the shelf for a month or more to absorb the brine and become truly pickled.

 Pickled items are going to have a salty flavor. They're meant to be eaten as a condiment, a single pickle or two at a time. Although pickles do have salt in the recipe, you aren't going to be making a meal of them.

Making Sense of Sweeteners

Many people are trying to cut back on sweeteners in their diet because many processed foods are sweetened unnecessarily, with too much sugar and manmade sweeteners like high fructose corn syrup.

 When we talk about using sugar in canned goods, we're referring to natural sugars, such as granulated sugars and honey. High fructose corn syrup has no place in home-canned products; by eating sweet foods eaten from your home-canned pantry, you'll do a lot to reduce the high fructose corn syrup in your family's overall diet.

Sugars do have a purpose, though, in home canning. Sugar extends the shelf life, masks slight flavor changes in the foods, and helps keep an appealing color in the product. Although alternative and low-sugar recipes are available, if possible, use pure, cane sugar whenever you can.

If you prefer a lesser sugar content, use a light sugar syrup. You don't need to always have heavy syrups for all your fruits.

Book I

Getting Started with Canning and Preserving

Meeting the sugars

Many sugars work well in canned goods. Not all are the best choice, however. If sugar is needed in a canning recipe, your choices are

- **Cane or beetroot white sugar:** The cleanest and most available sugar on the market. Cane sugar is the first choice for home canners. When a recipe calls for sugar, this sugar is the one to use.

- **Brown sugar:** Brown sugar is used when making some butters and pie fillings. It has a richer flavor and works equally well. Because it is brown, it makes a sugar syrup dark and is not recommended. The amount of molasses determines whether a brown sugar is labeled light or dark, but they're interchangeable for the most part.

- **Honey:** When a recipe uses honey, any light-tasting honey is acceptable. Don't substitute honey for white sugar in a recipe on your own. For substitution rates and ideas, see Chapter 2 of Book II for more information.

- **Corn syrup:** Unlike high fructose corn syrup, this ingredient is commonly used in home cooking. Corn (or caro) syrup adds a less sweet taste and is sometimes desired. Find recipes that already contain corn syrup as part of the sweetener.

Getting to know the new sweeteners

It seems like every year a new alternative food hits the market. Lately, alternative sweeteners have gotten a lot of press. Numerous companies make different versions of essentially the same thing — sugar combined in different percentages with a naturally sweet herb called stevia. *Stevia* is a plant that has been used for thousands of years. It's extremely sweet, with a licorice aftertaste.

Containing no calories, and safe for diabetics, these new sweeteners are generally good sugar alternatives. However, they have various degrees of good taste, and when used for canning, they leave a bitter aftertaste.

Going sugar-free?

If you're trying to reduce the use of sugar in your diet, you can omit or reduce the amount of sugar in the liquid. Your fruit will be a little softer, but still good. Sugar offers no preservative for the fruit. Its value is purely in its taste and texture. To help avoid too-soft fruit, start with firm, newly ripened produce.

With the exception of Splenda, artificial sweeteners aren't recommended in canned products. If you prefer to use something other than Splenda, you can add it after you open the unsweetened, canned fruit to eat.

If you want to try using a stevia-type product in your canning recipe, use one that says that it measures the same as cane sugar and make the smallest batch possible. If you have time, allow your canned product to sit in the pantry for a week before committing to a larger canning session.

Chapter 3

Assembling Your Canning and Preserving Equipment

. . . .

In This Chapter

▶ Checking out your everyday kitchen utensils and equipment

▶ Exploring and using canning and preserving gear

▶ Looking into your options for freezing and drying foods

▶ Tracking down gear for smoking, fermenting, and juicing

. . . .

*H*ow many times have you heard the phrase, "Use the right tool for the job"? At no time is this advice truer than when you're canning and preserving. The majority of the items discussed in this chapter won't break the bank, but they'll make your canning and preserving tasks more efficient. The faster you process your fresh ingredients, the better the quality and flavor of your final product.

In this chapter, you find a list of the tools and utensils you need to complete your tasks. You use some tools, like a jar lifter or a lid wand, only for canning. Other tools, like pots, pans, and knives, are used with more than one technique.

Assembling Your Tools

The tools that make canning and preserving easier are many of the very same tools that are in most well-stocked kitchens. When our recipe recommends a tool for canning, we have a practical reason for doing so. Using the proper tool for the job decreases the chance of a jar failing to seal or being able to harbor bacteria. The proper tool can also reduce the chance of mishaps and injuries.

Always purchase good-quality tools and equipment; their quality and durability will pay for themselves many times over.

Basic tools and utensils

If you're serious about any work in the kitchen, these basic tools are indispensable.

- **Knives:** You need three basic knives: a paring knife, a multipurpose knife with a 6-inch blade, and an 8-inch (some people prefer a 10-inch) chef's knife. When purchasing quality knives, look for two options: stamped or forged blades and blades made of stainless or high carbon steel. (Tempered steel knives are no longer the epitome of high-quality cutlery.) Ceramic knives are also high quality, but these high-priced knives are easier to damage than their steel counterparts. Also, if you select knives that are balanced, the knife will do the work for you.

- **Measuring cups:** Accuracy in measuring ingredients is essential to achieve the correct balance of ingredients for canning. There are two types of measuring cups: those for measuring dry ingredients, like flour, sugar, and solid fats, and those for measuring liquid ingredients (see Figure 3-1).

  Liquid measuring cups are made from glass, plastic, or metal. With glass measuring cups, you can easily see the amount of liquid in the cup.

Figure 3-1: Measuring cups for dry and liquid food products.

liquid measure cup   dry measure cups

- **Measuring spoons (see Figure 3-2):** These come in graduated sizes from ⅛ teaspoon to 2 tablespoons. *Note:* Don't use adjustable measuring spoons for canning foods; they move too easily and can give you the wrong measurement.

  To avoid having to stop and clean your measuring spoons whenever you measure the same amount of wet and dry ingredients, have two sets handy, one for dry ingredients and the other for wet ingredients.

- **Spoons:** You need at least a couple of cooking spoons made of nonreactive metal (like stainless steel) that won't change the taste of acidic foods they come in contact with. Some choices for nonreactive metals are stainless steel, anodized aluminum, glass, or enameled cast iron. You can also use an assortment of different-sized wooden spoons (see Figure 3-2).

Figure 3-2:
Mis-
cellaneous
kitchen
tools:
wooden
spoon,
box grater,
timer,
measuring
spoons,
rubber
spatula,
and lemon
juicer.

Everyday Utensils

✔ **Rubber spatulas:** These spatulas (refer to Figure 3-2) are available in a variety of colors and sizes, from flat to spoon-shaped. Use heat-resistant spatulas for cooking items containing sugar. Check that the end doesn't easily come off the handle, a common problem with less expensive spatulas.

✔ **Tongs:** Tongs are handy for all types of kitchen chores, especially moving large pieces of food into and out of hot water. Try the spring-loaded variety in different lengths. Don't overlook a locking mechanism. It keeps the tongs closed when you're not using them.

✔ **Ladle:** Use a ladle that's heatproof with a good pouring spout.

✔ **Potholders:** Protect your hands from hot items. Have twice the amount of potholders available that you think you'll need.

Potholders often get wet during canning. Have enough on hand so that you don't have to use wet potholders. Heat quickly transfers through a wet potholder (in the form of steam), causing a severe burn.

✔ **Kitchen towels and paper towels:** Use them for cleaning your jar rims and as a pad for your cooling jars. They also are handy for wiping up small spills as you go, making your work area a safer place to be.

✔ **Graters:** A box grater (refer to Figure 3-2) gives you four or more options for shredding and grating. A microplane grater (see Figure 3-3) is an updated version of a rasp (a woodworking tool) that's perfect for removing the zest from citrus fruit.

MICROPLANE GRATER

ZESTER

Figure 3-3:
Microplane
grater and
zester.

✔ **Zester:** Before the microplane grater, a zester (see Figure 3-3) was the tool for removing citrus fruit *zest* (just the skin without the bitter white part). It's still an asset when you need a small amount of zest (a teaspoon or less), but for larger amounts, use a microplane grater.

✔ **Scissors:** Use scissors instead of knives to open food packages. Avoid cross-contaminating bacteria by washing your scissors after opening meat packages.

✔ **Timer:** Choose a timer (refer to Figure 3-2) that's easy to read, easy to set, and loud enough to hear if you leave the room. Consider getting two to ensure accuracy.

✔ **Waterproof pens and markers:** Select ones that don't rub off.

✔ **Labels:** You can make labels from masking or freezer tape, customize your own on your home computer, or order small quantities from a company like My Own Labels (see www.myownlabels.com).

✔ **Cutting board:** A good cutting board protects your knives while providing you with a movable work surface.

✔ **Candy thermometer:** A candy thermometer accurately registers the temperature of candy and sugar. In canning, it's used to check the temperature of cooked items. Some candy thermometers have marks indicating the gel point for jelly (220°). Purchase a candy thermometer that's easy to read with a base to support the thermometer so that the bulb portion doesn't touch the bottom of your pan, which can cause your temperature reading to be inaccurate. Many come with a clip attached to keep the bulb off of the bottom.

If you can, store a second thermometer in a handy location. If you accidentally break one while canning, you'll have a backup.

Book I

Getting
Started
with
Canning
and
Preserving

Nice-to-have tools

The following items aren't absolutely mandatory, but they're certainly nice to have. If you don't already have these items in your kitchen, add them as you need them. They don't take up a lot of room, and you'll find yourself constantly reaching for them when you can.

✔ **Vegetable peeler:** Use it for peeling carrots, potatoes, and apples.

✔ **Potato masher:** It makes quick work of smashing your cooked fruits or vegetables.

✔ **Lemon juicer:** This tool, shown in Figure 3-2, works on any citrus fruit and allows you to extract the juice in a hurry. Just cut your fruit in half, insert the juicer point into the fruit, and press away.

Measure your juice and keep seeds and pulp out at the same time by squeezing your fruit into a mesh strainer resting on the edge of a measuring cup.

✔ **Melon baller:** With a melon baller, you can easily remove the seeds from a halved cucumber without the seeds ending up all over your kitchen.

✔ **Corer:** This tool removes apple cores without damaging the fruit. A corer is a real timesaver when you're handling pounds of apples.

✔ **Cherry/olive pitter:** There's nothing better for removing cherry and olive pits. Purchase the size of pitter that holds your fruit size.

Pots, pans, bowls, and more

You probably already have an assortment of pots, pans, and mixing bowls. If not, don't worry: You don't need to purchase everything at one time. Start with a good basic assortment and add pieces as you find a need for them.

✔ **Pots:** Pots have two looped handles (one on each side of the pot), range in size from 5 to 8 quarts, are deep, and allow ample space for the expansion of your food during a hard-rolling boil. A good-quality, heavy-bottomed pot provides even heat distribution for cooking jams, jellies, or other condiments.

✔ **Saucepans:** Saucepans range in size from 1 to 3 quarts. They have a long handle on one side of the pan and usually come with a fitted lid.

✔ **Mixing bowls:** Keep a variety of mixing bowl sizes in your kitchen. Look for sets in graduated sizes that stack inside each other for easy storage. Bowls made from glass and stainless steel are the most durable.

Purchase mixing bowls with flat, not curved, bases. They won't slide all over your kitchen counter while you work. When mixing vigorously, place a damp dishtowel under the bowl to prevent the filled bowl from sliding.

✔ **Colander:** Colanders aren't just for draining pasta. They're perfect for washing and draining fruits and vegetables. Simply fill your colander with food and immerse it in a sink full of water. Remove the colander from the water and let your food drain while you move on to other tasks.

✔ **Wire basket:** A collapsible wire or mesh basket with a lifting handle makes blanching a breeze. Place your filled basket of food into your pot of boiling water. When the blanching time is up, lift the food-filled basket out of the boiling water.

Tried-and-true timesavers

All the items in this list are indispensable for your food preservation chores. These tools all save you loads of time.

✔ **Food processor:** Purchase the best-quality food processor you can afford. It should be heavy and sturdy so that it doesn't bounce around on your kitchen counter as it's processing away. Figure 3-4 is one example of a food processor.

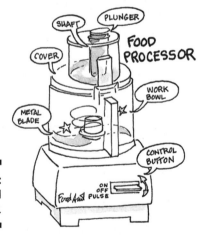

Figure 3-4:
A food processor.

✔ **Food mill:** A food mill (see Figure 3-5) purees fruits and vegetables as it removes the peel and seeds. You accomplish this seed removal by manually cranking the blade, which forces the pulp through the mill. Look for a food mill that rests on the edge of your bowl or pot, which enables you to use one hand to stabilize the mill while you crank the blade with your other hand.

Book I

Getting
Started
with
Canning
and
Preserving

FOOD MILL

Figure 3-5:
Food mill.

✔ **Blender:** A blender purees fruits and vegetables in a hurry, but you need to remove the peel and seeds first. Be cautious of incorporating too much air into your food.

✔ **Food scale:** A food scale is essential when your canning recipe lists your fruits or vegetables by weight. A food scale with metric quantity markings makes converting recipe ingredients a breeze. The two most common types of food scales are spring and electronic:

- A *spring scale* (sometimes referred to as a manual scale) allows you to place a bowl on the scale and manually adjust the weight setting to 0 before weighing your food. After placing your food on the scale, read the indicator on the dial to determine the weight.

- An *electronic scale* is battery operated with a digital readout. It's more costly than a spring scale but easier to read. Look for one with a *tare feature*. This feature allows you to set the scale to 0 if you add a bowl to hold your food. If you have a choice, choose an electronic or digital scale.

✔ **Vacuum-sealing machines:** A vacuum sealer is the most efficient appliance around for removing air from food-storage bags. Use vacuum sealers for packaging dried foods or for storing raw or cooked foods in the freezer. Although a vacuum sealer takes up room and can be costly, you'll realize its full value after you own one.

New on the market are hand-held vacuum sealers. They can provide a less expensive alternative to purchasing an electric version.

Choosing Your Canning Gear

The equipment in this section is especially designed for canning, which means you'll use it during canning season but not much otherwise. Make sure that you store these items in a safe, clean location. And be sure to look over every piece each time you use it to check for wear and tear.

Canning vessels

The kind of food you'll be canning determines the type of vessel you'll be using: a water-bath canner or a pressure canner:

- ✔ **Water-bath canner:** A water-bath canner, also referred to as a boiling-water canner, is a kettle used for processing high-acid foods (primarily fruits, jams, jellies, condiments, and pickled foods). The canner consists of a large enamelware or stainless-steel pot with a tight-fitting lid and a jar rack. Check out Chapter 1 of Book II for an illustration of a water-bath canner and instructions on how to use one.

- ✔ **Pressure canner:** A pressure canner, sometimes referred to as a steam-pressure canner, is used for canning low-acid foods (primarily vegetables, meats, fish, and poultry) in an airtight container at a specific pressure. A weighted gauge or a dial gauge measures steam pressure in the canner. This ensures that the high temperature of 240° is attained to safely process your food. Pressure canners and how to use them are described (and illustrated) in Chapter 1 of Book V.

Jars and lids

Even the most careful filling of jars is only as good as the lids themselves. Always use the proper lids for your jars, to keep the food clean and well-sealed.

Home-canning jars

Over the years, many types of jars with many varieties of seals have been used for home-canning. The most commonly used jars bear the names of Ball and Kerr and are commonly referred to as *Mason jars.* They use a two-piece cap to produce a vacuum seal in the jar after heat processing.

To ensure safe home-canning today, use only jars approved for home-canning and made from tempered glass. *Tempering* is a treatment process for glass that allows the jars to withstand the high heat (212°) of a water-bath canner, as well as the high temperature (240°) of a pressure canner, without breaking.

Home-canning jars come in many sizes: 4-ounce, half-pint, 12-ounce, 1-pint, and 1-quart (see Figure 3-6). They offer two widths of openings: regular-mouth (about 2½ inches in diameter) and wide-mouth (about 3⅛ inches in diameter). The smaller jars are usually reserved for jams and jellies, while quarts are usually filled with other foods.

Regular-mouth jars are used more frequently for jelly, jam, relish, or any other cooked food. Wide-mouth jars are mainly used for canning vegetables and pickles and meats, because it's easier to get the large pieces into the wide opening.

Figure 3-6: Varieties of canning jars: wide-mouth, regular-mouth, and jelly jars.

CANNING JARS

Two-piece caps

Two-piece caps consist of a lid and a metal screw band (see Figure 3-7). They're made specifically for use with modern-day home-canning jars.

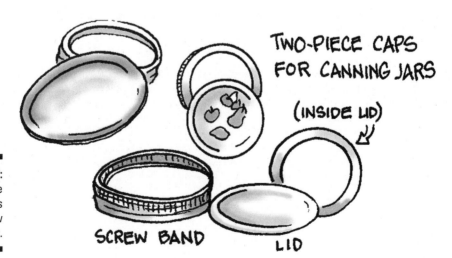

Figure 3-7: Two-piece caps: lids and screw bands.

TWO-PIECE CAPS FOR CANNING JARS

(INSIDE LID)

SCREW BAND   LID

- **Lids:** The underside edge of the lid has a rubberlike sealing compound that softens when it's heated. This compound adheres to a clean jar rim and creates an airtight seal after the heat-processing period.

- **Screw bands:** The screw band holds the lid in place during the processing period and secures it in place when storing an opened jar in the refrigerator. After verifying that your cooled jars have successfully sealed by pressing the center of each lid to check for a vacuum seal, you remove the screw band before you store the canned food. You can use the screw bands many times as long as there are no signs of corrosion or rust and they aren't bent or dented.

New on the market, reusable lids have been getting rave reviews. They're a good way to save money in the long run. You buy them once and reuse them each year. Check them out!

Canning tools

The tools in the following sections are must-haves for water-bath or pressure canning. Safety in the kitchen is No. 1, and the right tools for handling hot, filled jars and other large canning equipment are indispensable.

Foam skimmer

A *foam skimmer,* shown in Figure 3-8, makes removing foam from the top of hot jelly, jam, or marmalade easy while leaving any pieces of fruit or rind in the hot liquid. (The openings in slotted spoons are too large to achieve quick and efficient foam removal.)

Mason jars

If the most commonly used glass home-canning jars bear the names of Ball and Kerr, why do we call them Mason jars? The Mason jar is named for its creator, James Landis Mason. He designed and patented a unique glass jar that uses a screw-top lid to create an airtight seal for food. This easy-to-seal jar replaced the large stoneware vessels that had previously been used for food storage.

The tapered jars we use today were introduced after World War II. They use a two-piece cap consisting of a lid and a metal screw band that fits the threaded jar top. Today, all home-canning jars are generically referred to as Mason jars. Thank you, Mr. Mason, for making the task of home-canning easy with the use of screw-top closures.

Book I

Getting
Started
with
Canning
and
Preserving

FOAM SKIMMER

Figure 3-8:
A foam
skimmer.

Jar lifter

A *jar lifter* is one tool you don't want to be without. It's the best tool available for transferring hot canning jars into and out of your canning kettle or pressure canner. This odd-looking, rubberized, tonglike item (check out Figure 3-9) grabs the jar around the *neck* (the area just below the threaded portion at the top of the jar) without disturbing the screw band.

JAR LIFTERS

Figure 3-9:
Jar lifters.

Lid wand

A *lid wand* (see Figure 3-10) has a magnet on one end of a heat-resistant stick. With it, you can take a lid from hot water and place it on the filled-jar rim without touching the lid or disturbing the sealing compound.

Place your lids top to top and underside to underside to prevent them from sticking together in your pan of hot water. If they do stick together, dip them into a bowl of cold water to release the suction. Reheat them in the hot water for a few seconds before using them. Also, offset the lids as you place them in the water, which keeps them fanned out and easier to pick up one by one.

LID WAND

Figure 3-10:
A lid wand.

Thin plastic spatula

A thin, flexible plastic spatula is the right tool for releasing air bubbles between pieces of food in your filled jars (check out Figure 3-11). Buy a package of chopsticks for an inexpensive alternative.

Don't use a metal item or a larger object for this job because it may damage your food and crack or break your hot jar.

Figure 3-11:
A thin
plastic
spatula for
releasing air
bubbles.

PLASTIC SPATULA
FOR RELEASING AIR BUBBLES

Wide-mouth canning funnel

A wide-mouth funnel fits into the inside edge of a regular-mouth or a wide-mouth canning jar and lets you quickly and neatly fill your jars. This funnel is an essential tool for canning.

Jelly bag or strainer

A jelly bag is made for extracting juice from cooked fruit for making jelly. These bags aren't expensive, but if you'd rather not purchase one, you can make your own using a metal strainer lined with cheesecloth. Use a strainer that hangs on the edge of your pot or mixing bowl and doesn't touch the liquid. Head to Book II, Chapter 4 for instructions on making jelly.

Book I

Getting
Started
with
Canning
and
Preserving

Gathering Your Pickling Gear and Utensils

In addition to the basic equipment for water-bath canning (refer to Chapter 1 of Book II), you need nonreactive utensils and equipment for handling, cooking, and brining your food. Nonreactive items are made of stainless steel, nonstick-surfaced items (without a damaged nonstick surface), enamelware, or glass.

Don't use enamelware with chips or cracks or equipment or utensils made from or containing copper, iron, or brass. These items react with the acids and salt during the pickling process, altering the color of your food and giving the finished product a bad taste. *Definitely* don't use galvanized products, which contain zinc. These produce a poison when the acid and the salt touch the zinc, which is transferred to your food causing serious illness (or worse).

Grabbing Your Freezing Tools

Some of the items required for this simple form of food preservation are already in your kitchen. For a more detailed list, check out Book VI, Chapter 1.

An obvious piece of equipment you need is a freezer. If you're just getting started with freezing and aren't looking for long-term storage, the freezer attached to your refrigerator will suffice. It doesn't get and stay as cold as a dedicated freezer, however. For long-term freezing, a dedicated freezer unit is necessary.

Freezers come in a wide array of sizes to fit any household. They can be upright, resembling a refrigerator, or chest style, with a top opening lid.

Buy the largest freezer that you think you may ever need and be certain to measure the area that you want to fit the freezer into. Keep it in an out of the way area, but close enough for convenient "shopping."

Regardless of how you wrap and pack your preserved food, perhaps the most important element of the process is figuring out a way to organize your goods in your freezer so that they're sorted and easy to access. Nothing is worse than throwing away a package of home-grown food that has migrated to the back of the freezer and spent its freezer life buried.

These are the containers that you need to start your freezing adventure:

- ✔ **Rigid containers:** These containers can be made of plastic or glass. Use only containers approved for the cold temperatures of a freezer. Plastic containers should be nonporous and thick enough to keep out odors and dry air in the freezer. Glass containers need to be treated to endure the low temperature of a freezer and strong enough to resist cracking under the pressure of expanding food during the freezing process.

- ✔ **Freezer bags:** Use bags made for freezing in sizes compatible with the amount of your food.

- ✔ **Freezer paper and wraps:** This laminated paper protects your food from freezer burn, which results when air comes in contact with your food while it's in the freezer. Tape this paper to keep the wrap tightly sealed. Heavy-duty aluminum foil is another great freezer wrap and requires no taping.

For extra protection against freezer damage, wrap food items in foil and place them in a freezer bag.

Gathering Your Drying Equipment

Dehydrating food is a long, slow process of removing moisture from your food while exposing it to low heat.

Don't let the fancy name fool you; *dehydrating appliances* are simply ways to produce gentle heat and airflow around the things you're drying. You have two options:

- ✔ **A conventional oven:** If your oven maintains a low temperature and you can stand to be without it for up to 24 hours, use it for drying before making the investment in an electric food dehydrator.

  An oven thermometer tells you whether your oven temperature is low enough to dry your food without cooking it. (See Book VII, Chapter 1 for detailed instructions for how to check your oven's temperature).

- ✔ **An electric dehydrator:** This machine dries your food in an enclosed chamber while it circulates warm air around your food.

Most people don't realize how useful electric dehydrators can be and give them away to thrift stores. They can usually be found for less than $10, in perfect working order.

In addition, you can use trays and racks to hold your food while it's drying. They're included with an electric dehydrator. For oven-drying, use mesh-covered frames or baking sheets. For sun-drying, clean screens are necessary, along with clean cheesecloth to keep hungry bugs off the food as it dries.

For more details on this equipment, head to Book VII, Chapter 1.

Setting Up for Smoking

Back in the olden days, people dug a pit to smoke meats, so don't think you have to spend a lot of money on your equipment. Using less expensive options may mean that you have to work a little harder and be a little more watchful to keep the temperature steady.

From high-end to homemade, there's a smoker out there for anyone interested in trying this preservation method. Some prefer charcoal smokers; others go with electric or gas smokers; and still others are happy rigging up the kettle grill they already own. (Check out Book VIII, Chapter 2 for information about what you can do with the various kinds of smokers available and what makes them desirable or not.)

However, the meat of the matter, when it comes to smoking, actually is the wood. Smoke gives the meat unique flavor, and you get the smoke from putting hardwood between your charcoal and your meat so that the slow-burning wood sends its heavenly smoke up into whatever you're cooking. (Refer to Chapter 2 of Book VIII for more on flavoring with wood.)

In most cases, unless you're using an electric or gas smoker, you use charcoal as your heat source, and you use wood to add smoke and flavor.

Why not use wood as heat and smoke, you ask? Because oversmoking is a common mistake when you try to kill two birds with one pile of wood — you have better luck and better smoke and heat control if you use charcoal. Use too much smoke, and you're likely to end up with a very unwelcome bitterness in your meat. (Check out Chapter 2 of Book VIII for more on charcoal.)

You also need some special tools to make the smoking magic work:

✔ **Fire:** You need matches or a long butane lighter to get your charcoal going.

✓ **Chimney starter:** A chimney starter is the best way to get your charcoal going. (Check out Chapter 2 of Book VIII to get the details on chimney starters.)

✓ **Tongs and a long-handled metal spatula:** You don't want to pierce meat with a fork and let the juices run out. Tongs or spatulas let you move meat without damaging it.

✓ **Basting brush or mop:** Choose a sturdy brush or buy a cotton basting mop (see Figure 3-12), which gives you great coverage quickly — a plus considering you're working hard to maintain a steady temperature.

Figure 3-12:
A well-made brush or basting mop allows you to quickly sauce whatever you're cooking.

✓ **Thermometer:** If your smoker doesn't have a built-in thermometer, stick a candy thermometer into a vent. You can find digital, dial, and notched versions.

✓ **Grill brush:** A thorough scrape with a grill brush goes a long way toward maintaining the flavor of your food and keeping it from sticking.

✓ **Smoke pouch or pan:** Damp wood chips and hot charcoal aren't a good combination. Keep the two separate by using a smoke pouch, a small foil pouch, filled with wood chips. A pie tin, cake pan, or a pan you fashion from heavy-duty aluminum foil works great.

✓ **Spray bottle:** Use a spray bottle to discourage flames that may lick up from your grill or to add moisture to meat as you smoke it.

✓ **Heat-resistant gloves:** Big cuts of meat need hands-on attention, which means you need heat-resistant gloves so that you can move them.

✓ **Heavy-duty aluminum foil:** You use foil to wrap meat before you cook it and to keep the meat hot for residual cooking after it's out of the smoker.

Assembling Supplies for Salting and Curing

When you're getting ready for salting and curing meats, it's all about getting the flavor you want on and in the food. Here are some items that make salting and curing meats simple and effective:

- **Gloves:** Inexpensive gloves are great insurance for keeping your hands (and meat) as sanitary as possible. They're also protection against rubbing a salty, hot pepper mix into any little paper cut you might not know you had.
- **Food scale:** Many recipes for rubs and cures are listed by weight.
- **Meat injector:** This tool looks like a huge hypodermic needle and is used to inject brine directly into the meat. A meat injector is necessary for thicker cuts of meat.
- **Large container:** It will hold treated meat coated with cure. You want it to seal tightly.
- **Vacuum sealer:** Nice, but not essential. (See the earlier section "Tried-and-true timesavers" for more on vacuum sealers.) It's a great tool for speeding up the brining process, by creating a vacuum around the meat and drawing in the brine.

Fermenting Paraphernalia

Fermenting is a mysterious form of preserving. Though some may instantly picture ales and lagers when they think of fermenting, many of the foods you enjoy eating, like sauerkraut, vinegar, and yogurt, are actually fermented.

Take a look at the following sections, which outline the different equipment needed for the various types of fermentation.

Fermenting foods

You may be surprised to see the list of foods that are actually fermented. Sauerkraut and sourdough are just the start. Other foods, including fermented vegetables and drinks such as *kefir*, a fermented milk product, and Kombucha, a fermented tea drink, have benefits when added to your diet and are easy to make at home. (In other cultures, kefir is as familiar as apple cider vinegar is to us.)

Each fermented food requires the proper bacteria *(starter)* to begin working. The starter depends on what foods you're producing.

Containers can be summed up in two words: sanitary and nonreactive. There are traditional containers for all sorts of fermented foods. Your options include

✔ **Glass:** It's easy to clean and doesn't hold odors. Glass is also easy to find and easy to replace when you inevitably break something. With glass containers, you can also keep an eye on the fermentation process, without exposing the fermented food to unwanted handling. If you have a choice, go with glass.

✔ **Crocks:** Also referred to as stoneware crocks, these are food-safe containers that are opaque and usually have a lid. Crocks are wonderful units that come in all sizes, but they can be expensive to replace if broken. A small, baked bean crock is perfect for keeping sourdough in. Large stoneware crocks are available in sizes from 1 gallon to 5 gallons. They're nonreactive and are used for making pickles and olives. Uncoated aluminum or copper should not be used. Both of these metals react with the acidity and salinity of a fermenting food.

Make sure that you use only crocks that are glazed on the interior and certified free of lead and *cadmium,* a form of zinc ore used in pigments or dyes. (Because you can't know the history of secondhand crocks, it's best to purchase new ones.)

Fermenting brews

For the benefit of beginner homebrewers of lagers, ales, ciders, and meads, this section discusses only the minimal amount of equipment needed.

Many homebrew equipment suppliers sell prepackaged starter kits that can range from the bare-bones to the top-of-the-line — all-inclusive starter kits can run up to $200. All these kits include the basic equipment essentials, but some kits also throw in books, videos, or other unnecessary items that just inflate the price. Before you buy a kit, consider what you need and what you want to spend. To help you get the wheels turning, Table 3-1 gives you a starter list of necessary items and their approximate costs.

If you go high-end on all your equipment, your cost adds up to well over a couple hundred dollars, not including the cost of bottles. See Book IV, Chapter 6 for detailed information about this equipment, as well as bottles and their cost.

Book I

Getting
Started
with
Canning
and
Preserving

Table 3-1	Beginner Brewing Equipment and Its Cost
Equipment	*Approximate Cost*
Brewpot, 16 qt. minimum	$40/20 qt., $80/30 qt.
Brew spoon (HDPE plastic)	$4 or less
Primary fermenter (HDPE plastic) with spigot, lid	$20 or less
Airlock	$2 or less
Drilled rubber stopper for airlock	$2 or less
3 to 4 feet of food-grade plastic hose, ½ inch in diameter	$3
Bottling or "priming" bucket (HDPE plastic) with spigot	$15 or less
Bottles (must be the reusable type that don't use twist-off caps)	$20–$30 for one batch of beer (5 gallons); the exact number of bottles depends on their size: 12 oz., 16 oz., 22 oz., or 1 qt.
Bottle rinser	$12
Bottle brush	$3
Bottling tube (HDPE plastic) with spring valve	$4 or less
Bottle capper	$35 (bench-type) or $15 (two-handed)
Hydrometer (triple scale) with cylinder	$10 ($5 or less for the cylinder)

Juicing Tools

Juicing is a simple process; use simple utensils and make it easy to create this healthful food! Use sharp, clean items that are designed to reduce hand fatigue.

One of the nicest things about juicing is that you need very few tools:

- **Paring knife:** The knife should be razor sharp and of good quality. A sharp knife is much safer than a dull one, because it takes less force to actually do the work.

- **Citrus peeler:** A citrus peeler makes short work of inedible peelings from citrus.

✔ **Mesh strainer:** This handy gadget is a great way to remove excess pulp for people who can't tolerate the texture. Place over your juice cup and strain fresh juice through it.

Juicers can vary from the old school hand juicer, to a high-powered, twin-geared juicer that costs hundreds of dollars. Depending on how much money you have and how much juice you plan on making, there's a juicing system out there for you. Check out Chapter 1 of Book IX for detailed information about the juicer choices you'll find on the market.

Book II
Water-Bath
Canning with Fruits

The 5th Wave   By Rich Tennant

"...and here's what we canned from the garden
this year. Beets, carrots, cucumbers...oh,
there's that glove I couldn't find."

In this book . . .

This book tells you all you need to know about the most popular method of canning: water-bath canning. Some of the products, such as jam, jelly, marmalade, relish, and salsa, may be familiar to you, while others, like chutney, conserves, and mincemeats, may be new. Packed with easy-to-follow instructions for canning a wide variety of fruits, jellies, savory spreads, and more, this part sends you well on your way to a pantry stocked with healthy and delicious items.

Chapter 1

Discovering Water-Bath Canning

· ·

· ·

With water-bath canning, you essentially boil jars filled with food in a special kettle for a certain amount of time. Common foods for water-bath canning include fruits and tomatoes, as well as jams, jellies, marmalades, chutneys, relishes, pickled vegetables, and other condiments.

You may be wondering whether water-bath canning is safe for canning food at home. Yes, it is — provided that you follow the instructions and guidelines for safe canning.

In this chapter, you discover which foods are safely processed in a water-bath canner and step-by-step instructions for completing the canning process. In no time, you'll be turning out sparkling jars full of homemade delicacies to dazzle and satisfy your family and friends.

Diving into Water-Bath Canning

Water-bath canning, sometimes referred to as the *boiling-water method,* is the simplest and easiest method for preserving high-acid food, primarily fruit, tomatoes, and pickled vegetables.

To water-bath can, you place your prepared jars in a *water-bath canner,* a kettle especially designed for this canning method; bring the water to a boil; and then maintain that boil for a certain number of minutes, determined by the type of food and the size of the jar. Keeping the water boiling in your jar-filled kettle throughout the processing period maintains a water temperature of 212°. This constant temperature is critical for destroying mold, yeast, enzymes, and bacteria that occur in high-acid foods.

You can safely water-bath can only high-acid foods — those with a pH factor (the measure of acidity) of 4.6 or lower. So just what is a high-acid food? Either of the following:

- **Foods that are naturally high in acid:** These foods include most fruits.

- **Low-acid foods that you add acid to, thus converting them into high-acid foods:** *Pickled vegetables* fall into this category, making them safe for water-bath canning.

Using water-bath canning equipment

Just as you wouldn't alter the ingredients in a recipe or skip a step in the canning process, you don't want to use the wrong equipment when you're home-canning. This equipment allows you to handle and process your filled jars safely.

The equipment for water-bath canning is less expensive than the equipment for pressure canning. (Check out Book V, Chapter 1 to see what equipment pressure canning requires.) Water-bath canning kettles cost anywhere from $25 to $45. In some instances, you can purchase a *starter kit* that includes the canning kettle, the jar rack, a jar lifter, a wide-mouth funnel, and jars for about $50 to $60. (If you don't have a supplier near you, an online search for canning supplies will bring up dozens of merchants.)

Following is a list of the equipment you must have on hand, no exceptions or substitutions, for safe and successful water-bath canning:

- **A water-bath canner:** The water-bath canner consists of a large kettle, usually made of porcelain-coated steel or aluminum, that holds a maximum of 21 to 22 quarts of water, has a fitted lid, and uses a rack (see the next item) to hold the jars (see Figure 1-1). Do not substitute a large stock pot for a water-bath canner. Jars must sit off the bottom of the canner, and racks, included in your canner kit, are available to fit this purpose.

  Although aluminum is a *reactive metal* (a metal that transfers flavor to food coming in direct contact with it), it's permitted for a water-bath canner because your sealed jar protects the food from directly touching the aluminum.

WATER-BATH CANNING KETTLE

Figure 1-1:
A water-bath canning kettle with the rack hanging on the edge of the kettle.

Book II

Water-Bath Canning with Fruits

✔ **A jar rack:** The jar rack for a water-bath canner is usually made of stainless steel and rests on the bottom of your canning kettle. It keeps your jars from touching the bottom of the kettle, or each other, while holding the filled jars upright during the water-bath processing period. The rack has lifting handles for hanging it on the inside edge of your canning kettle (refer to Figure 1-1), allowing you to safely transfer your filled jars into and out of your kettle.

✔ **Canning jars:** Canning jars are the only jars recommended for home-canning. Use the jar size recommended in your recipe. For more on canning jars, refer to Book I, Chapter 3.

✔ **Two-piece caps (lids and screw bands):** These lids and screw bands, explained in detail in Book I, Chapter 3, create a vacuum seal after the water-bath processing period, preserving the contents of the jar for use at a later time. This seal protects your food from the reentry of microorganisms.

The older-style rubber rings are no longer recommended. Although they are sometimes still available secondhand, the seal is no longer dependable enough to result in a safe product. You can find these rubber rings in some specialty canning stores; however, due to their novelty, they are very expensive and sold in small quantities. Reserve this type of canning jar and kitschy design for your fun food gifts, not canning for a family's pantry.

In addition to the must-have items listed in the preceding, you may also want the following things. These items aren't critical to the outcome of your product, but you'll enjoy a more streamlined, efficient level of work if you use them. (You can find out more about these and other helpful but not necessary tools in Book I, Chapter 3.)

- ✔ **A teakettle or saucepan** filled with boiling water to use as a reserve.

- ✔ **A jar lifter,** the best tool for transferring hot jars into and out of a canning kettle or pressure canner.

- ✔ **A ladle and wide-mouth funnel** to make transferring food into your jars easier. The funnel also keeps the rims of the jars clean, for a better seal.

- ✔ **A lid wand** so that you can transfer your lids from the hot water to the jars without touching them and a jar lifter so that you can safely and easily lift canning jars in and out of your canning kettle.

- ✔ **A thin plastic spatula** to use for releasing air bubbles in the jar.

- ✔ **A foam skimmer** to deftly remove foam from the top of a jelly or marmalade.

- ✔ **A jelly bag or strainer,** an inexpensive strainer that removes fruit from cooked juice when making jelly.

Packing your jars with care

How you fill the canning jars is also important:

- ✔ **Don't overpack foods.** Too much food packed into a jar may result in heat not evenly penetrating, and bacteria can remain.

- ✔ **Make sure that your jars have the proper headspace.** *Headspace* is the air space between the inside of the lid and the top of your food or liquid in your jar or container (see Figure 1-2).

- ✔ **Make sure that you release the air bubbles from the jar before sealing the lid.** No matter how carefully you pack and fill your jars, you'll always have some hidden bubbles.

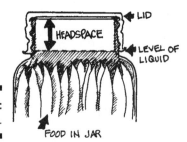

Figure 1-2:
Headspace.

The all-important headspace

When you're canning food, too little headspace in your canning jars restricts your food from expanding as it boils. Inadequate space for the expanding food may force some of it out of the jar and under the lid, leaving particles of food between the seal and the jar rim. If this occurs, your jar won't produce a vacuum seal.

Leaving too much headspace may cause discoloration in the top portion of your food. Excess headspace can keep your jar from producing a vacuum seal if the processing time isn't long enough to exhaust the excess air in the jar.

Always use the headspace stated in your recipe. If your recipe doesn't list a headspace allowance, use these guidelines:

Book II

Water-Bath Canning with Fruits

- For juice, jam, jelly, pickles, relish, chutney, sauces, and condiments, leave headspace of ¼ inch.

- For high-acid foods (fruits and tomatoes), leave headspace of ½ inch.

- For low-acid foods (vegetables, meats, fish, and poultry), leave headspace of 1 inch.

If you don't trust yourself to eyeball the headspace, use a small plastic ruler (about 6 inches long) to measure the correct headspace in the jar.

Releasing air bubbles from your jars

The most important thing to do when you're filling your jars is to release trapped air bubbles between the food pieces (see Figure 1-3). Air bubbles may seem unimportant, but they can play havoc with your final product:

- **Jar seals:** Too much air in the jar from trapped air bubbles produces excessive pressure in the jar during processing. The pressure in the jar is greater than the pressure outside the jar during cooling. This imbalance interferes with the sealing process.

- **Liquid levels:** Air bubbles take up space. When there's trapped air between your food pieces before sealing the jars, the liquid level in the jar drops when the food is heated. Release trapped air by inserting a plastic or wooden stick (a chopstick works well) into your jar to move the food, keeping the bubble from rising.

Never skip the step of releasing air bubbles.

RELEASING AIR BUBBLES

USE A NONMETALLIC SPATULA TO PRESS BACK GENTLY ON THE CONTENTS. GO ALL THE WAY AROUND THE JAR.

Figure 1-3: Releasing air bubbles from your filled jars.

Water-Bath Canning: From Prep to Product

Every aspect of the canning procedure is important, so don't skip anything, no matter how trivial it seems. When your food and canning techniques are in perfect harmony and balance, you'll have a safely processed product for use at a later time.

The following sections guide you through the step-by-step process for creating delicious, high-quality, homemade treats for your family and friends.

Always practice proper kitchen sanitation and cleanliness, carefully handle your food, and follow your recipe to the letter. Don't alter your recipe or skip any processing step.

Step 1: Preparing your gear

The first thing you do when canning is to inspect your equipment and get everything ready so that when you're done preparing the food (Step 2 in the canning process), you can fill your jars immediately.

Inspect and wash your jars, lids, and screw bands

Always review the manufacturer's instructions for readying your jars, lids, and screw bands. Then inspect your jars, lids, and screw bands for any defects as follows:

- **Jars:** Check the jar edges for any nicks, chips, or cracks in the glass, discarding any jars with these defects. If you're reusing jars, clean any stains or food residue from them and then recheck them for any defects.

- **Screw bands:** Make sure that the bands aren't warped, corroded, or rusted. Test the roundness of the band by screwing it onto a jar. If it tightens down smoothly without resistance, it's useable. Discard any bands that are defective or *out of round* (bent or not completely round).

  You can reuse screw bands over and over, as long as they're in good condition. And because you remove them after your jars have cooled, you don't need as many bands as jars.

- **Lids:** All lids must be new. Lids aren't reusable. Check the sealant on the underside of each lid for evenness. Don't use scratched or dented lids. Defective lids won't produce a vacuum seal. Don't buy old lids from secondhand stores. Older lids will not seal properly.

After examining the jars for nicks or chips, the screw bands for proper fit and corrosion, and the new lids for imperfections and scratches, wash everything in warm, soapy water, rinsing the items well and removing any soap residue. Discard any damaged or imperfect items.

Heating the water and jars

Fill your canning kettle one-half to two-thirds full of water and begin heating the water to simmering. Remember that the water level will rise considerably as you add the filled jars. Be sure to not overfill at this point.

Heat extra water in a teakettle or saucepan as a reserve. You want to make sure that the jars are covered with at least 1 to 2 inches of water. By adding preheated water, you don't have to wait for the entire canner to reheat before continuing.

While you're waiting to fill your jars, submerge the jars and lids in hot, not boiling, water and keep your screw bands clean and handy as follows:

- **Jars:** Submerge them in hot water in your kettle for a minimum of 10 minutes. Keep them there until you're ready to fill them.

- **Lids:** Submerge them in hot, not boiling, water in a saucepan. Keeping them separate from your jars protects the lid sealant.

- **Screw bands:** You don't need to keep your screw bands hot, but they do need to be clean. Place them where you'll be filling your jars.

Book II

Water-Bath Canning with Fruits

Step 2: Readying your food

Always use food of the highest quality when you're canning. If you settle for less than the best, your final product won't have the quality you're looking for. Carefully sort through your food, discarding any bruised pieces or pieces you wouldn't eat in the raw state.

Follow the instructions in your recipe for preparing your food, such as removing the skin or peel or cutting it into pieces.

Similarly, prepare your food exactly as instructed in your recipe. Don't make any adjustments in ingredients or quantities of ingredients. Any alteration may change the acidity of the product, requiring pressure canning (see Book V) instead of water-bath canning to kill microorganisms.

Step 3: Filling your jars

Add your prepared food (cooked or raw) and hot liquid to your prepared jars as soon as they're ready. Follow these steps:

1. **Transfer your prepared food into the hot jars, adding hot liquid or syrup if your recipe calls for it and being sure to leave the proper headspace.**

   Using a wide-mouth funnel and a ladle to quickly fill your jars eliminates a lot of spilling, and you'll have less to clean from your jar rims. It also helps cleanup and prevents slipping if you place your jars on a clean kitchen towel before filling.

2. **Release any air bubbles with a nonmetallic spatula or a tool to free air bubbles.**

   Before applying the two-piece caps, always release air bubbles and leave the headspace specified in your recipe. These steps are critical for creating a vacuum seal and preserving your food.

3. **Add more prepared food or liquid to the jar after releasing the air bubbles to maintain the recommended headspace.**

4. **Wipe the jar rims with a clean, damp cloth.**

   If there's one speck of food on the jar rim, the sealant on the lid edge won't make contact with the jar rim, and your jar won't seal.

5. **Place a hot lid onto each jar rim, sealant side touching the jar rim, and hand-tighten the screw band.**

   Don't overtighten because air needs to escape during the sealing process.

Step 4: Processing your jars

With your jars filled, you're ready to begin processing. Follow these steps:

1. **Place the jar rack in your canning kettle, suspending it with the handles on the inside edge of the kettle.**

2. **Place the filled jars in the jar rack, making sure that they're standing upright and not touching each other.**

   Although the size of your kettle seems large, don't be tempted to pack your canner with jars. Only place as many jars as will comfortably fit yet still allow water to move freely between them. And always process jars in a single layer in the jar rack.

   Never process half-pint or pint jars with quart jars because the larger amount of food in quart jars requires a longer processing time to kill any bacteria and microorganisms. If your recipe calls for the same processing times for half-pint and pint jars, you can process those two sizes together.

3. **Unhook the jar rack from the edge of the kettle, carefully lowering it into the hot water, and add water if necessary.**

   Air bubbles coming from the jars are normal. If your jars aren't covered by at least 1 inch of water, add boiling water from your reserve. Be careful to pour this hot water between the jars, instead of directly on top of them, to prevent splashing yourself with hot water.

   Make sure that the tops of the submerged jars are covered with at least 1 inch of hot water. Add water from your reserve teakettle or saucepan to achieve this level.

4. **Cover the kettle and heat the water to a full, rolling boil, reducing the heat and maintaining a gentle, rolling boil for the amount of time indicated in the recipe.**

   Start your processing time after the water boils. Maintain a boil for the entire processing period.

   If you live at an altitude above 1,000 feet above sea level, you need to adjust your processing time. Check out the section "Adjusting Your Processing Times for Altitude," later in this chapter, for details.

Step 5: Removing and testing your jars

After you complete the processing time, immediately remove your jars from
the boiling water with a jar lifter and place them on clean, dry, kitchen or
paper towels away from drafts, with 1 or 2 inches of space between the jars —
don't attempt to adjust the bands or check the seals — and allow them to
cool completely. The cooling period may take 12 to 24 hours. Do not try
to hurry this process by cooling the jars in any way. You may end up with
unsealed jars or cracked glass.

After your jars have completely cooled, test your seals by pushing on the
center of the lid (see Figure 1-4). If the lid feels solid and doesn't indent, you
have a successful vacuum seal. If the lid depresses in the center and makes
a popping noise when you apply pressure, the jar isn't sealed. Immediately
refrigerate unsealed jars, using the contents within two weeks or as stated in
your recipe.

TEST THE SEAL
BY DEPRESSING
THE CENTER OF
THE LID OF THE
COMPLETELY
COOLED JAR.

Figure 1-4:
Testing your
jar seal.

Reprocessing unsealed jars

Jars may not seal for several reasons: You may have miscalculated the processing time, pieces of food may not have been cleaned from the jar rim, you may have left an improper amount of headspace, or the sealant on the lids may have been defective. The safest and easiest method for treating processed jars that didn't seal is to refrigerate the jar immediately and use the product within two weeks.

If you want to reprocess jars that didn't seal, you can do that. But keep in mind that reprocessing your food takes almost as much time as making the recipe from the beginning. The only time to consider reprocessing jars is if every jar in the kettle doesn't seal.

To reprocess unsealed jars, follow these steps:

1. **Remove the lid and discard it.**

2. **Check the edge of the jar for damage.**

   If the jar is damaged, discard the food in case a broken piece of glass fell into the food.

3. **Discard any damaged jars.**

4. **Reheat the food.**

5. **Follow the step-by-step instructions in this chapter for filling your jars, releasing air bubbles, and processing your sterilized, filled jars.**

6. **Reprocess the filled jars for the recommended time for your recipe.**

7. **Check the seal after your jars have completely cooled.**

Book II

Water-Bath
Canning
with Fruits

Step 6: Storing your canned food

After you've tested the seal and know that it's good (see the preceding section), it's time to store your canned food:

1. **Remove the screw bands from your sealed jars.**

2. **Wash the sealed jars and the screw bands in hot, soapy water.**

   This step removes any residue from the jars and screw bands.

3. **Label your filled jars, including the date processed.**

4. **Store your jars, without the screw bands, in a cool, dark, dry place.**

Heeding Some General Directions

Some general directions apply to all the recipes in Book II. Be sure to heed the following instructions as you prepare the upcoming recipes:

- ✔ Prepare your canning jars and two-piece caps (lids and screw bands) according to the manufacturer's instructions. Keep the jars and lids hot until you fill them.

- ✔ When you fill your jars, release any air bubbles with a nonreactive utensil. Add more of the food you're canning and liquid as necessary to maintain the headspace noted in the recipe.

- ✔ After filling your jars (but before placing them in the water-bath canner), wipe the jar rims. Then seal the jars with the two-piece caps, hand-tightening the bands.

- ✔ It doesn't matter if you have a less-than-full canner. Simply arrange the jars so that they're evenly spaced, if possible.

- ✔ When your jars are done processing, remove them from the canner with a jar lifter. Place them on a clean kitchen towel away from drafts to cool.

- ✔ After the jars cool completely, test the seals. If you find jars that haven't sealed, refrigerate them and use them within the time specified in the recipe.

Safety First: Checking for Spoilage

The best way to detect food spoilage is by visually examining your jars. Review the following checklist. If you can answer True for each of the following statements, your food should be safe for eating:

- ✔ The food in the jar is covered with liquid, is fully packed, and has maintained the proper headspace.

- ✔ The food in the jar is free from moving air bubbles.

- ✔ The jars have good, tight seals.

- ✔ The food has maintained a uniform color.

- ✔ The food isn't broken or mushy.

- ✔ The liquid in the jar is clear, not cloudy, and free of sediment.

After your food has passed the preceding checklist, examine your jars more closely. If you discover any spoilage during any step of this process, don't continue your search, but properly dispose of your product.

1. **Hold the jar at eye level.**

2. **Turn and rotate the jar, looking for any seepage or oozing from under the lid that indicates a broken seal.**

3. **Examine the food surface for any streaks of dried food originating at the top of the jar.**

4. **Check the contents for any rising air bubbles or unnatural color.**

   The food and liquid should be clear, not cloudy.

5. **Open the jar.**

   There shouldn't be any spurting liquid.

6. **Smell the contents of the jar.**

   Take note of any unnatural or unusual odors.

7. **Look for any cottonlike growth, usually white, blue, black, or green, on the top of your food surface or on the underside of the lid.**

Spoiled low-acid food may exhibit little or no visual evidence of spoilage. Treat any jars that are suspect as if they contained botulism toxins. Follow the detailed instructions for responsibly disposing of spoiled, low-acid food in Book V, Chapter 1. Never use or taste any canned food that exhibits signs of spoilage or that you suspect is spoiled.

Removing the screw bands from your cooled, sealed jars before storing them allows you to easily detect any broken seals or food oozing out from under the lid that indicates spoilage.

Adjusting Your Processing Times for Altitudes

When you're canning at an altitude higher than 1,000 feet above sea level, you need to adjust your processing time (see Table 1-1). Because the air is thinner at higher altitudes, water boils below 212°. As a result, you need to process your food for a longer period of time to kill any microorganisms that can make your food unsafe.

If you live higher than 1,000 feet above sea level, follow these guidelines:

- ✓ **For processing times of less than 20 minutes:** Add 1 minute for each additional 1,000 feet of altitude.

- ✓ **For processing times of more than 20 minutes:** Add 2 minutes for each 1,000 feet of altitude.

Table 1-1	High-Altitude Processing Times for Water-Bath Canning	
Altitude (in feet)	*For Processing Times Less Than 20 Minutes*	*For Processing Times Greater Than 20 Minutes, Add This*
1,001–1,999	Add 1 minute	Add 2 minutes
2,000–2,999	Add 2 minutes	Add 4 minutes
3,000–3,999	Add 3 minutes	Add 6 minutes
4,000–4,999	Add 4 minutes	Add 8 minutes
5,000–5,999	Add 5 minutes	Add 10 minutes
6,000–6,999	Add 6 minutes	Add 12 minutes
7,000–7,999	Add 7 minutes	Add 14 minutes
8,000–8,999	Add 8 minutes	Add 16 minutes
9,000–9,999	Add 9 minutes	Add 18 minutes
Over 10,000	Add 10 minutes	Add 20 minutes

If you don't know your altitude level, you can get this information from many sources. Try contacting your public library, a local college, or the cooperative extension service in your county or state. Check your local phone book for contact numbers. Or check out `http://national4-hheadquarters.gov/Extension/index.html`. Just find your state on the map and then your location on the individual state's site.

Chapter 2

Canning Fruit

In This Chapter

▶ Preserving freshly picked fruit for optimum flavor

▶ Preventing fruit from lightening and darkening

▶ Choosing jar-filling liquids

▶ Making easy fruit pies and side dishes

Canning fresh fruit is a great way to preserve large quantities of ripe fruit in a short period of time. Buying fruit when it is in season saves money, and you can be assured of the best-flavored fruit. Canning fruit is easy to do: Just fill your jars with fruit and hot liquid and then process them! With canned fruit readily available, you have an easy snack or a quick side dish.

This chapter explains the importance of using freshly picked, perfectly ripe fruit and keeping your fruit looking and tasting its best.

Picking and Preparing Fruit

When selecting your fruit, think fresh, fresh, fresh! The best fruit for canning is freshly picked, ripe fruit. You're lucky if you grow your own fruit or have a friend who shares hers with you. Some growers offer a pick-your-own option in their growing area for a fee. (Ask growers at farmers' markets or check your local phone directory for locations in your area.) You'll need to bring your own containers for the fruit.

Fruit from your supermarket isn't the best choice because it's often picked before it's fully ripened in order to compensate for the time it takes to get the fruit from the field to the store shelf. Don't boycott your supermarket; just be finicky when selecting your fruit for canning.

The sooner you process your picked fruit, the better the texture and flavor of your final product. Your fruit can wait a few hours or overnight before you process it, but be sure to refrigerate it until you're ready.

Almost all fresh fruits can well with these exceptions: bananas, lemons, limes, melons, persimmons, and strawberries.

Identifying the proper degree of ripeness

How do you know if your fruit is ripe? *Ripe* fruit is defined as being fully developed, or mature, and ready for eating. If you grow your own fruit, you can check its development and maturity daily.

To check the fruit's ripeness:

- ✔ **Hold the fruit in the palm of your hand and apply gentle pressure with your thumb and fingers.** The fruit should be firm to the touch. If you see an impression in the fruit that doesn't bounce back, the fruit is overripe. If the fruit is as hard as a rock, it's underripe. Don't can overripe or underripe fruit. If you're picking your fruit for canning, you can perform the same test, with a slight difference: Do it while the fruit's still attached to the tree.

- ✔ **Smell the fruit.** Ripe fruit has a rich, full fruit aroma. A peach should smell like a peach; an apple should smell like an apple. The fragrance should be strong enough to entice you to devour the fruit on the spot.

Always use fruit picked directly from the bush or tree. Fruit collected from the ground (referred to as *dropped fruit* or *ground fruit*) is an indication that the fruit is overripe. Don't use it for canning.

Preparing your fruit properly

Use fresh, firm (not overripe) fruit. Wash and prepare your food well to remove any dirt and bacteria: Wash it in a large bowl filled with water and a few drops of detergent and then rinse it in a separate bowl of fresh water (see Figure 2-1). Can fruits (and vegetables) as soon as possible after they're picked.

No, you don't have to wash berries individually: Put them in a colander and submerge the colander, berries and all, in the wash bowl; then rinse them off with a running spray of water.

Figure 2-1:
How to wash fruits and vegetables well.

Book II

Water-Bath Canning with Fruits

Peeling and cutting: Necessary evils?

When you can fruit, should you leave the skin on or take it off? It depends on the recipe. Sometimes leaving the skin on your fruit is optional. Other times, you must remove the peel (see Figure 2-2). Always follow your recipe for specific guidelines.

Similarly, you may wonder whether cutting your fruit is necessary. The answer here depends on the fruit. The fruit you select dictates using it whole or cutting it into pieces. For example, fitting whole apples into a canning jar is difficult, but peeled apples cut into slices easily pack into a jar. You leave small fruit, like berries, whole.

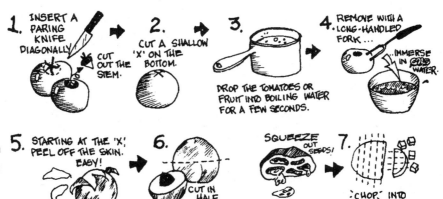

Figure 2-2:
Peeling soft-skinned fruits and tomatoes.

Preventing Discoloration

There's probably nothing more unattractive than a piece of perfectly ripe cut fruit that's *oxidized* — discolored, as in dark or brown. Discoloration primarily occurs in apples, apricots, nectarines, peaches, and pears but may occur in other fruits.

Meeting the antioxidants

You can protect your fruit from oxidation by slicing it directly into one of the following *antioxidant solutions,* a liquid to keep your fruit from darkening:

- ✔ **An ascorbic acid or citric solution:** Mix 1 teaspoon lemon or lime juice with 1 cup cold water. You can also use a commercial product, like Ever-Fresh or Fruit-Fresh, available in most supermarkets. When using one of these products, follow the instructions on the container.

  Ascorbic acid or citric acid is simply vitamin C. It doesn't change the fruit flavor. It's sold in powder form and is usually found in drugstores.

- ✔ **Vinegar, salt, and water:** Make this solution with 2 tablespoons vinegar (5 percent acidity), 2 tablespoons salt (pickling or kosher), and 1 gallon cold water.

Soak for 10 to 20 minutes, but don't leave your fruit in this solution longer than 20 minutes because the solution extracts nutrients from your fruit and changes its flavor.

After your fruit's dip in your antioxidant solution, you just rinse and drain your fruit before packing it into your prepared jars.

Knowing the limits

Even doing all the right things, when canning foods, you're subjecting the product to high heat and sustained cooking times. The canning process can cause unexpected color and texture changes in the food. Keep in mind that canned foods, although stored fresh, are not fresh foods. They are healthy foods that have been suspended in their best form for later eating.

Do not expect foods that are canned to resemble their raw state. Expect clean, fresh flavors, with a cooked texture.

Packing Particulars

The importance of properly packing jars cannot be diminished. Jars that are overpacked may not allow the heat to penetrate the food inside, resulting in dangerous bacteria surviving the canning process.

Jars that are too loosely packed will allow the product to float to the surface of the fluid inside, and oxidation will result on the parts that float in the headspace.

It is also just as important that all air bubbles are removed manually, before heat is applied. You don't want pockets of air because the food won't be properly vacuum packed while in the canner.

Raw pack and hot pack

Raw pack and *hot pack* refer to two methods of getting the product into the jars:

- **Raw pack:** A raw pack is the preferred method for fruits that become delicate after cooking, such as peaches and nectarines. This method is what it says: packing raw fruit into hot jars.

- **Hot pack:** Hot packing heats your fruit in a hot liquid before packing it into your prepared jars. The advantages of hot packing over raw packing include fitting more fruit into the jars because the fruit's softer and more pliable, using fewer jars because you can fit more fruit into the jars, and spending less time waiting for the water in your kettle to boil because the filled jars are hot in the middle.

With a few exceptions, most fresh fruits may be packed raw or hot. Always start with clean, ripe fruit and follow your recipe's instructions.

Generally, you can use either method for water-bath canning or pressure canning (see Book V). Which method you use is determined by the texture of the food and its tendency (or not) to fall apart from a lot of cooking. Whether you raw pack or hot pack also affects the processing times of the foods. Always refer to your recipe for guidance.

Lining your jars with liquid

You always add liquid when canning fresh fruit. Your options are boiling water, sugar syrup, or fruit juice. Determining which liquid you use is up to you, but consider the final use for your canned fruit. For example, if you're using your canned berries in a fruit cobbler, boiling water may be the better choice because you'll add sugar to the cobbler. If you'll be eating your canned fruit out of the jar, use a sugar syrup or fruit juice.

 After adding the hot liquid to your filled jars, release any trapped air bubbles in the jar. If the headspace drops after releasing the air bubbles, add more liquid to maintain the proper headspace. (See Book II, Chapter 1 for information about headspace.) If the fruit level drops, you need to add fruit.

Sugar syrups

Sugar syrup is simply a mixture of sugar and water. It adds flavor to your canned fruit, preserves its color, and produces a smooth, firm texture. You can add other sweeteners, such as honey, in addition to or without the sugar.

Use these guidelines for making your sugar-syrup choice:

- **Super-light syrup:** This syrup adds the least amount of calories. The sweetness level is the closest to the natural sugar level in most fruits.
- **Extra-light syrup:** Use this syrup for a sweet fruit, such as figs.
- **Light syrup:** This syrup is best with sweet apples and berries.
- **Medium syrup:** This syrup complements tart apples, apricots, nectarines, peaches, and pears.
- **Heavy syrup:** Use this syrup with sour fruit, such as grapefruit.

Table 2-1 offers you five concentrations of sugar syrup. Allow ½ to ¾ cup of liquid for each filled pint jar and 1½ cups of liquid for each filled quart jar of fruit. Bring your syrup ingredients to a boil in a saucepan over high heat; stir to dissolve the sugar.

Table 2-1	Sugar Syrup Concentrations		
Syrup Strength	*Granulated Sugar*	*Water*	*Approximate Yield*
Super-light	¼ cup	5¾ cups	6 cups
Extra-light	1¼ cups	5½ cups	6 cups
Light	2¼ cups	5¼ cups	6½ cups
Medium	3¼ cups	5 cups	7 cups
Heavy	4¼ cups	4¼ cups	7 cups

Always prepare your hot liquid before you prepare your fruit, to ensure your fruit is canned as soon as possible. The liquid should be waiting for you; you shouldn't be waiting for your liquid to boil.

Water or fruit juice

Packing fresh fruit in boiling water or fruit juice produces fruit with a soft texture. Two good choices for fruit juices are unsweetened pineapple juice or white grape juice. Use water you like to drink, without minerals and not the sparkling variety.

Always use the hot-pack method (see the section "Raw pack and hot pack" earlier in this chapter) when using water or unsweetened fruit juice for your canning liquid.

Book II

Water-Bath Canning with Fruits

Following Fresh Fruit Canning Guidelines

The following sections list foods that are commonly grown in home gardens. The quantity guide for each fruit fills a 1-quart jar. If you're using pint jars, cut the quantity in half.

The recipes in the following sections use the water-bath canning method. For detailed instructions on water-bath canning, filling and processing your jars, and releasing air bubbles, refer to the step-by-step guidelines in Book II, Chapter 1. And for a more extensive list of fruits, refer to the *Complete Guide to Home Canning and Preserving*, Second Revised Edition, by the United States Department of Agriculture.

Stone fruits – Fruits with pits

Peaches are a wonderful fruit, and by canning them yourself, you can save a lot of money. Use a light syrup so that you can enjoy the full flavor of the peach. Trust us: Home-canned peaches are much nicer than the heavy sweetness you find in store-canned varieties.

Nectarines and apricots are just as tasty as peaches and have the benefit of not needing to be peeled, making them even easier to can.

Cherries and plums are locally available in many parts of the country. If you are lucky enough to find them, they can beautifully.

Apricots make a sunny-flavored addition to winter meals. They make a great substitute for apples in an apple crisp recipe, too — you'll love the results!

Apples

Canned apples are wonderful for apple crisp, breads, and other recipes calling for slices or chunks of fruit. Use any crisp, tart apple, like Macintosh or Granny Smith. These apples usually ripen in the fall. Summer-ripened apples tend to be softer and won't hold up well to canning. Try making them with a light sugar syrup for a fresh-tasting treat. Or get a quick start to your piemaking by creating apple pie filling ahead of time.

Prep is easy: Just peel and core the apples and then cut them into slices or quarters. To prevent discoloration, treat the fruit with an antioxidant. (Refer to the section "Preventing Discoloration," earlier in this chapter.)

Berries

Canned berries have so many uses! You can use them to make smoothies or pies and as a sweet addition to your oatmeal. If your pantry is like ours, your berries will be the first things used up.

For canning, you want perfect, not soft or mushy, berries. Leave them whole. Wash and drain the berries (handling them as little as possible); remove any stems or hulls.

Strawberries don't can well. During the processing, they turn mushy and lose their taste and red color. They do, however, freeze very well. See Chapter 2 of Book VI for complete instructions.

Depending on the type of berry, you'll use either the raw or hot-pack method:

- ✔ **Raw pack:** Raw packing is best for soft berries, like blackberries, boysenberries, and raspberries.
- ✔ **Hot pack:** Use this method for firmer berries, such as blueberries, cranberries, and huckleberries.

The best of the rest

Although not as common, these items are well worth a look. Once you taste fresh pear conserve or rhubarb pie filling, you'll be a fan for life.

- **Pears:** All varieties of pears can well, so use your favorite variety. After cutting and peeling the pears, treat your fruit with an antioxidant to prevent discoloring. (Refer to the "Preventing Discoloration" section, earlier in this chapter).

- **Rhubarb:** This super-tart plant is an old- fashioned favorite. It can be mixed with strawberries for a pie filling and is delectable when combined with tart apples. Because of its tart taste, rhubarb is always canned with sugar and makes a great pie filling. If you make the filling ahead of time, in the winter you can just open a jar and fill your pie crust. Delicious!

Rhubarb leaves are toxic. Always remove and discard any leaves from the stalks before preparing your rhubarb. After removing the leaves, simply chop into bite-sized pieces to use.

Book II

Water-Bath Canning with Fruits

Fruit sauces and syrups

What makes fruit sauces and syrups so useful is that they add such a lovely flavor dimension to simple meals. Use them as toppings for pancakes, add them to soda water for delicious natural sodas, and don't forget the tried-and-true topping for a scoop of ice cream. A family favorite in coauthor Amy's house is to make angel food cake and cut the cake into cubes. She says, "Everyone has a bowl of cake and chooses their favorite sauce to drizzle over the top. It always evokes stories of how we picked the fruit, and those memories are worth every bit of time it took to create these treats."

Canned Apricots, Nectarines, or Peaches

Prep time: 15 min • **Process time:** 30 min (quarts); 25 min (pints) • **Yield:** 4 quarts or 8 pints

Ingredients	*Directions*
10 pounds apricots, or 10 pounds nectarines, or 12 pounds peaches Sugar syrup, light	**1** Wash your fruit. To prepare peaches, peel them; then cut them in half and remove the pits (see Figure 2-2). To prepare nectarines or apricots, simply cut them in half and remove the pits. Meanwhile, bring the sugar syrup to a boil.
	2 Pack the fruit firmly into hot jars and pour the boiling hot sugar syrup over the fruit, leaving ½-inch headspace.
	3 Process the filled jars in a water-bath canner for 30 minutes (quarts) or 25 minutes (pints) from the point of boiling. After processing, if you find jars that haven't sealed, refrigerate them and use them within 2 weeks.

Per ½-cup serving apricots: Calories 118 (From Fat 5); Fat 1g (Saturated 0g); Cholesterol 0mg; Sodium 2mg; Carbohydrates 29g (Dietary Fiber 3g); Protein 2g.

Per ½-cup serving nectarines: Calories 118 (From Fat 5); Fat 1g (Saturated 0g); Cholesterol 0mg; Sodium 0mg; Carbohydrates 29g (Dietary Fiber 2g); Protein 1g.

Per ½-cup serving peaches: Calories 88 (From Fat 1); Fat 0g (Saturated 0g); Cholesterol 0mg; Sodium 4mg; Carbohydrates 23g (Dietary Fiber 2g); Protein 1g.

Vary It! To make a sweeter canned fruit, use a medium syrup.

Tip: To make peaches easy to peel, blanch them to loosen the skin: Dip them in boiling water for 30 seconds and then dip them in cold water.

Canned Cherries

Prep time: 20 min • **Process time:** 25 min • **Yield:** 4 quarts

Ingredients	Directions
10 pounds of cherries, washed, with stems and pits removed **4 cups sugar syrup, light**	**1** Bring your sugar syrup to a boil. Pack the cherries firmly into your jars and pour the boiling hot sugar syrup over them, leaving ½-inch headspace.
	2 Process the filled jars (quarts) in a water-bath canner for 25 minutes from the point of boiling. After processing, if you find jars that haven't sealed, refrigerate them and use them within 2 weeks.

Per ½-cup serving: Calories 125 (From Fat 1); Fat 1g (Saturated 0g); Cholesterol 0mg; Sodium 0mg; Carbohydrates 30g (Dietary Fiber 3g); Protein 2g.

Canned Plums

Prep time: 20 min • **Process time:** 25 min • **Yield:** 4 quarts

Ingredients	Directions
10 pounds of plums **5½ cups sugar syrup, heavy**	**1** Wash the plums; prick each plum with a sterilized needle to prevent bursting. Bring your sugar syrup to a boil.
	2 Pack the plums firmly into jars and pour the boiling hot sugar syrup over them, leaving ½-inch headspace. Process the filled jars (quarts) in a water-bath canner for 25 minutes from the point of boiling. After processing, if you find jars that haven't sealed, refrigerate them and use them within 2 weeks.

Per ½-cup serving: Calories 154 (From Fat 7); Fat 1g (Saturated 0g); Cholesterol 0mg; Sodium 0mg; Carbohydrates 38g (Dietary Fiber 2g); Protein 1g.

Canned Apples

Prep time: 15 min • **Process time:** 20 min • **Yield:** 4 quarts or 8 pints

Ingredients	Directions
12 pounds apples **Sugar syrup, light**	**1** Over medium-high heat, bring the sugar syrup to a boil. Meanwhile, wash, core, and peel your apples; then slice them into ¼-inch pieces or cut them into even chunks.
	2 Pack the apples firmly into hot jars and pour boiling hot sugar syrup over the apples, leaving ½-inch headspace. Process the filled jars in a water-bath canner for 20 minutes for quarts and pints from the point of boiling. After processing, if you find jars that haven't sealed, refrigerate them and use them within 2 weeks.

Per ½-cup serving: Calories 137 (From Fat 4); Fat 0g (Saturated 0g); Cholesterol 0mg; Sodium 0mg; Carbohydrates 36g (Dietary Fiber 3g); Protein 0g.

Vary It! For a sweeter canned apple, try a medium syrup instead.

Grape Juice

Prep time: 30 min • **Process time:** 10 min • **Yield:** 7 quarts

Ingredients	Directions
7 cups of grapes, washed, stems removed **3½ cups sugar**	**1** Place 1 cup of grapes into each quart jar. Place ½ cup of the sugar over the grapes in each jar and fill with boiling water, leaving ¼-inch headspace.
	2 Process the filled jars (quarts) in a water-bath canner for 10 minutes from the point of boiling. After processing, if you find jars that haven't sealed, refrigerate them and use them within 2 weeks. To use, strain canned juice through a colander, into a juice pitcher. Add cold water, if desired.

Per 1-cup serving: Calories 125 (From Fat 2); Fat 0g (Saturated 0g); Cholesterol 0mg; Sodium 1mg; Carbohydrates 32g (Dietary Fiber 0g); Protein 0g.

Canned Blueberries

Prep time: 20 min • **Process time:** 20 min (quarts); 15 min (pints) • **Yield:** 4 quarts or 8 pints

Ingredients	*Directions*
10 pounds blueberries **Sugar syrup, light**	*1* Wash the berries gently in cold water to firm them and remove any stems or hulls.
	2 Place the berries into a saucepan and cover them with sugar syrup. Bring the mixture to a boil over medium-high heat, stirring occasionally to prevent sticking. In a large pot, bring water for your reserve to a boil.
	3 Ladle the hot berries and liquid into your prepared jars, adding boiling water if you don't have enough liquid to fill the jars, leaving ½-inch headspace.
	4 Process the filled jars in a water-bath canner for 20 minutes (quarts) or 15 minutes (pints) from the point of boiling. After processing, if you find jars that haven't sealed, refrigerate them and use them within 2 weeks.

Per ½-cup serving: Calories 124 (From Fat 3); Fat 0g (Saturated 0g); Cholesterol 0mg; Sodium 2mg; Carbohydrates 32g (Dietary Fiber 6g); Protein 1g.

Vary It! For sweeter canned berries, use medium syrup.

Note: This recipe shows you how to can blueberries. Follow the same directions for any other type of hard berry.

Canned Pears

Prep time: 15 min • **Process time:** 25 min (quarts); 20 min (pints) • **Yield:** 4 quarts or 8 pints

Ingredients	Directions
12 pounds pears **Sugar syrup, light**	**1** Bring your sugar syrup to a boil. Meanwhile, wash, peel, and core the pears. Slice the pears into ¼-inch pieces or cut them into even-sized chunks.
	2 Pack the pears firmly into the hot jars and pour the boiling hot sugar syrup over them, leaving ½-inch headspace.
	3 Process the filled jars in a water-bath canner for 25 minutes (quarts) or 20 minutes (pints) from the point of boiling. After processing, if you find jars that haven't sealed, refrigerate them and use them within 2 weeks.

Per ½-cup serving: Calories 79 (From Fat 0); Fat 0g (Saturated 0g); Cholesterol 0mg; Sodium 2mg; Carbohydrates 21g (Dietary Fiber 1g); Protein 0g.

Note: Try canned pears in place of apples in any recipe calling for cooked fruit.

Canned Raspberries

Prep time: 15 min • **Process time:** 20 min (quarts); 15 min (pints) • **Yield:** 4 quarts or 8 pints

Ingredients	*Directions*
12 pounds raspberries **Sugar syrup, light**	*1* Wash the berries gently in cold water to firm them and remove any stems or hulls. Meanwhile, bring the sugar syrup to a boil.
	2 Pack the berries loosely into your prepared jars and pour boiling hot sugar syrup over them, leaving ½-inch headspace.
	3 Process the filled jars in a water-bath canner for 20 minutes (quarts) or 15 minutes (pints) from the point of boiling. After processing, if you find jars that haven't sealed, refrigerate them and use them within 2 weeks.

Per ½-cup serving: Calories 138 (From Fat 8); Fat 1g (Saturated 0g); Cholesterol 0mg; Sodium 0mg; Carbohydrates 34g (Dietary Fiber 12g); Protein 2g.

Vary It! For sweeter canned berries, use medium syrup.

Note: This recipe explains how to can raspberries, but you can use it to can any other soft berry the same way.

Canned Oranges

Prep time: 30 min • **Process time:** 10 min • **Yield:** 5 quarts

Ingredients	Directions
10 pounds of fresh oranges, washed **Sugar syrup, light**	**1** Peel and section the oranges, removing all white membrane and seeds. Bring your sugar syrup to a boil. Pack the fruit firmly into your jars and pour the boiling hot sugar syrup over them, leaving ½-inch headspace.
	2 Process the filled jars (quarts) in a water-bath canner for 10 minutes from the point of boiling. After processing, if you find jars that haven't sealed, refrigerate them and use them within 2 weeks.

Per ½-cup serving: Calories 85 (From Fat 3); Fat 0g (Saturated 0g); Cholesterol 0mg; Sodium 0mg; Carbohydrates 22g (Dietary Fiber 4g); Protein 1g.

Canned Pineapple

Prep time: 40 min • **Process time:** 20 min • **Yield:** 7 quarts

Ingredients	Directions
10 pounds of fresh pineapple (about 5 medium) **Sugar syrup, light**	**1** Peel, core, and cut the pineapple into bite-sized pieces, removing the eyes of the pineapple and any tough flesh. Combine the pineapple and sugar syrup; bring to a boil. Simmer on medium heat until the pineapple is soft.
	2 Pack the hot fruit firmly into your jars and pour the boiling hot sugar syrup over them, leaving ½-inch headspace. Process the filled jars (quarts) in a water-bath canner for 20 minutes from the point of boiling. After processing, if you find jars that haven't sealed, refrigerate them and use them within 2 weeks.

Per ½-cup serving: Calories 57 (From Fat 2); Fat 0g (Saturated 0g); Cholesterol 0mg; Sodium 1mg; Carbohydrates 27g (Dietary Fiber 1g); Protein 0g.

Blueberry Pie Filling

Prep time: 20 min • **Process time:** 30 min • **Yield:** 7 quarts

Ingredients	Directions
6 quarts blueberries	*1* Wash and drain the blueberries. Combine the sugar, water, and Clearjel in a 6-quart pan. Bring the mixture to a boil, over medium heat, until thick and bubbly. Add the lemon juice and boil 1 minute more. Add the berries; stir gently.
6 cups sugar	
2¼ cups Clearjel	
7 cups water	
½ cup lemon juice	*2* Fill your jars, leaving ½-inch headspace. Process the filled jars (quarts) in a water-bath canner for 30 minutes from the point of boiling. After processing, if you find jars that haven't sealed, refrigerate them and use them within 2 weeks.

Per ½-cup serving: Calories 117 (From Fat 8); Fat 1g (Saturated 0g); Cholesterol 0mg; Sodium 1mg; Carbohydrates 30g (Dietary Fiber 4g); Protein 0g.

Peach Pie Filling

Prep time: 30 min • **Process time:** 20 min • **Yield:** 7 quarts

Ingredients	Directions
15 pounds peaches, peeled and pitted	*1* Mix the ClearJel and 2 cups of the water. Set aside. Combine the sugar, water, and salt in a 6-quart pan. Bring to a boil, over medium heat. Add the ClearJel and water mixture. Boil 1 minute. Add the peaches; stir gently.
2 cups ClearJel	
6 cups sugar	
1 teaspoon salt	*2* Fill your jars, leaving ½-inch headspace. Process the filled jars (quarts) in a water-bath canner for 20 minutes from the point of boiling. After processing, if you find jars that haven't sealed, refrigerate them and use them within 2 weeks.
6 cups water	

Per ½-cup serving: Calories 130 (From Fat 0); Fat 0g (Saturated 0g); Cholesterol 0mg; Sodium 42mg; Carbohydrates 32g (Dietary Fiber 1g); Protein 1g.

Cherry Pie Filling

Prep time: 20 min • **Process time:** 30 min • **Yield:** 7 quarts

Ingredients	Directions
6 quarts cherries	**1** Rinse and pit the cherries. Combine the sugar, water, and Clearjel in a 6-quart pan. Stir in the cinnamon and almond extract.
7 cups sugar	
1¾ cups Clearjel	
9 cups water	**2** Bring the mixture to a boil, over medium heat, until thick and bubbly. Add the lemon juice and boil 1 minute. Add the cherries; stir gently.
½ cup lemon juice	
1 teaspoon cinnamon	
2 teaspoons almond extract	**3** Fill your jars, leaving ½-inch headspace. Process the filled jars (quarts) in a water-bath canner for 30 minutes from the point of boiling. After processing, if you find jars that haven't sealed, refrigerate them and use them within 2 weeks.

Per ½-cup serving: Calories 144 (From Fat 2); Fat 0g (Saturated 0g); Cholesterol 0mg; Sodium 1mg; Carbohydrates 37g (Dietary Fiber 2g); Protein 1g.

Rhubarb Pie Filling

Prep time: 15 min, plus standing time • **Process time:** 15 min • **Yield:** 6 quarts

Ingredients	*Directions*
12 pounds rhubarb **6 cups sugar, or to taste**	**1** Wash, trim, and remove the leaves from the rhubarb. Cut the stalks into ½-inch pieces. Place the rhubarb pieces in a 6-quart pan. Add sugar to the cut pieces and let them stand for 4 hours to draw out the juice. Taste the mixture with a clean spoon to check that it's sweet enough. If not, add more sugar, to taste.
	2 When the standing time is complete, heat the rhubarb and sugar mixture to boiling over high heat. Pack the hot rhubarb mixture into your canning jars, leaving ½-inch headspace. Process the filled quart jars in a water-bath canner for 20 minutes from the point of boiling. After processing, if you find jars that haven't sealed, refrigerate them and use them within 2 weeks.

Per ½-cup serving: Calories 115 (From Fat 2); Fat 0g (Saturated 0g); Cholesterol 0mg; Sodium 4mg; Carbohydrates 29g (Dietary Fiber 2g); Protein 1g.

Apple Pie Filling

Prep time: 15 min • **Cook time:** 45 min • **Process time:** 25 min • **Yield:** 6 pints

Ingredients	*Directions*
6 pounds apples	**1** Peel and slice or cube the apples. Place the apples and the other ingredients into a heavy pan. Allow the mixture to stand about 30 minutes or until it becomes juicy. Cook the apple mixture over medium heat until the apples are softened, about 7 minutes. Ladle the pie filling into the pint jars, leaving ¼-inch headspace. Process the filled jars in a water-bath canner for 25 minutes from the point of boiling. After processing, if you find jars that haven't sealed, refrigerate them and use them within 2 weeks.
2 cups sugar	
2 teaspoons cinnamon	
½ teaspoon nutmeg	
2 tablespoons lemon juice	

Per ½-cup serving: Calories 121 (From Fat 3); Fat 0g (Saturated 0g); Cholesterol 0mg; Sodium 0mg; Carbohydrates 31g (Dietary Fiber 2g); Protein 0g.

Vary It! Substitute or add to the spices listed to create the pie your family likes.

Tip: To thicken this filling to just the right consistency, add a tablespoon of flour to the filled pie before adding the top crust.

Applesauce

Prep time: 15 min • **Cook time:** 1 hr • **Process time:** 20 min • **Yield:** 4 quarts

Ingredients	Directions
10 pounds apples **2½ cups sugar**	**1** Cut the apples in half (don't peel or core them) and place them in a 12-quart pot. Add enough water to cover the bottom of the pot and to keep the apples from scorching. Cook the apples over medium heat until they're soft, about 20 minutes. Press the softened apples through a food mill or sieve to remove the skins and seeds.
	2 Return the apple puree to the pot and add the sugar. Bring the mixture to a boil, stirring often to prevent scorching.
	3 Ladle the hot applesauce into your prepared jars, leaving ½-inch headspace. Process the filled jars in a water-bath canner for 20 minutes from the point of boiling. After processing, if you find jars that haven't sealed, refrigerate them and use them within 2 weeks.

Per ½-cup serving: Calories 129 (From Fat 3); Fat 0g (Saturated 0g); Cholesterol 0mg; Sodium 0mg; Carbohydrates 34g (Dietary Fiber 2g); Protein 0g.

Vary It! Try adding cinnamon and cloves for a spicy version. For a richer flavor, use a variety of apples.

Tip: To help prevent scorching, use a stovetop heat diffuser under the pot.

Rhubarb Sauce

Prep time: 45 min, plus standing time • **Process time:** 20 min • **Yield:** 4 quarts or 8 pints

Ingredients	*Directions*
8 pounds rhubarb **8 cups sugar, or to taste**	*1* Wash, trim, and remove the leaves from the rhubarb. Cut the stalks into ½-inch pieces. Place the rhubarb pieces in a 6-quart pot and add the sugar. Let the rhubarb-sugar mixture stand for 4 hours to draw out the juice.
	2 Heat the rhubarb and sugar mixture to boiling over high heat and cook the mixture until it's slightly chunky (about 30 minutes) or until the rhubarb is the consistency you desire.
	3 Ladle the boiling hot rhubarb sauce into your prepared jars, leaving 1-inch headspace. Process the filled jars in a water-bath canner for 20 minutes (both quarts and pints) from the point of boiling. After processing, if you find jars that haven't sealed, refrigerate them and use them within 2 weeks.

Per ½-cup serving: *Calories 211 (From Fat 2); Fat 0g (Saturated 0g); Cholesterol 0mg; Sodium 4mg; Carbohydrates 54g (Dietary Fiber 2g); Protein 1g.*

Raspberry Syrup

Prep time: 40 min • **Process time:** 10 min • **Yield:** 6 half-pints

Ingredients	Directions
5 cups fresh raspberries, hulled and cut in half **3 cups water** **1 tablespoon grated lemon zest** **2½ cups granulated sugar** **3½ cups corn syrup** **2 tablespoons fresh lemon juice (about ½ a lemon)**	*1* Place the raspberries in a 4- to 5-quart pot. Crush the berries with a potato masher. Add 1½ cups of water and the lemon zest. Bring the mixture to a boil; reduce the heat and simmer 5 minutes. Strain the hot mixture through a jelly bag or a cheesecloth-lined mesh strainer. *2* Place the sugar and the remaining 1½ cups of water in a 4-quart saucepan. Bring the mixture to a boil over high heat, stirring to dissolve the sugar. Cook the mixture until the temperature registers 260° on a candy thermometer. Add the strained berry juice and the corn syrup and return the mixture to a boil, boiling the syrup for 4 minutes. Remove the pan from the heat and stir in the lemon juice. Remove any foam from the surface with a foam skimmer. *3* Ladle your hot syrup into the prepared jars, leaving ¼-inch headspace. Process the filled jars in a water-bath canner for 10 minutes from the point of boiling. After processing, if you find jars that haven't sealed, refrigerate them and use them within 2 months.

Per 2-tablespoon serving: Calories 114 (From Fat 1); Fat 0g (Saturated 0g); Cholesterol 0mg; Sodium 0mg; Carbohydrates 0g (Dietary Fiber 1g); Protein 0g.

Vary It! Substitute other berries, or a combination of berries, for different syrup flavors.

Tip: This syrup is delicious on thick, grilled French toast sprinkled with ground cinnamon and powdered sugar.

Chapter 3

Canning Tomatoes

*N*o matter how carefully you can your tomatoes, it all starts with the perfect fruit. You can preserve any type of tomatoes, from typical canning types to little cherry tomatoes. In this chapter, you discover all types of tomatoes and then explore the many types of sauces you can craft using your imagination.

Picking and Preparing Tomatoes

Tomatoes are misunderstood. Are they a fruit or a vegetable? By definition, a *fruit* is a sweet, edible plant containing seeds inside a juicy pulp — which defines tomatoes perfectly. We use tomatoes as a vegetable, though, and as a rule, they're used in savory foods like vegetables are. How to classify them in your refrigerator is up to you.

Each tomato variety has its own color, flavor, and texture. Roma or paste tomatoes and slicing varieties are all used for canning. Paste varieties simply have less juice and therefore require less cooking to remove excess water for paste and thick sauces. You can use both interchangeably, but cooking times will vary.

Not all tomato varieties are suitable for canning due to their lack of taste and mass-production genetics. Stick with those that boast good canning results on the plant's tag or use a proven heirloom variety. Some varieties that work well include Ace, Amish Paste, Homestead 24, and Rutgers.

Appreciating heirloom tomatoes

Heirloom. You've probably heard this term being tossed around, but what does it mean? An *heirloom* tomato comes from a seed that has remained "true to type," meaning it has been open pollinated naturally, growing the same type of tomato for generations.

What makes heirlooms so wonderful is that they have proven themselves for hundreds of years.

If you save the seeds, you can grow more of the varieties that you love every year.

Heirlooms are not always perfectly red and round. They haven't been changed genetically to look attractive in the produce section of the grocery store. They have irregular shapes and interesting colors, with strong track records for handling the canning process just fine.

Knowing your choices

If you think that a tomato is just a tomato, think again. They may look a lot alike, but hundreds of varieties of tomatoes are out there. Take a look at some of the basics:

- ✔ **Canning tomatoes,** or canners, are varieties that hold up well under the high heat and extended cooking time of a water bath. Canning tomatoes also tend to be of similar size, making it easier for you to fit them into jars evenly. A common variety of canning tomato is Rutgers.

- ✔ **Paste tomatoes** are more oblong, ripening even later in the season. If you cut them open, you'll find they're much drier, with less seed and pulp. Because they're lower in moisture, they require less time to cook down to a thick sauce. A dependable paste tomato is Amish Paste.

- ✔ **Cherry and pear tomatoes** are small, sweet tomatoes, either round or slightly pear shaped. You can use them the same way as larger tomatoes, but remember that canning a quart of little tomatoes takes far longer. An heirloom variety that works well for canning is Matt's Wild Cherry.

Prepping for success

As always, choose nice, ripe, unblemished tomatoes. To ensure the proper acidity level for your variety (4.6 or lower), add an acid, like bottled lemon juice or powdered citric acid: Add 2 tablespoons lemon juice per quart jar or 1 tablespoon lemon juice per pint. If you're using citric acid, add ½ teaspoon per quart and ¼ teaspoon per pint.

Canned tomato recipes refer to whole or halved (even quartered) fruit. This simply means fitting the fruit into the jar in the most efficient way you can. If your tomatoes are smaller sized, they can fit into the jar whole. If they won't fit into the opening in the jar, they'll need to be cut into halves or quarters.

Coauthor Amy says that she usually cuts her tomatoes into halves. They seem to fit much better, filling every nook and cranny of the jar. This technique helps when using irregularly shaped tomatoes.

To make peeling tomatoes easier, blanch them first to loosen the skins: Dip them in boiling water for 30 seconds and then plunge into cold water.

Dipping into Tomato Sauces and Ketchups

Sauces are a fantastic way to add your own touch to any meal. You make sauces just as you'd make a spaghetti sauce and ladle them into jars when complete. You will be making a whole grilling season's worth at a time. You may never run out again!

The tomatoey, sugary barbecue sauce that so many people equate with barbecue itself is not a good match for the heat of the grill and tends to burn, so save it for the last few minutes of cooking, brush it on after you've pulled cooked meat from the smoker, or serve it as a dipping sauce.

Ketchups and chili sauces

Ketchup is an all-American condiment. From fries to meat to basically anything you can imagine, ketchup has a place on American tables. Modern ketchup is tomato-based, with added spices, sugars, and vinegar. You can season your ketchup to taste, from spicy to extra sweet, and your family will eat every jar you put up.

Chili sauces are somewhat similar to ketchup because they're tomato-based sauces, but chili sauce takes a spicy turn. Chili sauces vary around the world, but they're basically tomato-based with onions and hot peppers cooked into them. Chili sauces give a spicy kick (with a sweet tang) and are more like ketchup that is all grown up.

No rule says that you have to make your chili sauce (or ketchup, for that matter) super-hot. When you make it yourself, you can make a batch of mind-blowing hot stuff for the spice lovers and a milder version for everyone who enjoys the tingle of a good chili sauce, but can't stand too much heat.

Sampling spicy salsas

Salsa is the Mexican word for sauce. Traditionally, salsa was made with tomatoes, cilantro, chilies, and onions and served at room temperature. Today's versions can include fruits and other interesting additions. No matter the recipe, it's readily available in most supermarkets in mild, hot, or fiery intensities and is used on almost any food.

Not every sauce is a hot sauce, but even sweet salsas and sauces do well with a little something spicy, which, if you add it with a very cautious hand, actually underscores the sweet effect you're going for.

Then, of course, four-alarm-fire sauces throw the balance in the opposite direction, using a little something sweet to create depth and complement the tongue-scorching elements within the sauce.

Adding prepared hot sauce is a reasonable shortcut and creates good results. Here are additional suggestions for fueling a fire:

- ✔ Black pepper (fresh ground)
- ✔ Cayenne pepper
- ✔ Chili powder
- ✔ Chipotle (smoked jalapeño) peppers or sauce
- ✔ Crushed red pepper
- ✔ Dry mustard
- ✔ Horseradish
- ✔ Minced fresh hot peppers (jalapeño, habanera, serrano, and so on)
- ✔ Paprika

Adding fruits and other flavors

There's no limit to the ingredients you can add to make a sauce your own. Keep track of your additions as you tweak the recipe, and soon a new sauce that is all your own will take shape. As you work on your own sauce recipe, don't make changes all at once. If you mess with too many elements at a time, you can't pin down what's keeping the sauce from working. Change just one part of the recipe for a subsequent batch, and you leave no mystery as to what's making the difference. Then you know better how to proceed toward your masterpiece.

Don't be afraid to try unconventional tastes and ingredients. Once you mix that perfect combination, everyone will be glad you were so creative. Some unexpected ingredients that may help get you started include

- ✔ Maple syrup
- ✔ Pineapple or other fruits
- ✔ Lemon or lime juice

When you start dreaming up your own sauce, keep in mind that you want one element to do most of the work. A sauce needs an identity if it's to become a standout. If you prefer a sweet sauce, let an element like apricot preserves take the stage and give hot elements the role of backup singer. If you want a sour, vinegary sauce, heat and sweet do the doo-wop work.

Canned Tomatoes

Prep time: 15 min • **Process time:** 35 min (pints); 45 min (quarts) • **Yield:** 4 quarts or 6 pints

Ingredients	*Directions*
12 pounds whole tomatoes **Bottled lemon juice or citric acid** **Canning salt (optional)** **Boiling water**	**1** Wash and peel the tomatoes. Cut the larger tomatoes into halves or quarters. Place the tomatoes into your prepared canning jars, leaving ½-inch head space and pressing them to release their juice. (Use a canning funnel to keep the rims clean.)
	2 To each pint jar, add 1 tablespoon lemon juice or ¼ teaspoon citric acid and, if desired, ½ teaspoon salt. To each quart jar, add 2 tablespoons lemon juice or ½ teaspoon citric acid and, if desired, 1 teaspoon salt. If there's not enough juice to cover the tomatoes, add boiling water to the jars, retaining the ½-inch headspace.
	3 Process the filled jars in a water-bath canner for 35 minutes (pints) or 45 minutes (quarts) from the point of boiling. Use any unsealed jars within 2 weeks.

Per ½-cup serving: Calories 44 (From Fat 6); Fat 1g (Saturated 0g); Cholesterol 0mg; Sodium 19mg; Carbohydrates 10g (Dietary Fiber 2g); Protein 2g.

Tip: Use wide-mouth pint or quart jars for ease in filling. Although not necessary, they'll make the entire process go faster, and you'll have less mess.

Tomato Paste

Prep time: 15 min • **Cook time:** 4 hr • **Process time:** 30 min • **Yield:** 16 half-pints

Ingredients	*Directions*
16 pounds plum or paste tomatoes, cubed **3 cups sweet pepper, chopped** **2 bay leaves** **2 tablespoons salt** **3 cloves garlic** **Bottled lemon juice or citric acid**	*1* Combine all ingredients in a 6-quart pot and cook slowly over medium heat for 1 hour, stirring frequently to prevent sticking. Remove the bay leaves and press the mixture through a food mill or sieve. Return the mixture to the pot and continue to cook for another 3 hours over medium-low heat, stirring often.
	2 Pour the hot mixture into your canning jars, leaving ¼-inch headspace. Add ½ tablespoon lemon juice or ⅛ teaspoon citric acid to each half-pint jar.
	3 Process the filled half-pint jars in a water-bath canner for 30 minutes from the point of boiling. Use any unsealed jars within 2 weeks.

Per ½-cup serving: *Calories 48 (From Fat 6); Fat 1g (Saturated 0g); Cholesterol 0mg; Sodium 455mg; Carbohydrates 11g (Dietary Fiber 2g); Protein 2g.*

Tip: To check for sauce thickness, put a spoonful of sauce onto the center of a plate. Wait for 60 seconds and see whether any water seeps from it. If so, cook for 30 minutes more and recheck.

Tomato Ketchup

Prep time: 30 min • **Cook time:** 3–4 hr • **Process time:** 20 min • **Yield:** 3–4 pints

Ingredients	*Directions*
4 quarts ripe tomatoes, chopped	**1** Place chopped tomatoes, onions, and peppers in a 5- to 6-quart pot. Bring the mixture to a boil over medium-high heat, stirring often to prevent sticking. Reduce the heat to medium low; simmer, uncovered, for 45 minutes.
1 cup chopped onion	
¾ cup sweet pepper, chopped	
1 teaspoon mustard seed	**2** Blend cooked vegetables and run through a handmill or press through a wire strainer. Return strained vegetables back to pan and heat on medium 45 minutes to 1 hour, until reduced by half. Stir often.
1 teaspoon celery seed	
½ teaspoon whole allspice	
1 teaspoon whole cloves	
1 cinnamon stick	**3** Tie spices into a cheesecloth bag and add to the reduced vegetable mixture. Add the sugar, salt, and paprika to the sauce. Cook over medium heat for 1 to 1½ hours, or until very thick. Stir often to prevent scorching. Add the vinegar and cook gently for 10 minutes. Remove the spice bag.
1 cup brown sugar	
1 tablespoon salt	
1 tablespoon paprika	
1½ cups apple cider vinegar	**4** Ladle the hot ketchup into the prepared jars, leaving ½-inch headspace. Process the filled jars in a water-bath canner for 20 minutes from the point of boiling. Use any unsealed jars within 2 months.

Per tablespoon: Calories 32 (From Fat 3); Fat 0g (Saturated 0g); Cholesterol 0mg; Sodium 118mg; Carbohydrates 7g (Dietary Fiber 1g); Protein 1g.

Tomato Soup

Prep time: 15 min • **Cook time:** 45 min–1 hr • **Process time:** 40 min • **Yield:** 5 quarts

Ingredients	Directions
12 pounds of tomatoes **1 tablespoon sugar** **2 tablespoons pickling spices** **2 tablespoons salt** **1 teaspoon peppercorns** **4 medium onions, chopped** **2 carrots, sliced**	*1* Cut the tomatoes into quarters and place them in a 6-quart pot. Sprinkle them with sugar. Tie the pickling spices, salt, and peppercorns in a cheesecloth bag and place the bag in the pot with the tomatoes. *2* Add the remaining vegetables and bring to a boil over medium-high heat. Reduce heat and simmer until reduced to desired thickness, 45 minutes to 1 hour. *3* Remove the spice bag. Strain the soup and return it to the pot. Reheat the soup to a boil. *4* Ladle the hot soup into the prepared jars (quarts), leaving ½-inch headspace. Process the filled jars in a water-bath canner for 40 minutes from the point of boiling. Use any unsealed jars within 2 weeks. Prior to eating or tasting, boil the food for 15 minutes.

Per 1-cup serving: Calories 64 (From Fat 8); Fat 1g (Saturated 0g); Cholesterol 0mg; Sodium 724mg; Carbohydrates 14g (Dietary Fiber 3g); Protein 2g.

Jalapeño Salsa

Prep time: 30 min • **Process time:** 15 min • **Yield:** 3 pints

Ingredients	*Directions*

2 pounds tomatoes, peeled and chopped, to measure 3 cups

One 7-ounce can diced jalapeño chilies, or 12 fresh jalapeño chilies, finely chopped, seeds removed

1 onion, peeled and chopped

6 garlic cloves, minced

2 tablespoons finely chopped fresh cilantro

2 teaspoons ground oregano

1½ teaspoons kosher or pickling salt

½ teaspoon ground cumin

1 cup cider vinegar

1 Place all the ingredients in a 5- to 6-quart pot. Bring the mixture to a boil over high heat, stirring to combine. Reduce the heat to low; simmer, uncovered, for 10 minutes.

2 Ladle your hot salsa into the prepared jars; leaving ¼-inch headspace. Process the filled jars in a water-bath canner for 15 minutes from the point of boiling. Use any unsealed jars within 2 months.

Per 2-tablespoon serving: Calories 6 (From Fat 0); Fat 0g (Saturated 0g); Cholesterol 0mg; Sodium 99mg; Carbohydrates 2g (Dietary Fiber 0g); Protein 0g.

Chapter 4

Sweet Spreads: Jams, Jellies, and Butters

In This Chapter

▶ Exploring the world of preserves

▶ Unlocking the mystery of pectin

▶ Firming up your jams and jellies

▶ Meeting the marmalades and butters

▶ Satisfying your sweet tooth with tasty spreads

Sweet spreads aren't just for toast anymore! In this chapter, we include a variety of our favorite recipes with unique flavor combinations. The recipes utilize a variety of preparation techniques that take you step by step through each process. In addition to fresh fruit, some recipes use frozen fruit and fruit juice.

Getting to Know the Sweet Spreads

Making sweet spreads is basic chemistry, using exact proportions of fruit and sugar, cooking the two, and sometimes adding acid or pectin. Don't worry if chemistry wasn't your strong suit in school. Good recipes do the homework for you. Your responsibility is to follow the recipe exactly, using the correct ingredients and measuring them accurately.

Never double a sweet spread recipe or adjust the sugar amount. Recipes are balanced to achieve a specific consistency and texture. Any alteration or adjustment to the recipe upsets the perfect chemical balance and adversely affects your spread by producing inferior results. If you want more of the same recipe, make it twice. If you would like to use less sugar, find another recipe that uses your desired amount.

Sweet spreads, generically referred to as *preserves,* come in many forms and textures. The various types of sweet spreads are as follows:

- **Jam:** Jam is a combination of fruit (crushed or chopped), sugar, and sometimes pectin and acid, cooked until the pieces of fruit are soft and almost lose their shape. Common uses for jam include bread spreads, cookie and pastry fillings, and a topping for cheesecake.

- **Jelly:** This mixture combines fruit juice, sugar, and sometimes pectin. It's transparent with a bright color and should be firm, yet jiggly. If you use fresh fruit, you may be instructed to strain it. Use jelly as a bread spread or as a filling for cakes and cookies.

- **Marmalade:** These are soft jellies with pieces of fruit rind, usually citrus fruit, suspended in them. In addition to bread spread, marmalades are great as a glaze on a baked ham. (Use your favorite flavor!)

- **Preserves:** In addition to the generic term representing all sweet spreads, preserves have a definition of their own. They contain cooked fruit, sugar, and sometimes pectin and have a jamlike consistency, but with whole or large pieces of fruit. The fruit maintains its shape during the cooking process.

- **Butter:** This smooth, thick spread is made from fruit puree and sugar cooked for a long period of time. The results are a thick spread. Butters normally use less sugar than other sweet spreads and may have spices added to enhance the flavor of the fruit.

If you're looking for a low-sugar option, some of the alternative sweeteners, such as Splenda, offer their own recipes right on the package.

Processing with Fruit Pectin

Pectin is a natural, water-based substance that's present in ripe fruit. It's essential for thickening jams, jellies, and other types of preserves. Some recipes add commercial fruit pectin when more than the naturally occurring amount of pectin is needed (like when you want to thicken a fruit juice into a jelly). If your recipe does include such an ingredient, you'll see the kind of pectin (powdered or liquid) listed.

Never alter the amount of sugar your recipe calls for or use sugar substitutes. Exact amounts of sugar, fruit, and pectin are a must for a good *set* — that is, a consistency that isn't too thick to spread or too runny.

Commercial pectin basics

Commercial pectin is available in most supermarkets or where canning supplies are sold. Pectin may be in short supply in the spring and summer months because these are such popular times of year for canning. So be sure you have enough pectin on hand before you start preparing your recipe.

Inspect the pectin container for water stains, holes, or any other sign that it has come into contact with food (like food stuck to the package). Check to make sure that the package is sealed and that the use-by date hasn't passed.

Using pectin after the date on the package may affect your final product because the quality of the pectin may have deteriorated. Pectin wasn't always marked with a date. If your pectin container doesn't provide an expiration date, don't use it; it may be a sign that your product is extremely old.

Pectin is available in two forms: liquid and powdered (dry). Although both products are made from fruit, they're not interchangeable. Be sure to use the correct type and amount of pectin your recipe calls for.

Book II

Water-Bath Canning with Fruits

Using liquid fruit pectin

Liquid pectin is usually made from apples. Today, a box contains two 3-ounce pouches. The most common brand is Certo.

Liquid fruit pectin was originally sold in 6-ounce bottles. Older recipes may call for "one-half of a bottle." If you read a pouch of liquid pectin today, it states, "1 pouch equals ½ bottle."

Because you have to add your liquid pectin at the specified time and temperature, have it ready: Cut off the top of the pouch and stand it in a measuring cup or other container to keep it from spilling (see Figure 4-1). Then, when it's time to add the liquid pectin, add it all at the same time, squeezing the pouch with your fingers like you do to get the last bit of toothpaste out of the tube.

LIQUID PECTIN AT THE READY!

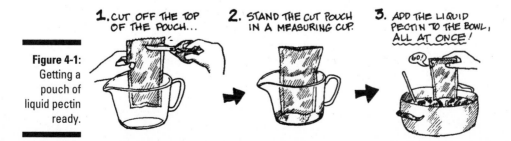

Figure 4-1: Getting a pouch of liquid pectin ready.

1. CUT OFF THE TOP OF THE POUCH...

2. STAND THE CUT POUCH IN A MEASURING CUP.

3. ADD THE LIQUID PECTIN TO THE BOWL, ALL AT ONCE!

Using powdered (dry) fruit pectin

Powdered pectin is made from citrus fruits or apples. It comes in a box similar to a gelatin- or pudding-mix box and contains 1.75 ounces (the most commonly used size) or 2 ounces. Use the size stated in your recipe ingredients and add it before you heat the fruit mixture.

In addition to different sizes, powdered pectin comes in two varieties: fruit pectin for homemade jams and jellies, and fruit pectin for lower-sugar recipes. Use the variety your recipe calls for; they're not interchangeable.

Gelling without pectin

Not all recipes require the addition of extra pectin. Some recipes cook the fruit mixture for a long period of time, which reduces the liquid in the mixture to achieve the desired consistency.

For this process, you need patience and the knowledge of what to look for when testing your cooked product. Basically, you need to know what the spread's gel point is. (*Gel point* is the cooking point at which jelly is considered done.)

The gel point temperature is 8° above boiling at an elevation of 1,000 feet above sea level or lower (220°). If you're at an altitude higher than 1,000 feet above sea level, you can determine the temperature of your gel point by bringing a pot of water to a boil. When the water boils, check the temperature on your thermometer and add 8 degrees. This number is the gel point for your altitude.

Use one of the following methods for testing the gel point:

- ✔ **A candy thermometer:** This is the most accurate method for testing the gel point of your spread. Use a thermometer that's easy to read. One degree over or under the gel point makes a difference in your final product.

    It's a good idea to have two candy thermometers. They're inexpensive and critical for perfect jelly-making. If one breaks, you'll have a second one for backup during canning.

- ✔ **The spoon, or sheet, test:** Dip a cool metal spoon into your cooked fruit and hold it so that the fruit runs off the spoon (see Figure 4-2). When the temperature of the fruit approaches the gel point, it falls off in a couple of drops. When it slides off the spoon in one sheet, the fruit's done. Proceed with your next step.

This test takes a bit of practice to master. Until you master it, use a candy thermometer in conjunction with this test. When the temperature of the fruit climbs toward the gel point, you'll be able to see the changes in the liquid and compare it to the sheeting from the spoon.

✔ **The plate test:** Place about 1 tablespoon of cooked fruit onto a chilled plate (see Figure 4-2). Put the plate in the freezer and cool the spread to room temperature. If the fruit is set and doesn't roll around on the plate, the mixture is done. Proceed to your next step.

SPOON TEST

WHEN THE JUICE HAS ALMOST REACHED THE GEL POINT, IT WILL SLOWLY COME TOGETHER AND FALL OFF THE SPOON IN 2 DROPS. WHEN IT SLIDES OFF THE SPOON IN A SHEET, THE JELLY IS READY!

Figure 4-2: Gel testing your food: the spoon test and the plate test.

PLATE TEST

PLACE A SMALL AMOUNT OF SPREAD ON A CHILLED PLATE. SET THE PLATE IN THE FREEZER UNTIL THE MIXTURE COOLS TO ROOM TEMPERATURE. IF THE MIXTURE IS SET, IT IS READY TO CAN.

The Road to Sweet Canning Success

The only method for safely processing your sweet spreads, as approved by the United States Department of Agriculture (USDA), is water-bath canning. The harmful bacteria and microorganisms living in high-acid foods are destroyed at the temperature of boiling water (212° at 1,000 feet or lower above sea level) by sterilizing the food and vacuum-sealing the jar. For that reason, the recipes in the following sections all use water-bath canning. For complete details on water-bath canning, refer to Book II, Chapter 1.

Here are a couple of other tips to help ensure your canning success:

✔ **Stick with tested recipes.** They're always the best. Don't experiment with different quantities of ingredients in any canning method. Quantity adjustments to your fruit or your sugar can seriously change the acid (pH level) in your food. And if the acidity changes, you may not use the correct home-canning method to produce a safe product, free from microorganisms.

✔ **Always practice safe food-handling procedures.** Complete each recipe, start to finish, without interruption. Any break between cooking your fruit to filling the jars and processing them may produce a product of inferior quality and one that may be unsafe for eating.

Coauthor Amy's mother always made jam and then added a paraffin wax seal instead of using a hot water bath. She then placed these jars of jam into the pantry. This technique has fallen out of style and is no longer recommended for safe food storage.

Jamming and canning

Jams and jellies are a great way to begin your canning journey. The process is simple, calling for just a few ingredients, and takes just a few minutes. Talk about instant gratification! Jams and jellies are not just sweet, however. Savory and spice have their place in your jelly jars and on your table as well.

What makes jelly and jam recipes so interesting is that even the super-hot ingredients are tempered by the sweetness. If you find that hot peppers are just too much for your palate, don't let that stop you from trying a red pepper jelly.

Savory mixes sweeten and bring a depth of flavor as a glaze to meats or as topping on a homemade biscuit. When you make jams and jellies, don't be afraid to break the traditional idea of jelly and go for something with a little more excitement.

Coauthor Amy's family can eat a half-pint of jam in one meal. Amy says, "At times, I simply take a batch of whatever fruit is ripe, make jam, and put it in the refrigerator. Although jams put up this way keep much longer than a few days, they certainly don't in my house!" If you have impatient eaters, don't forget to make a few batches of these easy jams.

Making refrigerator jams is even easier than making canned jams. They use the same recipes, but you simply put the finished jars into the refrigerator instead of water-bath canning them. What could be simpler? If you make a larger batch than you want to keep in the fridge, you can certainly freeze them, but let the jars cool to room temperature and solidify before freezing, or the jam may ooze up one side if it's not perfectly level in the freezer.

Fresh jams that are being frozen still need to have headspace to accommodate the swelling of the product as it freezes.

Jiggling with jelly

Jelly always has such a bright, cheerful look. It's a great last-minute appetizer that doesn't taste last-minute.

For a quick appetizer, spoon a tart jelly, such as cranberry, over a block of cream cheese, allowing it to cascade over the sides. Serve it with rich, buttery crackers.

Quick jellies are also the perfect answer for any extra fruit you have. Because quick jellies require few ingredients, most of which are in your pantry, if you know exactly how to make jelly, you'll be able to put up the fruits as they ripen.

Savory jellies are the grown-up answer to a treat. They're great for impromptu guests, paired with crackers and cheese, or used to dress up a roast as a glaze. Savory jellies are a must-have on your shelf.

In order to achieve a bright, crystal-clear jelly, you need to properly strain your fruit. You can use a commercially manufactured stand and a jelly bag, or you can make your own by using a mesh strainer lined with several layers of cheesecloth (see Figure 4-3).

Dry fabric absorbs flavor from your fruit, weakening the flavor of your final product. Moisten your jelly bag (or cheesecloth) with cold water, wringing out any excess moisture before straining your liquid through it.

Book II

Water-Bath Canning with Fruits

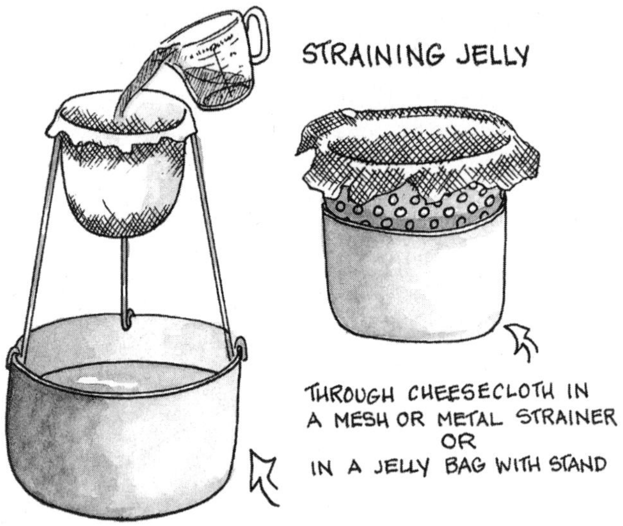

STRAINING JELLY

Figure 4-3:
Straining
jelly using
a jelly bag
and stand or
a cheese-
cloth-lined
strainer.

THROUGH CHEESECLOTH IN
A MESH OR METAL STRAINER
OR
IN A JELLY BAG WITH STAND

Mastering marmalades and butters

Introduce your family and friends to the spreads that were once more common than jams and jellies. Add variety to your canning pantry while you share the wonderful flavors and textures with those lucky enough to be around when you open a jar. After all, there's more to marmalade than oranges.

Marmalades take jams to the next level. Instead of a smooth product, marmalades have ingredients that combine into a more complex taste. Not just for grownups, many kids love the fruity, piquant mixtures as well.

Reminiscent of grandmother's kitchen, butters offer the richness of the fruits and the creamy texture of a nut butter. Fruit butters are perfect for the end of season abundance of fruit we experience every fall.

Strawberry-Rhubarb Jam

Prep time: 45 min • **Process time:** 20 min • **Yield:** 3 pints

Ingredients	Directions
4 cups strawberries, crushed **2½ cups chopped rhubarb** **¼ cup lemon juice** **One 1.75-ounce package pectin powder** **6 cups sugar**	**1** Hull and crush the strawberries. Clean the rhubarb, trim the ends, and remove the leaves. Cut the rhubarb into ½-inch pieces.
	2 Combine the strawberries, rhubarb, lemon juice, and pectin powder in a large saucepan. Bring the mixture to a boil over medium-high heat. Add the sugar, stirring to dissolve. Return the mixture to a full, rolling boil and boil hard for 1 minute. Remove the saucepan from the heat. Skim any foam from the surface with a foam skimmer, if necessary.
	3 Ladle the boiling-hot jam into your hot jars, leaving ¼ inch headspace.
	4 Process the filled pint jars in a water-bath canner for 20 minutes from the point of boiling. Use any unsealed jars within 2 weeks.

Per 1-tablespoon serving: Calories 53 (From Fat 0); Fat 0g (Saturated 0g); Cholesterol 0mg; Sodium 1mg; Carbohydrates 14g (Dietary Fiber 0g); Protein 0g.

Tip: You can make this jam throughout the year because frozen rhubarb works just like fresh.

Rhubarb Jam

Prep time: 20 min, plus refrigeration time • **Process time:** 15 min • **Yield:** 6 half-pints

Ingredients	Directions
5 cups rhubarb 2½ cups sugar One 3-ounce box gelatin (any flavor)	**1** Wash the rhubarb and cut it into ¼-inch pieces. Combine the rhubarb and sugar in a large mixing bowl. Let stand in the refrigerator for 2 hours. **2** In a 6-quart saucepan, bring the sugar and rhubarb mixture to a simmer over medium heat. Cook 15 minutes or until the rhubarb is soft. Remove from heat and stir in the gelatin until dissolved. **3** Pour the hot jam into hot jars, leaving ¼-inch headspace. **4** Process the filled jars in a water-bath canner for 15 minutes from the point of boiling. Use any unsealed jars within 2 weeks.

Per 1-tablespoon serving: Calories 49 (From Fat 0); Fat 0g (Saturated 0g); Cholesterol 0mg; Sodium 5mg; Carbohydrates 13g (Dietary Fiber 0g); Protein 0g.

Honey Jelly

Prep time: 20 min • **Process time:** 15 min • **Yield:** 6 half-pints

Ingredients	Directions
3 cups honey 1 cup water ½ bottle of liquid pectin	*1* Combine the honey and water in a 6-quart saucepan. Bring to a boil over medium-high heat and add the pectin. Return the pectin and honey to a rolling boil and remove from heat.
	2 Pour the hot jelly into hot jars, leaving ¼-inch headspace. Process the filled jars in a water-bath canner for 15 minutes from the point of boiling. Use any unsealed jars within 2 weeks.

Per 1-tablespoon serving: Calories 65 (From Fat 0); Fat 0g (Saturated 0g); Cholesterol 0mg; Sodium 1mg; Carbohydrates 18g (Dietary Fiber 0g); Protein 0g.

Herb Tea Jelly

Prep time: 30 min • **Process time:** 20 min • **Yield:** 5 half-pints

Ingredients	Directions
2 cups water 12 tea bags of your favorite herbal tea 3 cups sugar 1 cup apple juice One 3-ounce package of liquid pectin	*1* Bring the water to a boil in a 3-quart saucepan over high heat. Remove the pan from the heat and steep the tea bags, covered, for 30 minutes.
	2 Remove the tea bags and stir in the sugar and apple juice. Boil the mixture for 2 minutes; then remove the pan from the heat and stir in the pectin. Boil for 2 more minutes.
	3 Fill the prepared jars with boiling liquid, leaving ¼-inch headspace. Process the filled jars in a water-bath canner for 20 minutes from the point of boiling. Use any unsealed jars within 2 weeks.

Per 1-tablespoon serving: Calories 41 (From Fat 0); Fat 0g (Saturated 0g); Cholesterol 0mg; Sodium 0mg; Carbohydrates 11g (Dietary Fiber 0g); Protein 0g.

Hot Pepper Jelly

Prep time: 20 min • **Process time:** 15 min • **Yield:** 6 half-pints

Ingredients	Directions
¾ **cup hot peppers**	**1** In a 3-quart saucepan, combine the peppers and vinegar. Bring to a boil over medium-high heat. Add the sugar and stir until dissolved. Remove from the heat. Strain the jelly and add the remaining ingredients.
¾ **cup sweet bell peppers, washed and chopped**	
1½ **cup white vinegar**	
6½ **cups sugar**	**2** Ladle the hot mixture into jars, leaving ¼-inch headspace. Process the filled jars in a water-bath canner for 15 minutes from the point of boiling. Use any unsealed jars within 2 weeks.
6 **ounces liquid pectin**	
3 **drops red food coloring (optional)**	

Per 1-tablespoon serving: Calories 106 (From Fat 0); Fat 0g (Saturated 0g); Cholesterol 0mg; Sodium 0mg; Carbohydrates 27g (Dietary Fiber 0g); Protein 0g.

Kumquat Marmalade

Prep time: 30 min • **Cook time:** 30 min • **Process time:** 10 min • **Yield:** 7 half-pints

Ingredients	*Directions*
2 pounds kumquats, unpeeled **1½ cups water** **⅛ teaspoon baking soda** **½ cup fresh lemon juice (about 2 to 3 lemons)** **5 cups granulated sugar** **One 3-ounce pouch liquid fruit pectin**	*1* Slice the kumquats in half lengthwise; then slice each half into fourths lengthwise. Discard the bitter seeds. Place the kumquats into a 6- to 8-quart pot. Add the water and the baking soda.
	2 Bring the mixture to a boil over medium-high heat. Reduce the heat and simmer, covered, for 20 minutes, stirring occasionally. Add the lemon juice and simmer, covered, for 10 minutes longer, stirring occasionally.
	3 Stir the sugar into your cooked fruit. Bring the mixture to a full, rolling boil over high heat. Boil hard for 1 minute, stirring constantly.
	4 Remove the pan from the heat. Add the pectin, stirring to combine. Remove any foam from the surface with a foam skimmer.
	5 Ladle your hot marmalade into the prepared jars, leaving ¼-inch headspace. Process the filled jars in a water-bath canner for 10 minutes from the point of boiling. Use any unsealed jars within 2 months.

Per 1-tablespoon serving: Calories 40 (From Fat 0); Fat 0g (Saturated 0g); Cholesterol 0mg; Sodium 2mg; Carbohydrates 10g (Dietary Fiber 1g); Protein 0g.

Lime-Ginger Marmalade

Prep time: 20 min • **Cook time:** 1 hr • **Process time:** 10 min • **Yield:** 4 half-pints

Ingredients	*Directions*
3 to 4 limes, cut in half lengthwise and sliced crosswise (about ⅛-inch thick), to measure 1½ cups of fruit	*1* Place the lime slices, lemon zest, water, and ginger in a 5- to 6-quart saucepan. Bring the mixture to a boil over medium-high heat and boil rapidly until the fruit is tender, about 30 minutes. Remove the pan from the heat.
½ cup grated lemon zest (about 2 to 4 lemons)	*2* Measure the hot mixture into a heatproof measuring cup and return it to the pan. For each cup of fruit, add 1 cup of sugar. Return the pan to the stove and bring the mixture to a boil over high heat, stirring often to dissolve the sugar.
5 cups water	
¼ cup finely shredded fresh ginger (about a 5- to 6-inch piece)	
4¼ cups granulated sugar	*3* Cook the marmalade about 30 minutes until it sheets off a spoon (see Figure 4-2) or registers 220° on a candy thermometer. Remove the pan from the heat and cool the mixture for 5 minutes. Remove any foam from the surface with a foam skimmer.
	4 Ladle your hot marmalade into the prepared jars, leaving ¼-inch headspace. Process the filled jars in a water-bath canner for 10 minutes from the point of boiling. Use any unsealed jars within 2 months.

Per 1-tablespoon serving: Calories 53 (From Fat 0); Fat 0g (Saturated 0g); Cholesterol 0mg; Sodium 0mg; Carbohydrates 14g (Dietary Fiber 0g); Protein 0g.

Any-Time-of-the-Year Strawberry Preserves

Prep time: 10 min • **Cook time:** 5 min • **Process time:** 10 min • **Yield:** 6 half-pints

Ingredients	*Directions*
Three 10-ounce packages of frozen, sliced strawberries, thawed **¼ cup water** **1.75-ounce package powdered fruit pectin** **6 cups granulated sugar** **⅓ cup orange liqueur** **3 tablespoons fresh lemon juice**	*1* Combine the strawberries with the water and pectin in a 5- to 6-quart pot. Bring the mixture to a boil over high heat, stirring occasionally to dissolve the pectin. Boil hard for 1 minute. Stir in the sugar and return the mixture to a full, rolling boil. Boil hard for 1 minute, stirring constantly. *2* Remove the pan from the heat. Stir in the liqueur and the lemon juice. Cool for 5 minutes, stirring occasionally. Remove any foam from the surface with a foam skimmer. *3* Ladle your hot preserves into the prepared jars, leaving ¼-inch headspace. Process the filled jars in a water-bath canner for 10 minutes from the point of boiling. Use any unsealed jars within 2 months.

Per 1-tablespoon serving: Calories 53 (From Fat 0); Fat 0g (Saturated 0g); Cholesterol 0mg; Sodium 0mg; Carbohydrates 14g (Dietary Fiber 0g); Protein 0g.

Apple Butter

Prep time: 20 min • **Cook time:** 1 h, 10 min • **Process time:** 15 min • **Yield:** 6 half-pints

Ingredients	Directions
3½ cups apple cider **8 large apples (about 4 to 4½ pounds), peeled, cored, and sliced** **1½ cups granulated sugar** **¼ teaspoon kosher or pickling salt** **¾ teaspoon ground cinnamon** **One 3-inch cinnamon stick**	**1** Place the cider in a 5- to 6-quart pot and bring it to a boil over high heat. Add the apple slices and reduce the heat. Simmer the fruit, uncovered, for 45 minutes. Stir the fruit every 10 to 15 minutes to prevent sticking. **2** Stir in the sugar, salt, and the ground and stick cinnamon. Cook the mixture uncovered over medium-low heat, stirring occasionally, until the mixture thickens, about 20 to 25 minutes. (The consistency should be like applesauce.) Remove and discard the cinnamon stick. **3** Ladle your hot fruit into the prepared jars, leaving ¼-inch headspace. Process the filled jars in a water-bath canner for 15 minutes from the point of boiling. Use any unsealed jars within 2 months.

Per 1-tablespoon serving: Calories 23 (From Fat 0); Fat 0g (Saturated 0g); Cholesterol 0mg; Sodium 7mg; Carbohydrates 6g (Dietary Fiber 0g); Protein 0g.

Chapter 5

Savory Spreads and Conserves: Chutneys, Relishes, and Mincemeats

In This Chapter

▶ Expanding your world of condiments and accompaniments

▶ Celebrating chutney

▶ Relishing your fruits and vegetables

Condiments and accompaniments are to food what accessories are to clothing. They're not necessary, but they enhance what's there. They cover a wide range of flavors, including savory, spicy, salty, sweet, or a combination. Think of condiments and accompaniments as the bright spot on an otherwise dull winter plate.

In this chapter, we open the door to flavors and tastes from around the world. Chutneys are common in Asia and Middle Eastern countries, and relish is very popular in North America. Mincemeats were more common in days of old, and they have changed over time to leave out the actual meat. Enjoy the mincemeat recipe at the end of this chapter — it includes the more traditional meat — and see how this version of mincemeat pie is much more filling and satisfying to eat than the version without meat. Expand your taste experience as you visit the world of fascinating and enticing flavors.

The water-bath canning principles and step-by-step instructions explained in Book II, Chapter 1 (and used in Chapters 2 through 4) apply to the recipes in this chapter. As always, use the freshest fruit and other products you need to make your recipes.

Defining Conserves, Chutneys, Relishes, and Mincemeats

For many people, once you get past the jams and jellies (see Book II, Chapter 4), definitions start to get a little fuzzy. No need to be confused! More than just sweet spreads, conserves, chutneys, relishes, and mincemeats have a heartier texture, and their taste is a welcome accompaniment that brightens many dishes. Make up a few jars and enjoy a more flavorful meal.

✔ **Conserves** usually contain two fruits mixed with sugar and nuts and cooked to achieve a consistency similar to jam. Traditionally, conserves were used as a spread on biscuits and crumpets.

✔ **Chutney** is a condiment that contains fruit, vinegar, sugar, and spices. Chutneys range in flavor from sweet to spicy and mild to hot and have textures ranging from smooth to chunky. Chutneys usually accompany curry dishes, but don't limit them to that usage. Use chutneys as bread spreads, such as on biscuits for a soup supper. Chutneys have rich flavors, and they go well with a warm bowl of stew or soup.

Toasting nuts

Toasted nuts are delicious and simple to make. Pay close attention during the toasting process. If the nuts become overtoasted (very dark), there's no going back. You have to start over. Toast more nuts than your recipe calls for and use them in salads. Store cooled nuts in an airtight container in the refrigerator.

Toasting nuts takes only minutes (literally), so stay right by the oven:

1. **Spread your nuts evenly on a baking sheet and place it in a preheated 350° oven.**

2. **Set your timer for 3 minutes.**

   The size of the nut determines the toasting time. Three minutes will be enough for some nuts, not enough for others.

3. **After 3 minutes, check the nuts for doneness; shake or stir them.**

   If they're a color you're looking for (usually a light golden brown), remove them from the oven and cool them on the baking sheet.

4. **If the nuts aren't quite done, return them to the oven, checking them again in 2 minutes.**

   Toasting takes place quickly. Your nuts are done, or close to being done, when you can smell their wonderful aroma. If the skin is on the nut, it'll split to show you the color of the nut.

5. **Remove the finished nuts from the baking sheet to cool.**

   If you leave them on the sheet, they'll continue to cook.

✔ **Relish** wears many hats and complements a wide variety of foods, from hamburgers and hot dogs to meat and poultry. Relish is a cooked mixture of fruits or vegetables preserved with vinegar. Flavor can be sweet to savory and hot to mild with textures ranging from smooth to finely chopped or chunky. My family and I (Amy) like our relish to be a bit on the chunky side. That way, you can still see pieces of individual ingredients. Either way, relish is a must-have for your pantry.

✔ Back in the day when **mincemeat** was commonplace, it always included actual meat and fat. You can use these rich, filling pies as a quick breakfast on the run, keeping you full until lunch. As time progressed, mincement stopped including meat and fat and instead contained raisins and nuts for a thick, meatlike texture. This chapter contains both a traditional and a vegetarian recipe so that you can decide for yourself which is better for you!

Book II

Water-Bath Canning with Fruits

Creating Your Savory Spreads and Conserves

It can be difficult to think of spreads as savory. We get used to thinking of sweet jams on bread. However, if you can open yourself to the idea of the savory component, you'll have a multitude of tastes to combine together. Often, a savory spread or conserve will be special enough to serve at a dinner party — making them perfect hostess gifts!

Pectins can be considered the thickener of the jarred world. Some foods are cooked until they are a thick consistency, or they utilize their own natural pectin, but for the most part, you'll be adding pectin. Use the variety that's recommended in the recipe and don't substitute without the directions mentioning that you can do so.

Although the recipes are pretty simple, processing your items in a sanitary workspace is just as important as it is when canning other foods. When filling jars, use the proper headspace for the best results and always look for and remove trapped air bubbles, especially in the substantially thick mincemeats.

Always use the same caution when sealing these sweet and savory foods as you do with any other canned item. If the jars don't seal, you can store them in the refrigerator and use them within 2 weeks.

If your product grows mold on the surface, starts to smell off, or becomes foamy or bubbly, consider it spoiled and discard it properly.

Green Tomato Chutney

Prep time: 15 min **Cook Time:** 45 min • **Process time:** 10 min • **Yield:** 8 half-pints

Ingredients	*Directions*
4 pounds green tomatoes, chopped	*1* Place all the ingredients in a 6-quart pot and simmer on medium heat until the mixture is thick and rich, the consistency of very thick, chunky applesauce, about 45 minutes. Stir often to prevent scorching.
2 medium onions, chopped	
1½ green apples, peeled, cored, and chopped	
1 cup golden raisins	*2* Ladle the mixture into prepared half-pint jars. Leave ¼-inch headspace.
1 teaspoon salt	
½ teaspoon ground red pepper	*3* Process the filled half-pint jars in a water-bath canner for 10 minutes from the point of boiling. After processing, if you find jars that haven't sealed, refrigerate them and use them within 2 weeks.
1 teaspoon allspice	
1 teaspoon curry, or to taste	
1 cup brown sugar	
2 cups cider vinegar	

Per 1-tablespoon serving: *Calories 16 (From Fat 0); Fat 0g (Saturated 0g); Cholesterol 0mg; Sodium 21mg; Carbohydrates 4g (Dietary Fiber 0g); Protein 0g.*

Summer Squash Relish

Prep time: 10 min, plus soaking • **Cook time:** 30 min • **Process time:** 15 min • **Yield:** 6 pints

Ingredients	*Directions*
5 pounds (about 10 to 12) medium zucchini **6 large onions** **½ cup kosher or pickling salt** **Cold water to cover the vegetables (about 4 to 5 quarts)** **2 cups white wine vinegar** **1 cup granulated sugar** **Two 4-ounce jars pimentos, undrained** **2 teaspoons celery seed** **1 teaspoon powdered mustard** **½ teaspoon ground cinnamon** **½ teaspoon ground nutmeg** **½ teaspoon freshly ground black pepper**	*1* On the first day, finely chop the zucchini and onions. (If you're using a food processor, chop them in three batches.) Place the vegetables in a 5- to 6-quart mixing bowl and sprinkle them with the salt. Add water to cover them, place a cover on the bowl, and refrigerate overnight or at least 12 hours.
	2 On the second day, drain the vegetables in a colander. Rinse well with running water; drain. Transfer the vegetables to a 5- to 6-quart pot. Add the vinegar, sugar, pimentos, celery seed, mustard, cinnamon, nutmeg, and pepper. Stir to combine.
	3 Bring the vegetables to a boil over medium-high heat, stirring occasionally. Reduce the heat and simmer, uncovered, until the mixture reduces to 3 quarts, about 30 to 40 minutes. Stir the vegetables every 10 minutes to prevent sticking.
	4 Spoon the hot relish into your prepared jars, leaving ¼-inch headspace. Process your filled jars in a water-bath canner for 15 minutes from the point of boiling. After processing, if you find jars that haven't sealed, refrigerate them and use them within 2 months.

Per 2-tablespoon serving: Calories 16 (From Fat 1); Fat 0g (Saturated 0g); Cholesterol 0mg; Sodium 14mg; Carbohydrates 4g (Dietary Fiber 1g); Protein 0g.

Vary It! Use 3 pounds of zucchini and 2 pounds of patty pan or yellow crookneck squash.

India Relish

Prep time: 2 hr • **Cook time:** 45 min • **Process time:** 15 min • **Yield:** 10 pints

Ingredients	Directions
8 pounds tomatoes 3 cups celery 2 medium onions 2 medium red peppers ¼ cup salt 3 cups brown sugar 4 cups vinegar ½ cup mustard seed 1 teaspoon cinnamon 1 teaspoon allspice 1 teaspoon cloves	**1** Peel and chop the tomatoes. Chop the celery and onions. Seed and chop the peppers. **2** Combine the chopped vegetables, salt, mustard seed, cinnamon, allspice, cloves, brown sugar, vinegar, and water in a 6-quart pot. Allow the mixture to sit for 2 hours. **3** Heat the mixture over medium heat, simmering gently for 45 minutes or until thick. Raise the heat and bring the mixture to a boil. **4** Pack the boiling hot relish into jars, leaving ¼-inch headspace. Process the filled jars (pints) in a water-bath canner for 15 minutes from the point of boiling. After processing, if you find jars that haven't sealed, refrigerate them and use them within 2 weeks.

Per 2-tablespoon serving: Calories 24 (From Fat 2); Fat 0g (Saturated 0g); Cholesterol 0mg; Sodium 178mg; Carbohydrates 5g (Dietary Fiber 0g); Protein 0g.

Pear Relish

Prep time: 40 min, plus standing time • **Process time:** 20 min • **Yield:** 9 pints

Ingredients	*Directions*
16 pounds pears	*1* Wash, peel, and core the pears. Peel the onions. Wash and seed the peppers. Wash the celery. Finely chop the pear, onion, pepper, and celery or use a food processor.
6 onions	
6 green peppers	
8 stalks celery	
1 tablespoon allspice	*2* Combine the finely chopped pears and vegetables, allspice, sugar, salt, vinegar, and water in a 6-quart pot. Allow the mixture to sit for 2 hours.
3 cups sugar	
1 tablespoon salt	*3* Heat over medium-high heat and bring the mixture to a boil. Pack the boiling hot relish into pint jars, leaving ¼-inch headspace.
5 cups vinegar	
¼ cup water	
	4 Process the filled jars (pints) in a water-bath canner for 20 minutes from the point of boiling. After processing, if you find jars that haven't sealed, refrigerate them and use them within 2 weeks.

Per 2-tablespoon serving: Calories 22 (From Fat 0); Fat 0g (Saturated 0g); Cholesterol 0mg; Sodium 52mg; Carbohydrates 5g (Dietary Fiber 0g); Protein 0g.

Mincemeat

Prep time: 30 min • **Cook time:** 1 hr • **Process time:** 20 min • **Yield:** 6 quarts

Ingredients	*Directions*
10 pounds combined of apples and cherries	*1* Wash, core, and chop the apples. Wash and pit the cherries.
2 quarts sour cherries	
3 pounds sugar	*2* Combine the apples with remaining ingredients in a large 6-quart pot. Over medium heat, simmer gently for 60 minutes, stirring frequently to prevent burning.
½ teaspoon cloves	
½ teaspoon cinnamon	
1 quart apple cider	*3* Pack the mincemeat into jars, leaving 1-inch headspace.
2 pounds lean ground beef	
1½ pounds seedless raisins	*4* Process the filled jars (quarts) in a pressure canner at 10 pounds pressure for 20 minutes. When the processing time is done, allow the pressure to return to 0, wait an additional 10 minutes, and then carefully open the canner lid.
¼ cup melted butter	
	5 After processing, if you find jars that haven't sealed, refrigerate them and use them within 2 weeks. Prior to eating or tasting, boil the food for 15 minutes.

Per ½-cup serving: Calories 256 (From Fat 23); Fat 3g (Saturated 1g); Cholesterol 8mg; Sodium 16mg; Carbohydrates 56g (Dietary Fiber 3g); Protein 4g.

Vegetarian Mincemeat

Prep time: 20 min • **Cook time:** 20–25 min • **Yield:** Enough for 1 pie

Ingredients	Directions
3 large green apples	*1* Peel and chop the apples into ½-inch pieces. Chop the dates into ½-inch pieces. Chop the walnuts into ¼-inch pieces. Lightly dice the sunflower seeds.
½ cup dates	
¼ cup walnuts or cashews	
2 tablespoons sunflower seeds	*2* Place all ingredients in a 3-quart saucepan, over low heat. Bring to a simmer, stirring often to prevent sticking. Simmer for 20 to 25 minutes.
⅓ cup honey	
1 teaspoon cinnamon	
¼ teaspoon cloves	*3* Pack the mincemeat into a wide-mouth jar and seal with a tight-fitting lid. Refrigerate for up to 2 weeks before use.
¼ teaspoon nutmeg	
¼ teaspoon ginger	
1 teaspoon lemon zest	

Per ½-cup serving: Calories 158 (From Fat 34); Fat 4g (Saturated 0g); Cholesterol 0mg; Sodium 1mg; Carbohydrates 33g (Dietary Fiber 4g); Protein 1g.

Book III

Mastering the Art of Pickling

The 5th Wave   By Rich Tennant

"Quit moping. You won first place in the
pickled beets category, and that's good.
I'm the only one that knows it was
strawberry preserves you entered."

In this book . . .

Mosts meals benefit from the piquant taste of a pickled side dish. You may be surprised to find that you can make pickles in many ways other than the tried-and-true dill. Expand your pickle vision and create a shelf full of pickled foods that can accompany your regular meals or be the star performer on a platter of other edibles. From sweet to spicy, pickles are for everyone!

Chapter 1

Getting Started with Pickling

There is nothing like the sharp, crisp taste of a perfectly pickled cucumber. The flavors of pickled foods add such a fresh dimension to everyday meals, they should have a place on any pantry shelf.

You can use pickling for a wide range of foods, including fruits, vegetables, meats, and eggs. Although pickling isn't practiced much today, don't overlook this rewarding process. This chapter gives you an overview of pickling, describing the ingredients, the utensils, and the methods you can use. In no time, you'll be making easy-to-prepare pickled food and condiments to wow your taste buds.

Taking a Look at Pickling

Pickling preserves food in a *brine solution,* a strong mixture of water, salt, vinegar, and sometimes sugar or another sweetener. Brining is what gives food the pickled texture and flavor you're going for.

Knowing the sights and smells of pickling

The pickling process creates its own sights and smells. The smell of boiling vinegar and strong spices, as well as the idea of simply pouring boiling liquid over packed jars of raw ingredients, all require some practice. Knowing how pickling will change the color, shape, and size of the product is important. Some color changes and flavorings don't taste good as you pour them on, but they'll change the food into delectable treats over time.

Understanding the difference between pickling and fermenting

Pickling and fermenting aren't the same thing. Both take a fresh fruit or vegetable and change the flavor, immersed in a fluid, but that's where the similarities end. It gets confusing because many people refer to the fermenting liquid as a *brine,* which by definition is a mixture of salt and water. Pickling recipes also use the word brine, to define the salt, water, vinegar, and seasonings you add to the fresh product in jars. Using the same word for both techniques muddies the waters a bit.

To clarify, I look at both processes and define them further:

✔ **Pickling:** The fresh product sits in the flavored pasteurized brine and becomes pickled over time through osmosis. This time needed is why, if you reopen a freshly pickled cucumber, it may taste salty on the outside, but plain inside. The pickling process takes days and usually weeks to complete. As time passes, the flavors mellow and become delicious, without the worry of becoming contaminated by unwanted bacteria, thanks to the high heat of canning, which kills all the bacteria — both good and bad.

✔ **Fermenting:** You submerge food into liquid that contains salt and other seasonings (if desired), but the fermenting process is accomplished by the beneficial bacteria *lactobacillus* rather than by heat. Because the process is completed under the liquid, the food is protected from unwanted bacteria while the beneficial bacteria flourish. This *Lacto* bacteria needs to be kept in an oxygen-free (anaerobic) environment, which the brine provides. Fermented foods will often have a tingly tart taste, even effervescent. They're not just vinegary and salty, like pickled foods.

Think of pickling as the process that happens on the pantry or refrigerator shelf. You add the flavoring to the proper food, but the pickling happens on its own, over time.

Getting a handle on the process

For the best tasting pickled foods, check out these tips:

✔ Pick blemish-free produce and pickle it within 24 hours of harvesting. Never use foods that have spoiled or moldy parts.

✔ To ensure that every piece is pickled at the same time, always pack your jars with uniformly sized pieces.

✔ Scrub the produce well to get rid of any dirt, which contains bacteria, and trim ⅛ inch from the blossom and stem ends if you're using cucumbers. These ends may have enzymes that will spoil or soften your pickles.

✔ Pack your jars tightly. Pickling causes food to shrink slightly, and tightly filling the jars helps to prevent them from floating.

✔ Wait the recommended period of time before tasting the results. Many pickled foods need weeks to complete the pickling process. Tasting earlier than recommended will give you an inaccurate representation of the recipe.

✔ Be sure your foods remain submerged throughout the process, in order to be exposed to the brine.

Assembling Your Ingredients

The basic ingredients for pickling are salt, vinegar, water, and herbs and spices. Use high-quality ingredients for the best results. Of course, the quality of the food you use is important, too. (See Chapter 2 of Book I for more on picking perfect foods.)

The perfect balance of salt, vinegar, water, and herbs and spices safely preserves your pickled food. You can achieve this balance by precisely measuring your ingredients and following each step in your recipe.

Salt

In the pickling process, salt serves as a preservative and as a way to add both crispness and flavor. However, not just any salt will do. Use only the following pure, additive-free salts:

✔ Pickling and canning salt

✔ Kosher salt

✔ Sea salt

Don't use table salt, iodized salt, or rock salt. Chapter 2 of Book I tells you more about the salts for canning and preserving.

Vinegar

Vinegar is a tart liquid that prevents the growth of bacteria. For pickling, you must use vinegar with an acidity level of 5 percent. If the level of acidity isn't on the label, don't use the vinegar — the strength of the acid may not be adequate for safe food preservation.

The preferred vinegar for pickling is distilled white vinegar, which has a sharp, tart flavor, maintains the color of your food, and is relatively inexpensive. For a milder flavor, you can substitute apple cider vinegar. Keep in mind, though, that using cider vinegar changes the overall color of your finished foods, and not always for the better. You may get unappetizing gray or brown results from using the wrong type of vinegar.

To avoid cloudy pickles, use vinegar that's clear of sediment. Cider and wine vinegars often have sediment, and you may even be able to see things floating around. What causes the sediment? Vinegars that still contain the *mother,* a harmless bacterium that creates the vinegar but also causes sediment to form on the bottom of the bottle.

Never dilute or reduce the amount of vinegar in a recipe. To ensure a safe product, the brine must have the right acidity level. Never use vinegar with less than 5 percent acidity.

If the flavor's too tart, add ¼ cup granulated sugar for every 4 cups vinegar. Treating flavors in this manner doesn't upset the balance of your vinegar. If you don't like the flavor when you make the recipe, try another recipe. Don't forget to jot down your changes on your recipe card!

Water

Soft water is the best water for your brine solution. Too much iron in your water can cause discoloration of the finished product. *Distilled water,* water with all minerals and other impurities removed, is also a good choice. If you use tap water, make sure it's of drinking quality; if it doesn't taste good to you, it won't taste better in your food. Also, avoid using sparkling water. Check out Chapter 2 of Book I for everything you need to know about water.

Herbs and spices

Use the exact amount of herbs or spices called for in your recipe. If your recipe calls for a fresh herb, use the fresh herb. If your recipe calls for a dried spice, use one with a strong aroma. (For more information on drying herbs and spices, check out Chapter 3 of Book VII.)

Pickling spices are blends of many spices including allspice, bay leaves, cardamom, cinnamon, cloves, coriander, ginger, mustard seed, and peppercorns. They're mixed by the manufacturer and vary in flavor. Although these spices are generally whole and therefore good keepers, it is best to buy fresh, new spices each year, before you start canning.

Gathering Your Pickling Gear and Utensils

In addition to the basic equipment for water-bath canning (refer to Chapter 3 of Book I), you need nonreactive utensils and equipment for handling, cooking, and brining your food. Nonreactive items are made of stainless steel, nonstick-surfaced items (without a damaged nonstick surface), enamelware, or glass.

Don't use enamelware with chips or cracks or equipment or utensils made from or containing copper, iron, or brass. These items react with the acids and salt during the pickling process, altering the color of your food and giving the finished product a bad taste. *Definitely* don't use galvanized products, which contain zinc. These produce a poison when the acid and the salt touch the zinc, which is transferred to your food causing serious illness (or worse).

When it comes to the canning process, your equipment is simple to find and easy to use. You don't have to worry about pressure canning, which means your time frame for finishing a batch of jars is much shorter.

Pickling requires basic steps, no matter what recipe you use. Therefore, after you have the items you need, you'll become familiar with the pickling steps and, as you gain experience, find that the process is actually very quick and simple to do. Pickling is especially nice when you're overrun or when you find a good deal on a particular item that needs to be put up quickly, like after a long day of work. Pickling gets the food into the jars in record time.

Book III

Mastering the Art of Pickling

Mastering the Basics of Brining

Some recipes (usually older ones) include a brining step before the actual canning. Other pickling recipes add the brine solution to the raw food and the brining happens in the sterile canning jar as it sits on your shelf. These recipes generally have a recommendation for how many weeks to wait for best flavor.

The brining process is a key part of the pickling process because it does these important things:

- ✔ Chemically, it draws out the natural juices and replaces them with a salty/vinegar solution, giving your foods that familiar pickled flavor and texture.

- ✔ It extracts juice and sugar from your food, forming *lactic acid,* a bitter-tasting tart acid. This lactic acid serves as the preservative in your pickled food.

✔ Because the brining solution typically includes vinegar (an acid), it safely converts your low-acid fruits and vegetables (those with a pH level over 4.6) to high-acid foods (with a pH level of 4.6 or less), making it safe for water-bath canning. (This is why you must prepare your recipe as it's written and *not* modify the amounts.)

Sometimes you brine your food before canning; other times, you add the brine solution to the raw food and let the brining occur without adding high heat to stop the bacterial and enzyme action. The following sections explain how to prepare your chosen food for each.

Fresh packing

In this method, you place fresh raw food in prepared jars and then cover them with hot flavored liquid, usually a spicy vinegar, and process the filled jars in your water-bath canner. To ensure the pickling process can occur uniformly, make sure that your vegetables are completely submerged in the brining solution. Most of the pickling recipes in this book require raw packing.

Complete precooking

In this method, you cook your food completely before filling your jars. Precooking is common for most relish recipes. You follow a two-step process of soaking the shredded or chopped ingredients in a salt and water bath, sometimes overnight, and then adding them to the flavored brine and heating them to boiling before placing them into jars.

Brining before canning

When brining your produce before canning, how long you soak them can vary anywhere from a few hours to several weeks. Your recipe provides the details. Here's what you need to know about these long or short brines:

✔ **Long brine:** You primarily use this process to make a fermented food out of a fresh one. The product stays in the brine anywhere from 5 days to 6 weeks. The brine solution is quite heavy with salt and may contain some vinegar and spices. None of the pickling recipes in this book require a long brine. For more on this method, see the fermenting content in Book IV. (And for more on the differences between pickling and fermenting, see the sidebar earlier in this chapter.)

✔ **Short brine:** The soaking period for this method is 24 hours or less. Follow your recipe for the correct proportions in your brine solution. You use a short brine for the Sweet Pickle Relish and Zucchini Bread and Butter Pickles in the following chapter.

In both cases, you submerge the food in the brine solution, where it remains for the recommended period of time. (Your recipe gives you the details.) After brining, follow your recipe and make a fresh brine solution for filling your jars.

Be sure to keep your food completely submerged in the brine solution, whether it's for a few hours or longer. To do this, place a sealed, water-filled glass jar on top of your food. The jar applies pressure to keep the foods submerged when you cover your brining container.

Stoneware crocks are excellent choices for brining food. You can find them at specialty cookware stores or where canning supplies are sold. But there's an important caveat: Don't use a crock that you've gotten from a thrift store or other secondhand store. Without the original packaging, you have no way of knowing whether it's lead-free and suitable for brining.

Heeding Some General Directions

Some general directions apply to all the recipes in Book III. Be sure to heed the following instructions as you prepare the upcoming recipes:

✔ Prepare your canning jars and two-piece caps (lids and screw bands) according to the manufacturer's instructions. Keep the jars and lids hot until you fill them.

✔ When you fill your jars, release any air bubbles with a nonreactive utensil (refer to Book 1, Chapter 3). Add more of the food you're canning and liquid as necessary to maintain the headspace noted in the recipe.

✔ After filling your jars (but before placing them in the water-bath canner), wipe the jar rims. Then seal the jars with the two-piece caps, hand-tightening the bands.

✔ When your jars are done processing, remove them from the canner with a jar lifter. Place them on a clean kitchen towel away from drafts to cool.

✔ After the jars cool completely, test the seals. If you find jars that haven't sealed, refrigerate them and use them within the time specified in the recipe.

Chapter 2
Pickling Fruits and Veggies

In This Chapter

▶ Prepping your produce for pickling

▶ Outlining the pickling process

▶ Considering pickled fruits

The pickled cucumber may be the most common type of pickle, but don't limit your pickling to cukes. This chapter covers tips on pickling different vegetables and fruits and offers a selection of recipes certain to pique your interest and your taste buds.

The art of pickling comes into play when you start combining flavors. Many families have their own specific pickling recipes, known as "the best" or "Grandma's secret." The recipes in this chapter not only adhere to the safety of using proper acidity, but also use their own blends of sugars, spices, and even hot additions like peppers!

Preparing Produce for Pickling

Pickles are that one thing that finishes a plate of delicious food. The piquant, salty flavor is the component that rounds out a meal and brightens up an everyday dish. Pickles are also a wonderful way to add more variety to the same foods in your pantry. Because pickling completely changes the taste of a food, it's a good way to provide more options with the foods you have available to put up.

Although the following sections specifically talk about cucumbers, these guidelines apply to pickling vegetables of all kinds.

Picking pickling cucumbers

So what's so important about what kind of cucumber you use for pickles? After all, a cucumber is a cucumber, right? Definitely not. The common salad cucumber has a thick, dark-green, waxy skin. Don't use this cucumber for making pickles because the brine solution won't penetrate the waxy coating. Use this cucumber when your recipe doesn't specify "pickling cucumbers."

English cucumbers are another popular slicing cucumber. They're also unsuitable for pickling because they tend to become mushy.

A pickling cucumber is the only cucumber to use for making pickles. The skin of a pickling cucumber is thin, not waxy, and is left on the cucumber. Pickling cucumbers are about 4 inches in length, smaller than salad cucumbers. Don't eat pickling cucumbers raw; their flavor can be extremely bitter. Some varieties are now sold for both pickling and slicing. These varieties are fine to use. For pickling, use the smaller size of this variety; for slicing, use the larger size. Always look for cucumbers that are recommended for pickling, such as Kirby or Boston Pickling.

Slicing and peeling

Some love them whole, others in spears; pickles come in all shapes and sizes. You can choose your favorite cut (or not) for your pickles, but stick with the recipe directions. If you want to slice a pickle, don't use a whole pickle recipe, or it may make your slices soggy.

Pickles usually aren't peeled, but you do seed them (see Figure 2-1). If you find that your peels are tough after pickling and you're certain they are a pickling variety, the cucumbers may be old or not as fresh as you thought they were.

How to Seed a Cucumber

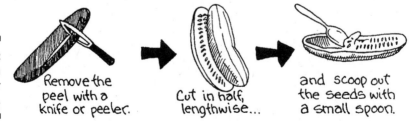

Figure 2-1: Seeding a cucumber with ease.

Remove the peel with a knife or peeler.

Cut in half, lengthwise...

and scoop out the seeds with a small spoon.

Keeping it clean

Because pickling is a precise process, it's important that your preparation area is scrupulously clean. Don't forget that a bumpy pickling cucumber has plenty of nooks and crannies where bacteria can lurk. Be certain all your produce is fresh and clean before use.

Diving into Pickled Veggies

Pickled vegetables are delicious additions to green salads or a relish plate. Enjoy these treats for a change of pace from plain, raw vegetables. They still retain their crisp texture but with an extra added bite from the brine.

Avoid long boiling periods for your vinegar solution. Lengthy boiling reduces the acetic-acid level in vinegar, changing the pH level of the food. This change may compromise the safety of your pickled food.

Getting a crash course on crunch

Book III

Mastering the Art of Pickling

The best method for maintaining crispness, crunch, and firmness in your vegetables during the soaking period is to add ice, preferably crushed ice, to your soaking solution. Adding ice works best for short brine soaking. (Check out the previous chapter for more on long and short brine soaking.)

After the soaking period, drain your vegetables in a colander, following your recipe instructions for any rinsing. Some recipes instruct you to roll the drained food in clean kitchen towels to dry it. This method works well for larger pieces of food, but not for finely chopped relishes. (Speaking of relishes, this chapter contains two relish recipes: Sweet Pickle Relish and Corn Relish.)

Note: In older pickling recipes, you may see the addition of alum or pickling (slaked) lime for the sake of crispness. The recipes in this chapter don't add either of these products because they aren't necessary when you're using modern canning methods.

Sweetening up

My grandmother made one kind of pickle: the sweet pickle. You could read a newspaper through the paper-thin slices of cukes and onions. Although my favorite is a garlic-dill recipe, I try to replicate her sweet slices, just to get a picture of her in my mind.

Pickles can be made sweet with the addition of white sugar. Using any other type of sweetener can cause cloudiness and a soft result.

Layering and packing

Pickled items will shrink a little, so be sure to pack them tightly as you fill the jars. Layers should be even and neat, allowing for brine to flow over and around each piece. Expect some floating and rearranging of the contents after going through the canner — this is normal.

Not Your Average Pickle: Fruit

Pickling fruit may seem odd, but don't be put off! The natural sweetness marries well with the acidity and slight saltiness of pickling brine. After you taste the results, the recipes in this chapter will be first on your list for fruits.

The spices you use in pickling fruits are warm and slightly sharp. Cinnamon, cloves, allspice, even peppercorns are just some of the flavors that work perfectly in a pickled fruit recipe. Keep your total measurements the same, but don't be afraid to create your own pickling mix.

Sweet Pickle Relish

Prep time: 55 min, plus soaking time • **Process time:** 10 min • **Yield:** 7 half-pints or 3 pints

Ingredients	Directions
5 to 6 medium cucumbers **3 to 4 green or red peppers** **3 to 4 medium onions** **¼ cup kosher or pickling salt** **4 to 6 quarts cold water** **3 cups granulated sugar** **2 cups cider vinegar** **2½ teaspoons celery seeds** **2½ teaspoons mustard seed** **½ teaspoon turmeric**	**1** Peel the cucumbers, cut them in half lengthwise, and remove the seeds (refer to Figure 2-1). Remove the stems and seeds from the bell peppers. Remove the skin of the onions.
	2 Using a food processor fitted with a metal blade, finely chop the cucumbers to measure 6 cups, the bell peppers to measure 3 cups, and the onions to measure 3 cups.
	3 Combine the cucumbers, peppers, and onions in a 5- to 6-quart bowl. Sprinkle them with salt and add cold water to cover them.
	4 Cover the bowl; let the veggies stand at room temperature for 2 hours. Rinse the vegetables with running water in batches in a colander. Drain well.
	5 Combine the sugar, vinegar, celery seeds, mustard seeds, and turmeric in a 5- to 6-quart pot. Bring the liquid to a boil over high heat, stirring occasionally to dissolve the sugar. Add the drained vegetables and return the mixture to a boil.
	6 Reduce the heat to medium-high and simmer, uncovered, stirring occasionally, for 20 to 30 minutes or until most of the excess liquid has evaporated.
	7 Spoon and lightly compact the hot relish into the prepared jars. Process your filled jars in a water-bath canner for 10 minutes from the point of boiling. Use any unsealed jars within 2 months.

Per 2-tablespoon serving: Calories 51 (From Fat 1); Fat 0g (Saturated 0g); Cholesterol 0mg; Sodium 499mg; Carbohydrates 13g (Dietary Fiber 0g); Protein 0g.

Tip: This recipe is ready to eat as soon as you're done precooking it. So save one jar to cool for dinner the night you make it.

Speedy Dill Pickles

Prep time: 35 min • **Process time:** 10 min (pints); 15 min (quarts) • **Yield:** 6 pints or 3 quarts

Ingredients	Directions
4 pounds pickling cucumbers **6 tablespoons kosher or pickling salt** **3 cups distilled white vinegar** **3 cups water** **1 tablespoon whole mixed pickling spices** **18 black peppercorns** **3 tablespoons dill seed** **Fresh dill sprigs (optional)**	**1** Wash your cucumbers. Leave them whole if they're smaller than 4 inches in diameter. Cut larger cucumbers into slices or lengthwise in halves or quarters. **2** Combine the salt, vinegar, and water in a 3- to 4-quart saucepan. Bring the liquid to a boil over high heat, stirring occasionally to dissolve the salt. Keep the liquid hot over medium heat. **3** Snugly pack the cucumbers into your prepared jars. To each pint jar, add ½ teaspoon pickling spices, 3 peppercorns, and 1½ teaspoons dill seed. To each quart jar, add 1 teaspoon pickling spices, 6 peppercorns, and 1 tablespoon dill seed. If you're using fresh dill, add a sprig or two to each pint or quart jar between the inside edge of the jar and the cucumbers. **4** Ladle the hot liquid into your filled jars, leaving ¼-inch headspace in the pint jars and ½-inch headspace in the quart jars. Completely submerge the cucumbers in the liquid. If they protrude from the jar, adjust them until you have the proper headspace, because the lids may not properly seal from the internal pressure. **5** Process your filled jars in a water-bath canner for 10 minutes (pints) or 15 minutes (quarts) from the point of boiling. Use any unsealed jars within 2 months. Keep the pickles on the pantry shelf for at least 2 weeks for the taste to develop.

Per 2-ounce serving: Calories 11 (From Fat 1); Fat 0g (Saturated 0g); Cholesterol 0mg; Sodium 1,308mg; Carbohydrates 2g (Dietary Fiber 1g); Protein 1g.

Vary It! For kosher-style dill pickles, add 2 cloves of peeled, halved garlic to each jar of pickles.

Zucchini Bread and Butter Pickles

Prep time: 40 min, plus soaking time • **Process time:** 10 min • **Yield:** 12 pints

Ingredients	Directions
6 pounds thinly sliced zucchini 2 cups thinly sliced onions ½ cup kosher or pickling salt 2 quarts ice water 2 cups sugar 2 quarts distilled white vinegar ¼ cup whole mustard seed ¼ cup celery seed 1 teaspoon turmeric	**1** Slice the zucchini into ¼-inch-thick rounds. Peel the onions and cut them in half lengthwise from the tip to the bottom core. Lay them on a cutting board, cut side down; then slice them, starting at the top of the onion, to a thickness of ¼ inch.
	2 Place the zucchini and onion slices in a 12-quart nonreactive stock pot. Sprinkle them with salt. Add ice water to cover the vegetables. Stir them once; then cover the bowl and let the veggies stand at room temperature for 3 hours.
	3 Transfer the veggies to a colander and rinse them thoroughly with running water. (You may need to do this in more than one batch.) Drain well. Roll the pieces in a clean, dry kitchen towel to partially dry them.
	4 In the nonreactive pot, combine the sugar, vinegar, mustard seed, celery seed, and turmeric. Bring the liquid to a boil over high heat, stirring occasionally to dissolve the sugar and mix the spices. Add the vegetables and return the mixture to a boil.
	5 Pack the boiling hot pickles into the prepared jars and add the hot liquid, leaving ½-inch headspace. Process your filled jars in a water-bath canner for 10 minutes from the point of boiling. Use any unsealed jars within 2 months.

Per 2-ounce serving: Calories 22 (From Fat 0); Fat 0g (Saturated 0g); Cholesterol 0mg; Sodium 116mg; Carbohydrates 6g (Dietary Fiber 1g); Protein 0g.

Note: These pickles are ready to eat as soon as they cool.

Tip: Pick your zucchinis when they're cucumber sized and use that day for the best texture.

Dilly Beans

Prep time: 16 min • **Process time:** 10 min • **Yield:** 4–5 pints

Ingredients	*Directions*

Ingredients

2½ **cups distilled white vinegar**

2½ **cups water**

¼ **cup coarse kosher or pickling salt**

2½ **pounds fresh green beans, washed, with the ends and strings removed**

4 **sprigs fresh dill, washed and drained**

4 **cloves garlic, peeled**

4 **dried whole red chile peppers**

1 **teaspoon cayenne pepper**

1 **teaspoon dill seed**

Directions

1 Combine the vinegar, water, and salt in a 6- to 8-quart pot. Bring the liquid to a boil over high heat; boil for 1 minute, stirring to dissolve the salt. Reduce the heat to low and keep the mixture hot.

2 Pack the beans into the prepared jars, leaving ¼-inch headspace, as shown in Figure 2-2. (Trim the tops of the beans, if necessary.) Add the following to each jar: a sprig of dill, 1 garlic clove, 1 dried red chile pepper, ¼ teaspoon cayenne pepper, and ¼ teaspoon dill seed.

3 Ladle the hot liquid over the beans, covering the tops of the beans and leaving ¼-inch headspace. Process your filled jars in a water-bath canner for 10 minutes from the point of boiling. Use any unsealed jars within 2 months. Let the beans sit for 2 weeks on your pantry shelf for the flavors to fully develop.

Per ½-cup serving: Calories 40 (From Fat 2); Fat 0g (Saturated 0g); Cholesterol 0mg; Sodium 167mg; Carbohydrates 10g (Dietary Fiber 2g); Protein 1g.

Vary It! Use a combination of green and yellow string beans.

Figure 2-2: Packing raw beans into a jar.

PACK RAW BEANS INTO A JAR BY HOLDING THE JAR AT AN ANGLE ON ITS SIDE.

Pickled Asparagus

Prep time: 10 min • **Process time:** 10 min • **Yield:** 8 pints

Ingredients	Directions
12 pounds young asparagus spears	*1* Wash the asparagus thoroughly and cut it into lengths to fit your pint jars.
8 small dried peppers (optional)	*2* Place 1 hot pepper (if desired), ½ teaspoon dill seed, ½ teaspoon mustard seed, and 1 clove of garlic in each jar.
4 tablespoons dill seed	
4 teaspoons whole mustard seed	*3* Firmly pack the asparagus spears vertically into the jars, but don't force them. If necessary, trim the spears to leave ½-inch headspace.
8 cloves garlic	
5 cups distilled vinegar	*4* In an 8-quart nonreactive pot, combine the vinegar, water, and salt, and heat to boiling. Pour the boiling hot solution over the asparagus spears, leaving ½-inch headspace.
5 cups water	
½ cup canning salt	
	5 Process the filled jars in a water-bath canner for 10 minutes from the point of boiling. Use any unsealed jars within 2 weeks. Let the spears sit for 2 weeks on the pantry shelf for the flavors to develop.

Per ¼-cup serving: Calories 26 (From Fat 5); Fat 1g (Saturated 0g); Cholesterol 0mg; Sodium 358mg; Carbohydrates 4g (Dietary Fiber 2g); Protein 2g.

Tip: Put these up in pints — part of their charm is the look of the straight spears packed like soldiers inside.

Spiced Pickled Beets

Prep time: 1 hr, 35 min • **Process time:** 30 min • **Yield:** 4–5 pints

Ingredients	Directions
4 pounds beets **3 cups thinly sliced white or yellow onions (about 3 medium)** **2½ cups cider vinegar** **1½ cups water** **2 cups granulated sugar** **1 teaspoon kosher or pickling salt** **1 tablespoon whole mustard seed** **1 teaspoon whole allspice** **1 teaspoon whole cloves** **3 cinnamon sticks, broken into pieces**	*1* Trim your beets, leaving the taproots and 2 inches of the stems. Wash and drain the beets, using a stiff brush to remove any clinging soil.
	2 Cover the beets with water in a 5- to 6-quart pot. Bring the water to a boil over high heat and cook the beets until they pierce easily with a fork, about 20 to 30 minutes.
	3 Drain the beets. Run cold water over them and remove the skin. Remove the stem and taproot. Slice the beets into ¼-inch-thick slices. Place the beets in a bowl; set aside.
	4 Place the onions, vinegar, water, sugar, salt, mustard seed, allspice, cloves, and cinnamon sticks in the pot. Bring the mixture to a boil over high heat; reduce the heat and simmer for 5 minutes. Add your beet slices and simmer the mixture to heat the beets, about 3 to 5 minutes. Remove the cinnamon stick pieces.
	5 Pack the hot beets and onions into the hot jars and ladle the hot liquid over the beets, leaving ¼-inch headspace.
	6 Process your jars in a water-bath canner for 30 minutes from the point of boiling. Use any unsealed jars within 2 months.

Per ¼-cup serving: *Calories 71 (From Fat 2); Fat 0g (Saturated 0g); Cholesterol 0mg; Sodium 107mg; Carbohydrates 17g (Dietary Fiber 1g); Protein 1g.*

Tip: Use beets that are small, tender, and no larger than 2 inches in diameter. Purchase beets with the top leaves attached. If the leaves are wilted and quite dark, the beets aren't fresh; continue your search for fresher beets.

Note: Once canned, these beets are ready for eating.

Pickled Beet Salad

Prep time: 45 min • **Process time:** 15 min • **Yield:** 10 pints

Ingredients	Directions
12 small beets **6 stalks celery** **1 small head cabbage** **2 medium onions** **3 cups vinegar** **1½ cups red beet juice** **4 cups sugar**	**1** In a 6-quart saucepan, cook whole beets until fork tender (40 minutes). Peel and grate.
	2 Grate the celery, cabbage, and onions. Add them to the grated beets and return all grated vegetables to the 6-quart saucepan.
	3 Add the vinegar, beet juice, and sugar to the grated vegetables. Bring the vegetable mixture to a simmer over medium heat, stirring often to prevent burning. Simmer until the vegetables are tender, about 5 minutes.
	4 Pack the vegetable mixture firmly into jars, leaving ¼-inch headspace. Process the filled jars in a water-bath canner for 15 minutes from the point of boiling. Use any unsealed jars within 2 weeks.

Per ½-cup serving: Calories 99 (From Fat 1); Fat 0g (Saturated 0g); Cholesterol 0mg; Sodium 48mg; Carbohydrates 25g (Dietary Fiber 1g); Protein 1g.

Tip: This recipe is great for using up your extra beets.

Pickled Brussels Sprouts

Prep time: 15 min • **Process time:** 10 min • **Yield:** 6 pints

Ingredients	Directions
12 to 14 cups young Brussels sprouts	*1* Wash the Brussels sprouts and remove any outer leaves that have insect damage or brown edges. Cook the sprouts for 5 minutes in boiling water and then dip them immediately into cold water. Drain.
3 tablespoons dill weed	
2 cups distilled vinegar	*2* Pack the sprouts into your hot pint jars, leaving ½-inch headspace. To each jar, add 1½ teaspoons dill weed. Combine the vinegar and salt and pour this solution over the sprouts, leaving ½-inch headspace.
½ cup canning salt	
	3 Process the filled jars in a water-bath canner for 10 minutes from the point of boiling. Use any unsealed jars within 2 weeks. Let your pickled Brussels sprouts sit for 2 weeks so the flavors can develop.

Per ¼-cup serving: Calories 26 (From Fat 2); Fat 0g (Saturated 0g); Cholesterol 0mg; Sodium 475mg; Carbohydrates 6g (Dietary Fiber 1g); Protein 1g.

Pickled Onions

Prep time: 20 min, plus standing time • **Process time:** 1 min • **Yield:** 8 pints

Ingredients	Directions
4 quarts pickling onions 1 cup salt 1 gallon cold water 8 cups vinegar 2 cups water 1 cup sugar 8 cloves peeled garlic 2 tablespoons pickling spice	**1** Place the onions in a medium mixing bowl and cover with boiling water. Let stand for 2 minutes. Drain, cool, and peel.
	2 Combine the salt with 1 gallon of water. Pour over the onions. Let stand overnight. The next day, drain the onions and rinse them in cold water.
	3 In an 8-quart saucepan, combine the vinegar, water, sugar, garlic, and pickling spices. Bring to a boil and reduce heat to simmer for 15 minutes.
	4 Pack the onions into jars, adding 1 clove of garlic to each jar. Pour boiling pickling solution over them, leaving ½-inch headspace.
	5 Process the filled jars in a water-bath canner for 10 minutes from the point of boiling. Use any unsealed jars within 2 weeks.

Per ½-cup serving: Calories 43 (From Fat 1); Fat 0g (Saturated 0g); Cholesterol 0mg; Sodium 71mg; Carbohydrates 11g (Dietary Fiber 1g); Protein 1g.

Tip: After about 2 weeks, the pickles will start to taste "pickled enough" for eating.

Pickled Green Tomatoes

Prep time: 30 min • **Process time:** 15 min • **Yield:** 8 pints

Ingredients	Directions
5 pounds green tomatoes	**1** Wash and quarter the green tomatoes. In a 6-quart saucepan, combine vinegar, water, and salt. Heat on high to a boil.
3 cups vinegar	
3 cups water	
¼ cup canning salt	**2** Place 1 clove of garlic and 1 tablespoon of dill seed in each jar. Pack the tomato halves into the jars and pour the hot pickling mixture over them, leaving ¼-inch headspace.
6 cloves garlic	
6 tablespoons dill seed	
	3 Process the filled jars in a water-bath canner for 15 minutes from the point of boiling. Use any unsealed jars within 2 weeks.

Per ½-cup serving: Calories 16 (From Fat 1); Fat 0g (Saturated 0g); Cholesterol 0mg; Sodium 893mg; Carbohydrates 3g (Dietary Fiber 1g); Protein 1g.

Corn Relish

Prep time: 20 min • **Process time:** 15 min • **Yield:** 10 pints

Ingredients	Directions
20 ears sweet corn	*1* Cut corn from cobs. Roughly chop the cabbage, onion, green pepper, and celery.
1 medium head cabbage	
1 medium onion, chopped	*2* Combine the corn, chopped vegetables, sugar, dry mustard, celery seed, mustard seed, turmeric, vinegar, and water in a 6-quart pot. Heat the mixture over medium heat and simmer gently for 20 minutes. Increase the heat to bring the mixture to a boil.
2 medium green peppers	
4 stalks celery	
2 cups sugar	
1½ tablespoons dry mustard	
1 tablespoon celery seed	*3* Pack hot relish into jars, leaving ¼-inch headspace. Process the filled jars in a water-bath canner for 15 minutes from the point of boiling. Use any unsealed jars within 2 weeks.
1 tablespoon whole mustard seed	
1 tablespoon turmeric	
1 quart vinegar	
1 cup water	

Per ½-cup serving: Calories 85 (From Fat 6); Fat 1g (Saturated 0g); Cholesterol 0mg; Sodium 8mg; Carbohydrates 20g (Dietary Fiber 2g); Protein 2g.

Pickled Hot Peppers

Prep time: 10 min, plus standing time • **Process time:** 15 min • **Yield:** 12 pints

Ingredients	*Directions*
8 pounds hot peppers 1½ cups salt 1 gallon cold water 10 cups vinegar 2 cups water ½ cup sugar 6 cloves garlic	**1** Wash the peppers and cut a small nick in each pepper to prevent them from exploding. **2** In a large mixing bowl, place all the peppers, the salt, and 1 gallon of water. Let stand overnight. The next day, drain and rinse the peppers. **3** Combine the vinegar, 2 cups water, the sugar, and the garlic in a 6-quart saucepan. Bring to a boil over high heat. Simmer 20 minutes. **4** Pack the peppers into jars and pour the hot pickling mixture over them, leaving ¼-inch headspace. Process the filled jars in a water-bath canner for 15 minutes from the point of boiling. Use any unsealed jars within 2 weeks.

Per pepper: Calories 29 (From Fat 1); Fat 0g (Saturated 0g); Cholesterol 2mg; Sodium 344mg; Carbohydrates 7g (Dietary Fiber 1g); Protein 1g.

Spiced Apple Rings

Prep time: 60 min • **Process time:** 20 min • **Yield:** 7 quarts

Ingredients	Directions
15 pounds apples 9 cups sugar 6 cups vinegar 2 cups water 5 sticks cinnamon 1½ tablespoons whole cloves	*1* Wash the apples; then peel, core, and slice them into ¼-inch rings. *2* Combine the sugar, vinegar, water, cinnamon, and cloves and bring the sugar syrup to a boil. Add the apple rings and simmer gently for 30 minutes. *3* Pack the apples loosely into jars and pour the hot sugar syrup over them, leaving ½-inch headspace. Process the filled jars in a water-bath canner for 20 minutes from the point of boiling. Use any unsealed jars within 2 weeks.

Per ½-cup serving: Calories 183 (From Fat 3); Fat 0g (Saturated 0g); Cholesterol 0mg; Sodium 0mg; Carbohydrates 47g (Dietary Fiber 2g); Protein 0g.

Pickled Pears

Prep time: 1 hr • **Process time:** 20 min • **Yield:** 8 pints

Ingredients	*Directions*
10 pounds small green pears	*1* Peel the skin from the pears and remove the bottom ends, but keep them whole.
4 tablespoons pickling spice	
2 cups sugar	*2* Tie the pickling spice in a piece of cheesecloth and place in a 6-quart saucepan. Add the sugar, water, vinegar, and cinnamon sticks to the saucepan. Bring to a boil over medium-high heat. Turn down the heat and simmer for 30 minutes.
2 cups water	
¾ cup vinegar	
8 sticks cinnamon	
	3 Carefully place the pears into the simmering syrup and bring to a boil. Lower the heat and simmer 30 minutes.
	4 Pack the hot pears into jars, placing a cinnamon stick into each jar, and pour the syrup over them, leaving ½-inch headspace.
	5 Process the filled jars in a water-bath canner for 20 minutes from the point of boiling. Use any unsealed jars within 2 weeks.

Per ½-cup serving: Calories 81 (From Fat 0); Fat 0g (Saturated 0g); Cholesterol 0mg; Sodium 2mg; Carbohydrates 21g (Dietary Fiber 2g); Protein 0g.

Watermelon Rind Pickles

Prep time: 15 min, plus standing time • **Process time:** 15 min • **Yield:** 8 half pints

Ingredients	Directions
4 quarts of cubed watermelon rind **Water to cover cubed rind** **½ cup salt** **1 tablespoon whole cloves** **1 tablespoon whole allspice** **4 sticks cinnamon** **2 cups vinegar** **4 cups water**	*1* Peel the green skin and the pink flesh from the rind. Cut the rind into 1 inch cubes (about 16 cups). *2* Place the cubed rind in a large mixing bowl. Sprinkle the salt on the rind and pour enough water over the rind to cover it. Place the bowl in the refrigerator overnight. *3* The following day, drain the rind and place it in an 8-quart saucepan. Cover with fresh water. Bring to a boil and simmer 10 minutes. Drain. *4* Place the cloves, allspice, cinnamon, vinegar, and 4 cups water into the 8-quart saucepan. Bring to a boil and stir in the rind. Return the mixture to a boil. Lower the heat and simmer until tender, about 20 minutes. Continue to simmer until the rind is transparent, another 10 minutes. *5* Pack the pickles into the jars and pour the syrup over them, leaving ½-inch headspace. Process the filled jars in a water-bath canner for 15 minutes from the point of boiling. Use any unsealed jars within 2 weeks.

Per ½-cup serving: Calories 7 (From Fat 0); Fat 0g (Saturated 0g); Cholesterol 0mg; Sodium 350mg; Carbohydrates 1g (Dietary Fiber 1g); Protein 1g.

Chapter 3

Pickling Meat, Fish, and Eggs

In This Chapter

▶ Discovering which cuts of meat taste great when pickled

▶ Knowing all about pickled fish

▶ Trusting the safety of a pickled egg

*P*ickling meats is an old way of making cuts of meat taste great when they may otherwise be tough or unusual. Pickled meats are often the budget meats and are extremely affordable. Pickling is a wonderful way to get the most mileage out of the meat you may not know what to do with.

Pickling improves the flavor of fish that would otherwise taste too fishy if prepared another way. Eggs are made even more delicious when pickled and are a common way to use up the spring flush of eggs that chicken owners sometimes face.

Although often reserved for the budget meats, pickling is useful for adding flavors to the pantry, with the same base ingredients.

Experimenting with Pickled Meats

The term *pickling* here is the art of soaking meat, fish, or eggs in a flavorful brine, in a refrigerator, for an extended period of time. You use little vinegar when pickling these proteins, and what you do use is simply for flavor.

Pickling meats often aren't called *pickled* at all. They're commonly known as *corned* or by the cut of meat they come from, such as the tongue or heart. These meats are the least expensive, and usually they're discarded portions that you may not know how to prepare. Don't think of them as lesser quality meats because the finished product is usually extremely flavorful.

Pickling infuses the meat with rich flavors. And because of the long cook time usually involved in preparing it for the plate, these underestimated meats may end up being one of the finest tasting meals you can offer your family.

Not all pickled meats have to be tough cuts or organ meats, although that's traditionally the case. Pickling adds a wonderful flavor to any meat you choose to use. Because the process adds tenderizing as well as infuses flavor, this method is typically reserved for meats that need that help.

If you find that you enjoy the overall flavor of a particular pickling recipe, you can use that recipe with a different cut of meat.

Pickling Fish Safely and Effectively

Fish takes well to being pickled. Like other meats, the fish most often pickled don't have the most prized flavors when cooked fresh. Of course, you can use any fish that you want to pickle, but those with mild, white flesh are most common.

The delicate nature of fish means that the older it is, the stronger the taste. For the freshest tasting pickled fish, use the freshest fish you can find.

Pickling fish is no different than pickling meat, other than the fragile nature of fish means that you must work quickly to keep the freshness. You first soak fish in a plain, salty brine to draw out any fishiness or unwanted flavors. Then you cover the fish with a flavorful brine (cooked and cooled) to infuse the meat and pickle it. This entire process is done in the refrigerator to keep the fish from decaying.

Fish should be moved from the water to the jar as quickly as possible.

Fish is especially delicate. Unlike beef, fish has no period of aging that improves its flavor. Fish must be from clean waters, as fresh as possible, and prepared in an efficient manner to keep it as cold as possible throughout the entire process.

Appreciating Pickled Eggs

Pickled eggs are most often thought of as bar food. Although it's true that they may taste great washed down with an ice cold draft, pickled eggs deserve some acknowledgement as a tasty and unique food. You can add pickled eggs to a garden salad for a zippy flavor addition. They also taste spectacular in egg salad. I like to add one pickled egg for every two plain eggs, and I adjust my seasoning in consideration of the salt and seasonings the pickled egg brings.

Don't feel confined to eating just chicken eggs! Any egg will benefit from the pickling flavors. Fresh eggs are difficult to peel, but you can use quail, goose, duck, or any other bird egg you like for this process.

A small egg, like a quail's egg, takes less time to fully pickle than a larger duck or goose egg does. Feel free to taste as you go to get the perfect timeframe for pickling these exotic eggs.

Because eggs are particularly fragile, you have to keep them cold throughout the pickling process. You may know someone who has pickled eggs that sat on his counter for an extended period of time, but modern science considers this practice unsafe. Eggs can harbor *botulism,* odorless bacteria with fatal results if eaten.

A refrigerator is the perfect place to pickle your eggs. They'll stay a safe temperature, and the pickling process will work just as well. A dozen eggs fit in a 1-quart jar perfectly, so your batch of eggs will take up very little room as it works.

Book III

Mastering the Art of Pickling

Pickled Sausage

Prep time: 20 min • **Process time:** 3 days • **Yield:** 1 quart

Ingredients	Directions
1 small onion	*1* Scald a 1-quart canning jar by filling it with boiling water and draining.
2 cups vinegar	
½ cup water	*2* Peel and slice the onion into ¼-inch rings.
¾ cup sugar	
1 teaspoon salt	*3* In a 3-quart saucepan, combine the onions with the vinegar, water, sugar, salt, hot pepper flakes, pickling spice, and cinnamon stick. Bring to a boil over medium heat. Remove from heat.
2 teaspoons hot pepper flakes	
1 tablespoon pickling spice	
1 cinnamon stick	
4 links hot Italian sausage, cooked and cut to fit jars	*4* Place the links, if they fit, or chunks of the sausage links, into a canning jar. Pour cooled pickling liquid over the sausage, leaving ¼-inch headspace. Refrigerate the jar immediately. The sausage will be pickled after 3 days.

Per 1-ounce serving: Calories 97 (From Fat 39); Fat 4g (Saturated 2g); Cholesterol 13mg; Sodium 320mg; Carbohydrates 11g (Dietary Fiber 0g); Protein 3g.

Pickled Pork

Prep time: 30 min • **Process time:** 4 days • **Yield:** 2 pounds

Ingredients	Directions
4 cups vinegar	*1* In a 3-quart saucepan, combine the vinegar, mustard seed, red pepper flakes, salt, peppercorns, bay leaf, cloves, and garlic. Bring the pickling brine to a boil over medium-high heat. Boil for 5 minutes. Remove it from the heat and cool it to room temperature.
½ cup whole mustard seed	
½ teaspoon red pepper flakes	
1 tablespoon salt	
1 tablespoon whole peppercorns	*2* In an airtight container, submerge the pork in the pickling brine. Refrigerate immediately. Pickle the pork for 5 days.
1 bay leaf	
1 teaspoon cloves	
8 garlic cloves	
2 pounds fresh pork butt, cut into 2-inch cubes	

Per 1-ounce serving: Calories 63 (From Fat 34); Fat 4g (Saturated 1g); Cholesterol 25mg; Sodium 349mg; Carbohydrates 0g (Dietary Fiber 0g); Protein 7g.

Corned Venison

Prep time: 30 min • **Process time:** 3 weeks • **Yield:** 10 pounds

Ingredients	*Directions*
5½ cups salt 3 gallons water 4 cloves garlic 1 cup brown sugar 3 tablespoons pickling spice 10 pounds venison roast, trimmed of fat	*1* In an 8-quart saucepan, dissolve the salt into the water. Add the garlic, sugar, and pickling spice to the salted water. Bring the pickling solution to a boil over medium-high heat. Reduce the heat and simmer for 5 minutes. Allow the brine to cool to room temperature.
	2 Place the venison in a container large enough to hold both the meat and the room-temperature brine. Cover tightly. Refrigerate immediately. Allow the venison to pickle for 3 weeks, skimming any foam that develops.
	3 After 3 weeks, remove the meat and place it in a clean, 8-quart saucepan. Add enough fresh water to cover the meat. Bring the water to a boil over high heat. Lower the heat to medium and simmer the meat for 4 hours.

Per 3-ounce serving: Calories 170 (From Fat 69); Fat 8g (Saturated 2g); Cholesterol 87mg; Sodium 1,502mg; Carbohydrates 1g (Dietary Fiber 0g); Protein 24g.

Pickled Beef Heart

Prep time: 15 min • **Cook time:** 45 min • **Process time:** 3 days • **Yield:** 3 pounds

Ingredients	Directions
1 beef heart	*1* Place the beef heart and 3 quarts of water in an 8-quart saucepan. Bring the water to a boil over high heat. Turn down the heat and simmer for 45 minutes.
3 quarts water	
1 large onion, sliced into rings	
2 cups vinegar	*2* Remove the meat from the water and allow the meat to cool for safe handling. Slice the heart into ¼-inch thick slices.
2 cups water	
1 tablespoon salt	
3 tablespoons pickling spice	*3* In an airtight container, place the heart slices, sliced onions, vinegar, 2 cups water, salt, and pickling spice. Seal and refrigerate immediately. The meat will be pickled in 1 week.

Per 3-ounce serving: Calories 105 (From Fat 28); Fat 3g (Saturated 1g); Cholesterol 108mg; Sodium 1,344mg; Carbohydrates 1g (Dietary Fiber 0g); Protein 17g.

Pickled Tongue

Prep time: 15 min • **Cook time:** 4 hr • **Process time:** 3 days • **Yield:** 1 quart

Ingredients	Directions
1 beef tongue	**1** Place the beef tongue in an 8-quart saucepan. Pour the water over the tongue. Sprinkle the salt over the water. Cover tightly and cook over medium-low heat until tender (3 hours).
3 quarts water	
1 tablespoon salt	
3 cups vinegar	**2** Remove the cooked tongue from the hot water and plunge it immediately into cold water to loosen the skin. Save the broth. Peel the skin from the tongue.
1 cup sugar	
1 teaspoon whole cloves	
1 teaspoon whole allspice	**3** Return the peeled tongue to the broth in the saucepan and add the vinegar, sugar, cloves, allspice, bay leaf, cinnamon stick, and pepper. Cover and simmer over low heat for 1 hour. Remove from heat and cool enough to handle safely.
1 bay leaf	
1 stick cinnamon	
½ teaspoon pepper	
	4 Place the tongue in a large mixing bowl and pour the pickling liquid over the top until covered. Seal and refrigerate for 2 days to finish pickling. Slice thinly to serve.

Per 3-ounce serving: Calories 238 (From Fat 154); Fat 17g (Saturated 7g); Cholesterol 88mg; Sodium 537mg; Carbohydrates 2g (Dietary Fiber 0g); Protein 18g.

Pickled Fish

Prep time: 3 days • **Cook time:** 10 min • **Process time:** 1 week • **Yield:** 1 quart

Ingredients	Directions
4 pounds white fish	**1** Cut the fish into 1-inch chunks. Peel and slice the onion into ¼-inch thin slices.
1 medium onion	
1 quart water	**2** In a large mixing bowl, combine the water and salt. Add the fish chunks. Cover the bowl tightly and refrigerate for 3 days.
1 cup pickling salt	
5 cups vinegar	**3** In a 3-quart saucepan, combine the vinegar, sugar, spices, and onion slices. Heat over medium-high heat until boiling. Boil for 10 minutes. Cool the brine completely.
2 cups sugar	
5 tablespoons pickling spice	
	4 Place the fish in a large mixing bowl. Pour the cooled brine and onions over the top. Cover tightly and refrigerate immediately. Allow the fish to pickle for 7 days.

Per 3-ounce serving: Calories 140 (From Fat 51); Fat 6g (Saturated 1g); Cholesterol 58mg; Sodium 638mg; Carbohydrates 3g (Dietary Fiber 0g); Protein 19g.

Spicy Pickled Eggs

Prep time: 15 min • **Process time:** 3 days • **Yield:** 1 quart

Ingredients	*Directions*
1 small onion **2 cups vinegar** **½ cup water** **¾ cup sugar** **1 teaspoon salt** **2 teaspoons hot pepper flakes** **1 tablespoon pickling spice** **1 cinnamon stick** **10 hard-boiled eggs, peeled**	*1* Scald a 1-quart canning jar by filling it with boiling water and draining. Peel and slice the onion into ¼-inch rings. *2* In a 3-quart saucepan, combine the onion with the vinegar, water, sugar, salt, hot pepper flakes, pickling spice, and cinnamon stick. Bring the mixture to a boil over medium heat. Remove from heat. *3* Place the peeled eggs into a prepared canning jar. Pour the hot pickling liquid over the eggs, leaving ¼-inch headspace. Refrigerate the jar immediately. The eggs will be pickled after 3 days.

Per egg: Calories 81 (From Fat 45); Fat 5g (Saturated 2g); Cholesterol 213mg; Sodium 300mg; Carbohydrates 2g (Dietary Fiber 0g); Protein 6g.

Pickled Eggs with Beets

Prep time: 1½ hr • **Cook time:** 1 hr, 15 min • **Process time:** 3 days • **Yield:** 2 quarts

Ingredients	Directions
4 pounds small beets	**1** Place the washed beets in a 6-quart saucepan and cover with water. Simmer 1 hour or until fork tender. Drain the beets and cover with cold water. Trim off the tops and roots and pull off the skins.
2 cups water	
1 cup sugar	
1 cup brown sugar	**2** Scald two 1-quart canning jars by pouring boiling water into them and draining. Divide the beets evenly between the jars.
2 cups water	
2 cups vinegar	
2 teaspoons whole mustard seed	**3** In a 4-quart saucepan, combine the water, sugars, vinegar, mustard seed, salt, cinnamon, cloves, allspice, and celery seed. Bring to a simmer over medium heat for 10 minutes.
1½ teaspoons salt	
1 teaspoon cinnamon	
½ teaspoon cloves	**4** Divide the liquid between both of the jars and cool completely. Once cold, add the peeled eggs. Refrigerate for 3 days before eating.
½ teaspoon ground allspice	
½ teaspoon celery seed	
12 hard-boiled eggs, peeled	

Per egg: Calories 255 (From Fat 49); Fat 6g (Saturated 2g); Cholesterol 212mg; Sodium 443mg; Carbohydrates 45g (Dietary Fiber 3g); Protein 8g.

Book IV

Fermenting and Brewing

The 5th Wave   By Rich Tennant

"Great homebrew! By the way, whatever happened to that buddy of yours, the Tin Man?"

In this book . . .

Fermenting is not some weird backroom hobby. In fact, you're probably eating fermented foods in your diet right now and don't know it. In this book, you find out how fermenting changes the flavor and nutrition of foods.

When it comes to homebrewing, you can't join in the fun until you have a little understanding of the craft as well as the necessary equipment. Fortunately, the chapters in this book give you just the information you need to get started: equipment, ingredients, and step-by-step guidelines for creating and bottling tasty ciders, meads, and beers.

Chapter 1

Fermenting for Nutrition

· ·

In This Chapter

▶ Understanding why and what you can ferment

▶ Discovering the difference between pickling and fermenting

▶ Appreciating the good guys of the bacteria world

▶ Fending off illness with scrupulous sanitation methods

· ·

Fermenting food is done to change the food in a controlled way, into something completely different. Fermenting is used in common foods and beverages like beer, mead, yogurt, cheese, and even vegetables. After a food has been fermented, it not only tastes different, but also *is* different on a molecular level.

Fermenting releases some nutrients that would otherwise be unavailable for digestion and creates an environment for *probiotic,* or beneficial, bacteria to thrive. This bacteria already lives in a healthy digestive tract and helps break down food properly. Antibiotics and digestive illnesses can reduce the number of good bacteria, making you susceptible to illness. Your immune system includes your digestive tract, and improving digestion can only help overall health.

Getting Familiar with Fermenting

When making fermented foods, you're actually souring the food rather than pickling it. Because *fermenting,* or souring, is a controlled decay of the food, you must follow all food safety rules. Always ferment in the most sanitary conditions possible and use very fresh, exceptional food. Adding fermented food to your food pantry is not only tasty but also healthy.

Fermenting is simply decaying with style. There's a fine line between going bad and fermenting, so the rules of a good fermenting system are stringent. These rules become easier to adhere to as you become proficient, and the benefits are worth it.

Bringing in the bacteria

The beneficial bacteria, called *Lactobacillus,* convert carbohydrates into acetic acid. This process is what ferments the food. Because *Lactobacillus* thrive only in *anaerobic* (without oxygen) conditions, brine is needed to keep oxygen off the food. *Lactobacillus* are found in the intestines of a healthy person, and you'll often hear the term *probiotic* used to refer to this and other beneficial bacteria that you want in your body.

Vinegar doesn't ferment food. It flavors it (as in pickling). To properly ferment food, you need to cultivate the proper bacteria in a controlled environment.

Appreciating the health benefits

Fermented foods benefit everyone. Your digestive tract works at its best when it has the proper number of bacteria available to do the work. *Lacto* bacteria are very important to this process. Eating fermented foods helps keep the digestive tract in balance and provides enzymes that aren't found anywhere else.

When first adding fermented foods to your diet, you may experience slight bloating or gassiness. These symptoms will soon pass, as your digestive tract becomes used to the new food.

Knowing the good guys

Not all bacteria are created equal. The bacteria that make you sick have no place in fermenting. By fermenting properly, you create the perfect environment for the beneficial bacteria to thrive, while keeping bad bacteria at bay.

All fermented products start with some sort of bacterial culture. This culture can be in many forms. The following are some of the more commonly used forms for home fermenting:

- ✔ **Vinegar mother:** To make vinegars, a mother is needed. This algae-like ingredient is seen floating at the bottom of a bottle of raw vinegar and is made up of yeast and acetic acid bacteria. It's harmless, and some people think it may make vinegar more healthful.

- ✔ **SCOBY:** This is an acronym for Symbiotic Colony of Bacteria and Yeast. Sometimes called a mat or mother, a SCOBY is necessary for making Kombucha, a fermented tea drink. This SCOBY replicates during the fermenting process and can then be shared.

✔ **Grains:** These are specific to kefir, which is living bacteria that ferments milk (or sometimes water) into a delicious fermented food. You can also find powdered kefir mixes at many health-food stores.

✔ **Wild yeasts:** Don't be afraid of this term. Yeast is found all around you in the natural environment. When you create a sourdough from scratch, you're making the perfect environment for the yeast bacteria to grow. After the first batch (or if you have a friend who has a starter), you add a small amount of successful starter to the fresh flour/water mixture.

Assembling Your Equipment

The items in this section aren't essential, but they are important for easy fermenting. These items are easy to find and handy to keep in the kitchen so that you have them on hand when you want to start a new batch of fermented food. (Items required for brewing beer, mead, and cider are covered in Book IV, Chapters 6 and 7.)

✔ **Coffee filters:** Filters are handy for creating breathable lids on jars of kefir and Kombucha. These good bacteria need to be able to release gas, but at the same time stay as clean as possible. Use a coffee filter and an elastic band to keep your jar contents clean.

✔ **Wooden utensils:** Don't stir and scrape fermented foods with metal utensils. Use wooden or bamboo utensils to keep your bacteria happy.

✔ **Bean pots:** Bean pots are great for fermenting foods. Because they're often discarded after losing their lid (a common occurrence), you can often find bean pots, sans lid, in thrift stores. To make your own lid, use a margarine or yogurt plastic top that fits perfectly.

Taking Sanitation Seriously

Working with any food means knowing and adhering to proper sanitation practices. When fermenting, this can't be worded strongly enough. Proper bacterial cultivation is key to safe fermenting, and keeping the environment as clean as possible of unwanted bacteria is essential.

Part of the sanitation process is monitoring and removing anything that doesn't appear to be part of the final product. You can have an imbalance of bacteria in your fermenting container, causing mildew or molds to grow. You must remove these molds or mildews carefully. Depending on what you're fermenting, you may need to add brine in order to properly cover the remaining food.

Odors are another indication of proper fermentation. No matter what the food is, you shouldn't detect a disagreeable odor. Fermented foods smell vinegary, sour, tart, or even a combination of these things. In the case of fermented food, your nose knows.

If your fermented food begins to smell off, check for unwanted bacterial growth. Remove and recheck that you've covered the food properly with brine and the temperature isn't too warm. Also make sure that the surface of the container keeps unwanted dirt from falling in. When all else fails, dump the fermented product and start again with clean ingredients.

Not all bacteria are bad. When fermenting, you're cleaning to remove as much of the bad bacteria as possible to avoid cross-contamination of your fermenting products.

Cleaning as you ferment

As you ferment, you're using the mother from one batch to inoculate a new batch of food. Keep things clean as you do so. Wash your hands with hot, soapy water and rinse well. Don't dry them unless you have a fresh, absorbent towel to use. Kitchen towels harbor an unbelievable amount of bacteria that can ruin the balance in a fermented food jar.

Your fermenting vessel should be scrupulously clean. Don't use a container with bits of dried food or visible dust on it.

Many fermented food enthusiasts recommend against using bleach when cleaning utensils and containers you plan to use for fermenting. Stick with hot, soapy water and dry upside down so that the excess water is allowed to drain.

Keeping your fermented foods happy

Fermented foods need to have two things:

- **Enough room to do their thing:** Don't overpack a crock with product. If you tightly smash the food together, some areas won't benefit from the fermenting liquid. Pack firmly, but don't go overboard.

- **Anaerobic conditions:** Keep the food under the fermenting liquid at all times. Remove the scum that naturally forms and keep the oxygen out of the crock.

Keeping your cool

All varieties and recipes for fermentation have one thing in common: They must be kept cool. This coolness prevents unwanted bacteria from taking hold and allows the good bacteria to flourish in a controlled way. If the heat is too high, your food will ferment faster than you expect, sometimes resulting in messy leakage. You're cleaning off the scum daily, so if the food is too warm, this scum can form too fast for you to keep up with and end up ruining the entire batch.

Keep your fermenting foods out of direct sunlight and cool. This reduces the chance of large temperature fluctuations and too-fast fermentation.

Chapter 2

Fermenting Fruits and Veggies

*P*utting up food means creating foods your family will enjoy. A simple way to extend what food you've put up is to ferment it. *Fermenting* is the controlled decay of food. That's right, decayed. Your food is decaying from the moment you pick it. If fermenting is done correctly, you create the perfect environment of temperature, liquid, and oxygen (or lack thereof) to change your food into a delectable, sometimes healthier, food.

If you've never had fermented food, don't worry. The piquant taste is something that's enjoyable for most people and unforgettable to anyone who tries it. Fermenting is more than making sauerkraut. Vegetables and fruits change their flavor profile in a pleasant way when fermented. Fermenting is a great way to use up the overabundance of fruit that happens to ripen all at once, often resulting in wasted produce. Try to create at least a few jars of fermented foods for your pantry. You'll love the texture, zing, and bright taste they provide.

Selecting Produce for Fermenting

Because you want to develop perfectly fermented food, you must start with perfect produce. Any cuts or bruising is where decay is happening, and you don't want to give unwanted bacteria any chance to be present in the fermenting container.

The produce you choose for fermenting can't be too soft. Overripe items and those that have a particularly mushy nature won't turn out well after going through the fermentation process. If your food is naturally crisp and crunchy, it's most likely a good candidate for fermenting.

Perfecting your choices

Choosing the fruits and vegetables to ferment requires some simple rules to follow. No matter what produce you're working with, these guidelines are the same:

- ✔ Choose unblemished fruits or vegetables. Bruising and dents, cuts in the skins, and broken areas are breeding grounds for unwanted bacteria.
- ✔ Choose items that are perfectly ripe or slightly underripe. Foods that are past their prime have a higher rate of recipe failure and may result in soft, mushy fermented food.
- ✔ Choose items based on how much room you can devote to storage and the condition of the space in which you'll be fermenting.

Planning your location and quantities

Planning your quantities requires a bit of thought before you begin. Because you're going to store your items for long periods of time in locations that must not freeze or become too hot, your choices are limited. It's best to not move the jars around during the fermentation process, so the location you choose should be one where jars can sit undisturbed for weeks.

Also consider that the foods will sit in full-sized containers. Kombucha and kefir are made in quart- or gallon-sized jars. Crocks for fermenting sauerkraut range in size from 1 gallon to more than 5 gallons. Jars and crocks take up more room than neatly stacked freezer bags, and the location is going to be full for quite some time.

Fermenting foods also need tending to. They have to be watched carefully and monitored. Even the best fermenting process requires you to skim foam off the top, replace evaporating liquids, and check for discolorations and other things going on. You have to keep your fermenting items in an out of the way but *accessible* place.

Despite all these considerations, fermenting is an easy process to learn. Planning the location for your fermenting is well worth the extra effort. After you taste the results, you'll be on your way to a lifetime of perfecting the best fermented food.

The ideal location for fermenting food has the following attributes:

- ✔ It's out of direct sunlight.
- ✔ The temperature is stable. Avoid being next to the stovetop or butted up against the toaster.
- ✔ It's a quiet spot. Don't allow your fermenting product to be jostled and shaken.
- ✔ It's clean and draft free. Avoid a particularly dusty area. Drafts must be avoided, too, to help maintain an even temperature.

Some ideal locations are in a cupboard, in a broom closet, in a quiet corner of your kitchen counter, or in another area that's not only easy to get to but also easy to avoid.

Mastering the Basic Brining Process

The word *mastering* may be a misnomer. After you learn the correct way to properly ferment, the mastering comes in making the perfect recipe for your own taste. I've tried other people's fermented vegetables that had so much onion flavor that the food was unpalatable to me; meanwhile, the proud owner ate the entire jar over a cup of coffee! Other people like or dislike certain seasonings. You'll always have room for improvement in your fermenting process. However, you need to perfect the actual fermenting itself by knowing and recognizing when things are going right or wrong.

Welcoming anaerobic

An anaerobic bacterium is the secret ingredient that makes fermentation work. This bacterium can thrive only in the absence of oxygen, which is why fermentation must be done in a fluid. More than keeping the food moist, the fluid keeps atmospheric oxygen away so that these bacteria can do their magic.

If the food floats to the surface, it can then allow bacteria that you don't want (molds as well) to grow. The naturally occurring bacteria in the air will ruin the entire batch if you don't remove them every day.

WARNING!

Don't resubmerge fermenting food if it becomes covered with mold. Remove the offending piece, along with the surface mold.

Book IV

Fermenting and Brewing

Keeping things exact

When fermenting, these basics are the same no matter what you're working with:

- ✔ Use fresh, unblemished products
- ✔ Use a sterilized, nonreactive container
- ✔ Keep fermenting in an undisturbed place that can be easily monitored
- ✔ Check daily for any problems

When fermenting, the *process* has to remain exact. The liquid must remain at the correct level, the container must be nonreactive and sterile, the produce must be perfect and packed properly, and no air can touch any of the fermenting items. The *product* you're fermenting, however, can be changed up a bit to offer different flavors.

Adding flavors

You can include additional flavoring in the fermenting liquid, if desired. You can use other produce or spices, such as cinnamon sticks, allspice, peppercorns, or dill seeds or heads. Choose whatever you like! The spice flavors will develop over time and grow stronger as the food absorbs them.

Try a fermenting recipe without adding any extra flavorings to see how you like it. Then, as you become proficient in the process, add your extras to spice it up perfectly.

Surveying the Krauts

If you love the tang of a crisp pickle, then you'll surely love the taste of homemade sauerkraut. Canning it ensures you'll have enough to last the entire winter season. Sauerkraut is simply cabbage and salt, covered and allowed to ferment for a few weeks. You can find many recipes for creating your own. Sauerkraut is a tangy, fermented food that may take some getting used to. After you enjoy the taste, however, you'll find different ways to bring this delicious treat into your diet. Sauerkraut is a well-known pairing for sausages and hotdogs, it's used in German cooking, and it's a flavorful addition to a sandwich. What you may not know is that sauerkraut can include more than just cabbage.

Sauerkraut in its basic form is cabbage and salt. The salt draws out the natural juice in the cabbage through the firm pounding the cabbage gets as you layer it in the jar or crock. The liquid of natural juice covers the cabbage, and the fermenting process can begin.

Sauerkraut doesn't end there. After you make plain sauerkraut a few times, try adding your own spices to create your favorite version. Additions like caraway seeds, onions, apples, and dill are all delicious ways to get more from your cabbage — without much extra effort.

Here's an easy sauerkraut you can use in the Canned Sauerkraut recipe later in this chapter:

1. **Finely shred the cabbage and layer it with salt in a glass or stoneware crock; layer until the crock is full.**

   Use 1 tablespoon salt for every 5 pounds cabbage.

2. **Make an airtight seal by using a food-safe plastic bag of water to seal the top.**

   Just fill a plastic bag with water and place it over the top of the container. It doesn't have to overlap; it just sits on top like a plug.

3. **Allow the cabbage to ferment at room temperature (68° to 72°) for 5 to 6 weeks.**

Discovering Kimchis

To the American palate, *kimchi* may be an exotic food. In other countries, kimchi is as commonplace as ketchup. Kimchi is a Korean condiment that contains a variety of ingredients, including cabbage, spicy peppers, radishes, garlic, onions, and ginger to name a few. You can find hundreds of varieties, all ranging from mild to volcanic in heat. Kimchi is eaten at every meal, including breakfast! If you develop a taste for fermented food, include it in your diet just as much!

Although you can find too many kimchi varieties to count, the one thing that kimchis have in common is that they're all fermented foods.

Book IV

Fermenting and Brewing

No matter what variety of kimchi you eat, all are crispy and piquant. The vegetables used are of a crunchy nature, and although the flavor develops during the fermentation process, the crunch factor remains. This crunchiness is a sign of fresh ingredients and proper handling of the fermentation.

Choosing sides: Cabbages, cucumbers, and more

Authentic kimchi usually includes Napa cabbage. You can, of course, use whatever variety you have available, which is part of the attraction of this pungent food.

To choose your kimchi ingredients, choose what you like to eat. If you can't take the heat of super-hot chilies, add just a bit to flavor your kimchi. (And if other members of your family crave that heat, add copious amounts of the chilies and clearly label the jars for the more daring eaters in the family.)

Your ingredients have to be as fresh as possible. Don't buy produce of questionable age and plan on creating your kimchi as soon as you can. Your end product will depend on how perfectly crisp and ripe your beginning product was.

Some ingredients to experiment with include

- Cabbages of any type
- Hot peppers
- Sweet peppers
- Carrots
- Onions
- Cucumbers
- Garlic

Storing your kimchi

Kimchi is a true fermented food. It can remain under the fermenting fluid, where it will just continue to ferment as you eat from the top. By the time you get to the bottom, however, it may become too strong for your taste. In order to slow down the fermentation process, allow your kimchi to arrive at the flavor you like and then refrigerate it. The kimchi will still continue to develop stronger flavors, but at a much slower pace, allowing you to savor it over a longer period of time.

Stopping the process

Fully stopping the process of fermentation isn't necessary. Your food isn't going to turn bad all of a sudden, unless it's improperly handled. You can slow the process through refrigeration, if desired; if you enjoy your kimchi cold, use this method.

You can stop the fermentation process completely by sterilizing or canning the kimchi. This process will preserve the fermented food, but it will also destroy the probiotic, or good bacteria, that you created. If you eat your fermented food for the health benefit, you may want to avoid canning it.

Canning your fermented food isn't bad; it simply isn't necessary. After it's canned, the fermentation stops, and the food no longer has the benefit of living, healthy, probiotic bacteria.

Stocking Fermented Food Safely

Stocking up on fermented foods is slightly different from stocking up on other items. Unless you're particularly lucky, space will eventually become limited if it's filled with rows of fermenting jars and crocks.

To make the most of your storage, ferment in the largest jars possible and add fermented foods to your diet on a regular basis by trying to use them up daily. Doing so not only offers you the biggest health benefit, but also keeps your stock on rotation, avoiding the risk of forgetting something or not monitoring your foods regularly.

To store the most fermented food without waste, coauthor Amy says, "I like to have one jar in the refrigerator that we're actively consuming, one jar that's timed to be finished as that one is used up, and a third jar that's just started so that as I use up the first one, the next one is ready to take its place."

Sauerkraut with Apples

Prep time: 30 min • **Ferment time:** 3–4 weeks • **Yield:** 4 quarts

Ingredients	*Directions*
4 medium apples	*1* Wash, peel, and core the apples. Peel off damaged outer leaves of cabbage. Quarter the cabbage and remove the hard core. Finely shred the cabbage and apples by hand or use a food processor.
5 pounds cabbage	
3 tablespoons canning salt	
	2 Scald a glass gallon jar with boiling water. Add a 1-inch layer of the cabbage and apple mixture to the jar. Sprinkle with salt. Tamp firmly with a wooden utensil to remove any hidden air pockets and bruise the cabbage, making it release juice. Repeat Step 2 until all ingredients are used up.
	3 Cover the jar with a coffee filter and leave for 2 hours to allow time for the salt to draw out water from the ingredients. Every 30 minutes, tamp down the ingredients to help draw out brine and force the cabbage mixture to be submerged.
	4 After 2 hours, if you still don't have enough natural brine, mix 1 teaspoon canning salt to 1 cup water and pour over mixture. When the mixture is fully submerged, place a small saucer that fits just inside the top of the jar so it rests directly on the submerged cabbage. Add a weight, such as a water-filled quart jar, to keep the saucer and product under the brine.
	5 Cover with a clean dishcloth to keep out dust and insects. Place the jar out of the way, at room temperature. Check the jar daily, for 3 to 4 weeks. Skim off any scum that may build up on the top. Replace the clean dishcloth with another each time you remove scum buildup.

Per ½-cup serving: Calories 26 (From Fat 2); Fat 0g (Saturated 0g); Cholesterol 0mg; Sodium 676mg; Carbohydrates 6g (Dietary Fiber 2g); Protein 1g.

Tip: Glass gallon jars can be found anywhere that serves food: restaurants, school lunchrooms, sandwich shops, and so on. Just ask!

Brined Green Beans

Prep time: 30 min • **Ferment time:** 3 weeks • **Yield:** 6 quarts

Ingredients	*Directions*
8 pounds green beans **3 cups canning salt**	*1* Wash and trim the ends of the green beans. Cut into 2-inch pieces.
	2 Scald a glass gallon jar with boiling water. Sprinkle a layer of salt in the jar. Add a layer of beans. Repeat Step 2 until all ingredients are used, ending with a layer of salt.
	3 Cover the jar with a clean muslin cloth and add a saucer that fits inside the top of the gallon jar, so it rests on the beans. Allow the mixture to sit for 24 hours to draw out the moisture. After 24 hours, if you don't have enough brine to cover the beans, combine 3 tablespoons salt per cup of cold water and pour over the top.
	4 Store the covered jar in a cool place for 3 weeks. Check daily to see whether enough brine is covering the beans and change the cloth.
	5 To cook, freshen the beans by soaking them in cold water for 15 minutes. Change the water and soak for another 15 minutes. Simmer over medium heat until beans are softened as desired.

Per ½-cup serving: *Calories 26 (From Fat 0); Fat 0g (Saturated 0g); Cholesterol 0mg; Sodium 710mg; Carbohydrates 6g (Dietary Fiber 2g); Protein 1g.*

Fermented Cucumbers

Prep time: 20 min • **Ferment time:** 3–4 weeks • **Yield:** 9 pints

Ingredients	Directions
4 pounds pickling cucumbers **2 quarts water** **½ cup canning salt** **¼ cup dill** **20 cloves peeled garlic**	**1** Wash and trim the blossom ends of the cucumbers. Scald a glass gallon jar with boiling water. Combine the water with the salt, stirring to dissolve the salt. **2** Place the dill and peeled garlic cloves in the bottom of a jar. Add the cucumbers to the jar. Pour the saltwater brine over the cucumbers. Weigh the cucumbers down with a saucer to keep them submerged. **3** Cover the jar with a clean muslin cloth and place the jar in a cool place for 3 to 4 weeks. Check daily to see whether enough brine is covering the cucumbers, and change the cloth. After 3 to 4 weeks, place the jar in the refrigerator for storage.

Per ½-cup serving: Calories 9 (From Fat 0); Fat 0g (Saturated 0g); Cholesterol 0mg; Sodium 788mg; Carbohydrates 2g (Dietary Fiber 0g); Protein 0g.

Making fermented pickles

Fermented pickles have many names. They're sometimes called sour pickles, or lacto fermented pickles. They're all the same thing: fermented cucumbers. Through the fermenting process, the cucumbers become tart and pleasantly sour tasting. Unlike the pickling process (see Book III), you don't use vinegar in the process; the tartness is the result of the lacto bacteria working its magic.

Sour isn't spoiled. Your fermented pickles will be crisp and pleasantly tangy when finished. The addition of onions and garlic to the mixture will enhance the sour flavor, but it isn't necessary. Using good fermenting techniques is still imperative, and so is watching the process carefully for any sign of problems.

Kimchi

Prep time: 20 min, plus standing • **Ferment time:** 2–3 days, plus refrigeration • **Yield:** 1–2 qts

Ingredients	Directions
1 medium Napa cabbage **1 to 2 inches fresh ginger** **1 medium onion** **1 head garlic** **½ cup salt** **3 tablespoons soy sauce or tamari** *+ Red peppers (hot)* *+ Jalepenos*	**1** Wash, core, and chop the cabbage into ½- to 1-inch pieces. Peel and shred the ginger and onion. Peel the garlic, but leave the cloves whole.
	2 Place a layer of cabbage in a glass gallon jar. Sprinkle the salt over the cabbage. Repeat until all cabbage is used. Allow the cabbage and salt to sit at room temperature for 6 hours. Rinse the salt off the cabbage and place the cabbage in a large mixing bowl.
	3 Mix the ginger, onion, garlic, and soy sauce with the cabbage. Place the mixture in a glass gallon jar. Cover the filled jar with cheesecloth.
	4 Allow to ferment at room temperature for 2 to 3 days. Place the jar in the refrigerator to ferment for another week, or until the desired taste has developed.

Per ½-cup serving: Calories 22 (From Fat 0); Fat 0g (Saturated 0g); Cholesterol 0mg; Sodium 1,049mg; Carbohydrates 4g (Dietary Fiber 1g); Protein 2g.

Vary It! Traditional Kimchi is quite spicy. Add red chile flakes, if desired.

Fermented Garden Vegetables

Prep time: 20 min • **Ferment time:** 1 week • **Yield:** 1 gallon

Ingredients	*Directions*
1 green pepper **1 red pepper** **1 yellow pepper** **1 head garlic** **2 medium onions** **1 head broccoli** **1 head cauliflower** **2½ tablespoons canning salt** **2 quarts water**	*1* Scald a glass gallon jar with boiling water. Remove the seeds from all the peppers and thinly slice them into rings. Peel the garlic cloves. Peel and thinly slice the onions. Cut the broccoli and cauliflower into florets. *2* In a large pot, combine the salt and water. Place all the vegetables in the gallon jar and pour the saltwater brine over all. Place a saucer that fits inside the jar directly onto the vegetables to hold them under the brine. *3* Cover the jar with a muslin cloth and place it in an out-of-the-way place at room temperature. Check the jar daily, removing any scum, washing and replacing the saucer, and recovering the jar with a clean cloth. *4* After the fourth day, taste for desired flavor. After 1 week, place the jar in the refrigerator for up to a month.

Per ½-cup serving: Calories 13 (From Fat 0); Fat 0g (Saturated 0g); Cholesterol 0mg; Sodium 561mg; Carbohydrates 3g (Dietary Fiber 1g); Protein 1g.

Vary It! Use any of your favorite garden vegetables in the mix.

Fermented Onions

Prep time: 20 min • **Ferment time:** 7 days • **Yield:** 1 quart

Ingredients	Directions
6 to 8 medium onions 3 tablespoons canning salt 1 quart water	**1** Peel and thinly slice the onions. Combine the salt and water. Place onions in a glass quart jar, pour the salted water over them, and press down the onions so they stay under the brine.
	2 Cover the jar with a muslin cloth and place it in an out-of-the-way location at room temperature. Check the jar daily, removing any visible scum and replacing the cloth. After 1 week, place the jar in the refrigerator and enjoy.

Per ½-cup serving: Calories 22 (From Fat 1); Fat 0g (Saturated 0g); Cholesterol 0mg; Sodium 2,657mg; Carbohydrates 5g (Dietary Fiber 1g); Protein 1g.

188

Book IV: Fermenting and Brewing

Fermented Dandelion Greens

Prep time: 20 min • **Ferment time:** 3–5 days • **Yield:** 1 quart

Ingredients	Directions
4 cups fresh dandelion leaves **1 tablespoon canning salt** **3 cups water**	*1* Wash the dandelion greens. Combine the salt and water, mixing until the salt is dissolved.
	2 Pack the dandelion greens into a quart jar, tamping firmly and pouring the salted water over the packed layer. Repeat the greens layer and the saltwater layer, ending with the greens fully submerged.
	3 Cover tightly and place at room temperature to ferment for 3 to 5 days. Place the fermented leaves in the refrigerator and enjoy.

Per ½-cup serving: *Calories 12 (From Fat 2); Fat 0g (Saturated 0g); Cholesterol 0mg; Sodium 893mg; Carbohydrates 3g (Dietary Fiber 1g); Protein 1g.*

Fermented Fruit

Prep time: 20 min • **Ferment time:** 2 weeks • **Yield:** 1 quart

Ingredients	*Directions*
2 cups canned peaches with liquid **2 cups canned pineapple with liquid** **1½ cups sugar** **1 package dry yeast**	**1** Combine all ingredients and place them in a glass gallon jar. Cover loosely to keep out dust and insects and let sit at room temperature.
	2 The first day, stir every 4 hours. Then stir once a day for 2 weeks. After 14 days, the fermented fruit can be covered and placed in the refrigerator to enjoy.

Per ½-cup serving: Calories 238 (From Fat 3); Fat 0g (Saturated 0g); Cholesterol 0mg; Sodium 3mg; Carbohydrates 61g (Dietary Fiber 1g); Protein 1g.

Canned Sauerkraut

Prep time: 15 min • **Process time:** 20 min • **Yield:** 7 quarts or 14 pints

Ingredients	*Directions*
7 quarts sauerkraut **Boiling water**	*1* Prepare your canning jars and two-piece caps (lids and screw bands) according to the manufacturer's instructions. Keep the jars and lids hot.
	2 Place your sauerkraut in an 8-quart pot and bring it to a simmer over medium heat, stirring often to prevent sticking. In a separate pan, bring additional water to a boil to use as a reserve for filling the jars to the recommended level.
	3 Ladle the boiling hot sauerkraut and juice into the prepared jars. Add additional water from your reserve to cover the tightly packed sauerkraut, leaving 1-inch headspace. Release any air bubbles with a nonreactive utensil, adding water as necessary to maintain the proper headspace (refer to Book II, Chapter 1). Wipe the jar rims; seal the jars with the two-piece caps, hand-tightening the bands.
	4 Process the filled jars in a pressure canner at 10 pounds pressure for 20 minutes (quarts or pints). Allow the pressure to return to 0, wait an additional 10 minutes, and then carefully open the canner lid. (Head to Book V, Chapter 1, for detailed processing instructions for pressure canning.)
	5 Remove the jars from the canner with a jar lifter. Place them on a clean kitchen towel away from drafts. After the jars cool completely, test the seals (refer to Book II, Chapter 1). If you find jars that haven't sealed, refrigerate them and use them within 2 weeks. Prior to eating or tasting, boil the food for 15 minutes.

Per ½-cup serving: Calories 13 (From Fat 2); Fat 0g (Saturated 0g); Cholesterol 0mg; Sodium 429mg; Carbohydrates 3g (Dietary Fiber 2g); Protein 0g.

Chapter 3

Fermenting Beans

Fermenting beans is an interesting way to add flavor and nutrition to an inexpensive food. When fermentation takes place, beans actually become easier to digest, and your body can get more nutrition from the same package.

For vegetarians and vegans, fermented beans add nutrition and versatility to the diet. The fermentation produces new textures and tastes that pair well with many common foods in the vegetarian diet, like whole grains.

Some fermented foods, like tempeh, can be flavored and cooked to resemble bacon — a savory addition that many people miss when they stop eating meat.

Selecting and Preparing Beans

Any beans can be fermented. The process is the same, combining cooked beans and whey, no matter the type. But the final product will have a different taste, depending on the variety of bean you start with. Soybeans are the traditional choice for the Asian fermented food called *natto*. Natto is slimy and not wildly appealing to most non-Asian diets, but it has been shown to provide health benefits, especially for the heart.

Knowing your choices

To prepare fermented beans, you can use any type of bean you have. Some good choices are

- ✔ Black beans
- ✔ Garbanzo beans
- ✔ Kidney beans
- ✔ Pinto beans
- ✔ Soybeans

Use the beans that are locally available to you. Keep a quantity of them dried in the pantry, so you can keep the fermentation going as your family eats the finished product.

Planning your quantities

Although there's no hard and fast rule, fermenting beans is best done in the quantity that you'll use up regularly. For my family of seven, I make two quart jars of mashed beans at a time, a week apart. That way, I have enough to use as a condiment or filling throughout the week. A smaller family may do well with a quart whereas for a couple, a pint would probably be sufficient.

Making the most of miso

You may have heard of another popular fermented bean product called *miso*. Miso is sold as a very thick paste and comes in a variety of flavors, all with different levels of salty, sweet, and savory. Depending on the flavor and color, miso is known as red, white, or even mixed types. Traditionally made from soybeans, miso is now made from other things, including buckwheat, corn, and rice.

Miso is a living food. It's healthful and delicious, but you can't expose it to too high a heat. A cup of very hot, but not boiling, water with a spoonful of miso is an invigorating drink that tastes fantastic and still contains the probiotic benefit that miso has to offer.

Because miso can take anywhere from days to years, depending on the variety, it's worth purchasing miso from your local health food store. A jar goes a long way, and it may just be the introduction to fermented food that your family needs.

Testing the Tempeh Waters

Tempeh is one of those foods that may seem peculiar at first glance. It's a matted bunch of fuzzy beans. After you come to love tempeh, though, you'll see its strange look as a delight.

Tempeh is fermented soybeans. The beans are slightly cooked, and a bit of vinegar is added to improve the pH for the inoculant, an edible mold called *Rhizopus oligosporus.*

After a carefully controlled fermenting, the mold grows on the beans and creates a mat. This mat is the tempeh. The beans are changed through the fermentation process, and they become more digestible. The fermentation also changes the soybeans to increase the nutrients within, making them easier for your body to absorb. Soybeans are great, but fermented soybeans are fantastic!

Starting with a starter

Tempeh requires the proper starter, a powdered mold. You have to buy this starter because the mold isn't found wild (from the air) in today's kitchens. Tempeh starter is available online and in well-stocked health-food stores. If you don't see it on the shelf, ask whether the store can order it for you.

Tempeh starter can be kept tightly sealed in the freezer until you need it.

Gathering the tools

To make tempeh at home, you need these basic items:

- ✔ **Soybeans:** Purchase the base for your recipe from your local health-food store or even online.

- ✔ **Tempeh starter:** Purchase the starter from a company that specializes in starter cultures. (See the preceding section for more information.)

- ✔ **Plastic bags:** You perforate these bags to allow the mold spores to breathe properly as they ferment. Use a new bag each time you make a new batch.

- ✔ **Accurate thermometer:** Use this tool to monitor the beans and ensure that they remain at the proper temperature during the fermentation process.

Book IV

Fermenting and Brewing

Storing and serving your yield

After you ferment tempeh, keep it in the refrigerator until you use it. Purchased tempeh has an expiration date, but your homemade version will keep for up to one week. Keep it in a tightly closed container so that it remains moist.

Freeze any extra tempeh for up to three months. The jury is still out on whether the probiotic benefit remains after the tempeh is frozen, but the other health benefits certainly remain. Freezing tempeh gives you a hearty meat substitute on hand.

Eating tempeh is easy! Slice the mat of tempeh into serving sizes as desired. I like to slice mine in ¼-inch-thick slices. Steam lightly to improve the flavor even more. Then use it like you would meat: Marinate, fry, deep fry, grill, cut up, or sauté — let your imagination be your guide.

TIP

The edible white mold doesn't have to be removed from the surface of the tempeh. It's up to you!

Bacon Tempeh

Prep time: 20 min • **Marinate time:** 4 hr • **Yield:** 4 servings

Ingredients	Directions
8 ounces tempeh	**1** Slice tempeh into ¼-inch-thick slices.
5 tablespoons tamari	
1 tablespoon honey	**2** Combine the tamari, honey, garlic, and liquid smoke and place the mixture in a zippered plastic bag.
1 clove garlic, minced	
1 tablespoon liquid smoke	**3** Place the sliced tempeh in the bag of marinade for 4 hours, turning after the first 2 hours.
5 tablespoons oil for frying	
	4 Fry the tempeh in oil until crispy.

Per 3-slice serving: Calories 192 (From Fat 131); Fat 15g (Saturated 2g); Cholesterol 0mg; Sodium 299mg; Carbohydrates 7g (Dietary Fiber 3g); Protein 11g.

Vary It! Sprinkle coarse ground black pepper onto the slices before frying.

Tempeh

Prep time: 1 hr, 15 min • **Cook time:** 45 min • **Ferment time:** 36–38 hr • **Yield:** 1 quart

Ingredients	*Directions*
2 cups dry soybeans **2 tablespoons cider vinegar** **¾ teaspoon tempeh starter**	**1** Put the soybeans in a 6-quart pot and cover them with water. Bring to a boil over medium-high heat and boil for 15 minutes. Remove from heat and let sit for 2 hours to loosen the hulls.
	2 Drain the soybeans and place them back in the pan. Mash them to split all the beans. Mashing helps loosen the hulls as well.
	3 Add fresh water to cover the beans. Remove the hulls as they float to the surface.
	4 Bring the water and the split, dehulled soybeans to a gentle boil over medium-high heat. Boil for 30 minutes, or until tender. Remove the cooked soybeans and drain. Place the drained beans on a linen kitchen towel to dry the outsides.
	5 In a clean mixing bowl, pour the cooked, mashed beans and add the vinegar and starter. Mix well to combine.
	6 Place the bean mixture in 2 quart-sized bags so they're thinly spread out, with ventilation holes poked at ½-inch intervals over one side.
	7 Place the bags into a dehydrator with an accurate thermometer at 85° to 95° for 12 hours, or until the tempeh generates its own heat due to fermentation.
	8 Monitor the tempeh for 24 hours to be certain it remains at 85° to 95°. After 24 hours, it will have grown a white, edible mold over the entire surface.

9 The tempeh is finished when it is completely layered with white mold (around 25 to 30 hours after you put it in the dehydrator). Remove it from the plastic bags and steam it for 25 minutes to stop the fermentation process. Refrigerate until ready to use.

Per 4-ounce serving: Calories 183 (From Fat 77); Fat 9g (Saturated 1g); Cholesterol 0mg; Sodium 2mg; Carbohydrates 15g (Dietary Fiber 11g); Protein 16g.

Tip: If you like, you can cut the mold off before eating. Store-bought tempeh usually has the mold removed.

Chapter 4

Fermenting Cheese, Dairy, and Vegan Foods

Despite the strange name, fermented dairy is very common and probably found in your refrigerator right now in the form of cheese and yogurt. Fermented dairy products are common around the world, where they're sometimes referred to as *cultured* dairy products. In this chapter, I tell you everything you need to know about fermenting cheese, dairy, and vegan foods.

Introducing Fermented Dairy

Fermenting dairy provides not just delicious tasting food, but improved nutritional value as well. Many people who can't tolerate milk in its regular form have no problem eating it after it has been fermented.

Although this list is by no means exhaustive, some of the more common forms of fermented dairy include

✔ **Buttermilk:** True cultured buttermilk isn't a grocery store item. It's fermented with a variety of *Lacto* bacteria that gives it the tang and health benefit of a fermented product.

✔ **Cheese:** The largest class of fermented milk products, cheese is created by using specific bacteria and molds developed for specific flavors and textures.

✔ **Cultured butter:** This product is made by adding some cultured buttermilk to the cream you'll be churning. Allow it to ripen and then make your butter.

✔ **Kefir:** A fermented product, kefir is created with bacterial grains that resemble cauliflower. These gelatinous grains are removed and reused over again. They eventually grow in size and can be divided to share.

✔ **Koumiss:** Koumiss is a fermented, carbonated dairy drink that was traditionally made from mares' milk in central Asia. Koumiss has been used medicinally in various times. Depending on the level of fermentation, it can contain varying degrees of alcohol. The recipe for the version at the end of this chapter uses yeast to start the fermentation.

✔ **Sour cream:** Cultured sour cream is also different from the product found on most grocery shelves. The fermenting process results in a deliciously acidic food, using *Lactococcus lactis,* a bacterium that's also used in the making of buttermilk and many cheeses.

✔ **Yogurt:** Yogurt is usually made from dairy milk and beneficial bacteria such as *Lactobacillus bulgaricus* and *Streptococcus thermophilus.* A small scoop of finished yogurt can be used to start a new batch, in an endless cycle.

Savoring Cheeses

Not all cheeses have to be complicated. You can make many basic cheeses at home and then vary the flavorings forever. With a few simple ingredients, making cheese will become a weekly hobby that can provide nutrient-dense food your family will enjoy.

To make your own cheese, use packets of bacteria that are premeasured (called *direct set*) or create your own culture by sterilizing a portion of milk and adding the proper bacteria to store for future cheesemaking. This is referred to as a *mother.* Many places online cater to home cheesemakers and offer these supplies in manageable amounts.

Spreading the soft cheeses

Spreading cheeses are soft, even when cold. They usually contain herbs or other seasonings and are delicious on a party tray. Spreading cheese is a staple ingredient for many rich-tasting dishes as well. It's used as stuffing for noodles and fillings for crêpes. You can make a simple soft cheese base and flavor it however you like, for a variety of recipes. Using only milk and an acid, you can make this healthy food that's both delicious and useful.

Nibbling the hard cheeses

Hard cheeses are made using *rennet,* which can be derived from plant or animal material and comes in liquid or tablet form. Rennet, combined with heat, is what separates the curd from the whey in milk. Milk is heated to a specific temperature (depending on the variety of cheese you make), and then you add the rennet.

Left to rest, the milk and rennet mixture solidifies into a gelatinous mass that's cut easily. The cheesemaker then cuts the curds into the proper size bits called for, and, if the recipe requires it, the curds are cooked in order to develop the desired flavor and become the right texture.

This period of time that the curds are allowed to cook and shrink down is called *cheddaring.*

Saying Yes to Yogurts

Yogurt is made from a number of milks, such as cow, sheep, and goat. Most commonly, yogurt is made from milk that has been pasteurized to destroy all the bacteria, to make a sterile environment for the desired bacteria to proliferate. After the sterilized milk is inoculated with yogurt starter, it's left to incubate. Incubation is done at a warm temperature in a location where the yogurt won't be disturbed.

Avoid moving the cultured milk while it's incubating. Otherwise, it may remain runny and not set up.

When fermenting, all milks aren't created equal. They're all nutritious, but the flavor and texture of the finished product can be wildly different. As you start fermenting your own dairy products, remember that they won't be the same as store-bought examples. Your fermented foods won't contain thickeners and sweeteners like the products on the grocery shelves usually do.

If you're trying to start your own home fermented products by using store-bought varieties, check that the beneficial bacteria is present. You need a living food to use as a starter for the next batch of living food. If you're shopping at a health-food store, ask the clerk for the most natural form of fermented food you want.

Book IV

Fermenting and Brewing

Preparing Vegan Ferments

A growing number of people prefer to avoid dairy products. Fermented products are still available to you even if you're avoiding dairy. You can use soymilk to make tofu (soured, not fermented) and you can make kefir by adding sweetener. Kefir grains that have been living in soymilk may not thrive and will have to be replaced.

Soy yogurt is made by using soymilk and a starter culture from soy yogurt. Other than that, the yogurt is made in the same way as dairy yogurt. The final product is runnier than dairy yogurt, but you can add a vegan thickener.

Finding alternative milks

You can use a variety of delicious milks for fermenting. Locating sheep and goat dairies is easier than ever; even buffalo and camel milk are available if you know where to look.

An enthusiastic group of people enjoys making and eating fermented foods, so try looking online for forums that match what you're interested in. Many of them list suppliers and can connect you with someone who may even be local!

Selecting starters

Starters are living bacteria. They're best kept at the proper temperature and fed regularly. Many fermented food enthusiasts enjoy trading starters for little more than postage. Find the most local supplier to avoid your culture losing strength due to age or lack of food.

Starter cultures are readily available directly from others who are actively using them. Beware of sites posing as experts with superior starters. If you find the cost to be prohibitive, keep looking.

Storing and Serving

Fermented products are cultured at room temperature or above. After the desired fermentation is reached, they're chilled to slow the fermentation. For cheeses, fermentation may take weeks, or even years, to reach. Follow the cheese recipe to the letter, taste it, and decide whether you'll stick with the same storage time based on how well you like the flavor. While fermented food doesn't go bad, it does eventually become too sour-tasting to enjoy eating.

Serve fermented products at their optimal flavor, especially when you're introducing someone to the idea of home fermented items. For someone who's new to the taste, the tanginess may be off-putting if the product is overripe.

When serving things like yogurt and kefir, many people expect a highly sweetened taste. In order to retrain their palate, add natural sweeteners like honey, maple syrup, or organic sugar to the recipe. You can slowly cut back as their taste develops for the unsweetened product.

As with any fermenting, use nonreactive containers for the products in this chapter. Plastic is never recommended and is even discouraged. Glass is the perfect vessel for most of your fermenting. It's easy to clean, won't harbor odors, and can be recycled. Other choices are stainless steel and enamel-coated containers, or lead-free crocks.

When starting out with any new food, moderation is key. Try eating (or drinking) your new food in small amounts to gauge your reaction to it. Although you should never feel ill, fermented foods can produce gas or slight bloating in some people at first. A good rule is to start with no more than ¼ cup of fermented product a day for the first week. Then increase the amount the following week to give your system time to adjust.

If your fermented food seems too strong, try reducing the time of fermentation for the next batch. Chilling it, sweetening it, and adding it to other foods are also good ways to help you get used to the natural tang.

Book IV

Fermenting and Brewing

Queso Blanco (White Cheese)

Prep time: 20 min • **Drain time:** 2 hr • **Yield:** 1 pound

Ingredients	*Directions*
1 gallon cow or goat milk	*1* Heat the milk in a 6-quart pot over medium heat. Stir it often to prevent scorching. When the milk becomes steamy and bubbles are just forming around the edges of the pan, turn off the heat.
½ cup cider vinegar or lemon or lime juice	
	2 Pour the vinegar into the milk and stir gently until curds form. After the curds start to form, cover the pan and let it sit until you see a deep layer of whey on top with the mass of curds at the bottom of the pan.
	3 Place a linen- or cheesecloth-lined colander into the sink and scoop the curds into it. Discard the remaining liquid in the pot. Tie the corners of the cheesecloth together and hang until it stops dripping. (You can do this right in the sink or in the refrigerator if room is a factor.) Your cheese is ready to use!

Per 2-ounce serving: Calories 151 (From Fat 73); Fat 8g (Saturated 5g); Cholesterol 33mg; Sodium 120mg; Carbohydrates 12g (Dietary Fiber 0g); Protein 8g.

Vary It! For a dessert cheese, use lemon or lime juice in place of the vinegar.

Quick Feta-Style Cheese

Prep time: 20 min • **Yield:** 2 cups

Ingredients	Directions
1 pound queso blanco cheese made with vinegar 1 cup water 1 tablespoon salt	**1** Shape fresh queso blanco into a flattened wheel shape. Wrap it in a dampened cheesecloth. Place the cheese on a sandwich plate with a second plate on top. Place a foil-wrapped brick or other heavy object on top of the second plate. Press overnight at room temperature in an undisturbed place.
	2 Remove the weight, plates, and cheesecloth. Cut the pressed cheese into ½-inch cubes.
	3 Combine the water and salt and stir until the salt is dissolved. Place the cubed cheese in a quart jar. Pour the saltwater brine over all.
	4 Cover the jar tightly and keep it in the refrigerator for 3 to 5 days, tasting daily until desired saltiness is reached.

Per 2-ounce serving: Calories 151 (From Fat 73); Fat 8g (Saturated 5g); Cholesterol 33mg; Sodium 556mg; Carbohydrates 12g (Dietary Fiber 0g); Protein 8g.

Sweet Dessert Dip

Prep time: 20 min • **Yield:** 2 cups

Ingredients	Directions
1 pound queso blanco cheese made with lemon or lime juice	**1** Quarter the cheese so it fits into your food processor and then drain the cheese. Place the drained cheese in a food processor. Process until smooth and creamy.
1 tablespoon honey	
Zest from 1 lemon or lime	**2** Scrape the smooth cheese into a serving bowl. Add honey and lemon or lime zest and stir well. Store cheese in a tightly closed container in the freezer for up to 3 months.

Per ¼-cup serving: Calories 155 (From Fat 73); Fat 8g (Saturated 5g); Cholesterol 33mg; Sodium 120mg; Carbohydrates 13g (Dietary Fiber 0g); Protein 8g.

Savory Cracker Dip

Prep time: 10 min • **Yield:** 2 cups

Ingredients	Directions
1 pound queso blanco cheese made with vinegar	**1** Quarter the cheese so that it fits into your food processor and then drain the cheese. Place the drained cheese in a food processor. Process until smooth and creamy.
½ teaspoon salt	
1 tablespoon dried Italian herbs	**2** Scrape the smooth cheese into a serving bowl. Add the salt and herbs and stir well. Store cheese in a tightly closed container in the freezer for up to 3 months.

Per ¼-cup serving: Calories 151 (From Fat 8); Fat 8g (Saturated 5g); Cholesterol 33mg; Sodium 192mg; Carbohydrates 12g (Dietary Fiber 0g); Protein 8g.

Tip: Serve with crusty bread or crackers.

Feta Cheese

Prep time: 10 min • **Cook time:** 75 min, plus hanging time • **Yield:** 2 pounds

Ingredients	*Directions*
2 gallons goat milk	*1* Warm the milk to 86° and stir in the mesophilic culture. Let the mixture ripen for 1 hour. Mix the rennet into the cool water and stir into the milk. Cover and allow the mixture to sit for another hour to coagulate.
¼ teaspoon mesophilic culture	
¼ teaspoon liquid vegetable rennet, or ½ of a rennet tablet	
¼ cup cool water	*2* Cut the curds into ½-inch cubes and then allow them to rest for 5 minutes.
Kosher or any noniodized salt	
	3 Stir gently for 15 minutes, keeping the curds at 86°. Cut any pieces that were missed so the pieces are uniform in size. Pour the curds into a cheesecloth-lined colander. Tie the bag of curds and hang it to drain for 4 to 6 hours or overnight.
	4 Remove the cheese from the cheesecloth, slice it in half, and lay it in a bowl. Salt all surfaces, cover it with a plate or plastic wrap, and allow it to sit at room temperature for 24 hours. During the 24 hours, intermittently drain the whey that's expelled from the cheese and re-salt the cheese.
	5 Put the cheese in a covered container and refrigerate it. The cheese will keep for 5 to 7 days.

Per 2-ounce serving: Calories 270 (From Fat 146); Fat 16g (Saturated 10g); Cholesterol 43mg; Sodium 958mg; Carbohydrates 17g; Dietary Fiber 0g; Protein 14g.

Note: Mesophilic culture is a culture that's destroyed at higher temperatures. You can get it at a cheese supply store when you're buying rennet.

Note: The beauty of this cheese is that it's very forgiving. If you add the rennet late, cut the curds late, or let it hang or expel whey for a longer time than the recipe calls for, it will still turn out fine. You also can't oversalt it because it's a salty cheese, and the salt helps remove the whey.

Marinated Goat Cheese

Prep time: 10 min, plus marinating • **Yield:** 1 quart

Ingredients	Directions
¼ **pound goat cheese**	**1** Scald a quart canning jar by filling it with boiling water and then draining it. Pack the goat cheese, peppercorns, coriander seeds, bay leaf, thyme, rosemary, and garlic into the jar. Pour the olive oil over all, submerging all the ingredients with oil. Add more oil, if necessary.
½ **teaspoon peppercorns**	
⅛ **teaspoon coriander seeds**	
1 fresh bay leaf	
1 sprig thyme	**2** Use a clean lid, seal the jar tightly, and refrigerate it immediately. Marinate for 7 days. Store cheese in a tightly closed container in the freezer for up to 3 months.
1 sprig rosemary	
2 cloves peeled garlic	
½ **cup olive oil**	

Per 2-ounce serving: Calories 316 (From Fat 297); Fat 33g (Saturated 8g); Cholesterol 13mg; Sodium 105mg; Carbohydrates 0g (Dietary Fiber 0g); Protein 5g.

Tip: This oil becomes fragrant and delicious as well.

Making the most of your results

The one thing to remember about culturing foods at home is that they're best used continuously. In order to get into the habit of doing this, these foods should become important in your diet. The following are some ways to begin and continue to use fermented foods:

✔ Use kefir in smoothies. Try using natural sweeteners to entice your family's taste buds. Reduce the sweetness as they become used to the flavor.

✔ Culture your own cream into sour cream and use it in place of store-bought sour cream.

✔ Create fresh cheese at least once a week and use it for snacks and dips, as after-school snacks or the first course for dinner.

✔ Eat yogurt with fresh fruit or granola as a healthy breakfast.

✔ Place yogurt in a cheesecloth-lined strainer and allow liquid (whey) to drain away. The resulting cheeselike product makes wonderfully rich tasting cream cheese–style food.

Simple Goat Cheese

Prep time: 15 min • **Cook time:** 15 min, plus hanging time • **Yield:** About 1 lb

Ingredients	*Directions*
1 gallon goat milk **¼ cup vinegar or lemon juice** **Kosher or any noniodized salt, to taste**	*1* Slowly heat the milk to 195°. Stir in the vinegar and keep the milk at 195°, stirring occasionally, for 10 to 15 minutes. The milk will gradually start to curdle, first with very small curds and then with larger curds. When the curds stay separate from the milk when you stir, they're ready. When a soft curd has formed, pour into a cheesecloth-lined colander.
	2 Sprinkle salt, according to taste, over the curd, and then remove the cheese in cheesecloth and hang it to drain for several hours. When the cheese reaches the desired consistency, refrigerate it. The cheese keeps for about a week.

Per 2-ounce serving: Calories 271 (From Fat 146); Fat 16g (Saturated 10g); Cholesterol 43mg; Sodium 195mg; Carbohydrates 18g; Dietary Fiber 0g; Protein 14g.

Note: This straightforward recipe is a good place to start your goat-milk recipe exploration.

Tip: Never use ultrapastuerized goat milk from the store, because it won't turn into cheese.

Vary It! Add whatever ingredients you like to flavor the cheese. Try salt, herbs, or even fruit and powdered sugar to taste.

Koumiss

Prep time: 30 min, plus standing and storing • **Cook time:** 30 min • **Yield:** About 1 gall

Ingredients	Directions
1 gallon goat milk	**1** Heat the goat milk to 180° in a stainless steel pot and remove any film that forms. Add the honey and allow the mixture to cool to 70°.
2 tablespoons honey	
⅛ teaspoon champagne yeast	
¼ cup warm water	**2** Dissolve the champagne yeast in 115° water and let it stand for 10 minutes. Stir the yeast mixture into the milk. Cover it with a clean cloth and allow it to stand at room temperature until it foams (about 24 hours).
	3 Pour the koumiss into sanitized beer bottles that can withstand carbonation pressure. Fill only to 1 inch below the bottom of the neck of the bottle.
	4 Store the koumiss at room temperature for 24 hours and then refrigerate. Shake the bottles *gently* every few days but not just before opening. Koumiss will keep for 6 to 8 weeks but then becomes increasingly acidic. You can add honey to hide the acidic taste.

Per 1-cup serving: Calories 177 (From Fat 91); Fat 10g (Saturated 7g); Cholesterol 27mg; Sodium 122mg; Carbohydrates 13g; Dietary Fiber 0g; Protein 9g.

Tip: You can buy the champagne yeast at a beermaker's shop.

Herbed Yogurt Dressing

Prep time: 20 min • **Ferment time:** 2 weeks • **Yield:** 1½ cups

Ingredients	*Directions*
1 cup plain yogurt ¼ cup mayonnaise 1 tablespoon lemon juice 2 teaspoons honey ¼ cup shallots ¼ cup fresh herbs	*1* In a medium mixing bowl, combine the yogurt, mayonnaise, lemon juice, and honey. *2* Finely chop the shallots and add them to the yogurt mixture. Chop the herbs and add them to the mixture. Stir well. *3* Chill for 30 minutes to thicken before using. Store dressing for up to 2 weeks in the refrigerator.

Per 2-tablespoons serving: *Calories 65 (From Fat 45); Fat 5g (Saturated 1g); Cholesterol 8mg; Sodium 47mg; Carbohydrates 4g (Dietary Fiber 0g); Protein 2g.*

Homemade Yogurt

Prep time: 20 min • **Ferment time:** 2 weeks • **Yield:** 1 quart

Ingredients	*Directions*
2 quarts cow or goat milk **2 tablespoons yogurt that contains active cultures**	**1** In a 6-quart pot, bring the milk to 185°. Don't allow the milk to boil over. Cool the milk to 110° by placing the entire pan into an ice-filled sink and swirling around.
	2 Add the yogurt to the cooled milk, stirring well. Pour the yogurt into the container that you'll be storing it in and place it in a dehydrator with an accurate thermometer gauge. Keep the yogurt at 110° for 7 hours, or until thickened and as tangy as you like.
	3 Refrigerate the finished yogurt until ready to eat. Store yogurt for up to 2 weeks in the refrigerator. Keep 2 tablespoons of this yogurt as the starter for the next batch.

Per 1-cup serving: Calories 303 (From Fat 147); Fat 16g (Saturated 10g); Cholesterol 66mg; Sodium 242mg; Carbohydrates 23g (Dietary Fiber 0g); Protein 17g.

Note: Goat's milk yogurt is naturally looser than cow's milk yogurt. This is normal.

Kefir

Prep time: 20 min • **Ferment time:** 24 hr • **Yield:** 1 quart

Ingredients	*Directions*
4 tablespoons kefir grains **1 quart milk**	**1** Place the grains in the bottom of a quart canning jar. Pour the milk over the grains, leaving ½-inch headspace.
	2 Cover a jar with a coffee filter and place an elastic band around the coffee filter, if desired. Place the jar in an out-of-the-way place at room temperature.
	3 After 24 hours, the kefir is ready. Strain out grains for the next batch and refrigerate the finished kefir. Store kefir in the refrigerator for up to 1 week.

Per 1-cup serving: Calories 159 (From Fat 78); Fat 9g (Saturated 5g); Cholesterol 33mg; Sodium 126mg; Carbohydrates 12g (Dietary Fiber 0g); Protein 9g.

Tip: You can find kefir grains by doing a search online. A huge community of kefir drinkers willingly share grains through the mail.

Note: Kefir is carbonated at first. Be aware that it can bubble over if agitated too much after it's finished. Never use metal utensils in any part of kefir making.

Kefir Smoothie

Prep time: 5 min • **Yield:** 2 servings

Ingredients	Directions
2 cups kefir 2 large bananas 2 cups frozen strawberries 1 tablespoon honey	**1** Pour the kefir into a blender. Peel the bananas and cut them in half. Add the bananas, frozen strawberries, and honey to the blender.
	2 Cover and blend until smooth and thick. Kefir smoothies can keep for up to 1 week in the refrigerator.

Per 1-cup serving: Calories 343 (From Fat 79); Fat 9g (Saturated 5g); Cholesterol 29mg; Sodium 114mg; Carbohydrates 62g (Dietary Fiber 7g); Protein 10g.

Vary It! Try this recipe with a sprinkle of cinnamon.

Pumpkin Kefir Smoothie

Prep time: 5 min • **Yield:** 2 servings

Ingredients	Directions
2 cups kefir ¼ cup pumpkin puree ⅛ teaspoon pumpkin pie spice ¼ teaspoon vanilla 4 ice cubes	**1** Pour the kefir into a blender. Add the pumpkin puree, pumpkin pie spice, vanilla, and ice.
	2 Cover and blend until smooth and thick. Kefir smoothies can keep for up to 1 week in the refrigerator.

Per 1-cup serving: Calories 151 (From Fat 70); Fat 8g (Saturated 5g); Cholesterol 29mg; Sodium 112mg; Carbohydrates 13g (Dietary Fiber 1g); Protein 8g.

Vary It! Add a medium banana for extra sweetness.

Tip: The thickness of kefir varies from batch to batch — sometimes it's thick; other times, it's thin. The thicker the kefir, the thicker your smoothie will be.

Chapter 5

Working with Breads and Grains

There's nothing like the smell of fresh bread. You can instantly taste the butter and jam. Some cooks think of making bread as too time consuming or too difficult to master, and therefore they never try it. The truth is that homemade bread never fails to taste better and offer more than mere packaging for sandwich meat. In this chapter, I show you the basics of breadmaking, and I share my tried-and-true recipes for anyone who wants to bake her own delicious loaves!

What You Knead to Know about Breads

No matter what type of bread you're making, it usually has the same basic ingredients: flour, water, yeast, and salt. Mixing these ingredients together makes a crusty, chewy loaf of bread. After you know the basic recipe for a loaf of bread, you can begin to add your own variations, using different flours, yeasts, salts, and sweeteners.

The rest of breadmaking comes from experience. You'll come to know how moist dough that's kneaded sufficiently feels. Your nose will recognize the yeasty smell of a good sourdough, and soon you'll know when a loaf of bread is finished baking, even before the timer goes off.

Zeroing in on Sourdough

The chewiness and special tang that sourdough brings to a loaf is hard to beat. Sourdough is in a class all its own, bringing additional texture and flavor to any sandwich. You can make your own sourdough and keep it for years! I've kept the same sourdough starter for more than 5 years, making everything from loaves of bread to cookies with it.

Sourdough is simply a yeasty mixture. Usually, it's made from flour and water and then left uncovered to gather the wild yeast that's naturally found all around you. This is why traditionalists believe that sourdough breads from certain locations taste different. Whether or not this belief is true, there's something almost magical about creating sourdough by harnessing the power of the wild yeast that you already have in your kitchen.

The tanginess you love in a slice of sourdough varies with how sour the starter actually is. You can easily change the sourness of your recipe in several ways. If you allow your sourdough to work without refrigeration, it becomes sourer. Using this mixture will flavor your final product tremendously.

If you prefer a more gentle sourdough, you can add a pinch of baking soda to the recipe to temper the flavor. Many people add baking soda when they know a recipe ends up just a bit more sour than they can take.

You can also refrigerate your starter after it reaches your desired flavor. Refrigeration will slow down and keep your starter at the perfect tanginess for your liking. Remove the amount needed from the refrigerator and allow it to return to room temperature before adding it to your bread recipe. The remaining starter should be fed and allowed to work before replacing.

Feed your starter once a week if you're not already using it within that time. You can add equal parts flour and water, stir, and let sit at room temperature until bubbly once again. I add ½ cup flour and ½ cup water at each feeding.

Mastering Rye and Pumpernickel

Rye and pumpernickel breads are richly colored, and the flavors are uniquely wonderful. Rye gets its flavor from rye flour and caraway seed. Keep rye flour in the freezer because it goes rancid rapidly and can bring a bitter flavor to the recipe.

Pumpernickel bread traditionally got its dark color from a long baking time. This long, slow baking could last for up to 16 hours! Today, pumpernickel gains its rich, delicious-looking color from things like coffee and cocoa. Rye flour is still used, and the combination of flavors gives pumpernickel a taste that's unforgettable.

Indulging in flours

Have you ever wondered what exactly the difference is between white flours? Here's a handy list:

- ✔ **All-purpose flour:** The most common flour for the home baker, it's made from a combination of hard and soft wheat kernel. The bran and germ of the wheat are removed during the milling process. This flour is used in a wide range of baking recipes. All-purpose flour, or APF, can be bleached or unbleached. Studies have shown that the two have no nutritional difference; bleached flour, however, gives a more delicate texture for cake baking.

- ✔ **Bread flour:** This flour is ground from a specific type of wheat, the hard red spring wheat. It's designed for commercial baking, although you can find it in large food stores. For breadmaking, it works exceptionally well, because it has a greater gluten strength.

- ✔ **Self-rising flour:** Although not as well known as the others in this list, this flour is simply all-purpose flour with leavening and salt added. You can substitute it for all-purpose flour, but you'd have to reduce the amount of salt and leavening in your recipe.

- ✔ **Cake flour:** Often used by specialty bakers, cake flour is made from soft wheat, resulting in a low gluten, higher starch content, which makes for lighter baked goods. For the most part, unless you're doing high-end baking, you can substitute all-purpose flour.

Flours are made from different types of things, including rye, corn, oatmeal, rice, soy, peanuts, chickpeas, and even beans. You can use all these ingredients to change the flavor and texture of a basic bread recipe. They all deserve experimenting with.

Adding flours other than white will result in a heavier, denser loaf of bread. This is normal. The *bite,* or chewiness of the bread, will be different as well. When you're trying new flours for the first time, add a cup at a time to your favorite recipe to see how much you like the flavor and texture.

Book IV

Fermenting and Brewing

Adding seeds and other extras

After you choose the flour you want to use in your recipe, you can consider an endless assortment of extras to add to a loaf of bread. Try any of the following to get started:

- Nuts
- Seeds
- Whole oats
- Dried fruits
- Dried herbs
- Alternative sweeteners
- Dried vegetable bits

Spotlighting Sprouted Grains

Something almost magical happens when you sprout grains. Sprouting changes the nutritional content of the grain, improving it. Adding sprouted grains to your bread, or even creating a loaf by using sprouted flour, creates a whole food that's full of essential nutrients. If you use the right grains, the bread can even be tolerated by those who can't digest gluten.

Soaking before cooking

To make your sprouts for use, you must soak them to start the sprouting process. The nuts, seeds, or grains all need a soaking in warm water to get started. The grains soak up moisture, swelling up to three times their size when dried.

This soaking process can be as short as 30 minutes, in the case of tiny seeds, to as long as 12 hours, for large beans. After soaking, thoroughly drain and rinse the swollen seeds, removing any broken or discolored pieces you may have missed when they were dry.

No matter what you're sprouting, all grains must be drained and allowed to sprout without sitting in water. If a grain is left to sit in water, it will quickly go rancid. Grains do, however, need to remain damp. To keep your grains moist enough to sprout properly, yet not wet enough to go rancid, you must rinse them. Rinse your grains at least twice a day; four times a day is optimal. Rinsing takes only a few seconds, and it keeps the sprouts fresh. To rinse, simple fill your sprouting container with cool water, drain, and repeat at least once.

You can sprout grains in either a dish with a saucer as a lid or a glass jar with a mesh lid — both make great sprouting containers.

Your sprouts should always be either odorless or have a fresh, green smell. If they ever smell rancid, fishy, or musty, throw them away and start again.

Releasing the nutritional power of sprouted grains

After they sprout, most grains and beans can be eaten raw (with the exception of kidney beans and soybeans, which must be cooked first). When adding sprouted grains to bread, some recipes call for the sprouts to be blended in a food processor, making a sort of thick paste-like dough that you bake. Other recipes require the sprouts to be dried first and then added. You'll benefit from the nutrients either way.

Book IV

Fermenting and Brewing

Sourdough Starter

Prep time: 5 min • **Ferment time:** 48 hr • **Yield:** 1 quart

Ingredients	Directions
2 cups flour	**1** Place all the ingredients in a small crock or quart jar. Stir until combined. Cover and store at room temperature for 48 hours, or until pleasantly yeasty smelling.
2 cups warm water	
1 package dry yeast	
	2 Store your finished sourdough starter in the refrigerator.

Note: To use, remove the amount required for your recipe and add 1 cup each of water and flour to the remaining starter. Stir and allow to stand at room temperature until bubbly once again.

Sourdough Pancakes

Prep time: 10 min • **Cook time:** 3–5 min • **Yield:** 15 pancakes

Ingredients	Directions
1 cup sourdough starter	**1** Place the starter in a medium mixing bowl. Add the remaining ingredients. Mix well.
2 eggs	
2¼ cups milk	**2** Cook the pancakes, pouring about ¼ cup of the batter for each pancake, on a hot, greased griddle, until golden brown.
1 teaspoon salt	
2 teaspoons baking soda	
2 cups flour	
3 tablespoons melted butter	
2 tablespoon sugar	
1 teaspoon vanilla	

Per pancake: Calories 138 (From Fat 41); Fat 5g (Saturated 3g); Cholesterol 40mg; Sodium 352mg; Carbohydrates 20g (Dietary Fiber 1g); Protein 4g.

Vary It! Add ¼ teaspoon of nutmeg to the batter.

Sourdough Bread

Prep time: 10 min, plus rising time • **Bake time:** 45 min • **Yield:** 1 loaf

Ingredients	*Directions*
2 cups sourdough starter	*1* In a large mixing bowl, combine the starter, sugar, and salt. Add flour 1 cup at a time, stirring as much as you can with a wooden spoon.
1 tablespoon sugar	
2 teaspoons salt	
4 cups flour	*2* When the dough is firm enough to knead by hand, turn it onto a lightly floured surface and add the remaining flour, kneading vigorously by hand, until the dough is no longer sticky, but is moist and flexible.
	3 Wash the mixing bowl with hot water, dry it, and place the dough in the warm bowl. Cover the bowl with a dishcloth and let the dough rise in a warm place until doubled.
	4 Punch down the dough, form it into one round loaf, and let it rise a second time on a lightly greased cookie sheet.
	5 Bake the loaf in a preheated 350° oven for 40 to 45 minutes, or until the crust is deep brown and sounds hollow when tapped.
	6 Cool for 1 hour before slicing.

*Per slice ($^1/_{16}$ **of a loaf**): Calories 146 (From Fat 4); Fat 0g (Saturated 0g); Cholesterol 0mg; Sodium 292mg; Carbohydrates 31g (Dietary Fiber 1g); Protein 4g.*

Sourdough Biscuits

Prep time: 35 min, plus rising time • **Bake time:** 15 min • **Yield:** 12–16 biscuits

Ingredients	Directions
¾ **teaspoon salt**	**1** In a medium mixing bowl, combine the salt, sugar, baking powder, baking soda, and ½ cup flour.
1 tablespoon sugar	
½ **teaspoon baking powder**	**2** In a large mixing bowl, add the combined dry ingredients to the starter.
½ **teaspoon baking soda**	
2½ **cups flour**	**3** Turn out the dough onto a floured counter and mix and knead it by hand. Add the remaining flour as needed to make a dough that's soft but holds together.
2 cups sourdough starter	
	4 Pat the dough into a 1-inch-thick rectangle. Cut the dough into square biscuits with a pizza cutter.
	5 Let the biscuits rise for 30 minutes.
	6 Bake at 375° for 15 minutes.

Per biscuit: Calories 138 (From Fat 3); Fat 0g (Saturated 0g); Cholesterol 0mg; Sodium 215mg; Carbohydrates 29g (Dietary Fiber 1g); Protein 4g.

Tip: By cutting square biscuits instead of round ones, you handle the dough only once, resulting in light, fluffy biscuits.

Sourdough English Muffins

Prep time: 20 min, plus rising time • **Cook time:** 7–8 min • **Yield:** 12–16 muffins

Ingredients	Directions
4 cups flour	*1* In a small mixing bowl, mix together the flour, 4 tablespoons cornmeal, baking soda, and salt.
7 tablespoons cornmeal	
1 teaspoon baking soda	
¼ teaspoon salt	*2* In a separate medium mixing bowl, combine the starter and soured milk. Add the dry ingredients to the wet ingredients.
2 cups sourdough starter	
¾ cup soured milk (¾ cup milk with 1 teaspoon vinegar) or buttermilk	*3* Combine until the dough is firm enough to knead by hand. Turn out the dough onto a lightly floured counter and knead by hand until smooth.
	4 Roll the dough to ½-inch thickness. Cover the dough and let it rise for 10 minutes. Cut out muffins by using a large water glass or a round cutter.
	5 Dip the muffins in the remaining cornmeal and place them on a nonstick cookie sheet. Cover and let rise for 45 minutes to an hour.
	6 Heat a dry griddle on medium-high heat and cook the muffins, 3 or 4 at a time, for 7 to 8 minutes total, turning carefully. To serve, split the muffins and toast them.

Per muffin: Calories 208 (From Fat 8); Fat 1g (Saturated 0g); Cholesterol 0mg; Sodium 171mg; Carbohydrates 43g (Dietary Fiber 2g); Protein 7g.

Farmer's Bread

Prep time: 20 min, plus rising time • **Bake time:** 30 min • **Yield:** 6 loaves

Ingredients	Directions
7 teaspoons yeast	**1** In a 2-cup measuring cup, combine the yeast and 1 cup warm water. Let the yeast work for 5 minutes. (Fresh yeast becomes foamy during this time.)
5 cups warm water	
1 cup sugar	**2** In a large mixing bowl, mix the remaining water, sugar, salt, and melted lard. Add the yeast mixture and stir well. Add 4 cups whole-wheat or multigrain flour, mix well, and let stand for 45 minutes, or until bubbly and slightly risen. The mixture will resemble pancake batter.
2 tablespoons salt	
1 cup lard, melted	
4 cups whole-wheat or multigrain flour	
8 to 10 cups flour	**3** Mix in the remaining flour until the dough is easy to handle. Turn the dough onto a lightly floured counter and knead until elastic (5 minutes). Let it rise in a warm place until doubled in size (1 hour).
	4 Punch down the dough and let it rise again (1 hour). Divide the dough into 6 equal portions and roll each into a loaf shape. Place into greased loaf pans and let rise until doubled (30 minutes).
	5 Bake at 325° for 30 minutes. Remove the bread from the loaf pans immediately and place the loaves on a cooling rack. For best results, brush the loaves with melted butter or lard.

*Per slice ($^1/_{16}$ **of a loaf**): Calories 83 (From Fat 21); Fat 2g (Saturated 1g); Cholesterol 2mg; Sodium 146mg; Carbohydrates 14g (Dietary Fiber 1g); Protein 2g.*

Note: This recipe gives you perfect sandwich bread that holds up to slicing. The lard keeps the bread soft and tasty for 3 to 4 days.

Vary It! For perfect white bread, use all white flour.

Oatmeal Bread

Prep time: 30 min, plus rising time • **Bake time:** 30 min • **Yield:** 2 loaves

Ingredients	Directions
1 cup quick-cooking oats	**1** Place the oats, wheat flour, brown sugar, salt, and butter in a large mixing bowl. Pour boiling water over all. Let cool to lukewarm.
½ cup whole-wheat flour	
½ cup brown sugar	
1 tablespoon salt	**2** Dissolve the yeast in warm water and add to the batter. Add enough flour to make a smooth, elastic dough. Knead for 5 more minutes. Place the dough in a greased bowl and let it rise until doubled (1 hour).
2 tablespoons butter	
2 cups boiling water	
1 package dry yeast	**3** Punch down the dough and divide it into 2 equal portions. Create 2 loaf shapes and place each in a greased loaf pan. Let rise until nearly doubled (45 minutes).
½ cup warm water	
5 cups flour	
	4 Bake at 350° for 30 minutes. Immediately remove the bread from the pans onto a cooling rack. Butter the crust, if desired.

Per slice (¹⁄₁₆ of a loaf): Calories 106 (From Fat 10); Fat 1g (Saturated 1g); Cholesterol 2mg; Sodium 220mg; Carbohydrates 21g (Dietary Fiber 1g); Protein 3g.

Vary It! After the bread is baked, mix 1 tablespoon honey with 1 tablespoon melted butter. Brush the loaves with this mixture and sprinkle 1 tablespoon oats over both loaves.

Sprouting: Timing the process

Beans have different soaking and sprouting times, depending on the size and variety of bean. Some beans and seeds are super-fast, and others take up to 4 days.

Type	Soaking Time	Sprouting Time
Soybeans	12 hours	2 days
Pinto beans	12 hours	2 days
Lentils	12 hours	2 days
Alfalfa	12 hours	4 days
Wheat berries	12 hours	3 days

Sprouted Grain Bread

Prep time: 15 min, plus rising time • **Bake time:** 1 hr • **Yield:** 1 loaf

Ingredients	*Directions*
4½ cups sprouted grains ½ cup plus 2 tablespoons vital wheat gluten 1 teaspoon salt 1 package dry yeast 2 tablespoons honey ¼ cup sesame seeds ¼ cup sunflower seeds ¼ cup warm water	**1** Grind the sprouted grains in a food processor until smooth. In a large mixing bowl, combine the ground sprouts, vital wheat gluten, salt, yeast, honey, sesame seeds, sunflower seeds, and warm water. Stir until blended. The dough will be sticky but manageable.
	2 Turn out the dough onto a dampened countertop and knead for 10 minutes. Form the dough into a ball. Place the ball back in the mixing bowl, cover, and let rise for 1 hour.
	3 Shape the dough into a loaf shape and place it in a greased loaf pan. Cover and let rise until almost doubled (1 hour).
	4 Preheat the oven to 425°. Turn the oven down to 350° and bake the bread for 1 hour. Remove the bread immediately from the pan onto a cooling rack. Cool for 1 hour before slicing.

*Per slice (¹⁄₁₆ **of a loaf**): Calories 100 (From Fat 21); Fat 2g (Saturated 0g); Cholesterol 0mg; Sodium 151mg; Carbohydrates 17g (Dietary Fiber 1g); Protein 4g.*

Tip: Try these sprouts in this recipe: lentils, wheat berries, rye berries, chickpeas, soybeans, barley, or spelt.

Rye Bread

Prep time: 25 min, plus rising time • **Bake time:** 45 min • **Yield:** 2 loaves

Ingredients	Directions
1½ cups warm water	**1** In a large mixing bowl, combine the warm water and yeast. Allow to proof for 5 minutes.
4 teaspoons yeast	
⅓ cup brown sugar	**2** Add the brown sugar, molasses, salt, caraway seed, rye flour, and lard. Mix well. Add flour until the dough forms a manageable ball. Turn out the dough onto a lightly floured countertop and continue to knead until the dough is smooth and elastic (15 minutes).
¼ cup molasses	
1 tablespoon salt	
2 tablespoons caraway seed	
2½ cups rye flour	**3** Return the dough to the mixing bowl, cover the bowl, and allow the dough to rise until doubled (1 hour).
2 tablespoons lard	
3 cups all-purpose flour	**4** Punch down the dough and let it rise again until doubled (45 minutes). Divide the dough into 2 equal portions and shape each into a loaf. Place the dough into greased loaf pans and let rise until doubled (1 hour).
	5 Bake at 375° for 45 minutes. Remove the bread from the pans immediately onto a cooling rack. Cool for 1 hour before slicing.

*Per slice (¹⁄₁₆ **of a loaf**): Calories 99 (From Fat 9); Fat 1g (Saturated 0g); Cholesterol 1mg; Sodium 220mg; Carbohydrates 20g (Dietary Fiber 1g); Protein 2g.*

Vary It! Add a medium banana for extra sweetness.

Winter Squash Braided Bread

Prep time: 20 min, plus rising time • **Bake time:** 25 min • **Yield:** 1 loaf

Ingredients	Directions
⅓ cup warm milk	**1** In a large mixing bowl, combine the milk, water, yeast, and salt. Let the mixture sit until bubbly (5 minutes). Add the remaining ingredients. Mix well until a soft dough is formed.
2 tablespoons warm water	
1 package dry yeast	
¼ teaspoon salt	
1 cup cooked, pureed winter squash	**2** Turn the dough onto a lightly floured countertop, and knead until smooth, 5 minutes. Place the dough back in the mixing bowl, cover the bowl, and let the dough rise until doubled (1 hour).
3 tablespoons brown sugar	
¼ cup soft butter	**3** Punch down and divide the dough into three equal portions. Roll each portion of dough into an 18-inch-long piece.
1 egg	
3½ cups flour	
	4 On a greased cookie sheet, place the 3 pieces side by side. Press the 3 pieces together at one end. Braid the pieces and press the other end together firmly to keep the braid together. Cover and let rise until doubled (60 minutes).
	5 Bake in a 350° oven for 25 minutes. Cool slightly before slicing.

Per slice (¹⁄₁₆ of a loaf): Calories 149 (From Fat 33); Fat 4g (Saturated 2g); Cholesterol 22mg; Sodium 9mg; Carbohydrates 25g (Dietary Fiber 1g); Protein 4g.

Vary It! Brush with egg whites before baking for a glossy finish, if desired. You can substitute pumpkin for the winter squash.

Beer Bread

Prep time: 5 min • **Bake time:** 45 min • **Yield:** 1 loaf

Ingredients	*Directions*
2½ cups flour	*1* In a large mixing bowl, combine the flour, baking powder, salt, and brown sugar. Melt the butter and add it to the dry ingredients. Pour in the beer and mix until a soft dough is formed.
2 teaspoons baking powder	
1 teaspoon salt	
2 tablespoons brown sugar	*2* Spoon the dough into a greased 8-x-4-inch loaf pan. Bake for 45 minutes, or until golden brown. Remove the hot loaf from the pan and cool on a wire rack before slicing.
¼ cup butter	
1 cup beer	

Per slice (¹⁄₁₆ of a loaf): Calories 103 (From Fat 27); Fat 3g (Saturated 2g); Cholesterol 8mg; Sodium 194mg; Carbohydrates 17g (Dietary Fiber 1g); Protein 2g.

Tip: This recipe doubles very well. To freeze the extra loaf, wrap it in foil and then place it in a freezer bag with excess air removed.

Focaccia

Prep time: 25 min, plus rising time • **Bake time:** 20 min • **Yield:** 2 loaves

Ingredients	*Directions*
2 cups warm water	*1* In a large mixing bowl, combine the warm water with the sugar and yeast. Allow to become foamy for 5 minutes. Add the flour, salt, and ¼ cup olive oil and mix until dough forms.
1 teaspoon sugar	
1 package dry yeast	
6 cups flour	
1 teaspoon salt	*2* Turn the dough onto a lightly floured surface and knead until smooth dough forms (10 minutes). Place the dough back into the cleaned mixing bowl and cover. Let rest 1 hour, or until doubled.
¼ cup plus 2 tablespoons olive oil, divided	
1 tablespoon fresh rosemary	*3* Punch down the dough and divide it into 2 even pieces. Press the dough onto 2 round pizza stones or a cookie sheet, creating slight indentations on the surface of the flattened dough.
½ teaspoon salt, optional	
	4 Drizzle 2 tablespoons olive oil over the surface of the focaccia. Sprinkle rosemary and ½ teaspoon salt, if desired, evenly over both pieces. Bake in a 425° oven for 20 minutes, or until golden brown.

*Per slice (¹/₁₂ **of a loaf**): Calories 145 (From Fat 33); Fat 4g (Saturated 1g); Cholesterol 0mg; Sodium 98mg; Carbohydrates 24g (Dietary Fiber 1g); Protein 3g.*

Chapter 6

Beer-Brewing Basics

· ·

In This Chapter

▶ Deciding what equipment and ingredients you need

▶ Ensuring the cleanliness of your homebrewing setup

▶ Brewing a batch step by step

▶ Priming and bottling your beer

▶ Taking homebrewing to the next level

· ·

Homebrewing is one of the most sublime hobbies. Like canning vegetables grown in your backyard garden or baking bread in your own kitchen, homebrewing enables you to recapture the hands-on rusticity of the olden days while producing something that's an absolute delight to consume. Just as nothing can substitute for preparing a meal from your own garden, nothing is as gratifying as sipping a fresh beer brewed on your own kitchen stove.

Gathering Your Gear

Every homebrewer is a first-time brewer at least once, which means that every homebrewer needs to start with at least the minimum amount of equipment. With its barest essentials, homebrewing requires three tools: a *brewpot* in which you boil the *wort* (the German term for beer before it's fermented), a container in which you ferment the beer (the *fermenter*), and bottles in which you package the beer.

If this list sounds overly simplistic, that's because it is. The following sections talk about the necessary equipment for beginner and intermediate home-brewing endeavors.

Sniffing out sources

The first step in your homebrewing expedition is to locate your local homebrew supply retailer. Start with the phone book; try looking under *Hobbies* or *Beer*.

Stop in at your local homebrew supply shop and ask for a catalog and price list (if they have one). To the first-timer, the vast quantities of equipment and ingredient choices can be somewhat intimidating.

Don't fret if you don't have a local retailer in your area. Check out the Internet for homebrew supply websites. Homebrewing equipment varies, as shown in Figure 6-1, and any homebrew-supply shop worth its salt can get you just about anything you need.

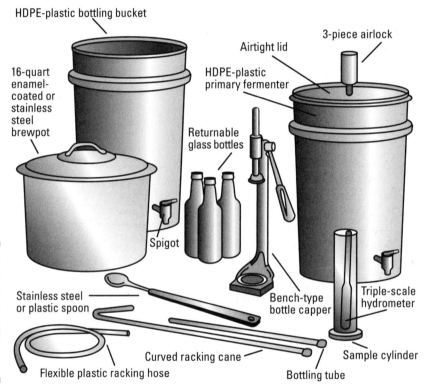

Figure 6-1:
Many homebrew shops sell this basic equipment as a startup kit.

HDPE-plastic bottling bucket

16-quart enamel-coated or stainless steel brewpot

Airtight lid

3-piece airlock

HDPE-plastic primary fermenter

Returnable glass bottles

Spigot

Stainless steel or plastic spoon

Bench-type bottle capper

Triple-scale hydrometer

Flexible plastic racking hose

Curved racking cane

Bottling tube

Sample cylinder

Finding equipment for the beginning brewer

For the benefit of beginning homebrewers, this section discusses only the minimal amount of equipment you need. Thrift is also a consideration, so we typically recommend cheaper alternatives over more expensive equipment and methods.

Many homebrew equipment suppliers sell prepackaged starter kits that can range from the bare-bones to the top-of-the-line — all-inclusive starter kits can run up to $300. All these kits include the basic equipment essentials, but some kits also throw in books, videos, or other unnecessary items that just inflate the price. Before you buy a kit, consider what you need and what you want to spend. To help you get the wheels turning, Table 6-1 gives you a starter list of necessary items and their approximate costs.

Table 6-1	Beginner Brewing Equipment and Its Cost
Equipment	*Approximate Cost*
Brewpot, 16 qt. minimum	$40/20 qt., $80/30 qt.
Brew spoon (HDPE plastic)	$5 or less
Primary fermenter (HDPE plastic) with spigot, lid	$20 or less
Airlock	$2 or less
Drilled rubber stopper for airlock	$2 or less
3 to 4 feet of food-grade plastic hose, ½ inch in diameter	$3
Bottling or "priming" bucket (HDPE plastic) with spigot	$15 or less
Bottles (must be the reusable type that don't use twist-off caps)	$30–$40 for one batch of beer (5 gallons); the exact number of bottles depends on their size: 12 oz., 16 oz., 22 oz., or 1 qt.
Bottle rinser	$15
Bottle brush	$3
Bottling tube (HDPE plastic) with spring valve	$4 or less
Bottle capper	$35 (bench-type) or $15 (two-handed)
Hydrometer (triple scale) with cylinder	$10 ($5 or less for the cylinder)

Okay, you've read the list in Table 6-1 and made your own list of what equipment you need. You're ready to go shopping, right? Not so fast. The following list gives you some insights into what all these gadgets do so that you can be a more informed consumer.

- **Brewpot:** Chances are good that you already have a large pot of some sort in your kitchen, but if your brewpot is made of enamel-coated metal, make sure that it's not chipped where it may come in contact with your beer. Your brewpot also needs to have a minimum 16-quart capacity, but we highly recommend you go ahead and upgrade to the 20- or 30-quart pot listed in Table 6-1.

The more of your wort you boil, the better for your finished beer. So, when it comes to brewpots, the bigger the better.

✔ **Brew spoon:** Regardless of how well equipped your kitchen is, every homebrewer needs to have a spoon dedicated for brewing beer and nothing else. A brew spoon needs to be stainless steel or HDPE (food-grade) plastic, and it needs to have a long handle — 18 inches or longer. Avoid wooden spoons because they can't be kept thoroughly sanitized (and they can splinter).

✔ **Primary fermenter:** The *primary fermenter* is where you pour the cooled wort shortly after you're done brewing. You must be able to seal this vessel airtight for the duration of the fermentation. A primary fermenter needs to have a minimum capacity of 7 gallons and an airtight lid with a hole in it (to accommodate an airlock with an attached rubber stopper). These specially made plastic fermenters come with removable plastic spigots positioned near the bottom for easy use.

✔ **Airlock:** An *airlock* is an inexpensive (but incredibly simple and efficient) tool that allows the carbon dioxide gases to escape from the fermenter during fermentation without compromising the antiseptic environment within. Filled halfway with water, this setup lets gas escape without allowing any air (and, therefore, germs) into the fermenter. A similar contraption, called a *bubbler,* is a two-chambered device that works on the same principle. The difference is that you can easily clean and sanitize the inside of an airlock (unlike the totally enclosed bubbler).

✔ **Drilled rubber stopper:** You need a rubber stopper to fit over the stem of the airlock or bubbler to act as a wedge when you insert the airlock into the hole in the fermenter lid. These drilled stoppers come in numbered sizes (for example, a #3 stopper). Be sure you buy a stopper that fits the opening in your fermenter lid. (Your homebrew equipment supplier can determine what you need.)

✔ **Plastic hose:** Flexible plastic hosing is a multifunctional piece of equipment you use to transfer your beer from vessel to vessel or from vessel to bottle. It's an important part of your equipment package and one that you need to always keep clean and undamaged. You want to have 3 to 5 feet of hosing.

✔ **Bottling bucket:** You need this vessel on bottling day. It doesn't require a lid, but it's considerably more efficient if you buy a bucket with a removable spigot at the bottom. The bottling bucket is also called a *priming vessel* because you prime your fermented beer with corn sugar just prior to bottling.

- **Glass bottles:** Your bottles must be the thick, heavy, returnable kind. Don't use any bottle with a threaded (twist-off) opening — a bottle cap doesn't seal properly across the threads. You need enough bottles to hold 5 gallons of beer: 54 12-ounce bottles, 40 16-ounce bottles, or any combination of bottles that adds up to 640 ounces. You can buy brand-new bottles from a homebrew supply shop, but you can get used bottles much more cheaply from commercial breweries.

- **Bottling tube:** This hard plastic tube is about a foot long and comes with a spring-loaded valve at the tip. You attach the bottling tube to the plastic hosing (which you then attach to the spigot on the bottling bucket) and insert the tube into the bottles when filling them.

- **Bottle brush:** Another inexpensive but important piece of equipment. You need this soft-bristle brush to properly scrub the inside of the bottles prior to filling.

- **Bottle rinser:** You attach this curved plastic or brass apparatus to a faucet. It works as an added convenience for rinsing bottles. This device isn't an absolute necessity, but for the money it's a good investment.

  If you buy a bottle rinser, take note of which faucet in your home you plan to use. Utility faucets usually have larger hose threads while others, such as bathroom and kitchen faucets, have fine threads where you may need an adapter. Make sure the bottle rinser and any adapters have a rubber washer (gasket) in place.

- **Bottle capper:** You need a bottle capper to affix new bottle caps to the filled bottles. These cappers come in all shapes, sizes, and costs.

  Most cappers work equally well, but we suggest that you choose a bench-type capper over the two-handed style. A *bench capper* is free-standing and can be attached to a work surface (permanently, if you like), which leaves one hand free to hold the bottle steady.

- **Triple-scale hydrometer:** A *hydrometer* is a fragile glass measuring device used to calculate the density of your beer as well as the amount of alcohol that the yeast has produced in your homebrew. *Triple scale* refers to the three different measuring scales within the hydrometer.

Book IV

Fermenting and Brewing

Assembling intermediate equipment

After you master homebrewing techniques at the novice level, you may be looking for a bigger challenge. This section is for the budding homebrewer who intends to get more personally involved in the brewing processes.

The list of equipment in Table 6-2 is based on the additional needs of the homebrewer who endeavors to try the intermediate brewing procedures.

Table 6-2   Intermediate Brewing Equipment and Its Cost

Equipment	Approximate Cost
Glass carboy (5 gallon)	$28 or less
Another airlock	$2 or less
Rubber stopper for carboy (drilled)	$2 or less
Carboy brush	$5 or less
Racking tube or cane	$3
8-inch plastic funnel	$10 or less
Kitchen strainer	$10 or less
Sparge bags	$5 (reusable nylon) $0.50 (disposable)
Lab immersion thermometer (or similar)	$10
Grain mill	$100 and up
Kitchen or postal scale	$20–$30

The following list explains why you need each gizmo in Table 6-2:

- ✔ **Glass carboy:** *Carboys* are the large cylindrical jugs that water delivery companies used for years until they switched to the plastic carboys used today. Because plastic carboys aren't really appropriate for homebrewing use, you need to purchase a glass carboy from your local homebrew supply store. The principal use for a glass carboy in homebrewing is as a secondary fermenter, where you age and mature your beer.

   Carboys may come in 3- to 15-gallon capacities, but the 5-gallon size best matches the typical batch of homebrew; therefore, it's probably the best choice for homebrewing purposes.

- ✔ **Rubber stopper:** If you intend to use the carboy as a fermenter, you need another drilled rubber stopper to fit the carboy's neck (usually a #6 or #7 stopper). As with the plastic primary fermenter, the carboy needs to be sealed with an airlock while the beer inside is aging.

- ✔ **Airlock:** You may not actually need another airlock in the brewery, but you may find you like to have a spare one around — besides, it costs less than a couple of bucks!

   Having a second airlock allows you to brew two batches in quick succession. While one batch is aging in the carboy, another can be fermenting in the primary fermenter.

- ✔ **Carboy brush:** If you want to continue to use the carboy as a fermenter, you need a carboy brush. This heavy-duty, soft-bristle brush is specially designed to reach every curve and corner of the carboy during cleaning.

✔ **Racking tube:** *Racking* is the act of transferring beer from one vessel to another, or into bottles, while leaving yeast sediment and particulate matter behind. Because carboys don't offer the convenience of a spigot, you need a hard-plastic, curved racking tube — also called a *cane* — to siphon the beer out.

✔ **Funnel:** Because the opening of the carboy is so small, a good funnel is a handy thing to have around. We recommend one with an opening at least 8 inches in diameter.

✔ **Kitchen strainer:** With the addition of loose grain, hops, and other ingredients to your brewpot, a strainer with a handle becomes a necessary piece of equipment. Food-grade steel mesh is better than plastic; don't settle for a strainer with a diameter of less than 10 inches or one without a strong handle. You may have to go to a culinary specialty store to find the right one.

✔ **Sparge bags:** Regardless of whether you have a strainer, *sparge bags* are effective for steeping grain or keeping whole-leaf hops under control in the brewpot. You can buy reusable nylon bags with drawstrings, or you can buy the inexpensive disposable kind.

✔ **Lab immersion thermometer:** Because temperature control becomes more and more important in brewing at the intermediate level, you probably want to have an immersion thermometer in your brewery. A lab-quality immersion thermometer is capable of temperature readings above the boiling point (212° Fahrenheit or 100° Celsius at sea level) and as low as 40° Fahrenheit (or 4.4° Celsius).

✔ **Grain mill:** A *grain mill* is one of the more expensive items you need. You use the grain mill to crack the grain prior to brewing with it. You can buy precracked grain, but many homebrew stores don't crack it properly (and precracked grain can also go stale more quickly). The mill-less homebrewer can find inventive ways to crack the grain, such as putting it into a large sealable plastic bag and rolling it with a rolling pin or baseball bat.

Whatever you do, don't use a coffee grinder to do your grain milling. If you do, your grain ends up looking like sawdust — and the way it looks is just the beginning of your problems. Grinding your grain too finely causes your beer to have an unpleasant, bitter, astringent taste.

✔ **Kitchen or postal scale:** After you start to brew beer according to specific recipes, you may find that you need many ingredients in small quantities. A good kitchen or postal scale is vital to getting these quantities just right because it can measure fractions of ounces.

Knowing Your Ingredients

Four basic building blocks make beer — barley (malt), hops, yeast, and water. This section looks at these ingredients and their role in the brewing process.

Malt: Going with grain

Of the four main ingredients used to make beer, barley — really, grain in general — makes the biggest contribution. It's responsible for giving beer its color, its underlying flavor, its sweetness, its body, its head of foam, and its *mouthfeel* (or the textural qualities of beer on your palate and in your throat — *viscosity*, or thickness; carbonation; alcohol warmth; and so on). Grains also contribute the natural sugars that feed the yeast, which in turn converts the sugars into alcohol and carbon dioxide during fermentation.

The word *malt* generally refers to the natural maltose sugars derived from certain grains (mainly barley) that eventually become beer. At the commercial brewing level, as well as the advanced homebrewing level, brewers produce beer through procedures that create and capture the malt sugars from the grain. At the beginner and intermediate levels of homebrewing, however, you use commercially produced malt syrup that eliminates the need for these procedures.

Before you can brew with barley, it must undergo a process known as *malting*. The malting process, simply put, simulates the grain's natural germination cycle. Fortunately for homebrewers (particularly novices), you can make beer much more easily, without having to deal with grains. You can buy a product called *malt extract,* which has been nothing less than a boon to the homebrewing industry. (Some professional brewers use it, too.)

Malt extract comes in two distinct forms. One is *liquid,* which is quite thick and viscous, and the other is *dry,* which is a rather sticky powder. Dry malt extract has a longer shelf life, due to lack of water, while liquid malt ages faster and turns darker.

Heading to hops heaven

If malts represent the sugar in beer, hops surely represent the spice. As a matter of fact, you use hops in beer in much the same way that you use spices in cooking. The divine mission of hops is to accent the flavor of beer and, most importantly, contrast the sweetness of the malt. This spiciness, however, isn't all hops have to contribute.

Hops contribute five qualities to beer:

- **Bitterness** offsets the cloyingly sweet flavor of malt
- **A zesty, spicy flavoring** accents the malt character in beer
- **A pungent floral/herbal aroma**
- **Bacterial inhibitors**
- **Natural clarifying agents**

Traditionally speaking, brewers handpicked hops from the vine and air-dried them in bulk before tossing them whole into the brewkettle. Today, however, hops are processed and sold in three different forms (shown in Figure 6-2): whole-leaf hops, pellets, and hop extract.

Figure 6-2:
Some of the different ways that brewers process hops.

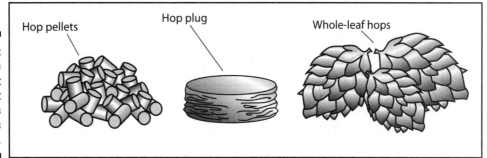

Hop pellets

Hop plug

Whole-leaf hops

More than 70 recognized hop varieties exist, and each hop variety offers different nuances in bittering intensity, flavor, and aroma. The differences between them are often so subtle that even the most experienced brewers and beer judges are hard-pressed to recognize their individual attributes in a given beer — especially when you consider that brewers often use blends of different hops in a single batch of beer.

How and when you use the hops determines the effect that they have on the finished brew. The longer you boil the hops, the more bitterness dissolves into the wort (up to a point). Boiling hops for 5 to 30 minutes imbues the beer with far less bitterness than the hops could potentially add, but you get some hop flavor. Adding hops very late in the boil and boiling them for less than 5 minutes provides the beer with aromatics and little else.

Many homebrew recipes tell you not only which hop varieties to use and in what quantities but also how long to boil them to get bittering, flavoring, or aromatizing characteristics from them.

Considering yeast and fermentation

Although yeast is an ingredient that the average beer consumer rarely contemplates, brewers often consider it the most important ingredient. In fact, yeast can have a greater influence and effect on the finished beer than any other single ingredient.

Book IV

Fermenting and Brewing

Yeast is a member of the fungus family. It's a living single-celled organism and one of the simplest forms of life. Because it has cell-splitting capabilities, it's also *self-reproducing*. Yeast is the one ingredient responsible for carrying out the fermentation process in brewing.

Fermentation, simply put, is the natural conversion of sugar to alcohol. Yeast has a voracious appetite for sweet liquids. And, in exchange for a good, sweet meal, yeast produces equal amounts of ethanol (ethyl alcohol) and carbon dioxide.

Fermentation is, indeed, magical and mystical. A simple yeast cell consumes sugar (in liquid form) and in turn excretes alcohol and carbon dioxide in addition to hundreds of flavor compounds. As part of the growth process, a single cell reproduces by cloning itself — splitting into two separate cells. Multiply this chain of events by billions, and you have fermentation.

Yeast for the homebrewer comes in both a dry form and a liquid form. Because of its convenience, we highly recommend dry yeast at the beginner level. Dry yeast comes in granular form in small foil packets. You simply tear these packets open and rehydrate the yeast in water before pitching it into fresh wort. However, because of dry yeast's lack of stylistic variety, you'll want to progress to liquid yeast cultures as soon as you're comfortable.

Factoring in water

Water is just one of the four primary ingredients used to make beer, but considering that it constitutes up to 95 percent of a beer's total ingredient profile, water can certainly have a tremendous influence on the finished product. The various minerals and salts found in water used for brewing can accentuate beer flavors or contribute undesirable flavor components.

Having said that, however, you can still make good beer with average tap water. Thousands of homebrewers are proving it every day. A very general rule says, "If your water tastes good, so will your beer." A caveat is important here, though: This general rule pertains solely to extract-based homebrews.

The importance of certain aspects of water composition becomes much more important when homebrewers begin mashing their own grains. And water chemical profiles are really important only to the small percentage of homebrewers who are determined to imitate the water found in famous brewing cities around the world.

At any skill level, keep the following things in mind:

- If your water is from a private underground well, it may be high in iron and other minerals that may affect your beer's taste.

- If your water is softened, it may be high in sodium.

- If your water is supplied by a municipal water department, it may have a high chlorine content. Other than chlorine, the *filtering* (the primary method of removing elements and impurities from water) performed at municipal water sources usually produces water that's sufficiently pure for brewing.

High iron, sodium, and chlorine contents in your brewing water aren't desirable. If these minerals are present in your brewing water, you may want to consider buying bottled water for your brewing needs.

Cleaning Up Your Act: Sanitation

Scrupulously clean brewing equipment and a pristine brewing environment are the keys to making good beer. And by clean, we don't mean just soap-and-water clean. In homebrewing, serious sanitation is necessary.

Take a closer look at a few important words used in this chapter. *Clean,* as it pertains to homebrewing, means that you've removed all dust, dirt, scum, stains, and other visible contaminants from your brewing equipment and bottles to the best of your ability. After the visible contaminants are history, you need to *sanitize* your equipment and bottles; sanitation is the elimination of invisible contaminants (bacteria and other microorganisms) that can ruin your brew. Clean requires a little elbow grease; sanitized requires chemicals.

Never assume that clean equipment is sanitized and never assume sanitized equipment is clean. For the good of your beer, practice good cleaning and sanitizing techniques — in that order.

A third and equally important word is *sterilize*. Sterilization is another method of germ-killing accomplished with very high temperatures (over 200°). Boiling your wort for at least an hour is an effective way of sterilizing the ingredients in your beer. After your wort cools, however, air-borne, water-borne, and human-borne germs can easily recontaminate it. For this reason, clean and sanitized equipment is imperative. From the boiling point forward, you need to treat your wort like a person without an immune system — safeguarded from the bacterial world.

Book IV

Fermenting and Brewing

Nothing is more important to your production of clean, drinkable, and enjoyable beer than utilizing proper sanitizing procedures prior to your brewing. You must sanitize or sterilize anything and everything that will come into contact with your beer at any time.

"What's the big deal?" you may ask. Well, millions of hungry *microbes* just love to make meals of freshly brewed beer. These microbes are in your home, on your body, and even in the air you breathe (cough, wheeze). Bacteria and fungi are the forms of microbes that you need to be wary of — they're both opportunistic, and if you let them have their way with your brew, they do so (always with negative results). Beer that bacteria have contaminated smells and tastes awful.

So, how can you get rid of these little beer-ruining pests? Well, in truth, you can't really get rid of them completely; the idea is to keep them away from your beer (or at least minimize their effect). We provide the following helpful tips to assist you in deterring these foes:

- ✔ Keep your brewery (kitchen, laundry room, basement, or wherever you make your beer) as clean and dust-free as possible.

- ✔ Quarantine all furry, four-legged family pets in another part of the house while you brew or bottle your beer.

- ✔ Consider every cough and sneeze a threat to your beer.

- ✔ Treat your equipment well. Clean and sanitize it properly prior to brewing, rinse it well, and dry it off after every use and before storing it away. Keep your equipment stored in a dust- and mildew-free location if at all possible. You may even want to go as far as sealing all your equipment in large-capacity garbage bags between brewing sessions.

The variety of chemicals that you can use to clean and sanitize your homebrewing equipment includes iodine-based products, chlorine-based products, *caustics* (which can burn your skin), ammonia, and a couple of environmentally safe cleansers that contain oxygen-based *percarbonates*. For my money, ordinary unscented household bleach is still the best bet.

Practicing safe sanitizing

The most effective methods of sanitizing involve soaking rather than intensive scrubbing. For this purpose, the best place to handle sanitizing procedures is in a utility basin or large-capacity sink.

Never use any abrasives or materials that can scratch your plastic or metal equipment, because pits and scratches are excellent hiding places for those wily bacteria. Using a very soft sponge that you've devoted to cleaning only homebrew equipment is a good idea.

When you're ready to begin sanitizing, follow these instructions:

1. **Place the items you want to sanitize in the plugged utility basin and begin drawing cold water into the basin.**

   Because chlorine is volatile, don't use hot water with bleach; the heat of the water causes the chlorine gas to leave the water much more quickly.

   If you're sanitizing the fermenter, carboy, or bottling bucket, you need to fill only those items rather than the whole basin or sink. You can place smaller items in the sanitizing solution within these larger items. However, for bottles, you need to fill the entire sink.

2. **As the water runs, add cleansing/sanitizing chemicals according to package directions or pour in 1 ounce unscented household bleach per gallon of water.**

3. **Completely immerse all the items you want to sanitize in the sanitizing solution.**

   Don't forget to include the fermenter lid, which you have to force into the fermenter sideways. Always allow 30 minutes for all bottles and equipment to soak.

4. **After 30 minutes, remove your equipment and thoroughly rinse the various pieces in hot water.**

5. **Sanitize the spigots on the fermenter and bottling bucket by draining the sanitizing solution through each spigot.**

6. **Allow everything to air dry.**

   The fermenter lid, placed upside down on a clean surface, is a good place to dry the smaller sanitized items.

Bottle cleanliness is a virtue

When you're ready for bottling, you need to clean and sanitize your bottles. You can clean your bottles pretty much at your convenience if you store them properly, but sanitizing your bottles too far ahead of time may lead to bacterial recontamination. Read more on sanitizing bottles in the section "Bottling Your Brew," later in this chapter.

Book IV

Fermenting and Brewing

Ready, Set, Brew: Beginners

Beginning brewers have to start somewhere, and that somewhere needs to be with an all-inclusive homebrewing kit. A *kit* is simply a package you buy from a homebrew supply store that includes all the ingredients (pre-hopped malt extract and a packet of yeast) that you need to brew a particular style of beer. The kits are ingredient kits only, mind you; they don't include any equipment.

But brewing beer from a kit also has a possible downside, depending on your perspective. At the beginner homebrewing level, you have little personal control over most of the beer-making process. When you use a kit, much of the thinking and the work have been done for you. This extra guidance is good if you're just starting out in the world of homebrewing and want to work with a net the first few times through the process.

You can master several aspects of homebrewing (sanitation, racking, observing fermentation, and bottling) at the beginner level. Thus, another simple rule at the beginner level: The more you brew, the better your beer gets. It's a delicious circle.

Assembling your tools

Before you start the brewing process, make sure you have all your homebrewing equipment (see the "Gathering Your Gear" section earlier in this chapter), you've properly sanitized it (see the previous section, "Cleaning Up Your Act: Sanitation"), and it's in place and ready to use. Here's a quick equipment checklist for you:

✔ Airlock

✔ Brewpot with lid

✔ Brew spoon

✔ Coffee cup or small bowl (for proofing the yeast)

✔ Fermentation bucket with lid

✔ Rubber stopper (to attach to the airlock)

✔ Hydrometer (the hydrometer cylinder isn't necessary at this time)

Now you just need a couple of simple household items to complete the ensemble. Gather and sanitize a long-handled spoon or rubber spatula (for scraping the gooey malt extract from the cans), hot pads (to hold onto hot pots and pans), and a small saucepan (to heat up the cans of extract). Speaking of which, be sure to have your homebrew kits on hand.

We recommend either two 3.3-pound cans of pre-hopped malt extract (plus yeast) or one 6.6-pound can. This is the appropriate amount for the average 5-gallon batch of beer. The style of beer or brand of malt extract is your choice.

Brewing your first batch

The following numbered list covers 24 steps that walk you all the way through the brewing process. Twenty-four steps may sound pretty intense, but they're easy, quick, and painless steps.

1. **Fill your brewpot about two-thirds full with clean tap water or bottled water and then place it on the largest burner of your stove.**

   The exact volume of water isn't terribly important during this step, because you add cold water to the fermenter later to bring the total to 5 gallons.

2. **Set the burner on medium-high.**

3. **Remove the plastic lids from the kits and set the yeast packets aside.**

4. **Strip the paper labels off the two cans of extract and place the cans in a smaller pot or saucepan filled halfway with tap water; place the pot or saucepan on another burner near the brewpot.**

   The water's purity isn't important here because you don't use this water in the beer.

5. **Set the second burner on medium.**

6. **Using hot pads, flip the cans in the warming water every couple of minutes.**

7. **As the water in the brewpot begins to boil, turn off the burner under the smaller pot (containing the cans), remove the cans from the water, and remove the lids from the cans.**

8. **Using a long-handled spoon or rubber spatula, scrape as much of the warmed extract as possible from the cans into the water in the brewpot.**

9. **Immediately stir the extract/water solution and continue to stir until the extract completely dissolves in the water.**

   This malt extract/water mixture is now officially called *wort*.

    If you don't stir the wort immediately, you risk scorching the extract on the bottom of the brewpot.

10. **Top off the brewpot with more clean tap or bottled water, keeping your water level a reasonable distance — about 2 inches — from the top of the pot to avoid boilovers.**

11. **Bring the wort to a boil.**

    Turn up the burner, if necessary.

Book IV

Fermenting and Brewing

12. **Boil the wort for about an hour, stirring the pot every couple of minutes to avoid scorching and boilovers.**

    Never put the lid on the brewpot during the boiling phase! Stove-top boilovers occur regularly when a brewpot's lid is on. Boilovers are not only a sticky, gooey mess, but also a waste of good beer!

13. **Turn off the burner and place the lid on the brewpot.**

14. **Put a stopper in the nearest sink drain, put the covered brewpot in the sink, and fill the sink with very cold water.**

    Fill the sink completely (or up to the liquid level in the brewpot if the sink is deeper than the brewpot).

15. **After 5 minutes, drain the sink and refill it with very cold water — repeat as many times as you need until the brewpot is cool to the touch.**

16. **While the brewpot is cooling in the sink, draw at least 6 ounces of lukewarm tap water into a sanitized cup or bowl.**

17. **Open the yeast packets and pour the dried yeast into the cup or bowl of water.**

    Called *proofing,* this process is a gentle but effective way to wake up the dormant yeast and ready it for the fermentation to follow.

18. **When the brewpot is relatively cool to the touch, remove the brewpot lid and carefully pour the wort into the fermentation bucket.**

    Make sure the spigot is closed!

19. **Top off the fermenter to the 5-gallon mark with cold, clean water, pouring it vigorously into the bucket.**

    This splashing not only mixes the wort with the additional water, but also aerates the wort well.

    The yeast needs oxygen in order to get off to a good healthy start in the fermentation phase. Because boiled water is virtually devoid of oxygen, you need to put some oxygen back in by aerating the wort. Failure to aerate may result in sluggish and sometimes incomplete fermentations.

20. **Take a hydrometer reading.**

    See the section "Brewing-day reading," later in this chapter, for specific information about this process.

21. **After you take the hydrometer reading and remove the hydrometer, pour the hydrated yeast from the cup or bowl into the fermenter and give it a good brisk stir with your brew spoon.**

22. **Cover the fermenter with its lid and thoroughly seal it.**

23. **Put the fermenter in a cool, dark location, such as a basement, a crawl space, or an interior closet.**

Don't put the fermenter in direct sunlight or where the temperatures fluctuate daily, as they do in your garage. This temperature fluctuation can mess with your beer's fermentation cycle.

24. **After the fermenter is in a good place, fill the airlock halfway with water and replace the cap; attach the rubber stopper and position it snugly in the fermenter lid.**

    Check to make sure that the fermenter and airlock are sealed airtight by pushing down gently on the fermenter lid. This gentle pressure causes the float piece in the airlock to rise; if it doesn't, you have a breach in the seal. Recheck the lid and airlock for leaks.

    Fermentation should begin within the first 24 hours and last anywhere from 7 to 10 days. This wait can be nerve-wracking for first-timers, but patience is rewarded with great beer.

How quickly the beer begins to ferment and how long the fermentation lasts depends on the amount of yeast, the health of the yeast, the temperature at which the beer is fermenting, and whether the wort was properly aerated. Healthy yeast, mild temperatures (65° to 70°), and an abundance of oxygen in the wort make for a good, quick ferment. Old, dormant yeast, cold temperatures, and under-oxygenated wort cause fermentations to start slowly, go on interminably, or even quit altogether.

After your beer has been in the fermenter for about a week or so, check the bubbling action in the airlock. If visible fermentation is still taking place (as evidenced by the escaping bubbles), continue to check the bubbling on a daily basis. When the float piece within the airlock appears to be still and the time between bubbles is a minute or more, your beer is ready for bottling. Before you begin the bottling procedures, however, you need to take a second gravity reading to make sure that the fermentation is complete. (See the section "Prebottling reading," later in this chapter, for specifics.)

Bottling beer before it's done fermenting may result in exploding bottles.

Taking hydrometer readings

The following information shows you specifically how to take hydrometer readings on brewing and bottling days.

Brewing-day reading

You want to take the first hydrometer reading on brewing day (see Step 20 in the earlier "Brewing your first batch" section of this chapter). To take a good reading, do the following:

1. **Lower the sanitized hydrometer directly into the cooled and diluted wort inside the fermenter.**

Book IV

Fermenting and Brewing

As you lower the hydrometer into the wort in the fermenter, give the hydrometer a quick spin with your thumb and index finger; this movement dislodges any bubbles clinging to the hydrometer that may cause you to get an incorrect reading.

2. **Record the numbers at the liquid surface on the hydrometer scales.**

   You need this information on bottling day to decide whether fermentation is complete and to figure out the alcohol content in your beer. The gravity of your malt extract and water mixture will determine the numbers you'll see on the scales. Typically, 6 or so pounds of malt extract diluted in 5 gallons of water appear on the hydrometer's O.G. scale as 1.048, and the alcohol potential (as noted on the hydrometer's alcohol potential scale) is around 6 percent.

Prebottling reading

When you think your beer is ready for bottling (based on the bubbling action in the airlock), it's time to take another hydrometer reading. When compared to the first (brewing day) reading, this reading helps you decide whether your beer is actually ready to be bottled.

1. **With your hydrometer test cylinder in hand, take a sample of beer from the spigot of the fermenter.**

   Fill the cylinder to within 1 inch of the opening, leaving room for liquid displacement of the immersed hydrometer.

2. **Immerse the hydrometer in the beer, record the numbers at the liquid surface of the hydrometer, and compare with those numbers recorded on brewing day.**

   Remember that the average healthy yeast consumes at least 65 percent of the available sugars in the wort. If the final gravity reading on your fermented beer isn't 35 percent or less of the original gravity, too much natural sugar may be left in your beer.

Calculating alcohol content percentage

Here's a sample figuring for your first batch of beer to help you figure out how much alcohol has been produced in your beer during fermentation. If you use about 6 pounds of liquid malt extract for your brew, your original gravity (or *O.G.* in homebrew lingo) is in the neighborhood of 1.048. If your yeast is good and hungry, your final gravity *(F.G.)* a week or so later (after fermentation) will be about 1.012. Because a *ten-forty eight* (also acceptable homebrewer lingo for the 1.048 gravity) represents an alcohol potential of 6 percent, and a *ten-twelve* (the 1.012 gravity) represents an alcohol potential of 2 percent, the yeast produced 4 percent alcohol in your brew. (Subtract the final alcohol potential from the original alcohol potential to derive the alcohol content percentage.)

Here's a sample equation: If your beer has an original gravity of 1.048, subtract 1 so that you have 0.048; then multiply 0.048 by 0.35, which results in 0.017. Now add the 1 back in. If the final gravity of your beer is higher than 1.017, you want to delay bottling a few more days.

After you take your hydrometer reading, *don't* pour the beer from the cylinder back in with the rest of the beer — if you do so, you risk contaminating your beer.

A Primer on Priming

As you may know, yeast is responsible for producing the natural carbonation in beer and other fermentable beverages. And, because carbon dioxide escapes from the fermenter, you may be wondering how you can put the carbonation back into your beer. The answer is a simple little trick called priming.

Priming means adding more fermentable sugar to the beer just prior to bottling it. The small number of yeast cells that remain in the solution when you bottle your brew gladly see to it that they eat the sugars you add and thus provide the desired carbonation within the bottle. Of course, this process doesn't happen overnight. You need to allow another one to two weeks before your beer is properly carbonated and ready to drink.

Getting ready to prime

When you choose a priming sugar for beer, you need to consider two things: the *quantity* and the *fermentability* of the priming ingredient you're going to use. The first factor is dependent on the second factor.

The idea of priming is to put more fermentable sugar into the beer so that the yeast can create the needed carbonation within the bottle. But consider the consequences of giving the yeast too little or too much sugar to eat: Too little priming sugar can result in an undercarbonated beer, but too much sugar may cause your bottles to explode! Don't panic — proper priming quantities are covered in the next section.

Two important points regarding beer priming: First, not all beer styles contain the same level of carbonation. The second important point is that high-gravity beers you intend to condition in the bottle over longer periods of time are likely to build up increasing carbonation levels as they age.

Book IV

Fermenting and Brewing

Making primer decisions

Different sugar sources (refined sugar, honey, molasses, and so on) have different levels of fermentability, which means that the more fermentable sugar a priming mixture has, the less of the mixture you need. Conversely, you need more of a priming mixture with less fermentable sugar. Note that because you use them in such small quantities, priming sugars have virtually no effect on the beer's taste.

To keep the priming process simple, use dextrose (corn sugar). Dextrose is highly fermentable, widely available, easy to work with, and inexpensive.

Regardless of what form of priming sugar you use to prime your beer, always dissolve and dilute it in boiling water first and allow the priming mixture to cool before adding it to the beer. The amount of water used to boil the sugar in is of little concern — 1 or 2 cups are typical.

In the average 5-gallon batch of beer, ¾ of a cup (*not* ¾ of a pound!) of dextrose is the maximum recommended amount for priming. Using more than this may result in exploding bottles but is more likely to result in overcarbonated beer and *gushers* — bottles that act like miniature volcanoes when your buddies pry the caps off. Hmmm, sounds like a good prank, come to think of it.

Bottling Your Brew

Bottling homebrew isn't a difficult procedure, but brewers often deride it as one that's tedious at worst and boring at best. But for millions of people who brew their beer at home, bottling represents the only option for packaging their finished brew.

Picking out bottles

Using good, sound, safe bottles is an important part of the bottling process. Your beer may start out as a world-class brew, but if the bottles aren't worthy, you can end up with leaks, explosions, and sticky messes. When you're buying bottles, don't skimp.

Bottles come in all sizes and shapes, but check out these very important suggestions. Your homebrew bottles

✔ **Should be the thick, returnable type (no cheap throwaways).** The thick, returnable-type bottles can withstand repeated uses; cheap throwaways mean thin glass and easy breakage.

✔ **Should be made of colored glass (the darker the better).** Light damages beer; tinted glass protects against light damage.

✔ **Shouldn't have a twist-off opening.** Bottle caps can't seal across the threads on twist-off bottles.

✔ **Should be of uniform size.** Although uniform bottles aren't a requirement, having all your beer in bottles of the same size and shape makes capping and storing much easier.

Using larger bottles is a way to expedite the bottling process as well as free you from its drudgery. The more beer the bottles can hold, the fewer bottles you need.

Preparing to bottle

Before you start any bottling procedures, take a hydrometer reading of the beer in the fermenter to verify that fermentation is sufficiently complete. Just steal a little beer out of the spigot to fill the hydrometer cylinder to within an inch of the top (but no more). (See the earlier section, "Prebottling reading," for more information.)

After you've made certain that the beer is done fermenting, retrieved the bottling equipment, and quarantined the family pets, you're ready to start the bottling process. As always, setup starts with sanitizing all the necessary equipment (see the "Cleaning Up Your Act: Sanitation" section, earlier in this chapter):

✔ A bottling bucket

✔ A racking cane (if bottling from a vessel without an attached spigot)

✔ A plastic hose

✔ A bottling tube (with spring-action or gravity-pressure valve)

✔ Bottles (enough to hold 640 ounces of beer)

✔ Bottle caps (enough to cap all your bottles, plus some extras — just in case)

You need to sanitize all these items before bottling, so you also need a sanitizing agent. You also need the following:

✔ A bottle brush

✔ A bottle rinser

✔ A bottle capper

✔ Two small saucepans

✔ ¾ cup dextrose (corn sugar) for priming (see "A Primer on Priming," earlier in this chapter)

Now, here are the steps for the bottling brigade:

1. **Fill your utility tub or other designated sanitizing basin with enough cold water to cover your submerged bottles, adding bleach or another sanitizing agent according to the package directions.**

2. **Submerge as many bottles as you need to contain your full batch of 5 gallons of beer.**

   Make sure that your bottles are scum-free before dunking them in the sanitizing solution. Any bottle with dried or living crud in the bottom needs to be scrubbed separately with a cleanser such as trisodium phosphate (TSP) before you sanitize it.

   You can fill and submerge the bottles in less than half the time if you place a drinking straw in the bottles; the straw enables the air within the bottle to escape through the straw instead of slowly bubbling through the opening (your bottling tube with the valve detached suffices here).

3. **Allow your bottles to soak for at least half an hour (or the time necessary according to package directions).**

4. **While the bottles soak, dissolve ¾ cup of dextrose in a pint or so of water in one of the saucepans, cover the solution, and place it on a burner over low heat.**

5. **Put your bottle caps into your other saucepan, fill the pan with enough water to cover all the caps, and place the pan on another burner over low heat.**

   Put enough bottle caps for as many bottles as you have soaking, plus a few extra; having too many sterilized caps ready for bottling is better than not having enough.

6. **Allow both pans to come to a boil, remove them from the heat, and allow them to cool.**

7. **After the bottles soak for half an hour, connect the bottle rinser to the faucet over the sanitizing tub.**

8. **With one hand over the opening (so that you don't get squirted), turn on the hot water.**

   After the initial spray, the bottle washer holds back the water pressure until a bottle is lowered over the stem and pushed down.

9. **Start cleaning the bottles one by one with the bottle brush and then drain the sanitizer, rinse your bottles with the bottle rinser, and allow them to air dry.**

   Continue this step until all bottles are clean.

   Visually check each bottle for cleanliness rather than just assume that they're all clean.

Four dozen free-standing bottles make one heck of a breakable domino effect. Always put your cleaned bottles back into six-pack holders or cardboard cases to avoid an aggravating and easily avoidable accident.

10. **Drain the utility tub of the bottle-cleaning water.**

11. **Place the bottling bucket in the tub and fill it with water and the sanitizing agent of your choice.**

12. **Place the bottling hose, bottling tube, and hydrometer cylinder into the bottling bucket and allow them to soak for half an hour (or according to sanitizing agent directions).**

13. **While the bottling equipment soaks, retrieve the still-covered fermenter from its resting place and place it on a sturdy table, counter, or work surface about 3 or 4 feet off the ground.**

    At this point, you need to set up your bottling station, making sure that you have the priming sugar mixture (still in the saucepan), bottle caps, bottle capper, bottles, and hydrometer with cylinder on hand.

    If you're bottling your brew directly from the primary fermenter, you want to have already taken a hydrometer reading to confirm completion of fermentation. If you're bottling from your secondary fermenter (glass carboy; see Chapter 7), incomplete fermentation isn't a concern, and you can take a hydrometer reading (to determine final gravity and alcohol content) as the beer drains into the bottling bucket.

14. **After half an hour, drain the sanitizing solution from the bottling bucket through the spigot on the bottom and, after the bucket is empty, thoroughly rinse the remaining pieces of equipment (hose, bottling tube), along with the bottles and caps, and bring them to your bottling station.**

Pouring a cold one: Getting your beer into bottles

As soon as your bottling station is all set up and ready to go, start bottling your brew by following these steps:

1. **Place the bottling bucket on the floor directly below the fermenter and connect the plastic hosing to the spigot on the fermenter, allowing the other end of the hosing to hang inside the bottling bucket.**

   If you're initiating the bottling procedures from your glass carboy (see Chapter 7), you can't rely on the convenience of a spigot to drain out the beer. You need to use your racking cane and siphon the brew.

2. **Pour the dextrose and water mixture into the bottling bucket.**

   See the earlier section, "A Primer on Priming," for more on dextrose.

The dissolved corn sugar mixes with the beer as the beer drains from the fermenter into the bottling bucket. After you've bottled the beer, this sugar becomes another source of food for the few yeast cells still remaining in the liquid. As the yeast consumes the sugar, it produces the beer's carbonation within the bottle. Eventually, the yeast again falls dormant and creates a thin layer of sediment on the bottom of each bottle.

If, by chance, you bottle a batch of beer that isn't fully fermented or you somehow add too much dextrose at bottling time, you may find out first-hand what a mess exploding bottles can make. Excess sugar (whether added corn sugar or leftover maltose from an unfinished fermentation) overfeeds the yeast in an enclosed bottle. With nowhere for the pressure to go, the glass gives before the bottle cap. Kaboom! Mess! Do not overprime. (Use no more than ¾ cup of dextrose in 5 gallons of beer.) See the "A Primer on Priming" section in this chapter for more advice on priming.

3. **Open the spigot on the fermenter and allow all the beer to run into the bottling bucket.**

Don't try to salvage every last drop from the fermenter by tilting it as the beer drains down the spigot. The spigot is purposely positioned about an inch above the bottom of the fermenter so that all the spent yeast and miscellaneous fallout remains behind.

4. **After the last of the beer drains, close the spigot, remove the hose, and rinse it.**

Avoid splashing or aerating your beer as you bottle it. Any oxidation that the beer picks up now can be tasted later. Yuck.

5. **Carefully place the bottling bucket up where the fermenter was, connect the rinsed hose to the spigot on the bottling bucket, and attach the bottling tube to the other end of the hose.**

6. **Arrange all your bottles on the floor directly below the bottling bucket.**

Keep them all in cardboard carriers or cases to avoid potential breakage and spillage.

7. **Open the spigot on the bottling bucket and begin to fill all the bottles.**

Gently push the bottling tube down on the bottom of each bottle to start the flow of beer. The bottle may take a short while to fill, but the process always seems to accelerate as the beer nears the top. Usually, a bit of foam rushes to the top of the bottle; don't worry! As soon as you withdraw the bottling tube, the liquid level in the bottle falls.

8. **Remove the tube from each bottle after foam or liquid reaches the top of the bottle.**

Figure 6-3 shows you how full you want your bottles to be.

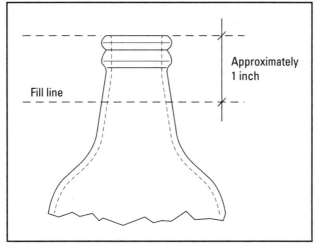

Figure 6-3:
Correct
bottle fill
level.

After you remove the bottling tube from the bottle, the level of the beer falls to about an inch or so below the opening. Homebrewers have differing opinions as to how much airspace (or *ullage*) is necessary. Some say the smaller the airspace, the less oxidation that can occur. Others claim that if you don't have correct ullage, the beer can't carbonate properly. Rather than jump into the fray, we say that if it looks like the space in bottles of beer from commercial breweries, go with it!

9. **After you completely drain the bottling bucket, close the spigot, remove the hose, toss it inside the bottling bucket, and set everything aside to be cleaned after all the bottling procedures are complete.**

10. **Place all the bottles on your tabletop or work surface; place a cap on each bottle, position your bottles in the capper (one at a time), and pull down on the capper handle or levers slowly and evenly.**

   You may want to do this task as soon as each bottle is full as insurance against everything that can go wrong when full bottles of your precious brew are sitting around open.

   Both bench- or two-handle-style cappers come with small magnets in the capper head designed to hold and align the cap as you start crimping. We don't trust the magnet to hold the caps in alignment and prefer to seat them on the bottles by hand.

   Occasionally, a cap may crimp incorrectly. If you suspect that a cap didn't seal right, tilt the bottle sideways and check for leakage. If you find you have a leaker, yank the cap and replace it. (You boiled extras — right?)

Book IV

Fermenting and Brewing

11. **Your homebrew needs to undergo a two-week conditioning phase, so store your liquid lucre in a cool, dark location (such as the same place that you kept the fermenter).**

    This phase is where the remaining yeast cells chow down on the dextrose and carbonate your beer.

    Putting your brew in the fridge isn't a good idea — at least for the first two weeks — because the very cold temperatures stunt the yeast's carbonating activity.

12. **Thoroughly rinse your brewing equipment in hot water and store it in a place that's relatively dust- and mildew-free; you may even want to go that extra step and seal all your equipment inside a large-capacity garbage bag.**

    This step may be the most important one of all, not so much for the brew just made but for the next one. Consider this step an insurance policy on your next batch of beer. Boring but worthwhile, like most insurance policies.

After two weeks pass, check to see whether the bottles have clarified (the yeasty cloudiness has settled out). Chill a bottle or two for taste-testing. Like any commercial beer, you need to decant homebrew before drinking, not only to release the carbonation and the beer's aromatics but also to pour a clear beer. Drinking homebrew out of the bottle stirs up the sediment, creating a hazy beer.

Brewing: Intermediate Steps

The basic differences between beginner and intermediate homebrewing can be easily — but not completely — summed up in a few lines. Intermediate brewers can

- ✔ Use specialty grains to add more color and flavor in your beer.
- ✔ Choose and add hops as opposed to using hopped extract.
- ✔ Use liquid yeast cultures instead of freeze-dried yeast.
- ✔ Perform secondary fermentation procedures.

The combination of ingredient changes and new procedures can make a world of difference in the quality of your homebrew. And you don't even have to apply these changes all at once.

Your first step away from being a novice brewer is to take effective but simple measures toward improving your beer. The first of these measures has to do with adding more and better ingredients.

Whenever you buy homebrewing ingredients, make sure you store them properly if you aren't going to use them immediately. You need to refrigerate all grains, hops, and yeast packets. (Freeze the hops if you plan to store them long term.) Never allow any of your ingredients to lie around in a warm environment or in direct sunlight, even if they ask you nicely. Think of beer ingredients as food products and think of the way most food products decay over time — especially in warmer environments.

Using different ingredients is only one way that intermediate homebrewers set themselves apart from the beginners. The other way is by using different methods of conditioning.

Conditioning means allowing your beer additional time to mature, mellow, clarify, and carbonate.

Conditioning for better beer with secondary fermentation

Secondary or *two-stage fermentation* is all about conditioning your beer. When you brewed at the beginner level, you put the fresh wort in the primary fermenter, let the yeast do its thing, and then you bottled the beer. The beer had about two weeks to condition in the bottle before you started drinking it. You did the right thing (within the limitations of your equipment and expertise), but now you can do more.

At the beginner level, taking the freshly fermented beer out of the primary fermenter was necessary not just because the initial fermentation was over, but also because all those little yeasties, fresh from a gluttonous feast, were about to start decomposing. That's right, enzymes in the sugar-starved yeast begin to break down the yeast cells. This horrific event is called yeast *autolysis.* Autolysis can impart a sulfury, rubbery stench and flavor to your beer. So leaving your fresh, young beer sitting on that bulging layer of self-destructing yeast dregs is akin to allowing your child to wallow with pigs in the mud — and you don't want to smell either one of them when they're done. Racking your beer over to a secondary fermentation vessel effectively leaves most of the sedimented yeast and other organic matter behind.

So if bottling the beer after one week worked before, why can't it now? It still can, but now that you're introducing more ingredients into the brewpot, the added flavors and textures in your beer need more time to blend together. By allowing the beer to undergo a secondary fermentation, you promote a mellowing process that makes a noticeable improvement in your beer.

Considering the advantages of secondary fermentation

Allowing your beer to age in a secondary fermenter before you bottle it also reduces *yeast bite,* the harsh flavor and mouthfeel associated with having excessive yeast sediment in the bottle.

Because the yeast has eaten most of the consumable sugars in the wort during primary fermentation, secondary fermentation yields very little yeast activity and rarely produces a measurable amount of alcohol. This second fermentation period is just an opportunity for all the beer's ingredients to acclimate to one another and establish a friendly (and tasty) relationship.

The secondary fermenter represents a world of new possibilities for your brew. You can add many different additives and flavorings to the secondary fermenter that may have a huge effect on the finished beer.

The two-stage aspect of secondary fermentation also allows you to perform some real beer-improving feats:

- **Dry hop:** You can impart more hop aroma to your beer by simply adding ¼ ounce to 2 ounces of hops (in pellet, plug, or whole leaf form) to the secondary fermenter and then draining your beer over them. You can do the same thing with spices, too.

- **Make true lagers:** In order to make genuine lager beers, you must age the beer in the secondary fermenter for at least a few weeks at very cold temperatures (32° to 40°) for proper flavor development.

- **Clarify your brew:** You can add various clarifying agents to the secondary fermenter to speed up the process of clarification.

One final vote in support of secondary fermentation: By using this procedure, you can not only quit worrying about unfinished primary fermentations (and exploding bottles), but also actually cut the primary ferment short by a day or two if that helps you rack the beer over to the secondary fermenter at a more convenient time. This shortcut is possible *only* after the peak fermentation activity subsides (usually by the fifth or sixth day of a normal, healthy fermentation).

Jumping into secondary fermentation

Secondary fermentation always needs to take place in either glass or stainless steel vessels. A 5-gallon glass carboy is the most popular secondary fermentation vessel, though a few homebrewers prefer to age their beer in stainless steel soda kegs. However, we don't recommend secondary fermentation in plastic vessels. Even the food-grade plastics used to make homebrewing equipment are penetrable by certain gasses (such as oxygen) over an extended period of time.

Remember that no phase of homebrewing is exempt from cleaning and sanitizing. When you add another fermentation phase, you must disinfect all the equipment that goes along with it. In addition to the use of a good sanitizing agent, you want to use a carboy brush to make sure you scrub the entire inner surface of the carboy. Rinse the carboy well with hot water and allow it to air-dry. Be sure to have an appropriately sized, sanitized rubber stopper to seal the carboy, as well as an airlock. Don't forget to sanitize all other equipment, especially the plastic hosing, before you use it. If necessary, review the sanitation methods we discuss earlier in this chapter.

If you decide to use liquid additives or flavorings (or the kind that can be dissolved in water), you can simply pour them into the carboy prior to adding the beer (which takes care of mixing). If your additive or flavoring is bulky or leafy, you want to place it in a hop bag or some kind of filter for easy removal. This bag saves you some work, because you have to strain whatever you put into the secondary fermenter out of the brew on bottling day.

Speaking of bottling, the procedure is delayed another week or two while the beer is mellowing in the carboy. A secondary fermentation isn't really worth the effort unless you allow it to last at least one week. Two to three weeks is the norm, and a month or more may be needed for barley wines, imperial stouts, and other complex and high-gravity beers and meads.

Before transferring your beer from the primary fermenter to the secondary fermenter, you want to be sure that the initial, vigorous fermentation (also called *high kraeusen*) is complete. You can do this check simply by watching the bubbles in the airlock. If they appear at half-minute or longer intervals, you can proceed with the following racking procedures:

1. **Place your primary fermenter on a table or sturdy work surface and position the empty carboy on the floor directly below the fermenter.**

2. **Connect one end of the plastic hose to the spigot on the primary fermenter and put the other end inside the carboy.**

   Be sure that you space the two vessels so that the dangling plastic hose reaches the bottom of the carboy — this practice prevents aerating the beer as you drain it. You may want to prop up the carboy on beer bottle cases, a step stool, or large books (basically, anything that can withstand the weight of a carboy full of beer).

3. **Fill the carboy with beer to within an inch or two of the opening.**

   In some cases, you may have to stop the flow of beer before it finishes draining out of the primary fermenter; in other cases, you may have to top off the carboy with clean water that you've boiled and cooled down. What little water you may need to add doesn't affect the beer's gravity.

Book IV

Fermenting and Brewing

Speaking of gravity, you don't need to take a hydrometer reading when you rack the beer from the primary to the secondary fermenter, but if you do, you can get an idea of how your brew is progressing and how long you need to consider leaving it in the carboy. Getting a beer sample from the hose into the hydrometer test cylinder can be tricky and may lead to a big mess if you're not careful. The key is to control the flow of beer with the spigot on the primary fermenter. Just remember to practice good sanitation and avoid aerating your beer.

4. **Place the appropriate rubber stopper in the neck of the carboy, fill your airlock halfway with water, and place it in the hole in the rubber stopper.**

5. **Store the filled carboy in a cool, dark place for a couple of weeks.**

   Padlock the door to the room where you've stashed the carboy and position a sentinel at the threshold. You're just 14 days away from some of the best beer you've ever tasted.

When you're ready to bottle your well-conditioned brew, you'll have no choice but to use siphoning procedures to drain the carboy, because carboys don't have spigots for convenience. Take a look at the "Mastering the art of siphoning" sidebar for more information.

Mastering the art of siphoning

The use of a carboy in homebrewing requires you to practice your siphoning techniques, because carboys don't come equipped with spigots. To perform such siphoning, you need a curved racking tube (or *cane*) and your plastic hosing.

The most effective siphoning occurs when the opening of the siphon hose is lower than the bottom of the vessel you're siphoning the beer out of (the lower the better). If you keep large air bubbles out of the siphon hose, you also increase the siphoning efficiency; air bubbles can actually slow or stop liquid flow. They can also oxidize the beer.

You can use a handful of ways to start a siphon, but not all of them are appropriate for homebrewing. For speed and simplicity, sucking on one end of the siphon hose sure gets a flow going, but it also opens the door to all kinds of contamination possibilities. Some brewers feel that a good gargle and rinse with

whiskey or vodka prior to sucking on the hose is a good temporary cure for this problem.

A better idea is to add a false end to the siphon hose that can be removed as soon as the beer begins flowing. A stiff straw, a piece of copper tubing, or a short piece of small-diameter hosing can be fitted snugly inside the siphon hose. After starting the flow of beer by sucking the false end, you can remove it and allow the flow to continue.

Another, more widely accepted practice is to fill the plastic hosing with water just prior to fitting it onto the racking tube. After you connect the tube and hose (with the tube resting in the carboy), just drop the open end of the hose into the bottling bucket, and the beer automatically starts to flow. This method may take a few tries before you get the system down. But what are a few beer stains on the floor in pursuit of a healthy libation?

Chapter 7

Making Your Own Ales, Lagers, and Other Beers

In This Chapter

▶ Discovering more about ales and lagers

▶ Delving into homebrew recipes

This chapter encourages you, the budding homebrewer, to get more personally involved in the brewing processes. You discover more information on what makes a beer an ale, a lager, or something else entirely. This chapter also includes a variety of recipes to get you going on your brewing journey.

Before attempting any recipes in this chapter, please read the brewing steps in Book IV, Chapter 6.

Looking at the Types of Beers

Before you join in on the fun of homebrewing, it's a good idea to start with a basic understanding of the cast of characters: the types of beers.

Testing out the ales

Ales, by traditional definition, are beers fermented with top-fermenting yeast at warm temperatures for relatively short periods of time. Ales are primarily associated with England and Ireland, but you can find them in a wide variety of styles in most brewing nations, such as Australia, Belgium, Canada, and the United States. Some examples include

- Irish red ale
- Extra special/strong bitter (ESB)
- American ale
- Brown ale
- Porter
- Stout
- India pale ale
- Belgian ale

The recipes in this chapter cover some of these ales; each offers a suggestion for beginners as well as instructions for an intermediate brew. Because certain beer styles are very difficult to produce at the homebrewing level, emphasis has been placed on popular beer styles. As a general guideline, all water treatments in intermediate recipes are assumed to be added to the brewpot unless otherwise noted.

Getting to know the lagers

Lagers are beers fermented with bottom-fermenting yeast at cool temperatures for relatively long periods of time. They're primarily associated with northern and eastern European countries, such as Germany, Denmark, the Netherlands, and Czechoslovakia. In fact, they're produced in a wide variety of styles in most brewing nations, including France, Belgium, the United Kingdom, Ireland, Russia, China, Japan, Australia, New Zealand, Canada, Mexico, and the United States. Examples include the following:

- American lager
- Bohemian pilsner
- Märzen/Oktoberfest
- German dark lager
- Bock beers

This chapter provides beer recipes for three lager varieties that can be produced at the homebrewing level. As a general guideline, all water treatments in intermediate recipes are assumed to be added to the brewpot unless otherwise noted.

Checking out the mixed beers

Mixed-style beers, or *hybrids,* are beers that cross the lines between conventional beer styles. These beers are fermented and aged with mixed traditions; one beer may be fermented with ale yeast at cold temperatures, and another is fermented with lager yeast at warm temperatures. Sometimes — depending on the whims of the brewer — they may be fermented either coolly or warmly as either ales or lagers. Some examples:

- Wheat beer
- Christmas and winter seasonal beer
- Smoked beer
- Fruit and vegetable beer

This chapter provides two beer recipes for the beer styles that don't fit neatly into the regular ale and lager categories.

Considering Specific Ales, Lagers, and More

Once the basics of homebrewing are in place, it's time to widen your palate with an endless variety of brews. Travel the world of ales, lagers, Porters, and even one-of-a-kind, herb and spice beer. Enjoy re-creating tastes from other countries, rich in both flavor and history.

Irish red ale

Traditional Irish ales are easy-drinking, but full-flavored, malt-accented brews. Consider the following:

- **Flavor profile:** Irish red ales are amber to deep copper/red in color (thus their name). This style's caramel malt flavor and sweetness sometimes has a buttered-toast or toffee quality. Irish ales often exhibit a light taste of roasted malt, which lends a characteristic dryness to the finish.
- **Commercial examples:** Smithwick's Irish Ale, Ireland; Kilgubbin Red Ale, Chicago.

If you're a beginner brewer and want to make an Irish red ale, you can use either pale extract or amber hopped extract — both finish within the generous color range for this style. If you choose the pale extract, try getting a little kettle caramelization by vigorously boiling the wort an extra 30 minutes or more. When you get a little more experience, try making Why'd You Kilkenny?, the Irish red ale recipe at the end of this chapter.

American pale ale

Americans have been brewing ale since the first wave of colonists reached the shores of the New World in the 1600s. With the recent upsurge in small-batch brewing, American ales are now leading the microbrewing renaissance.

- ✔ **Flavor profile:** Pale to deep amber to copper color. These beers offer medium hop flavor and aroma and are fruity and estery. Expect low to medium maltiness and high hop bitterness, with a bit of diacetyl and low caramel flavor. Medium-bodied.

- ✔ **Commercial examples:** Sierra Nevada Pale Ale, California; Great Lakes Burning River Pale Ale, Ohio.

Beginners, try making this beer by using two 3.3-pound cans of pale, unhopped extract. You can add hop character by boiling 2 ounces of Northern Brewer hops for 1 hour and 1 ounce of Cascade hops in the last 5 minutes of the boil for the classic American pale ale character. When you're confident in your brewing abilities, make the American pale ale at the end of this chapter, Give Me Liberty, or . . . Else.

Brown porter

The porter name is borrowed from a group of people known to consume large quantities of this beer: the porters at London's Victoria Station. The porters had a habit of ordering portions of several beers mixed into the same drinking glass. This concoction came to be known as *entire.* One enterprising brewer capitalized on this habit by marketing a beer that closely approximated this blend of brews, and he used the name porter to identify it.

- ✔ **Flavor profile:** This brew is medium to dark brown. Fruity esters are acceptable, and hop flavor and aroma are nonexistent to medium. No roast barley or strong burnt character is expected. Low to medium malt sweetness, with medium hop bitterness and low diacetyl. Light- to medium-bodied.

- ✔ **Commercial examples:** Samuel Smith Taddy Porter, England; Young's London Porter, England.

When you first try your hand at porter brewing, try producing the color and flavor in your porter by adding specialty grains (dark caramel, chocolate malt, black malt, roasted barley) to your pale malt extract rather than just buying a dark malt extract — the result is more satisfying. When you're ready to take the next step, try making a Coal Porter. (See the recipe at the end of this chapter for details.)

Stout

Stout is a hearty, top-fermented beer strongly associated with the British Isles and Ireland; it's known for its opaque-black appearance and roasty flavors.

- ✔ **Flavor profile:** Opaque black. No hop flavor or aroma. Roasted barley character is expected. Slight malt sweetness or a caramel malt character is okay. Medium to high hop bitterness with a slight acidity or sourness is possible. A very low diacetyl level is okay. Medium bodied.
- ✔ **Commercial examples:** Guinness Stout, Ireland; Murphy's Stout, Ireland.

The first time you attempt to brew a stout, try producing the color and flavor in your stout by using specialty grains (dark caramel, chocolate malt, black malt, roasted barley) rather than buying a dark malt extract — the result is more satisfying. Later on, we recommend brewing St. James Gate Stout, the stout recipe at the end of this chapter.

English India pale ale

One particular substyle of English-style pale ale is known as India pale ale, or IPA for short. The beer gets its name from Britain's colonial presence in India during the 1800s.

- ✔ **Flavor profile:** Golden to light copper. Very fruity and estery. Medium maltiness with high hop bitterness and low diacetyl. Hop flavor and aroma are medium to high. Alcoholic strength is often evident. Medium-bodied.
- ✔ **Commercial examples:** Samuel Smith's India Ale, England; Fuller's IPA, England.

American premium lager

The pale American-style premium lager represents the most-produced beer style in the United States. Despite the categorical name, they're still rather

Book IV

Fermenting and Brewing

one-dimensional beers compared to those made in Europe and elsewhere. The reasons for this condition are largely the cheaper ingredients used to make them and the treatment of beer in America as a beverage designed for mass consumption. American craft brewers, on the other hand, are producing premium lagers that are more deserving of the name.

✔ **Flavor profile:** Very pale to golden. No fruitiness, esters, or diacetyl. Low malt aroma and flavor are okay. Low hop flavor or aroma is okay, but low to medium bitterness is expected. Effervescent. Light-bodied.

✔ **Commercial examples:** Leinenkugel's, Wisconsin; Brooklyn Lager, New York.

Beginners, start with 5 pounds of the palest extract you can find and add 0.5 pound of brewer's rice syrup. Use high-quality lager yeast (preferably liquid) and allow a long, cool fermentation and aging period. When you're ready to try intermediate brewing techniques, we recommend the Gullywasher recipe at the end of this chapter.

Märzen/Oktoberfest

Oktoberfest beer, as an individual style, is an offshoot of another, larger lager style known as Märzen or Märzenbier. This fairly heavy, malty style of beer is brewed in the spring and named for the month of March (März). It was often the last batch of beer brewed before the warm summer months. This higher-gravity beer was then stored in Alpine caves and consumed throughout the summer. Whatever beer was left in storage at harvest time was hauled out and joyously consumed.

✔ **Flavor profile:** Amber to coppery orange. No fruitiness, esters, or diacetyl are evident. Low hop flavor and aroma are okay. The malty sweetness boasts of a toasty malt aroma and flavor. Low to medium bitterness is just enough to keep the malty character from becoming cloying. Medium-bodied.

✔ **Commercial examples:** Wurzburger Oktoberfest, Germany; Capital Oktoberfest, Wisconsin.

Oktoberfest/Märzenbiers are malt-accented beers. When you're just beginning, start with at least 6 pounds of pale extract and steep 1.5 pounds of 20-L crystal malt and 0.5 pound toasted malt in water and then strain into wort. Use high-quality lager yeast (preferably liquid) and allow a long, cool fermentation. Later, give the Dominion Day Oktoberfest recipe a try.

Traditional bock

Traditional bock beer is a hearty, bottom-fermented beer with a generously malty character and burnt toffee dark-grain flavors. It has a creamy mouthfeel, and the finish is lengthy and malty sweet. Hop bitterness is subdued — it's just enough to cut the cloying character of the malt. The color can run the spectrum from a deep burnt orange to mahogany. The alcohol content is usually considerable; a true German bock beer must have a minimum alcohol content of 6.5 percent to be called a bock.

✔ **Flavor profile:** Deep copper to dark brown. No hop aroma, fruitiness, or esters are evident. The malty-sweet character predominates in aroma and flavor, with some toasted chocolate-malt character. Low bitterness, low hop flavor, and low diacetyl are okay. Medium- to full-bodied.

✔ **Commercial examples:** Spaten Bock, Germany; Einbecker Ur-Bock, Germany.

Traditional bock beers are big beers; we suggest beginners start with no fewer than 8 pounds of amber extract; steep 1.5 pounds of 40-L crystal and strain into wort. Use high-quality lager yeast (preferably liquid) and allow a long, cool fermentation period. If you love traditional bock beers, check out the RE: Bock recipe later in this chapter.

Herb, spice, and vegetable beer

Although you don't see many herb and spice beers on your local beer retailers' shelves, a few do exist. If homebrewers had their say, many more would be available. The herb-and-spice-beer category is one of the more popular among homebrewers because it presents an almost unlimited number of choices.

Herb and spice beers may include lemon grass, ginger, cumin, allspice, caraway, mace, pepper, cinnamon, nutmeg, and clove, among myriad others. Vegetables in beer, on the other hand, are very few and far between — and, to my knowledge, no such thing as a vegetable extract is made for brewing — so you're pretty much limited to pumpkin and hot peppers here.

✔ **Flavor profile:** Herb, spice, and vegetable beers are often made with an anything-goes approach. In light of this practice, we have no way to accurately describe what you may expect from one of these beers.

✔ **Commercial examples:** Left Hand JuJu Ginger, Colorado; Fraoch Heather Ale, Scotland.

Book IV

Fermenting and Brewing

Here's an opportunity to go a little crazy. If you're a beginning brewer, pick a favorite herb or spice and either add it to your beer in the brewpot (in the last 20 minutes of the boil) or during the fermentation and aging phase. *Hint:* Too little is better than too much; you can always add more to the next batch you make. Add your veggies in the secondary fermenter for best results. More advanced brewers should try Wassail While You Work, the spice beer recipe later in this chapter.

Christmas/winter/spiced beer

Many breweries produce unique seasonal offerings that may be darker, stronger, spiced, or otherwise fuller in character than their normal beers. The special ingredients should complement the base beer and not overwhelm it.

- ✔ **Flavor profile:** These winter seasonal brews are often made with an anything-goes approach, so it's difficult to accurately describe what you may expect from one of these beers.

- ✔ **Commercial examples:** Anchor Our Special Ale, California; Harpoon Winter Warmer, Massachusetts.

Yule ales and winter warmers are made to toast the holidays and the winter season. Warm spice flavors and elevated alcohol levels are pretty effective at putting a flush in your cheeks. Beginners, start with at least 7 pounds of pale malt extract and then add whatever adjunct grains or flavorings evoke the holiday spirit for you. When you've had more practice, try Anne's Choice Christmas Ale (see the recipe later in this chapter).

Why'd You Kilkenny?

Malt extract:	6.6 pounds Northwestern Gold extract
Specialty grain:	1 pound 60-L crystal malt
	⅛ pound roast malt
Bittering hops:	0.5 ounce Fuggles (60 min)
	0.5 ounce Fuggles (40 min)
Flavoring hops:	1 ounce Fuggles (20 min)
Finishing hops:	0.5 ounce Kent Goldings (5 min)
Yeast:	Wyeast #1084
Primary:	6 days at 65°
Secondary:	12 days at 65°

Brewer: Marty Nachel

Give Me Liberty, or . . . Else

Malt extract:	6 pounds Northwestern light
Specialty grain:	2 pounds 40-L crystal malt
Bittering hops:	1 ounce Northern Brewer (60 min)
Flavoring hops:	1 ounce Northern Brewer (30 min)
	1 ounce Spalt (15 min)
Finishing hops:	1 ounce Cascade (5 min)
Dry hop:	1 ounce Cascade
Yeast:	Wyeast #2112
Primary:	7 days at 65°
Secondary:	21 days at 65°

Brewer: Marty Nachel

Book IV

Fermenting and Brewing

Coal Porter

Malt extract:	3.3 pounds Brewmaker Mild hopped extract
	3.3 pounds Munton and Fison amber
Specialty grain:	1.66 pounds caramel malt
	5 ounces chocolate malt
Bittering hops:	0.5 ounce Northern Brewer (8 AAU) (35 min)
Finishing hops:	0.25 ounce Northern Brewer (8 AAU) (2 min)
Dry hop:	0.25 ounce Cascade
	0.5 ounce Hallertauer
Yeast:	Wyeast #1028
Misc. fermentable ingredients:	6 ounces barley syrup
Water treatment:	0.5 teaspoon noniodized salt
Primary:	12 days at 65°
Secondary:	(not given)

Brewer: Dennis Kinvig

Award won: 1st Place, AHA Nationals

St. James Gate Stout

Malt extract:	6.6 pounds amber extract
Specialty grain:	0.5 pound black malt
	0.5 pound 40-L crystal malt
	0.25 pound roasted barley
Bittering hops:	2 ounces Fuggles (60 min)
Finishing hops:	1 ounce Willamette (10 min)
Yeast:	Wyeast #1084
Primary:	(not given)
Secondary:	(not given)

Brewer: Northwestern Extract Co.

Exchequer Pale Ale

Malt extract:	6.6 pounds Northwestern extract
Specialty grain:	1 pound 40-L crystal malt
	⅛ pound roast malt
Bittering hops:	1.5 ounces Northern Brewers (60 min)
Finishing hops:	1 ounce Kent Goldings (10 min)
Dry hop:	1 ounce Fuggles
Yeast:	Wyeast #1098
Misc. flavoring ingredients:	8 ounces malto-dextrin powder
Primary:	1 week at 65°
Secondary:	2 weeks at 65°

Brewer: Marty Nachel

Typical/unusual procedures used: Add 1 ounce Fuggles hops and malto-dextrin powder to secondary fermenter.

Gullywasher

Malt extract:	5 pounds Alexander's pale extract
Specialty grain:	1 pound 10-L crystal malt
Bittering hops:	1 ounce Northern Brewer (60 min)
Flavoring hops:	1 ounce Perle (20 min)
Finishing hops:	0.5 ounce Saaz (5 min)
Yeast:	Wyeast #2035
Misc. fermentable ingredients:	1 pound brewer's rice syrup
Fining agent/ clarifier:	2 teaspoons Irish moss
Primary:	6 days at 60°

Brewer: Marty Nachel

Book IV

Fermenting and Brewing

Dominion Day Oktoberfest

Malt extract:	6.6 pounds Bierkeller extract
	1 pound amber DME
Specialty grain:	0.5 pound 10-L crystal malt
	0.5 cup chocolate malt
Bittering hops:	1 ounce Cascade (60 min)
Flavoring hops:	1 ounce Hallertauer (30 min)
Finishing hops:	0.75 ounce Tettnanger (1 min)
Yeast:	Wyeast #2206
Primary:	11 days at 50°
Secondary:	10 days at 45°
Tertiary:	15 days at 35°

Brewer: John Janowiak

Award won: 1st Place, AHA Nationals

RE: Bock

Malt extract:	6 pounds pale liquid malt extract
	2 pounds pale DME
Specialty grain:	1 pound 60 L Crystal malt
	0.5 pound chocolate malt
Bittering hops:	0.5 ounce Hallertau (60 min)
	0.5 ounce Hallertau (45 min)
Flavoring hops:	0.5 ounce Hallertau (30 min)
Yeast:	Wyeast #2206
Fining agent/ clarifier:	1 teaspoon Irish moss
Primary:	8 days at 55°
Secondary:	14 days at 45°

Brewer: Marty Nachel

Wassail While You Work

Malt extract:	10 pounds Northwestern light
Specialty grain:	1 pound 40-L crystal malt
Bittering hops:	2 ounces Mount Hood (60 min)
Flavoring hops:	1 ounce Northern Brewer (30 min)
Finishing hops:	1 ounce Cascade (5 min)
Dry hop:	1 ounce Cascade
Yeast:	Pasteur Champagne (dry)
Misc. flavoring ingredients:	2 sticks cinnamon, 1 teaspoon cloves
Primary:	11 days at 60°
Secondary:	25 days at 60°

Brewer: Marty Nachel

Award won: 1st Place, Dukes of Ale Spring Thing

Anne's Choice Christmas Ale

Malt extract:	3.5 pounds Munton & Fison stout kit
	3.3 pounds Munton & Fison amber extract
	3 pounds Munton & Fison amber DME
Bittering hops:	0.5 ounce Hallertauer (55 min)
Finishing hops:	0.5 ounce Hallertauer (5 min)
Yeast:	Wyeast #1007
Misc. fermentable ingredients:	0.75 pound honey
Misc. flavoring ingredients:	Five 3-inch cinnamon sticks
	2 teaspoons allspice
	1 teaspoon cloves
	6 ounces grated gingerroot
	6 medium oranges (rinds only)
Primary:	14 days at 60°
Secondary:	(not given)

Brewer: Philip Fleming

Award won: 1st Place, AHA Nationals

Typical/unusual procedures used: Simmer all the flavoring ingredients in the honey for 45 minutes; strain into the brewpot.

Chapter 8

Brewing Other Liquids: Cider, Mead, Vinegar, and Kombucha

In This Chapter

▶ Celebrating ciders

▶ Mixing it up with meads

▶ Experimenting with vinegar and Kombucha

The art of homebrewing generally denotes brewing beer in your home. However, this definition doesn't necessarily exclude the options to make other somewhat-similar fermented beverages, such as cider and mead. Fermenting is also the foundation for certain vinegars and other more exotic brews such as Kombucha, a fermented tea. Although many homebrewers may never try their hand at making mead or vinegar, they already have all the equipment they need, so we present the information in case the occasion should arise.

Mulling Over Cider

Once the most popular beverage in America, hard cider is making a comeback of sorts, hot on the heels of the microbrewing revolution. In fact, some suggest that cider is now where craft brews were about 20 years ago and continues to grow in interest.

Hard cider, for the uninitiated, is a fermented beverage made from the juice of apples. (Regular, or *soft,* cider is unfermented and therefore contains no alcohol.) Hard cider is predominantly a British drink, although its traditions in the United States run deep. Its production may include optional ingredients, such as white and brown sugars, and various other fruits and spices, depending on the producer and the style.

Because of its combined acid and alcohol content, cider also has a shelf life that far exceeds that of beer.

Sorting cider styles

The antiquated *Anglo* style of cider, which originated in Britain, is generally more tannic and ale-like because of the cider makers' use of ale yeasts and bittersweet apples. The Anglo style is also more costly because it requires longer fermentations. The newer Continental style, popular in the United States, is generally sweeter and more like sparkling wine.

And speaking of sparkling wine, you can render ciders with various levels of carbonation from *still* (uncarbonated) to *sparkling* (highly carbonated). The level of mild carbonation between still and sparkling is called *petillant*.

According to the American Homebrewers Association, the following are some of the cider styles that you can produce:

✔ *Common cider* is made from culinary/table apples, with wild or crab apples often used for acidity/tannin balance.

✔ *English* and *French* ciders are made with bittersweet and bitter-sharp apple varieties cultivated specifically for cider-making. The main difference between the two is that the French use a slow or *arrested* fermentation, which leaves more apple flavor and sweetness.

Even though these style descriptions mention actual fruit, most cider brewers substitute high-quality natural fruit juice. Apple pressing is rather long and laborious and is a process best left to hard-core cider makers.

Ciders of any style may also range from sweet to dry, depending on the types of apples you use, as well as the yeast strain you use to ferment the juice. Furthermore, you may also serve cider *draft style,* which is pasteurized and filtered, or in the more natural *farmhouse style,* which is traditionally served unfiltered from a cask.

If you're looking for a few commercial ciders for comparison tasting, try the three most popular brands in the United States: Woodchuck, Seven Sisters Wild Horse, and Cider Jack. Two lesser-known brands, Ace and Hornsby's, come out of California. The leading non-U.S. brands include Woodpecker, Strongbow, and Blackthorn, all from the U.K.

Comparing apples to apples

The cider-making industry uses a wide variety of apples. At their most basic level, apples fall roughly into two categories:

> ✔ **Culinary:** You may be familiar with the culinary apple varieties, such as Granny Smith, Jonathan, Macintosh, and Golden Delicious. Cooks use these varieties in apple pies or applesauce, or you can eat them plain.
>
> ✔ **Bittersweet:** Less known are the bittersweet apples that go by monikers such as Northern Spy, Kingston Black, Golden Russet, and Newton Pippen. These varieties tend to have thicker skins and elevated tannin levels (which contribute the bitterness) and higher acid contents that make them less desirable for common consumption.

Most brand-name ciders are blends of the juices of different apple varieties, which creates a wider spectrum of flavors.

The key to making a good and enjoyable cider is to find the correct balance between the apple character (sweetness and flavor) and the natural acidity found in cider. Many people find the puckery tang of cider a little too assertive. If you count yourself among them, try adding a can of frozen apple concentrate to the mix to intensify the apple flavor or add honey or juices of other flavorful fruits to cut through the acid levels in your cider.

Making cider

Cider-making is still catching on with homebrewers. This may be because cider's tart taste isn't to everyone's liking, but it may just be that many homebrewers are unaware of how easy cider is to make. Technically, only one ingredient is necessary to make cider: apples (or apple juice)! No water, no yeast — just the forbidden fruit.

Okay, that statement may be a little misleading. Apples (and freshly squeezed apple juices), like grapes, *do* come complete with their own resident wild yeasts, but for better control over the cider-making process, you should destroy these uninvited apple yeasts by heating the juice to at least 180°, and then choose and add the proper yeasts. As far as water goes, apple juice naturally contains a high percentage of water and therefore doesn't require dilution.

Before you embark on your cider-making journey, be sure to check out the secondary fermentation procedures in Book IV, Chapter 6. Cider making is very similar to beginner extract brewing (also covered in Book IV, Chapter 6) except for the secondary fermentation process.

Because the amount of apple juice you buy represents the finished batch size (remember, you're not diluting), you must heat all your apple juice. This restriction means you either have to get a brewpot that can hold 5 gallons of liquid, or you have to heat your apple juice a couple gallons at a time until it's all heated. I don't recommend reducing your batch size because a lot of damaging airspace may be left in your primary and secondary fermenters that can cause oxidation problems later.

The first place to shop for apple juice is at your local grocer. Most large grocery stores carry at least a few different brands of apple juice and cider. But brand names aren't as important as product contents. Juice that's sugar-free and preservative-free is best.

Some serious cider makers prefer to buy their apple juice fresh from the local farmers' market or at roadside stands. This practice is fine, but keep in mind that this juice (which often comes as soft cider) isn't pasteurized, and you need to stabilize it before you pitch yeast into it. You also need to use such juice quickly because unpasteurized and preservative-free apple juice soon begins fermenting on its own! I don't recommend boiling unfiltered apple juice; the easiest way to stop wild and unintentional fermentations is to mix sulfur dioxide in the juice, which you can do simply by adding one crushed Campden tablet to the *must* (unfermented liquid). Winemakers use Campden tablets regularly, and most homebrew-supply shops stock them.

You can greatly enhance cider (like some beer styles) with the addition of fruits or fruit flavors, some spices, or even some other fermentable sugars such as honey or brown sugar. Cider also benefits from long periods of aging (anywhere from a couple of months to several months), so adding some more complex flavorings to your cider is no big deal. You can add some of these flavorings directly to the brewpot, and you should add some to the secondary fermenter. (See Book IV, Chapter 6 for flavoring ideas and procedures.)

With the cider recipes at the end of the chapter, you can produce an interesting libation appropriate for special occasions, competition, or just for sipping with friends. An added bonus is that you don't have to buy any extra equipment — your beer-brewing equipment is all you need.

Crafting Meads

Mead is a simple fermented beverage made from honey and water; it's also one of the more natural and uncomplicated beverages known to man. Despite its simplicity, however, mead is intoxicatingly enjoyable — pun intended, of course — and when well made, it can rival the world's finest Champagnes.

Knowing the power of honey

To understand and appreciate mead is to understand and appreciate honey. Mead is, after all, a simple dilution of honey in water fermented with yeast.

Honey is highly fermentable because it's mostly sugar. Taken as a whole, pure and natural honey is a healthy potion containing a handful of minerals, such as iron, potassium, and phosphorus, and vitamins A, B, C, and K.

Unfortunately, the more processed the honey is, the fewer of these goodies you're likely to find in it.

Estimates reveal over a thousand different kinds of honey in the world, each with a different color and flavor. Most commercially produced honeys are blends of various types, which tends to foster homogeneity among them. Lighter honeys, such as clover, alfalfa, and wildflower, are good for mead-making because their flavor contribution is mild. Orange blossom, mesquite, fireweed, and tupelo are some of the varietal honeys that produce very tasty mead.

Many brand-name meads are typically made from a homogenous blend of honeys, which pretty much guarantees consistency among batches. Those meads made from varietal honey usually broadcast that fact on their labels.

Making sense of mead styles

Fermenting plain honey and water produces traditional mead, but by simply adding other flavorings and fermentable sugars, you can produce different styles of mead.

According to the American Homebrewers Association competition guidelines, brewers can make mead at home in any of the following styles:

- **Traditional mead:** Dry, semisweet, sweet mead
- **Melomel (fruit mead):** Cyser (apple), pyment (grape), other fruit
- **Other mead:** Metheglin (spiced mead), braggot (barley mead), open category

All meads, regardless of style, should exhibit these three qualities:

- **Sweetness:** *Sweetness* simply refers to the amount of residual sugar in the mead; mead may be *dry, semisweet,* or *sweet*.
- **Carbonation:** Mead may be still, petillant, or sparkling. *Still* meads don't have to be totally flat — they can have some very light bubbles. *Petillant* meads are lightly sparkling and can have a moderate, noticeable amount of carbonation. *Sparkling* meads may have a character ranging from mouth-filling to an impression akin to Champagne or soda pop. (Making a petillant or sparkling mead is a simple matter of adding additional fermentable sugar to the mead at bottling time. Check out Book IV, Chapter 6 for more on bottling and carbonation.)
- **Strength:** Mead may be categorized as *hydromel, standard,* or *sack strength*. *Strength* refers to the alcohol content of the mead (and therefore to the amount of honey and fermentable ingredients used to make the mead). Stronger meads have a greater honey character and body (as well as alcohol content) than weaker meads, although this isn't a strict rule.

Book IV

Fermenting and Brewing

The vast majority of commercially made meads you encounter are likely middle-of-the-road meads: standard, semisweet, and still. Commercial mead is nowhere near as widely available as beer or wine, but if you're looking for a few commercial meads for comparison tasting, try scouting out Chaucer Mead, Lurgashall Mead, White Winter Mead, Redstone Mead, Rabbit's Foot Mead, or Jadwiga Mead.

Examining the process

Although homebrewing competitions have accepted mead with open arms, mead-making still isn't very common among homebrewers. This unpopularity may stem from the fact that mead is an acquired taste, but perhaps the main obstacle is that many homebrewers are unaware of how easy mead is to make.

Choosing your honey

Most large grocery stores carry at least a few different brands of honey, but the vast majority of commercial honeys are blended and homogenized — they're all virtually the same. You may want to travel that extra mile or spend that extra dollar to purchase a specialty or varietal honey from a specialty store, a roadside stand or farmers' market, or a local beekeeper.

Honey from a farmers' market or roadside stand often isn't pasteurized (or even filtered), and you need to stabilize it before you pitch yeast into it. The quickest way to kill unwanted wild yeast or bacteria is to mix sulfur dioxide into the *must* (unfermented honey and water dilution); you can do this by adding one crushed Campden tablet to the must. (You find Campden tablets at most homebrew-supply shops.)

Boiling your honey to kill any resident bacteria is also an option, but be careful: Boiling may also kill a lot of the delicate aromatics of the honey. The best way to boil safely is to pour the honey into water that's already boiling and immediately turn off the heat. Stir well.

Fermenting your mead

The brewer has a fair amount of control over the fermentation process; some sweet mead yeasts aren't very alcohol-tolerant and cease fermenting before they've consumed all the available sugars. On the other hand, liquid culture dry mead yeasts or Champagne yeasts are very alcohol-tolerant and consume as much available sugar as they can. Given honey's high degree of fermentability and some yeast strains' alcohol tolerance, your mead could conceivably end up with a final gravity of 0.999 or lower, which is even less dense than water.

Most meads start with original gravities greater than 1.080 and ferment down to final gravities below 1.020. This level of attenuation results in alcohol levels above 9 percent, which is equivalent to most table wines. For the homebrewer, it takes about 12 pounds of honey in a 5-gallon batch to get to this starting gravity point, but it's not unheard of for mead makers to use as many as 15 to 18 pounds of honey in a 5-gallon batch. Figure on a dilution rate of 2½ to 3 pounds of honey per gallon of water to achieve the appropriate starting gravity.

At high original gravities, however, yeasts have a tough time staying motivated. It helps to make sure that you've aerated the must before you pitch the proper amount of yeast. In order to keep fermentation moving along, you may need to rouse the yeast by agitating the fermenter or by racking the mead over to another vessel. Adding fresh, healthy yeast to mead already in the secondary fermenter isn't out of the question, either.

Don't be surprised if your primary mead fermentations continue for two weeks to a month. Three to 6 months is the norm, but 9 to 12 months isn't out of the ordinary for extremely high gravity meads or those with lots of flavor components that benefit from aging and melding, such as bold fruit flavors or aggressive spices.

Before you dive headlong into mead-making, take a look at the secondary fermentation procedures in Book IV, Chapter 6. Mead-making is similar to beginner extract brewing, except for the secondary fermentation process.

Taking your mead to the next level

Like certain beer styles, you can jazz up your mead by adding spices, fruits or fruit flavors, or even other fermentable sugars like brown sugar. Because mead benefits from long periods of aging, adding more complex flavorings is no problem. (See Book IV, Chapter 6 for flavoring ideas and procedures.)

The mead recipes at the end of this chapter allow you to create a tasty concoction perfect for special occasions (even if that occasion is Wednesday). As a bonus, you don't even need any new equipment; your beer-brewing gear is perfect.

Sampling Vinegars

Vinegar is more than the flavoring behind a dill pickle. Vinegar in its raw form is actually a living food, containing the beneficial bacteria you need to digest your food properly.

Several types of vinegars are used medicinally and in cooking. Some of them are commonly found in a well-stocked pantry, while others are usually found in either specialty stores or in the specific country where they're used. Here's a list of some vinegars you can find commercially:

- ✔ **White vinegar:** Actually a distilled product containing 5 to 8 percent acetic acid in water. This type of vinegar is used for many kitchen preparations, like pickling and baking, due to its plain flavor.

- **Apple cider vinegar:** Brown in color, this vinegar is available raw, with the mother still visible. Made from apples, this vinegar is thought to have the health benefits of a naturally fermented product.

- **Fruit vinegars:** These vinegars are made from fruit that's allowed to ferment. They have a delicious fruity flavor, and are wonderful for cooking.

- **Balsamic:** Made from grapes, this almost black vinegar is aged for many years. The flavor is complex, and it's used in dishes that can showcase the unique flavor.

- **Rice vinegar:** This vinegar is made from rice, the color denoting the type of rice used in the production. Rice vinegar is mild tasting and never overpowering.

Making use of peelings

If organic fruits are used, the peelings from the fruits can be allowed to ferment into delicious vinegars. These vinegars use wild yeast to work, so the outcome isn't always the same. Often, these vinegars will work for a while, and then suddenly a batch will fail. After that happens, do a thorough cleaning of the area where the vinegar sits to work and start with completely new items.

Always use a bit of good vinegar to start a new batch. This will ensure that the beneficial bacteria have a head start.

Understanding acidity science

The tartness of vinegar comes from acetic acid. This is a form of acid that, when at the proper pH, is beneficial to your health.

Too acidic, and vinegar can actually be caustic, causing injury or worse to anyone exposed to it. Luckily, the home vinegar hobbyist won't be able to make vinegar that strong.

Not acidic enough, and vinegar won't preserve foods properly. This is why you must use a specific type of vinegar (purchased and not homemade) for food preservation. Check the labeling to make certain that the acidity is adequate for preservation.

Considering Kombucha

Kombucha, a fermented tea often used for medicinal purposes, has a long history in other countries, perhaps going back to 250 BC in China. Today, Kombucha can be found commercially as well as made at home.

You can make Kombucha by adding a solid mass of yeast and bacteria, the starter culture, often referred to as the *mushroom* or the *mother,* to sugar and black or green tea; you then allow the mix to ferment. Typically, the tea is prepared by taking a sample of an existing culture and starting a new batch in a clean jar.

As a fermented food, Kombucha contains all the health benefits that fermenting brings, as well as a unique flavor that can be enhanced with the addition of fruits or mixed with juices.

Kombucha is acidic. If it's kept too long at a warm temperature, it will become too vinegary to drink in large quantities. However, it makes tasty vinegar and can be used in any cooking recipe that will be eaten fresh.

Use Kombucha as a replacement for any vinegar you like, but it's not adequate to use in any canning recipe that requires a specific acidity.

Book IV

Fermenting and Brewing

Rotten to the Corps Cider

Apple juice:	5 gallons (preservative-free)
Yeast:	Nottingham dry ale yeast
Nutrient:	2 ounces yeast nutrient
Primary:	8 days at 65°
Secondary:	21 days at 65°

Brewer: Denny Lake

Typical/unusual procedures used: Add priming sugar only at bottling for sparkling cider.

Note: You make common cider like Rotten to the Corps without the addition of adjunct sugars or flavorings. In England, where the cider tradition began, ale yeasts are preferable over Champagne or other types; this use results in fruitier ciders with more residual sweetness. Traditional ciders should be light-bodied with a crisp apple flavor.

Lindisfarne Libation Mead

Honey:	12 pounds wildflower (unpasteurized)
Yeast:	Pasteur Champagne (dry)
Nutrient:	2 ounces yeast nutrient
Primary:	16 days at 65°
Secondary:	21 days at 65°

Brewer: Marty Nachel

Typical/unusual procedures used: Add the yeast nutrient to the must in primary fermenter.

Note: Lindisfarne Libation is a traditional mead, one of the least complicated meads to make. It's a simple mix of honey and water that you can ferment to various levels of sweetness. Lindisfarne Libation is on the dry end of the sweetness scale.

Pride and Jay Cider

Apple juice:	5 gallons (unpasteurized, preservative-free)
Yeast:	None added (spontaneously fermented)
Misc. fermentable ingredients:	5 cups granulated white cane sugar
	0.5 cup dark brown sugar
Flavoring ingredients:	1.5 teaspoons grape tannin
	10 ounces raisins
	6 ounces oak chips
Primary:	10 days at 65°
Secondary:	14 days at 65°

Brewer: Jay Lubinsky

Typical/unusual procedures used: Use apple juice immediately. Boil and cool 5 cups white sugar with 5 cups apple juice. Add sugar, juice, and tannin to rest of juice. Let ferment naturally. After fermentation subsides, add the raisins and let sit about 10 days or until fermentation subsides again. Transfer to the secondary fermenter. Boil the oak chips in a little water for 10 minutes; add to the cider. Let sit for a week or two, depending on desired oakiness. Bottle and age for 3 months.

Note: Pride and Jay is a New England–style cider. This cider style is natural, so spontaneous wild yeast fermentations are okay. Because of the addition of white and brown sugars, New England–style cider also sports elevated alcohol levels (8 to 14 percent). Medium- to full-bodied, New England–style cider offers a pronounced apple aroma and flavor, ending with a throat-warming finish.

Book IV

Fermenting and Brewing

Winter Holiday Sweet Mead

Honey:	14 pounds wildflower
Apple juice:	4 gallons (unpasteurized, preservative-free), chilled
Yeast:	Red Star Cote des Blanc (dry)
Misc. fermentable ingredients:	2 pounds dark brown sugar
Flavoring ingredients:	0.5 ounce cinnamon stick
Clarifying agent:	3 teaspoons Sparkolloid
Primary:	10 days at 65°
Secondary:	14 days at 65°

Brewer: Tim Reiter

Award won: 1st Place in the First Round of the 2001 AHA Nationals

Typical/unusual procedures used: Heat the honey, brown sugar, and cinnamon in 1 gallon water in the brewpot. Cool with chilled apple juice and pitch rehydrated yeast. After primary fermentation is complete, stir in rehydrated Sparkolloid. Bottle or keg after 2 weeks.

Note: An open category mead like Winter Holidays Sweet Mead is one that combines elements of two or more other mead categories, or one that simply doesn't fit the style description of any other mead category. These meads are often made with an "anything goes" attitude.

Apple Peel Vinegar

Prep time: 15 min • **Process time:** 3-4 weeks • **Yield:** 1½ quarts

Ingredients	Directions
Organic apple peelings **2 tablespoons raw vinegar** **1½ quarts water**	**1** Fill a 2-quart glass container with apple peels. Tamp them down firmly with a wooden utensil. Pour raw vinegar over the peelings. Slowly pour the water over the peelings until they're fully submerged by 1 inch.
	2 Cover the glass container with a coffee filter and place an elastic band around the rim to hold it in place. Place the container at room temperature for 3 to 4 weeks, or until vinegar is reached.
	3 Strain through cheesecloth, to remove peelings, into glass jars and store tightly sealed in a dark place.

Tip: Allow your vinegar to mellow for a month for better flavor.

Ginger Vinegar

Prep time: 5 min • **Process time:** 1 week • **Yield:** 1 quart

Ingredients	Directions
1 quart white wine vinegar **One 2-inch piece gingerroot**	**1** Fill a quart canning jar with vinegar. Peel and chop the gingerroot. Add the gingerroot to the vinegar. Stir well.
	2 Cover the jar with a tight-fitting lid and place in an out-of-the-way place for 7 days. Strain and enjoy!

Pineapple Peelings Vinegar

Prep time: 5 min • **Process time:** 1½ months • **Yield:** 1 quart

Ingredients	*Directions*
Peel from 1 medium pineapple **2 tablespoons raw cider vinegar** **¼ cup sugar** **1 quart water**	**1** In a large mixing bowl, place the pineapple peelings, vinegar, sugar, and water. Cover the container with breathable material, like a muslin or linen dish towel, to keep out fruit flies and dust. Place the container in an out-of-the-way place, at room temperature.
	2 Stir once a day and replace the breathable cover. Check the odor of the vinegar every day. After 1 week, you should notice a vinegar odor. Continue fermenting until your vinegar is as strong as you like.
	3 Strain the vinegar into glass jars, through cheesecloth to remove peelings. Allow tightly capped jars to mellow for 1 month to improve the flavor.

Red Wine Vinegar

Prep time: 5 min • **Process time:** 3 months • **Yield:** 1 quart

Ingredients	Directions
1 quart red wine ¼ cup raw vinegar	**1** In a glass jar, place the wine and vinegar. Cover the jar with a coffee filter and place a rubber band around the top to hold the filter in place. Place the jar in an out-of-the-way place, at room temperature, for at least 3 months.
	2 Smell the vinegar, and filter it when it's to your taste. Pour the vinegar into fresh glass jars and cover tightly. Store until ready to use.

Vary It! For white vinegar, use white wine instead of red.

Kombucha

Prep time: 30 min • **Process time:** 2 weeks • **Yield:** 3 quarts

Ingredients	Directions
3 quarts cold water 1 cup sugar 6 black tea bags 1 SCOBY pad ½ cup Kombucha starter	**1** In a 6-quart saucepan, combine the water and sugar. Bring to a boil over high heat. Remove the boiled water from the heat. Add the teabags and cover tightly. Steep for 15 minutes. Remove the tea bags. Cover tightly. Allow the tea to cool to room temperature.
	2 Place the SCOBY into a glass gallon jar. Pour the Kombucha starter over the SCOBY. Pour the cooled tea into jar. Cover the jar with a coffee filter and hold it in place with an elastic band. Let sit in a warm place for 14 days, or until it smells like apple cider vinegar.
	3 Pour the finished vinegar into another jar to use, keeping ½ cup of Kombucha vinegar and SCOBY to start another batch.

Per 1-cup serving: Calories 64 (From Fat 0); Fat 0g (Saturated 0g); Cholesterol 0mg; Sodium 7mg; Carbohydrates 16g (Dietary Fiber 0g); Protein 0g.

Raspberry Kombucha

Prep time: 5 min, plus refrigeration time • **Yield:** 1 quart

Ingredients	Directions
1 quart Kombucha **½ cup freeze-dried raspberries**	*1* Fill a quart canning jar with Kombucha. Add the freeze-dried raspberries to the Kombucha and stir well.
	2 Cover the jar with a tight-fitting lid and refrigerate for 12 hours. Strain the raspberries and enjoy!

Per 1-cup serving: Calories 64 (From Fat 0); Fat 0g (Saturated 0g); Cholesterol 0mg; Sodium 7mg; Carbohydrates 16g (Dietary Fiber 0g); Protein 0g.

Ginger Clove Kombucha

Prep time: 5 min • **Yield:** 1 quart

Ingredients	Directions
1 quart Kombucha **One 1-inch piece gingerroot** **1 teaspoon whole cloves**	*1* Fill a quart canning jar with Kombucha. Peel and chop the gingerroot. Add the gingerroot and cloves to the jar. Stir well.
	2 Cover the jar with a tight-fitting lid and refrigerate for 12 hours. Strain and enjoy!

Per 1-cup serving: Calories 64 (From Fat 0); Fat 0g (Saturated 0g); Cholesterol 0mg; Sodium 8mg; Carbohydrates 16g (Dietary Fiber 0g); Protein 0g.

Note: This Kombucha tastes wonderful when you're fighting a cold.

Book V
Pressure Canning

"Oh, that gave me such a start! When you're pressure canning game birds, dear, remember to remove the heads."

In this book . . .

The chapters in this book explore the world of pressure canning, the canning method you use to preserve vegetables, meat, poultry, seafood, and other low-acid foods. Preserving low-acid foods requires more care than processing high-acid foods (see Book II), but the rewards are well worth the additional effort. Thanks to this book, you'll be safely preserving your favorite low-acid foods in no time.

Chapter 1

Holding Up Under Pressure

- -

In This Chapter

▶ Understanding low-acid foods

▶ Selecting a pressure canner

▶ Processing low-acid foods to perfection

- -

*P*ressure canning is a process for preserving food with a low-acid content by exposing the food to a high temperature (240°) under a specific pressure for a specific period of time in a specific type of pot: the pressure canner.

This chapter leads you step by step through the pressure-canning process, including an explanation of pressure canning, what to look for when purchasing a pressure canner, and how to fill your canner and safely process your filled jars.

Canning in a Low-Acid World

Low-acid foods contain little natural acid and require more care during the canning process than other types of foods. (If you're a techie, note that low-acid foods are foods with a *pH factor* — that's a measure of acidity in food — higher than 4.6.) Foods in this category include vegetables, meats, poultry, seafood, and combination foods (like soups, meat sauces, and salsas) that contain low-acid and high-acid ingredients. Exceptions to these low-acid foods sometimes include tomatoes, which are really a fruit and can be water-bath canned (although for safety's sake, you still add acid to tomatoes) and vegetables converted to high-acid foods, such as sauerkraut, pickles, or pickled vegetables (see Books III and IV).

Low-acid foods require pressure canning to kill microorganisms that are harmful if not destroyed before ingesting the food. Pressure canning at 240° kills the botulism bacteria. If this temperature isn't achieved and the bacteria isn't destroyed, one taste of this spoiled food can kill you. And to make matters worse, these botulism-causing bacteria are odorless, have no taste, and actually thrive in low-acid foods that are in a moist environment and not in contact with air — the exact condition provided in a jar of canned food. Simply boiling food on the stovetop will not kill any botulism and should not be considered a safety step.

In a water-bath canner, the temperature of boiling water never increases above 212° (the boiling point for water). While 212° is fine for water-bath canning high-acid foods, it's *not* sufficient to safely can low-acid foods. For that, you need to superheat your filled jars to a temperature of 240°, which only a pressure canner can achieve. Be sure to use a pressure canner that's approved for pressure canning by the United States Department of Agriculture (USDA).

Only one form of canning — pressure canning — is approved for safely processing low-acid foods. And only one piece of equipment — a pressure canner — is approved for safely processing low-acid foods. Don't think you can use a substitute process or piece of equipment.

Choosing Your Pressure Canner

A *pressure canner,* shown in Figure 1-1, is a heavy kettle made for processing home-canned food. It includes a locking, tight-fitting cover that makes the kettle airtight. The purpose of pressure canning is to sterilize the food by destroying hard-to-kill microorganisms, especially the bacteria that cause botulism (see Chapter 1 of Book I).

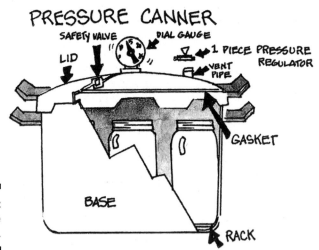

Figure 1-1: A pressure canner.

People who hear someone talking about pressure canning often ask, "Is it safe?" or "Won't the pressure canner explode?" These concerns are certainly valid ones, but rest assured, when you know the right way to use a pressure canner, you can safely process a variety of low-acid foods. While pressure cookers and canners of the past may have once exploded if not closed properly, the new generation of canners and cookers are much lighter in weight and have built-in safety features that release steam if the pressure gets too high. None of your grandparents' pressure cooking equipment had this.

Don't confuse pressure canners with pressure cookers. A pressure canner is used to process and sterilize home-canned, low-acid foods. The purpose of a pressure cooker is to cook food fast. Check out *Pressure Cookers For Dummies,* by Tom Lacalamita (Wiley), for the lowdown on pressure cooking. Pressure canners and pressure cookers are *not* interchangeable. Pressure cookers are not large enough to hold the jars and the amount of water necessary to can properly. They also do not have pressure gauges that allow you to maintain the constant pressure required.

When shopping for a pressure canner, keep these things in mind:

✔ **Size:** Pressure canners come in many sizes, holding from 4- to 19(!)-quart jars. For the home canner, however, a pressure canner with a capacity of 16 to 22 quarts is fine. This size holds seven 1-quart jars and permits good air circulation during processing.

✔ **Price:** The cost of a pressure canner may vary from $100 on the low end to upward of $600. Some reasons for the variance are size, features, and reputation of the manufacturer.

When making your purchasing decision, study your options and estimate how frequently (or infrequently) you plan to pressure-can. You may even consider co-owning a pressure canner with a friend. If you're buying a pressure canner secondhand, take it to your local county extension office to have it checked for proper seal and to be sure it's still safe to use.

✔ **Features:** All pressure canners — regardless of features — safely process your filled jars of low-acid food in the same manner because a pressure canner operates in only one way. Each pressure canner has a locking cover, a pressure gauge, and an overpressure plug. Manufacturers of pressure canners, however, slightly vary the same features and add accessories in much the same way car manufacturers add extras to a basic car model.

The following sections explain the different features various pressure canners offer so that you can determine which features you prefer. The type of pressure canner you choose doesn't matter as long as the model is made and approved for processing home-canned foods.

No matter which type or size of pressure canner you choose, the goal is always the same: to superheat and process low-acid food at a high temperature (240°) that destroys microorganisms.

Cover: With a gasket or without

You can find two types of covers for pressure canners: a lock-on cover and a metal-to-metal cover that's attached with wing nuts. The difference is that one has a rubber gasket to ensure an airtight seal; the other one doesn't. For a beginner, a lock-on cover is the easiest and most fail-proof to use.

Lock-on cover

A lock-on cover (see Figure 1-2) usually has a rubber gasket between the cover and the base unit to ensure an airtight seal. To securely fasten the cover to the pressure canner, rotate the cover on the base to the locked position (matching up the handles, arrows, or other markings on the unit). To ensure that the pressure canner is properly closed, refer to your owner's manual for precise instructions.

LOCK-ON COVER

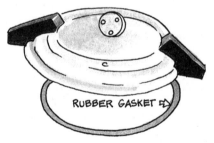

Figure 1-2:
A lock-on cover and rubber gasket.

RUBBER GASKET

Over time, the rubber gasket may stretch out of shape or begin to rot and deteriorate (indicated by cracking or splitting). If your gasket is in this condition, don't use your pressure canner until you've replaced the gasket. A gasket in poor condition may prevent the canner from reaching the pressure required to superheat the food and kill microorganisms.

After each use, carefully remove the gasket from the cover. Thoroughly wash the gasket in hot, soapy water and dry it well. After the gasket is completely dry, put it back on the cover so that your pressure canner is always ready for use. Some manufacturers suggest lightly coating the gasket with cooking oil, but check your owner's manual before doing this.

Metal-to-metal cover with wing nuts

A metal-to-metal cover (see Figure 1-3) doesn't require a gasket to create a tight seal; instead, this pressure canner uses wing nuts. To secure a cover with wing nuts, tighten two wing nuts on opposite sides of the canner at the same time by hand. (Don't use a tool and don't tighten one side at a time.) Repeat this process for the remaining wing nuts.

Never tighten one nut at a time because uneven results will occur. If your wing nuts aren't tightened properly, as soon as the pressure starts to rise, water leaks out. You then have to carefully remove the canner from the heat and wait for the pressure to subside before untightening and retightening all over again.

METAL-TO-METAL COVER

WING NUT ON
METAL-TO-METAL
COVER

Figure 1-3:
A metal-to-metal cover with wing nuts.

Every year, check for nicks and dents in the rim of both the lid and the canner itself. These imperfections will prevent the canner from making a seal.

Gauges

Gauges are located on the top of the pressure canner cover and regulate pressure within the canner. Two types of gauges are available: a weighted gauge and a dial gauge (see Figure 1-4). A dial gauge indicates the pressure of the canner, while a weighted gauge indicates and regulates the pressure of the contents. If you're a beginner, go with the weighted gauge.

Figure 1-4:
The two
types of
gauges
available
on pressure
canners.

DIAL GAUGE   WEIGHTED GAUGE

Weighted gauge

A *weighted gauge* is simple and accurate. It's sometimes referred to as an *automatic pressure control* or a *pressure regulator weight*. This gauge allows you to cook without looking: The weighted gauge automatically controls the pressure by jiggling as the canner reaches the correct pressure. When the pressure in the canner is too high, the weighted gauge jiggles faster and may hiss as it releases excess steam from the canner.

A weighted gauge has a preset control that needs no service or testing to ensure an accurate pressure measurement. The pressure settings are indicated by three numbers marked on the gauge: 5, 10, and 15. The numbers represent the pounds per square inch (psi) of pressure created by the trapped steam from the boiling water in the pressure canner.

The most common pressure used in pressure canning is 10 pounds, but never guess — always refer to your recipe.

Dial or steam pressure gauge

A *dial* or *steam pressure gauge* (refer to Figure 1-4) is a numbered instrument that indicates the pressure in the canner. You have to watch dial gauges carefully to be sure that they don't rise too high, and you have to turn the heat up or down to keep the pressure in the right area.

Unlike the weighted gauge that requires no service, you must check this control for accuracy each season or at least once every year of use. To obtain service, refer to your owner's manual for service locations, check with the store where you purchased the canner, or contact your local cooperative extension services.

If your annual service shows that your dial gauge is off by 5 or more pounds, replace the gauge. An inaccurate reading may not produce the temperature required to kill all microorganisms. You can have your canner checked for a nominal fee, if not free, at your local hardware store or county extension office.

Vent tube, pipe vent, or petcock

Whatever the name of this feature — *vent tube, pipe vent,* or *petcock* — the function is the same (see Figure 1-5). These terms refer to an opening in the pressure-canner cover for emitting steam. Sometimes the weighted gauge sits on the vent tube.

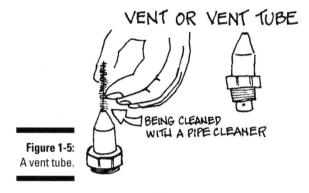

VENT OR VENT TUBE

BEING CLEANED
WITH A PIPE CLEANER

Figure 1-5:
A vent tube.

To work properly, the vent tube opening cannot be obstructed with food or other matter. Obstructions restrict the optimum pressure and temperature required for your recipe. To check the vent for obstructions, hold it up to the light. If the vent appears to be clogged, insert a piece of wire (or other item suggested in your owner's manual) into the tube. Rinse the vent with hot water. Repeat the procedure if you still see an obstruction.

Overpressure plug

An *overpressure plug* (see Figure 1-6) releases (pops up) if too much pressure exists in your pressure canner due to a blocked vent tube. The overpressure plug is a safety feature that's solely for your protection. If you follow the instruction manual for your pressure-canner operation, chances are this plug will never be used.

Figure 1-6:
An over-
pressure
plug.

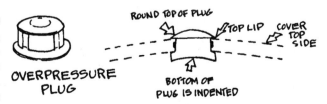

OVERPRESSURE
PLUG

ROUND TOP OF PLUG

TOP LIP   COVER
TOP
SIDE

BOTTOM OF
PLUG IS INDENTED

Rack

Your pressure canner should come with a rack. (If the rack is missing, contact the store where you made your purchase.) The perfect rack lies flat in the bottom of your canner and has lots of holes and openings that allow steam to circulate around your filled jars. Figure 1-7 is an example of a canner rack.

Figure 1-7:
A rack for holding jars in the bottom of your pressure canner.

A RACK FOR HOLDING
JARS IN THE BOTTOM OF
YOUR PRESSURE CANNER

Make sure that your rack is stable when you place it in the bottom of the canner. A stable rack holds jars in place, thus preventing the jars from tipping, touching other jars, or touching the sides of the canner.

Examining the Pressure Canning Process

In order to ensure a high-quality processed product that is free from microorganisms, be sure to follow each step in this section. Don't omit or modify any part. You may spend a bit more time canning low-acid foods with a pressure canner than you would canning high-acid foods in a water-bath canner, but the end result is worth the extra effort.

In this section, you begin your journey of pressure-canning low-acid foods. Avoid any temptation to omit any step or portion of any step in the process. Each step is important to produce safe, home-canned foods.

If you've never used a pressure canner, do a trial run with no jars: Heat up the canner and go through the steps of pressurizing and depressurizing to familiarize yourself with the sounds the pressure canner makes as it builds and then releases pressure. You'll hear the steam escaping, the weight gauge shaking, and the ticking of the canner as it heats and cools; if you don't know what to expect, you could misinterpret these noises as scary or wrong.

Step 1: Gear up

At least a couple of weeks before you do any pressure canning, you should check your equipment:

- ✔ Have the pressure gauge and seal on your pressure canner tested every year for accuracy. (Weighted gauges don't require testing.) This service is often offered for free at your local extension office.

- ✔ Use jars and two-piece caps made for home-canning. Discard any jars that are cracked or nicked.

- ✔ Never use sealing lids a second time. Always use new lids. The sealant on the underside of the lid is good for only one processing. If your jars don't seal the first time, always replace the lid with a fresh one. The sealant may have a problem, despite starting with a new lid, so check new lids for imperfections and scratches.

It's also a good idea to select your recipe and inventory your pantry for any nonperishable ingredients, adding any needed items to your shopping list. Your goal is to have all the supplies you need and your pressure canner in good working order on the day you're ready to can.

Preparing your pressure canner before the actual canning season means you won't find the store out of supplies and the extension agent too busy to check your gauge in time to begin canning when the produce is ripe.

On the actual canning day, get your tools ready by following these steps:

1. **Assemble your prechecked equipment and utensils.**

   In addition to your pressure canner and the standard canning supplies (jars with two-piece lids), other items can make your canning easier: things like a food scale, extra pans for cooking your veggies and keeping a water reserve on hand, a wide-mouth funnel, and so on. (Head to Chapter 3 of Book I for a list of canning supplies.)

2. **Wash your jars and screw bands in warm, soapy water, rinsing well to remove any soap residue.**

   Double-check for nicks and dents and discard any damaged items.

3. **Place your clean jars and lids in a kettle of hot — not boiling — water until you're ready to fill them.**

   Never boil the lids because the sealant material may be damaged and won't produce a safe vacuum seal.

4. **Ready your canner by filling it with 2 to 3 inches of water and heating the water.**

Always read the manufacturer's instructions for your pressure canner and follow them to the letter.

Also, assemble the other canning items you need. You can find a complete list in Chapter 3 of Book I.

Step 2: Prepare your food

Always start with food of the highest, freshest quality. Food that's spoiled or bruised doesn't improve in quality during the pressure-canning process! To prepare your food for pressure canning, follow these steps:

1. **Wash all food prior to packing it in the jars or precooking it.**

   For detailed instructions on washing your food, refer to Chapter 2 of Book II.

2. **Thoroughly cut away all evidence of spoilage or discard any inferior products.**

3. **Prepare the food by precisely following your recipe.**

   Some recipes call for you to fill your jars with raw food; others may want you to precook the food. If you're precooking your low-acid food before filling your jars, don't discard the cooking liquid; use this liquid for filling your jars.

Work in manageable batches. Your canner will determine the amount of produce you can process at one time.

Step 3: Fill your jars

Always place your product into hot jars. (You keep them hot by leaving them in a kettle of hot water, as explained in the earlier section "Step 1: Gear up.") To fill your jars, follow these steps:

1. **Remove a jar from the kettle with tongs, place it on a clean towel to catch any spills, and pack the food into the jar so that the food is snug, yet loose enough for liquid to circulate into the open spaces.**

2. **Ladle boiling water (or the liquid from precooking the vegetables) into the jars, leaving the amount of headspace stated in your recipe.**

   If you're adding cooking liquid, divide the cooking liquid evenly among the jars and finish filling the jars with boiling water, if necessary. That way, if you run short of the cooking liquid, you won't have one jar filled with only boiling water.

3. **Release any air bubbles with a nonmetallic spatula or a tool to free bubbles.**

   If the headspace drops, add food and liquid to the jar.

4. **Wipe the jar rims with a clean, damp cloth.**

   Have a few rags handy to be sure that you're using a clean one every time.

5. **Place a lid on the jar (seal side down) and secure the lid in place with a screw band.**

   Hand-tighten the band without overtightening it.

Always work quickly, stopping for nothing. Time is of the essence! Your hot foods need to remain hot, your lids seal best if placed on the jars while hot, and your food needs to be processed as quickly as possible to preserve the most flavor and quality.

Step 4: Place the jars in the canner

Place your filled and closed jars carefully on the rack in the pressure canner, making sure that you have the recommended amount of simmering water in the bottom of the canner. Don't crowd the jars or place more jars in the canner than is recommended for your size of pressure canner. Place them so that they're stable, won't tip, and don't touch each other or the side of the canner.

If your recipe makes more jars than your canner can hold, only fill enough jars for one canner load and do the rest in the next batch. Do not fill all the jars and leave a few waiting for the next canner load. You want your food to be as hot as possible, before adding to the canner. This cuts down on the time and effort it takes for the canner to get up to pressure.

Unlike water-bath canning (see Book II), you can process a second layer of pint or half-pint jars at the same time as long as your canner accommodates the height of the two layers. To build the second layer, place a second rack on top of the first layer of jars. Stagger the second layer of jars so that they aren't directly above the bottom layer. Staggering permits proper air circulation for achieving the proper pressure and temperature. After you have a few simple canning sessions successfully under your belt, try this technique to save a little time.

Step 5: Close and lock the canner

For optimum performance, steam must be allowed to steadily escape from the canner for a specified period. This process is called *exhaustion*. Properly closing and locking your pressure canner ensures that exhaustion can take place. Closely follow your owner's manual when closing and locking the pressure canner. (If not sealed properly, the canner won't build pressure and/or hot water will spit out.)

Step 6: Process your filled jars

Once your canner lid is locked on, you're ready to beginning processing your filled jars. Follow these steps:

1. **Allow a steady stream of steam to escape from the pressure canner for 10 minutes or the time recommended in your manual.**

2. **Close the vent, bringing the pressure to the amount specified in your recipe.**

   If you live in higher altitudes, see the upcoming section "Pressure Canning at Higher Altitudes" for information on how to adjust the pounds of pressure used during processing.

   Processing time starts when your canner reaches the required pressure. The pressure must remain constant for the entire processing time. If your pressure drops at any time during processing, so will your temperature. To remedy this problem, return the pressure to the specified amount by increasing the heat. After your pressure has been regained, start your processing time from the beginning.

3. **After the processing time has passed, turn the heat off and allow the pressure to return to 0.**

   Allowing the pressure to return to 0 may take as long as 30 minutes. Don't disturb the canner; jars that are upset may not seal properly.

Step 7: Release the pressure

Approximately 10 minutes after the pressure returns to 0, or at the time stated in the manual, remove the lid, opening the cover away from you and allowing the steam to flow away from you.

We can't emphasize enough the importance of following the instructions in your owner's manual, step by step, for releasing the pressure in the canner after your processing time is concluded. There's no quick-release method for a pressure canner as there is for a pressure cooker. Don't confuse the two!

Running water over your pressure canner to reduce the pressure is a definite no-no. The sudden change in temperature can cause the jars to burst.

Step 8: Remove and cool the jars

Ten minutes after you release the pressure (Step 7), remove the jars from the pressure canner with a jar lifter. Place them on a clean towel, away from drafts with 1 to 2 inches of space around the jars.

The jars may take as long as 24 hours to completely cool. Don't be tempted to play with the lids or adjust the bands.

As your jars cool, you'll hear a popping noise coming from them, indicating a vacuum seal. You'll soon start to look forward to these tiny pings and dings. Amy's children often give a shout each time they hear one. This canning music means you have successfully saved your summer bounty.

Step 9: Test the seal and store your bounty

The final pressure-canning step is to test the seals on your completely cooled jars: Push on the center of the lid. If the lid feels solid and doesn't indent, you've produced a successful seal. If the lid depresses when applying pressure, this jar isn't sealed. Refrigerate any unsealed jars immediately, using the contents within two weeks or the period stated in your recipe.

To store jars, do the following:

1. **Remove the screw bands of the sealed jars.**

2. **Remove any residue by washing the jars, lids, and bands in hot, soapy water; then dry them.**

3. **Label your jars with the content and date of processing.**

4. **Store the jars without the screw bands, in a cool, dark, dry place.**

Heeding Some General Directions

Some general directions apply to all the recipes in this chapter. Be sure to heed the following instructions as you prepare the upcoming recipes:

✔ Prepare your canning jars and two-piece caps (lids and screw bands) according to the manufacturer's instructions. Keep the jars and lids hot until you fill them.

✔ When you fill your jars, release any air bubbles with a nonreactive utensil (refer to Book II, Chapter 1). Add more of the food you're canning and/or liquid as necessary to maintain the headspace noted in the recipe.

✔ After filling your jars, wipe the jar rims. Then seal the jars with the two-piece caps, hand-tightening the bands.

✔ When the processing time is done, allow the pressure to return to 0, wait an additional 10 minutes, and then carefully open the canner lid.

✔ When your jars are done processing, remove them from the canner with a jar lifter. Place them on a clean kitchen towel away from drafts to cool.

✔ After the jars cool completely, test the seals. If you find jars that haven't sealed, refrigerate them and use them within the time specified in the recipe.

Disposing of Spoiled Products

Although you may follow all the steps and procedures for pressure canning low-acid foods (see the preceding section), you still have a chance for spoilage. Knowing the signs to look for is part of the food-preservation process.

Here are some visual signs that may indicate a spoiled product:

✔ A bulging lid or a broken seal

✔ A lid that shows signs of corrosion

✔ Food that has oozed or seeped under the lid

✔ Gassiness, indicated by tiny bubbles moving upward in the jar

✔ Food that looks mushy, moldy, or cloudy

✔ Food that gives off an unpleasant or disagreeable odor when the jar is opened

✔ Spurting liquid from the jar when the seal is broken

Storing your sealed jars without the bands allows you to see any signs of food seepage that indicates a potentially spoiled product.

Botulism poisoning can be fatal (see Book I, Chapter 1). Because botulism spores have no odor and can't be seen, you can't always tell which jars are tainted. *If you suspect that a jar of food is spoiled, never, never, never taste it.* Instead, dispose of the food responsibly.

When you need to dispose of spoiled low-acid foods, use one of the two disposal methods described in the following sections. The first method is for sealed jars, and second is for jars with broken seals.

If your jar is still sealed

If the jar has the seal intact, you can simply place your container in a garbage bag, tie it tightly, and discard it in the trash. Keeping the jar sealed keeps the product from coming in contact with any human or animal and eliminates the transfer of bacteria.

Be sure to thoroughly wash your hands and any surface that may have come in contact with spoiled food or its juices.

If your jar has a broken seal

If you see signs that the seal is broken or not tight, place the jar, the lid, the screw band, and the contents of the jar in a deep cooking pot. Cover the items with 1 to 2 inches of water, taking care not to splash any of the contents outside of the pot so that you don't cross-contaminate other foods in your household.

Cover the pot with a tight-fitting cover. Bring the contents to a boil. Keep the contents boiling for 30 minutes. Turn off the heat and allow the contents to cool while remaining covered. Discard the contents in a sealed container in the trash or bury them deeply in the soil.

Never pour the contents into a water source, a sink, or garbage disposal or down the toilet because the contents may come into contact with humans or animals through a water-reclamation process.

Using a solution made up of one part household chlorine bleach to four parts *tepid* (lukewarm) water, thoroughly wash all equipment, working surfaces, clothing, and body parts that may have come in contact with the jar or spoiled food. You may also add dishwashing soap. Dispose of the jar, the lid and screw band, and any sponges or dishcloths used in any phase of this process by wrapping the items in a trash bag, sealing the bag, and placing it in the trash.

Pressure Canning at Higher Altitudes

If you're canning at an elevation higher than 1,000 feet above sea level, adjust the pounds of pressure used during processing, according to Table 1-1. Your pressure-canner processing time will remain the same.

Table 1-1	High-Altitude Processing Times for Pressure Canning
Altitude	**Process at This Pressure**
2,000–3,000	11½ pounds
3,000–4,000	12 pounds
4,000–5,000	12½ pounds
5,000–6,000	13 pounds
6,000–7,000	13½ pounds
7,000–8,000	14 pounds
8,000–9,000	14½ pounds
9,000–10,000	15 pounds

If you don't know your altitude level, you can get this information by contacting your public library, a local college, or the cooperative extension service in your county or state. Or go to `http://national4-hheadquarters.gov/Extension/index.html`. Click your state on the map and follow the instructions on your state's website.

Chapter 2

Canning Veggies

....

In This Chapter

▶ Organizing your vegetables

▶ Filling your jars: Raw packing versus hot packing

▶ Processing vegetables perfectly

▶ Preparing nutritious meals from your canned vegetables

....

Recipes in This Chapter

▶ Canned Asparagus

▶ Canned Fresh Green Beans

▶ Canned Dried Beans

▶ Canned Beets

▶ Canned Bell Peppers

▶ Canned Carrots

▶ Canned Corn

▶ Canned Creamed Corn

▶ Canned Greens

▶ Canned Onions

▶ Canned Peas

▶ Canned White Potatoes

▶ Canned Sweet Potatoes

▶ Canned Summer Squash

▶ Canned Winter Squash

▶ Spaghetti Sauce

▶ Barbecue Sauce

Don't you just love the time of year when you're starting your garden — preparing the soil, sowing seeds, pulling weeds, looking for pests, and asking the gardening gods for perfect weather and an abundant harvest? Then, after months of hard work and dirty fingernails, you're rewarded with fresh vegetables.

At first, your garden produces enough each day for one or two meals, and then the explosion starts. Tomatoes, zucchini, and beans, to name a few, abound. You wonder, "How can just a few plants produce so many vegetables?" You're proud to share your bounty with friends, neighbors, and coworkers, but there's a limit to how much you can give away!

This chapter gives you basic information on selecting and preparing your vegetables, understanding which packing method (raw or hot) works best, knowing the correct pressure and processing times, and using the proper jar sizes for your vegetables.

Finding the Freshest Produce

When choosing which vegetables to can, be picky. The quality of your final product is affected by the quality of the food you start with.

Cracking the corn code

Starting with corn that has the husks on and the silk attached allows you to assess the freshness of the corn. Choose ears with brightly colored husks that are free of spots and moisture; silks should be golden, not matted or brown.

Here's a surefire way to select corn that is sure to be juicy and tender (see figure): Slightly peel back the husk to check for any pests. If all is clear (no bugs or mold), use your thumbnail to depress a kernel about an inch below the top of the corn. If the ear has adequate moisture, liquid will squirt out. Buy this ear! If no spitting occurs, select another ear and repeat the test.

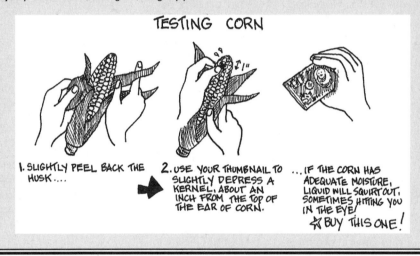

TESTING CORN

1. SLIGHTLY PEEL BACK THE HUSK....

2. USE YOUR THUMBNAIL TO SLIGHTLY DEPRESS A KERNEL, ABOUT AN INCH FROM THE TOP OF THE EAR OF CORN.

...IF THE CORN HAS ADEQUATE MOISTURE, LIQUID WILL SQUIRT OUT. SOMETIMES HITTING YOU IN THE EYE! ☆ BUY THIS ONE!

Whether harvesting your vegetables from the garden or shopping at a farmers' market, select vegetables that are free of bruises and imperfections. These marks may encourage the growth of bacteria in your food.

Follow this basic rule for evaluating damage on vegetables for canning: If you won't eat that portion of the vegetable fresh, don't buy it and can it.

The key to keeping all this wonderful, perfect freshness is to process the vegetables the day of harvesting or purchasing — the sooner, the better. If you need to wait a day, store the items in your refrigerator to preserve the quality and prevent deterioration of your food. Don't make your vegetables wait longer than one day! For more information on how to successfully process your canned vegetables, head to the section "Processing Tips for Successful Results," later in this chapter.

Even if you don't have a garden (or access to one), you can find high-quality vegetables at your local farmers' market. Purchasing vegetables in season (when they're abundant) is usually the best time to find the best pricing. Look for vegetables that are locally grown — they'll taste fresher and won't be covered with wax that prolongs the life of veggies.

Avoiding Certain Veggies

You shouldn't preserve some vegetables by pressure canning because the food may discolor, produce a stronger flavor when canned, or just lose its look (meaning it disintegrates or falls apart when placed under high heat and high pressure). Other methods, such as pickling (see Book III) or freezing (see Book VI), may be better preserving choices for these foods.

Table 2-1 lists some vegetables you may be tempted to pressure-can but that will preserve better in other ways.

Table 2-1	Vegetables Not Recommended for Pressure Canning
Vegetable	*Suggested Preservation Method*
Broccoli	Freezing
Brussels sprouts	Freezing
Cabbage	Pickling (to make sauerkraut)
Cauliflower	Pickling
Cucumbers	Pickling
Eggplant	Pickling
Mushrooms	Pickling
Parsnips	Pickling
Rutabagas	Pickling
Turnips	Pickling

If you're pickling mushrooms, for safety reasons, use ones that are commercially grown. Don't go out and pick them yourself.

Preparing Your Veggies

You can prep your clean vegetables for filling your jars in two ways: raw pack or hot pack. Not all vegetables are suited for both methods. Follow your recipe instructions.

Cleaning your vegetables

Properly cleaning your vegetables is important to your finished product. The method and amount of cleaning required is determined by where the vegetables were grown:

- **Vegetables grown above the ground:** These vegetables (like beans or squash) usually have a thinner, more tender skin than vegetables grown in the ground. Remove any stems and leaves. Run water over them, gently rub the skin with your fingers, and remove any dirt. Shake off the excess water and place your food on clean kitchen or paper towels.

- **Vegetables grown in the ground:** Root vegetables, such as carrots and beets, may require soaking to loosen any clinging soil. After first rinsing the vegetables, immerse them in a basin of cool water. Using a stiff brush (a new toothbrush works well), scrub the surface of the vegetables, removing any clinging soil. Rinse thoroughly with running water, placing the vegetables on clean kitchen or paper towels to drain.

Choosing a packing method

Raw packing and hot packing foods refers to the way the food is treated before it is placed in the jars. In *raw packing,* you don't cook the food prior to processing. In *hot packing,* you do. The following sections go into more details on which method is preferable when you're canning vegetables.

Packing food raw or hot doesn't change your processing time for either pressure canning or water-bath canning. Reaching the required pressure in your canner, usually 10 pounds, or returning a water-bath canner to a boil takes the same amount of time, regardless of the temperature of your raw- or hot-packed jars

Raw (cold packing)

The raw packing (also called cold packing) method uses raw, unheated vegetables for filling your prepared jars. Filling the jars with raw vegetables keeps them firm without being crushed during processing. Refer to your recipe instructions to decide whether to remove the skin or cut the vegetables into pieces.

Disadvantages of using raw vegetables include the following:

- ✔ **Floating food:** During the pressure-canning process, air is removed from the vegetable fiber, causing the food to shrink. With more room in the jars, the vegetables have room to float toward the top of the jar. (This is called *floating food.*) Floating food doesn't affect the quality of your final product, but it may be unattractive.

- ✔ **Discoloring:** *Discoloring* occurs when the food comes in contact with air in the jar, causing a color change in your food after two or three months of storage. The flavor of your product is not affected, but the change in color in a portion of the food may appear odd.

To fill your jars using a raw packing method, follow these instructions:

1. **Wash your vegetables.**

2. **Prepare the hot liquid (refer to your recipe) for filling your jars.**

3. **Fill the hot, prepared jars with your raw vegetables.**

4. **Add the hot liquid and canning salt, if required.**

5. **Release any air bubbles with a nonreactive tool (refer to Book II, Chapter 1).**

   If the headspace in your jar drops, add food and liquid to maintain the headspace stated in your recipe.

6. **Wipe the jar rims, add the two-piece caps, and process the filled jars in a pressure canner.**

   See Book II, Chapter 1.

Hot packing

When you hot pack, you precook or heat your vegetables prior to placing them in your prepared canning jars. Hot packing is the preferred method for the majority of vegetables, particularly firm ones, such as carrots and beets. Using precooked vegetables improves the shelf life of the processed food by increasing the vacuum created in the jar during the pressure-canning period.

Precooking your vegetables in a boiling liquid, usually water, preshrinks the food and makes it more pliable, which allows you to pack more food into your jars. You also use fewer jars when you hot pack.

The method is a simple one:

1. **Wash your vegetables.**

2. **Heat your liquid to a boil in a large pot and add the vegetables, precooking them as directed in your recipe.**

Using your canned vegetables

Seeing a shelf lined with pressure-canned vegetables is quite rewarding, knowing all the care and effort applied to the process. Are you wondering, though, what you can do with all this nutritious food? Try the following:

✔ **Serve a canned vegetable as a side dish:** Use vegetables that have a firm texture, such as corn or carrots, for a side dish. Softer vegetables, such as squash and onions, are better used as a flavor ingredient in a recipe.

✔ **Combine your canned vegetables with meats and other ingredients to create easy, nutritious meals.** The recipes in this chapter offer a few suggestions.

When using low-acid, pressure-canned vegetables, always boil your food for 15 minutes *before you taste the food*. For altitudes over 1,000 feet above sea level, extend the boiling period 1 minute for each increase of 1,000 feet.

3. **Immediately fill your prepared jars with the hot vegetables, followed with the hot cooking liquid.**

4. **Release any air bubbles with a nonreactive tool.**

   If the headspace in your jar drops, add food and liquid to maintain the headspace stated in your recipe.

5. **Wipe the jar rims, add the two-piece caps, and process the filled jars in a pressure canner.**

   See Book II, Chapter 1.

Processing Tips for Successful Results

Because vegetables are low-acid foods, you must use the pressure-canning method outlined in Book V, Chapter 1. In addition to those pressure-canner-processing steps, use these tips for producing a high-quality product that's safe for eating:

✔ **Get your supplies ready ahead of time.** About one week before you begin pressure canning, assemble and check your equipment (see Book V, Chapter 1). Locate your recipe and review the ingredients you need to have on hand. Stopping at any stage of food preparing or processing adversely affects the quality of your final product.

✔ **Take a few minutes before you begin to acquaint yourself with the steps for pressure-canner processing in Book V, Chapter 1.** Always check your recipe to ensure that you're processing your food for the correct time, pressure, and jar size.

✔ **Use only one size jar (pints or quarts) for each batch of food.** Using a consistent jar size allows you to complete the correct processing time required to evenly heat the jars and destroy microorganisms.

✔ **Using or not using salt in your vegetables is a personal preference.** Add ½ teaspoon to each pint jar and 1 teaspoon to each quart jar before adding the hot liquid. If you add salt, use pickling or canning salt, which doesn't have preservatives, to eliminate cloudiness in the liquid.

✔ **Cover the vegetables with liquid, allowing the proper headspace.** Completely covering the vegetables prevents discoloration and spoilage. Head to Book II, Chapter 1 for detailed information on why headspace is important.

✔ **Release air bubbles.** Releasing all trapped air bubbles between the food pieces prevents a decrease in the liquid level of your final product, keeping the correct air space in the jar. After releasing air bubbles, you may need to add food or liquid to the jar. Go to Book II, Chapter 1 for more information on how to release air bubbles.

✔ **Be ready to process your jars immediately after filling them and process them exactly as the recipe indicates.** Processing immediately decreases the opportunity for microorganisms to reenter the jars.

✔ **Cool your jars.** Let your jars cool naturally. You may need to cool them as long as 24 hours.

✔ **Adjust for altitude.** When canning at altitudes over 1,000 feet above sea level, refer to the altitude chart in Book II, Chapter 1 for pressure adjustments.

The following sections offer instructions and guidelines for pressure canning some of the more common fresh vegetables.

Asparagus

Canning asparagus is a great way to preserve this delicate vegetable. With only one short season, asparagus is usually a special treat or pricy delicacy during the rest of the year. Keeping plenty on hand will ensure that your family can enjoy this treat any time it wants. (In Book III, Chapter 2, you can find a recipe for Pickled Asparagus.)

To prepare for canning, select firm, bright-green stalks with tightly closed tips. Stalks with small diameters indicate a young, tender vegetable. Cut stalks into 1-inch pieces or can them whole, placing the tips of the stalks toward the top of the jar. (Be sure to trim stalks from the bottom to maintain the headspace indicated in the recipe.)

Beans

Garden fresh green beans are a staple for any pantry. The Canned Fresh Green Beans recipe in this chapter is great for the beginning pressure canner. Although the recipe specifically uses green beans, all colors of beans — green, yellow, or purple — work equally well.

When you can green, string, Italian, or wax beans, select ones that are tender and small. Remove the ends and strings from the beans. Can them whole or cut them into 1- to 2-inch pieces.

Dried beans

Dried beans are a great way to add protein and richness to many dishes. Beans are inexpensive and work well blended as a thickener, a recipe-extender, and a plain stick-to-your-ribs addition to any meal. Add rice to beans, and you have complete protein. Delicious! Dried beans suitable for canning include peas, navy, pinto, soy, lima, and so on.

To prepare dried beans, check for any nonbean material, such as stems or stones. Rinse the dried beans before you soak them to remove any dust or dirt particles: Simply place the beans in a colander and run cold water over them while stirring them with your hands or a spoon.

Beets

Select beets with a deep red color. A beet with a diameter of 1 to 2 inches is the most desirable size for pressure canning. Larger-size beets are best pickled. (See Book III, Chapter 2 for information on pickling and a Spiced Pickled Beets recipe.)

To preserve the bright, red color of the beet, add 1 tablespoon vinegar (with an acidity of 5 percent) to each quart of liquid before sealing the jars.

Carrots

Carrots are an inexpensive vegetable at farmers' markets during their season, and canning is an excellent way to preserve them. Canned carrots keep all their sweet flavor, and the texture remains very nice.

For canning, choose carrots with a diameter of 1 to 1½ inches.

Canned carrots make a favorite side dish even faster. Once reheated, add brown sugar and butter for a sweet treat.

Corn

Canned corn is a staple in most people's homes. Many people don't realize how easy it is to store this tasty vegetable.

Creamed corn doesn't actually contain cream. Its creaminess comes from the naturally sweet juice, or *milk,* of the kernel. To obtain the creaminess, simply cut off the kernels and run your knife against the cob a second time, even closer to release the milk. Creamed corn is a great base for soups and makes a classic comfort food.

The Canned Cream Corn recipe in this chapter uses pints. (Quarts aren't recommended.)

Corn can sometimes develop a brown hue during pressure canning. This darkening is due to the caramelization of sugars during the process. It affects only the corn's aesthetics — it's still safe to eat.

Greens

Greens is a catchall term that refers to the green, leafy portions of a variety of plants that, when cooked (traditionally simmered in water with some type of pork fat), creates a delicious addition to many meals. You can use any combination: beets, collard, kale, mustard, spinach, Swiss chard, and turnip.

Canned greens are a fast way to add nutrients to any meal. Add them to soups and stews during the last 15 minutes of cooking time.

Select tender stems and leaves to produce a superior product after cooking and pressure canning. Large, older stems and leaves tend to produce a strong-tasting or stringy product.

Onions

Canned onions are useful for any quick meal. They're great if eaten on a burger, heated and added to gravy, or just eaten as a condiment.

Onions are a staple ingredient in many recipes. Their savory flavor often is the finishing touch to your favorite meal. Canning onions leave them soft but flavorful. Keep these onions in your pantry as an important ingredient for your favorite recipe.

Peas

You can pack a lot of peas in a jar. There's nothing like the taste of garden fresh peas. If your kids have decided they don't like cooked peas, convince them that your own canned peas are worth a try.

Try canned peas mixed with rice and tamari sauce.

Peppers

Canned peppers come out tender and full of flavor. Heat them up with sautéed onions and hot sausage. Sweet, firm bell peppers produce the best results.

With so many beautiful colored peppers available, a jar of canned bell peppers makes a lovely gift.

Because of the extremely low acid level in this vegetable, you must adjust the acidity level of the bell peppers by adding bottled lemon juice. Use only pint or half-pint jars for this extremely low-acid vegetable.

To peel peppers easily, heat them in a 400° oven for 6 to 8 minutes, or until the skin blisters. Then cover the peppers with a damp cloth and let them cool. Voilá! You can now easily remove skins with a knife or simply by rubbing them with your hands as you run cool water over the pepper.

Potatoes

The only potatoes recommended for pressure canning are sweet potatoes, yams, and white, or Irish, potatoes:

- ✔ **White or Irish:** These potatoes are round and white with a thin skin. Peel the potatoes prior to precooking. Small potatoes (2 to 3 inches in diameter) may be left whole; cut larger potatoes into quarters before precooking. I (Amy) drain my canned potatoes and use them in homemade hash in the winter. They're hearty breakfast fare after a cold morning at the farm.

- ✔ **Sweet potatoes and yams:** Sweet potatoes are roots, and yams are tubers — so they're actually from two different plant species. Even though sweet potatoes and yams are unrelated, they're suitable for the same uses. Sweet potatoes have skin colors ranging from light yellow to dark orange and flesh colors ranging from pale yellow to medium orange. Sweet potatoes are also sweeter than yams. Yams contain more natural sugar and have a higher moisture content than sweet potatoes; they're white to deep red in flesh color with skin colors ranging from creamy white to deep red. Small potatoes may be left whole; cut larger ones into quarters before removing the skins.

Sweet potatoes and yams can complement a meal, with their rich, naturally sweet flavor. Their bright orange color makes a dish pop, and many who think they don't like any veggies are pleasantly surprised at the delicious taste of the sweet potato. The Canned Sweet Potatoes recipe in this chapter produces a firmer finished product with much more flavor — a definite improvement over store-bought sweet potatoes or yams from a can.

Using any other potatoes yields inferior results because of their chemical makeup (texture and composition).

Summer squash

Summer squash include crookneck, zucchini, and patty pan, to name a few. The skins are thin and edible, eliminating the need to peel them.

Summer squash is one of those vegetables that seems to grow faster than anyone can use it. The Canned Summer Squash recipe in this chapter is an easy way to keep that sunny flavor for the winter months and add some brightness to soups and stews.

Winter squash

Winter squash is good for canning. Winter squash varieties include banana, butternut, Hubbard, spaghetti, and turban squash.

Because pumpkins are similar in texture to winter squash, you can use the Canned Winter Squash recipe and instructions in this chapter to can pumpkin also. Canning winter squash and pumpkins is a bit labor-intensive — some of these winter vegetables can be difficult to peel and clean — but the rewards are oh, so good!

Add winter squash to stews, mash and sweeten them with brown sugar and butter for a great side dish, or simply heat and serve.

Canned Asparagus

Prep time: 15 min • **Process time:** 40 min (quarts); 30 min (pints) • **Yield:** 7 quarts or 14 pints

24 pounds fresh, young asparagus

Canning salt

1 Wash the asparagus spears. Cut them into 1-inch pieces. In a 12-quart pot, bring water to a boil. Heat the asparagus pieces in the boiling water for 2 to 3 minutes, until the spears are bright green but still firm inside. Do not drain.

2 Loosely pack the cut spears into jars. (Don't press them down.) Pour the boiling cooking liquid over the pieces, leaving 1-inch headspace. Add 1 teaspoon salt to each quart jar or ½ teaspoon salt to each pint jar.

3 Process the filled jars in a pressure canner at 10 pounds pressure for 40 minutes (quarts) or 30 minutes (pints).

4 After processing, if you find jars that haven't sealed, refrigerate them and use them within 2 weeks. Prior to eating or tasting, boil the food for 15 minutes.

Per ½-cup serving: Calories 23 (From Fat 3); Fat 0g (Saturated 0g); Cholesterol 0mg; Sodium 301mg; Carbohydrates 4g (Dietary Fiber 2g); Protein 3g.

Canned Fresh Green Beans

Prep time: 15 min • **Process time:** 25 min (quarts); 20 min (pints) • **Yield:** 8 quarts or 16 pints

Ingredients	*Directions*
4 pounds fresh green beans **Canning salt**	**1** In an 8-quart pot, bring 2 quarts water to a boil. While the water is boiling, trim off the ends of the beans and cut them into 2-inch pieces (see Figure 2-1).
	2 Tightly pack the cut beans into the prepared jars. Pour the boiling water over the beans, leaving 1-inch headspace. Add 1 teaspoon salt to each quart jar or ½ teaspoon salt to each pint jar.
	3 Process the filled jars in a pressure canner at 10 pounds pressure for 25 minutes (quarts) or 20 minutes (pints).
	4 After processing, if you find jars that haven't sealed, refrigerate them and use them within 2 weeks. Prior to eating or tasting, boil the food for 15 minutes.

Per ½-cup serving: Calories 10 (From Fat 1); Fat 0g (Saturated 0g); Cholesterol 0mg; Sodium 292mg; Carbohydrates 2g (Dietary Fiber 1g); Protein 1g.

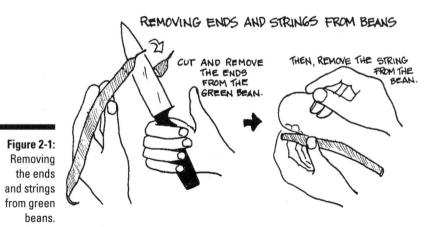

REMOVING ENDS AND STRINGS FROM BEANS

CUT AND REMOVE THE ENDS FROM THE GREEN BEAN.

THEN, REMOVE THE STRING FROM THE BEAN.

Figure 2-1:
Removing the ends and strings from green beans.

Canned Dried Beans

Prep time: 15 min, plus soaking time • **Process time:** 50 min (quarts); 40 min (pints) •
Yield: 7 quarts or 14 pints

Ingredients	Directions
3 pounds dried beans (or dried peas) **Canning salt**	**1** Rinse the beans in a colander and remove any stones or broken bean pieces. Place them in a 12-quart pot and cover them with cold water. Let the beans soak at least 12 hours or overnight.
	2 Pour out the soaking water and add more cold water to cover the beans. Bring the covered beans to a boil and allow them to boil for 30 minutes, or until tender. Do not drain.
	3 Using a slotted spoon, loosely pack the hot beans into your canning jars, leaving 1-inch headspace. Pour the cooking liquid over the beans, maintaining the proper headspace. Add 1 teaspoon salt to each quart jar or ½ teaspoon salt to each pint jar.
	4 Process the filled jars in a pressure canner at 10 pounds pressure for 50 minutes (quarts) or 40 minutes (pints).
	5 After processing, if you find jars that haven't sealed, refrigerate them and use them within 2 weeks. Prior to eating or tasting, boil the food for 15 minutes.

Per ½-cup serving: Calories 71 (From Fat 2); Fat 0g (Saturated 0g); Cholesterol 0mg; Sodium 292mg; Carbohydrates 13g (Dietary Fiber 4g); Protein 5g.

Canned Beets

Prep time: 15 min • **Process time:** 35 min (quarts); 30 min (pints) • **Yield:** 7 quarts or 14 pints

Ingredients	*Directions*
21 pounds beets, without tops **Canning salt**	*1* Scrub your beets clean of dirt and remove the tap roots. Place the cleaned beets in a 12-quart pot and cover them with water. Boil the beets for 15 to 20 minutes.
	2 When beets are cool enough to handle, the skins will peel off easily. Remove them from the water and peel. Trim the remaining root and stem. Leave small beets whole and cut larger beets in half for a better fit in the jar. Reserve the cooking liquid.
	3 Pack the beets into your prepared jars. Pour the cooking liquid over the beets, leaving 1-inch headspace. Add 1 teaspoon salt to each quart jar or ½ teaspoon salt to each pint jar.
	4 Process the filled jars in a pressure canner at 10 pounds pressure for 35 minutes (quarts) or 30 minutes (pints).
	5 After processing, if you find jars that haven't sealed, refrigerate them and use them within 2 weeks. Prior to eating or tasting, boil the food for 15 minutes.

Per ½-cup serving: *Calories 72 (From Fat 3); Fat 0g (Saturated 0g); Cholesterol 0mg; Sodium 416mg; Carbohydrates 0g (Dietary Fiber 0g); Protein 0g.*

Canned Bell Peppers

Prep time: 15 min • **Process time:** 40 min (pints); 35 min (half-pints) • **Yield:** 5 pints or 10 half-pints

Ingredients	Directions
5 pounds sweet peppers **Lemon juice** **Canning salt**	**1** Wash the peppers and cut them into quarters, removing the stems and seeds. Meanwhile, bring 2 quarts water to a boil.
	2 Pack flattened peppers firmly into jars. Pour the boiling water over the peppers, leaving 1-inch headspace. Add 1 tablespoon lemon juice and ½ teaspoon salt to each pint jar or ½ tablespoon lemon juice and ¼ teaspoon salt to each half-pint jar.
	3 Process the filled jars in a pressure canner at 10 pounds pressure for 40 minutes (pints) or 35 minutes (half-pints).
	4 After processing, if you find jars that haven't sealed, refrigerate them and use them within 2 weeks. Prior to eating or tasting, boil the food for 15 minutes.

Per ½-cup serving: Calories 32 (From Fat 2); Fat 0g (Saturated 0g); Cholesterol 0mg; Sodium 584mg; Carbohydrates 8g (Dietary Fiber 2g); Protein 1g.

Canned Carrots

Prep time: 15 min • **Process time:** 35 min (quarts) or 25 min (pints) • **Yield:** 3 quarts or 6 pints

Ingredients	*Directions*
12 pounds of carrots, peeled and without tops **Canning salt**	**1** Rinse and scrub the carrots with a brush to remove any dirt. Alternatively, remove the skin with a vegetable peeler. Remove the carrot tops. Cut the carrots into ¼-inch slices or dice the carrots, being sure that all the diced pieces are approximately the same size.
	2 Place the sliced or diced carrots in a 12-quart pot and cover them with water. Bring them to a boil. Reduce heat to medium and allow the carrots to simmer for 5 minutes, or until they're still slightly firm in the center but tender on the outside. Do not drain.
	3 Pack the hot carrots into your prepared jars. Pour the cooking liquid over them, leaving 1-inch headspace. Add 1 teaspoon salt to each quart jar or ½ teaspoon salt to each pint jar.
	4 Process the filled jars in a pressure canner at 10 pounds pressure for 35 minutes (quarts) or 25 minutes (pints).
	5 After processing, if you find jars that haven't sealed, refrigerate them and use them within 2 weeks. Before tasting, boil the food for 10 minutes.

Per ½-cup serving: *Calories 94 (From Fat 3); Fat 0g (Saturated 0g); Cholesterol 0mg; Sodium 424mg; Carbohydrates 22g (Dietary Fiber 7g); Protein 2g.*

Canned Corn

Prep time: 15 min • **Process time:** 1 hr, 25 min (quarts); 55 min (pints) • **Yield:** 6 quarts or 12 pints

Ingredients	Directions
24 pounds fresh corn on the cob **Canning salt**	**1** Remove the husk and silk from the corn. Using a sharp knife, slice the corn from the cob, measuring the corn as you go so that you know how many total pints or quarts of corn kernels you have. Meanwhile, bring 1 gallon water to a boil in an 8-quart pot. (You'll use this water in Step 3.)
	2 Place the corn in a 12-quart pot. For each quart of corn, add 2 cups boiling water; for each pint of corn, add 1 cup boiling water. Place the pot over medium-high heat and bring to a simmer. Then reduce the heat to medium and allow the corn to simmer for 5 minutes.
	3 Ladle the corn into your prepared jars and pour additional boiling water over it, if necessary, leaving 1-inch headspace. Add 1 teaspoon salt to each quart jar or ½ teaspoon salt to each pint jar.
	4 Process the filled jars in a pressure canner at 10 pounds pressure for 1 hour, 25 minutes (quarts) or 55 minutes (pints).
	5 After processing, if you find jars that haven't sealed, refrigerate them and use them within 2 weeks. Prior to eating or tasting, boil the food for 15 minutes.

Per ½-cup serving: Calories 136 (From Fat 15); Fat 2g (Saturated 0g); Cholesterol 0mg; Sodium 312mg; Carbohydrates 32g (Dietary Fiber 3g); Protein 4g.

Canned Creamed Corn

Prep time: 20 min • **Process time:** 1 hr, 35 min • **Yield:** 9 pints

Ingredients	*Directions*
20 pounds corn on the cob **Canning salt**	*1* In a 12-quart pot, bring 2 gallons water to a boil. Remove the husk and silk from the corn. Blanch the corn on the cob for 4 minutes in the boiling water. Allow the corn to cool enough to handle.
	2 In a large bowl, slice the corn kernels from the cob with a sharp knife. Then run the knife blade along the ear again to remove the extra juice or milk. Measure the corn as you go so that you know how many pints of corn and corn milk you have.
	3 Place the corn and corn milk in a 12-quart pot. For each pint of corn and corn milk, add 2 cups water. Heat the corn to boiling.
	4 Using a canning funnel, pour the corn and corn milk mixture into your prepared jars, leaving 1-inch headspace. Add ½ teaspoon salt to each jar. If necessary, add boiling water to the jars to attain the required headspace.
	5 Process the filled pint jars in a pressure canner at 10 pounds pressure for 1 hour, 35 minutes.
	6 After processing, if you find jars that haven't sealed, refrigerate them and use them within 2 weeks. Prior to eating or tasting, boil the food for 10 minutes.

Per ½-cup serving: Calories 151 (From Fat 16); Fat 2g (Saturated 0g); Cholesterol 0mg; Sodium 605mg; Carbohydrates 35g (Dietary Fiber 4g); Protein 5g.

Tip: For easier slicing, place a saucer upside down in the bottom of your bowl, to rest the ear of corn on. Kernels and milk will be caught in the bottom of the bowl.

Canned Greens

Prep time: 15 min • **Process time:** 1 hr, 30 min (qts) 1 hr, 10 min (pts) • **Yield:** 7 qts or 14 pts

Ingredients	Directions
28 pounds fresh, young greens	**1** Thoroughly wash the greens, changing the water in the sink once or twice to be sure all the grit is removed. Place the greens in a 12-quart pot and add enough water to cover. Heat the greens on medium-high until they're wilted, about 5 to 7 minutes.
	2 Using a slotted spoon, remove the greens from the water and cut them into small pieces (about 1 inch). Reserve the cooking liquid.
	3 Loosely pack the greens into jars (don't press down) and pour the boiling hot cooking liquid over them, leaving 1-inch headspace.
	4 Process the filled jars in a pressure canner at 10 pounds pressure for 1 hour, 30 minutes (quarts) or 1 hour, 10 minutes (pints).
	5 After processing, if you find jars that haven't sealed, refrigerate them and use them within 2 weeks. Prior to eating or tasting, boil the food for 15 minutes.

Per ½-cup serving: Calories 55 (From Fat 4); Fat 0g (Saturated 0g); Cholesterol 0mg; Sodium 53mg; Carbohydrates 10g (Dietary Fiber 7g); Protein 6g.

Canned Onions

Prep time: 20 min • **Process time:** 40 min (quarts and pints) • **Yield:** 10 quarts or 20 pints

Ingredients	Directions
20 pounds fresh onions **Canning salt**	**1** Peel and wash the onions. If you're using large onions, chop them or slice them into ½-inch pieces.
	2 Place the onions in a 12-quart pot, cover them with water, and bring them to a boil over medium-high heat. Boil them for 5 minutes, or until they're translucent.
	3 Using a slotted spoon, remove the onions from the cooking liquid (reserve the liquid for filling the jars) and firmly pack them into the prepared jars. Add 1 teaspoon salt to each quart jar or ½ teaspoon salt to each pint jar. Pour the hot cooking liquid over the onions, leaving 1-inch headspace.
	4 Process the filled jars in a pressure canner at 10 pounds pressure for 40 minutes (quarts or pints).
	5 After processing, if you find jars that haven't sealed, refrigerate them and use them within 2 weeks. Prior to eating or tasting, boil the food for 15 minutes.

Per ½-cup serving: Calories 42 (From Fat 2); Fat 0g (Saturated 0g); Cholesterol 0mg; Sodium 294mg; Carbohydrates 10g (Dietary Fiber 1g); Protein 1g.

Canned Peas

Prep time: 15 min • **Process time:** 40 min (quarts and pints) • **Yield:** 7 quarts or 14 pints

Ingredients	*Directions*
28 to 30 pounds fresh, young peas in the pod **Canning salt**	**1** Wash and remove the pods. Place the peas in an 8-quart pot, cover them with water, and bring to a boil over high heat. Allow the peas to boil for 3 to 5 minutes, or until they're bright green but not fully cooked.
	2 Remove the peas from the cooking liquid (reserve the liquid for filling jars) and loosely pack the peas into the prepared jars. Pour hot cooking water over them, leaving 1-inch headspace. Add 1 teaspoon salt to each quart jar or ½ teaspoon salt to each pint jar.
	3 Process the filled jars in a pressure canner at 10 pounds pressure for 40 minutes (quarts or pints).
	4 After processing, if you find jars that haven't sealed, refrigerate them and use them within 2 weeks. Prior to eating or tasting, boil the food for 15 minutes.

Per ½-cup serving: Calories 70 (From Fat 3); Fat 0g (Saturated 0g); Cholesterol 0mg; Sodium 295mg; Carbohydrates 13g (Dietary Fiber 4g); Protein 5g.

Canned White Potatoes

Prep time: 15 min • **Process time:** 40 min (quarts); 35 min (pints) • **Yield:** 7 quarts or 14 pints

Ingredients	*Directions*
7 pounds fresh, young potatoes **Canning salt**	*1* In a 12-quart pot, bring 2 gallons water to boil. Wash and peel your potatoes. Cube the potatoes into ½-inch pieces. Carefully place the potatoes in the boiling water and cook for 2 minutes or until potatoes are partially cooked but still firm.
	2 Pack the hot potatoes into the prepared jars, reserving the liquid you cooked them in. Add 1 teaspoon salt to each quart jar or ½ teaspoon salt to each pint jar. Pour the cooking liquid over the potatoes, leaving 1-inch headspace.
	3 Process the filled jars in a pressure canner at 10 pounds pressure for 40 minutes (quarts) or 35 minutes (pints).
	4 After processing, if you find jars that haven't sealed, refrigerate them and use them within 2 weeks. Prior to eating or tasting, boil the food for 15 minutes.

Per ½-cup serving: *Calories 36 (From Fat 1); Fat 0g (Saturated 0g); Cholesterol 0mg; Sodium 292mg; Carbohydrates 7g (Dietary Fiber 1g); Protein 1g.*

Canned Sweet Potatoes

Prep time: 15 min • **Process time:** 1 hr, 30 min (qts); 1 hr, 5 min (pts) • **Yield:** 7 qts or 14 pts

Ingredients	*Directions*
21 pounds sweet potatoes **Canning salt**	**1** In a 12-quart pot, bring 2 gallons water to boil. Wash and peel the sweet potatoes. Cube them into ½-inch pieces.
	2 Carefully place the sweet potatoes into the boiling water and cook for 10 minutes, or until the potatoes are partially cooked but still firm. Reserve the cooking liquid.
	3 Pack the hot sweet potatoes into the prepared jars. Add 1 teaspoon salt to each quart jar or ½ teaspoon salt to each pint jar. Pour the cooking liquid over the sweet potatoes, leaving 1-inch headspace.
	4 Process the filled jars in a pressure canner at 10 pounds pressure for 1 hour, 30 minutes (quarts) or 1 hour, 5 minutes (pints).
	5 After processing, if you find jars that haven't sealed, refrigerate them and use them within 2 weeks. Prior to eating or tasting, boil the food for 15 minutes.

Per ½-cup serving: Calories 139 (From Fat 4); Fat 0g (Saturated 0g); Cholesterol 0mg; Sodium 308mg; Carbohydrates 32g (Dietary Fiber 2g); Protein 2g.

Canned Summer Squash

Prep time: 15 min • **Process time:** 40 min (quarts); 30 min (pints) • **Yield:** 7 quarts or 14 pints

Ingredients	*Directions*
18 to 20 pounds summer squash **Canning salt**	*1* In a 12-quart pot, bring 2 gallons water to boil. Wash and cut the summer squash into ¼-inch slices or 1-inch cubes. Carefully place the cubed or sliced squash into your boiling water and return to a boil for 5 minutes, or until slightly softened. Reserve the cooking liquid.
	2 Using a canning funnel, loosely pack the squash into the prepared jars. Pour the hot cooking liquid over the squash, leaving ½-inch headspace. Add 1 teaspoon salt to each quart jar or ½ teaspoon salt to each pint jar.
	3 Process the filled jars in a pressure canner at 10 pounds pressure for 40 minutes (quarts) or 30 minutes (pints).
	4 After processing, if you find jars that haven't sealed, refrigerate them and use them within 2 weeks. Prior to eating or tasting, boil the food for 10 minutes.

Per ½-cup serving: *Calories 28 (From Fat 3); Fat 0g (Saturated 0g); Cholesterol 0mg; Sodium 294mg; Carbohydrates 6g (Dietary Fiber 3g); Protein 2g.*

Canned Winter Squash

Prep time: 15 min • **Process time:** 1 hr, 25 min (qts); 55 min (pts) • **Yield:** 7 qts or 14 pts

Ingredients	Directions
21 pounds winter squash (or pumpkin) **Canning salt**	*1* Cut the winter squash into 3-x-5-inch pieces. Scrape out the fiber and seeds. Place the squash in a 12-quart pot and cover with water. Bring the squash to a simmer on medium-high heat and allow it to simmer until soft, approximately 10 to 30 minutes, depending on the variety.
	2 Carefully remove the squash from the cooking liquid and discard the liquid. Scrape the pulp from the softened skin and place it in a sturdy mixing bowl.
	3 Using a potato masher, mash the pulp until smooth. Return the mashed pulp to the empty pot and bring it to a boil over medium-high heat. Boil for 10 minutes, stirring often to prevent sticking.
	4 Pack the boiling hot pulp into the prepared jars, leaving 1-inch headspace. Add 1 teaspoon salt to each quart jar or ½ teaspoon salt to each pint jar.
	5 Process the filled jars in a pressure canner at 10 pounds pressure for 1 hour, 25 minutes (quarts) or 55 minutes (pints).
	6 After processing, if you find jars that haven't sealed, refrigerate them and use them within 2 weeks. Prior to eating or tasting, boil the food for 15 minutes.

Per ½-cup serving: Calories 65 (From Fat 2); Fat 0g (Saturated 0g); Cholesterol 0mg; Sodium 295mg; Carbohydrates 17g (Dietary Fiber 5g); Protein 1g.

Spaghetti Sauce

Prep time: 30 min • **Cook time:** 1¹/₂ hrs • **Process time:** 25 min (qts); 20 min (pts) • **Yield:** 5 pts

Ingredients	*Directions*
10 quarts of tomatoes	*1* Peel and chop the tomatoes. Chop the onions and peppers and mince the garlic.
1 cup onions, chopped	
1 cup green pepper, chopped	*2* Combine the chopped vegetables and all the seasonings in a 6-quart pot and bring to a boil over medium-high heat. Reduce the heat and simmer until thickened as desired, about 1½ hours. Stir often to prevent scorching.
4 cloves minced garlic	
3 tablespoons salt	
¹/₄ cup sugar	
2 tablespoons Italian seasoning	*3* Ladle your spaghetti sauce into the prepared jars, leaving ½-inch headspace.
	4 Process the filled jars in a pressure canner at 15 pounds pressure, for 25 minutes (quarts) or 20 minutes (pints). When the processing time is done, allow the pressure to return to 0. Wait 10 minutes and then carefully open the canner lid.
	5 Prior to eating or tasting, boil the food for 15 minutes. Use any unsealed jars within 2 weeks.

Per ¹/₂-cup serving: Calories 23 (From Fat 3); Fat 0g (Saturated 0g); Cholesterol 0mg; Sodium 270mg; Carbohydrates 5g (Dietary Fiber 1g); Protein 1g.

Barbeque Sauce

Prep time: 30 min • **Cook time:** 1½ hrs • **Process time:** 20 min • **Yield:** 10 pints

Ingredients	*Directions*
4 quarts canned tomatoes	*1* Place the canned tomatoes in a 6-quart pot. Add the remaining vegetables and seasonings.
1½ cups chopped celery	
4 onions, chopped	
4 stalks of celery, chopped	*2* Bring to a boil over medium-high heat. Reduce heat and simmer until all the vegetables are soft, about 20 minutes.
2 green peppers, cored and chopped	
2 hot peppers (more or less as desired), seeded and chopped	*3* Strain the cooked vegetables through a food mill and return them to the pot. Simmer the sauce on medium heat until it's reduced by half, stirring often to prevent scorching.
4 cloves garlic, minced	
1 cup honey	
1 tablespoon dry mustard	*4* Ladle the boiling barbeque sauce into the prepared jars (pints), leaving ½-inch headspace.
1 tablespoon salt	
2 teaspoons hot sauce	*5* Process the filled jars in a pressure canner at 10 pounds pressure for 20 minutes. When the processing time is done, allow the pressure to return to 0, wait an additional 10 minutes, and then carefully open the canner lid.
1½ cups white vinegar	
½ teaspoon liquid smoke (adjust as desired)	
	6 Use any unsealed jars within 2 weeks. Prior to eating or tasting, boil the food for 15 minutes.

Per 2-tablespoon serving: Calories 56 (From Fat 4); Fat 0g (Saturated 0g); Cholesterol 0mg; Sodium 194mg; Carbohydrates 14g (Dietary Fiber 2g); Protein 1g.

Chapter 3

Canning Meats and Seafood

. . . .

In This Chapter

▶ Getting the lowdown on canning meats

▶ Keeping safety in mind

▶ Selecting the best cuts

. . . .

Canning meats are an often forgotten area of home canning, which is a shame. Canning a variety of meats is a great way to add a protein component to your pantry and build up a quantity of the most expensive part of your grocery bill as you can afford to.

In this chapter, you discover how to safely can meat, game, poultry, and fish and seafood. These items add variety to your pantry and give you delicious dinner foods that your whole family will want to eat. Book V, Chapter 4 covers ways in which to can meats with vegetables and other ingredients to make soups and stews.

The Basics of Canning Meats

Canning meat results in a tender product. Because canning meat draws out the natural juices but still keeps them intact, the meat is naturally succulent and delicious. Often, you don't need additional seasoning, so you can rest assured that your family is eating only healthy food and not flavor-enhancing additives and preservatives.

Without fail, canning meat, poultry, and seafood means using the pressure canner. These foods are low-acid foods and are unsafe to can using the water-bath canning method. You can't successfully can meats using any method other than pressure canning, regardless of stories you may have heard to the contrary.

You can can meat and poultry using either the hot pack or cold (or raw) pack methods. (Refer to Book V, Chapter 2 for more on these techniques.)

Be sure to follow the directions of the recipe carefully. Making changes can result in serious illness.

Tips for Safety and Efficiency

Meats need to be cut and canned as quickly as possible. Because bacteria can grow quickly in meat and poultry, your goal is to can the meat before it reaches room temperature, and not to allow your cut-up meat to sit out for any length of time between cutting and canning.

If you find that you have more meat cut than you can possibly process in one day, keep the extra in a refrigerator at 32° to 38° and can that meat first the next day, before cutting more. Keep canning all the meat until finished, even if it means working for more than one day. (Although you can freeze meat as soon as you purchase it for canning later, you risk canning an inferior product. You're better off buying it the day you plan to can it.)

Usually, when you can meats, you're processing a large portion at a time.

Canning meat is not the time to experiment with a recipe. Follow the recipe to the letter, making notes on your experience, so that you can then see how to change your technique, if desired, the next time.

Practice first

Every time you can — and no matter how many times you've canned in the past — set up all the necessary equipment and supplies and do a dry run to be sure you have everything ready and in the right place.

Be sure that you know how to close the canner properly and quickly; do it a few times if you need to. Once the canner is filled with steaming hot water and filled jars, closing it is a bit harder. If your canner doesn't close properly, you may not know it until after it's been filled and is coming to a rolling boil, at which point the canner may leak steam, hiss, and spit hot water. Then you'll be forced to wait until the canner cools and the pressure gauge returns to normal before you can reopen and reclose it. This mistake wastes valuable time because your raw meat is not being processed.

Check everything twice

Make sure that your pressure canner is in excellent condition, with no cracks or chips that might keep it from sealing properly. Before using the pressure canner, be sure to check its safety valve. You can test it with a string or fine wire, pushing the wire through the valve to make sure it's clean. A surefire way to know that the safety valve is clean is to hold the lid up to the light. When clean, you'll be able to see light through the hole. Check the safety valve every time you can. Check it between loads of jars during a single canning session as well. Double-checking it takes only a couple of seconds and can eliminate any major accidents.

Also make sure to check all your jars for nicked rims before and after sanitizing. (We recommend glass jars with lids and bands). Sometimes a jar will be perfect when coming out of storage but will get a small nick or crack in the cleaning process. A nicked rim won't keep a jar sealed.

Be as clean as a whistle

Wash all your work surfaces with hot soapy water and rinse well. You may want to add bleach to the rinse water and let the surfaces dry on their own to ensure that you have a sanitary work surface to sit your jars and utensils on.

Note: You don't have to sanitize the entire kitchen, just the area that you'll be working at. (Doing a trial run lets you know exactly where your work surfaces are.) You also need to ensure that your jars, rims, and lids are sanitized. (Go to Book V, Chapter 1 for details.)

Selecting and Preparing Meats for Canning

When canning meat, use only the best meat you can buy. The freshest meat has been raised and butchered in sanitary conditions.

Here are some ways to ensure that you're starting out with the best meat:

- ✔ Raise your own food animals
- ✔ Buy from a local small farmer
- ✔ Buy from a local butcher

You can certainly use meat from the local big-chain grocery store, but note that the store won't have the freshest meat available, and the meat itself may be raised in a way that you may not want to support.

When preparing meats to can, remove as much bruising, gristle, and fat as you can. You remove bruising and gristle because they're blemishes that don't can well. You remove the fat because fatty meat shouldn't be canned; it increases the chance of spoilage and can lend an off flavor to the finished product. You won't be able to remove every trace of fat, but cut off as much as possible during preparation.

How you cut the meat — into cubes, strips, and so on — depends on the type of meat you're canning. You can find specific guidance for the various types of meats in the upcoming sections.

Only prepare enough meat for one canner full of jars at a time. You do not want meat to sit out at room temperature for any longer than necessary. Meat is more susceptible to bacterial growth than other foods and must remain as cold as possible until used.

Meat Canning, Step by Step

Your equipment and supplies are checked and assembled, and you're ready to begin. The following steps provide a general overview of the process for canning meat.

1. **Place the wire jar rack into the canner and add the water to the canner following your canner's manufacturer's instructions**.

2. **Fill the jars following the recipe's instructions and close them hand tight.**

   For info on preparing your meat, refer to the earlier section "Selecting and Preparing Meat for Canning."

   Don't overtighten the jars. By hand-tightening them, you leave a miniscule amount of room between the rim and the lid, enabling the pressure of the canner to force air out of each jar as it becomes pressurized during the canning process. As the pressurized cans then cool, the lids will be sucked tightly onto the jars, providing an airtight seal.

3. **Place the hand-tightened jars in the canner and then place the lid on the canner and fasten, following the manufacturer's instructions.**

4. **Begin processing.**

   When the water comes to a boil, vent the steam for at least 10 minutes to ensure that the pressure gauge has an accurate reading.

5. **After the 10 minutes venting time, close the vent and watch the pressure build; then maintain the pressure specified in the recipe for the recommended period of time.**

   Stay nearby because you need to adjust the heat source so that the pressure builds high enough but not too high. Read your particular pressure canner's instructions to be sure of the technique the manufacturer recommends for your unit. If at any time your pressure falls below the recommended level during the canning process, you must bring it back up to the correct pressure and start timing all over again.

6. **After the specified cooking time has elapsed, allow the pressure to return to 0 and then remove the jars from the canner.**

7. **Allow the jars to cool completely and then store.**

8. **Before tasting or eating, boil the contents of each jar for 15 minutes.**

The remaining sections of this chapter provide specific instructions for various types of meats.

Canning Beef and Pork: Cubed Meat

Cubed meats, such as beef, pork, goat, and sheep, are easy to can and can be the main ingredient of many delicious dishes. Cubed meat is tender and delicious and is guaranteed to be one of the first things you reach for when you need a fast meal maker. You can use strips, cubes, and ground meats in any recipe that calls for that type of meat.

Canning is an excellent way to use the less expensive cuts of meat and still end up with a delicious dish. When you preserve meat this way, your family will never know that you started with a tougher cut of meat, and children often prefer canned meat to the noncanned version.

Preparing the meat

Before placing the meat into the jars, cut it into bite-sized pieces, about 1-inch square, and cook it in a frying pan on high heat until it's about halfway done and lightly browned on each side. You can soak meats that have a strong flavor in salted water for an hour before cooking. You can also use a tomato-based liquid in these strong-flavored meats (as the Wild Game in Gravy recipe does later in this chapter).

You can also cut strips of your desired meats from roasts and steaks. If you do so, make sure that you cut with the grain of the meat so that it will fit the length of the jar. Cutting in this way results in a more tender and aesthetic-looking piece of meat. Cutting across the grain can cause the meat to fall apart and result in a stringy texture.

Filling the jars

Pack the cubed meat while still hot into hot jars. (When canning chunky meats, use wide-mouthed jars, which makes filling the jars easier.) Leave 1-inch headspace.

Fill the jars until they're full but not overly packed. By leaving a bit of room, you allow all the air to be driven out of the meat. If packed too tightly, some air may become trapped, and your resulting meat won't be safe to use.

Pour your hot liquid of choice (tomato juice, boiling water, or stock) over the meat. This additional liquid fills in any air spaces that remain. (*Don't* use thickened gravy because it becomes gooey or too thick during the canning process, and you'll end up with an unsatisfactory product.)

Using a plastic or nonreactive utensil (not metal), release any air bubbles and add liquid as necessary to maintain the proper headspace. Then hand-tighten lids and process according to the recipe's instructions.

Canning Ground Meat

Ground meat is a family favorite. Canning it makes this handy staple even faster and easier to use. When canning ground meat, use any that your family enjoys. From poultry to red meat, all of it tastes wonderful when preserved this way.

You can use canned ground meat in the same way as you normally would — in any recipe that calls for already-cooked ground meat. You may find that your family prefers ground meat cooked this way, as it is far more flavorful than cooking in a frying pan.

When canning ground meat, keep these points in mind:

- ✔ **Preparing the ground meat:** Brown the meat just until it loses its pink color.
- ✔ **Filling the jars:** Using a wide-mouth canning funnel, carefully fill the jars with ground meat, leaving 1-inch headspace. You don't need to add any liquid because the canning process forces out the meat's natural juices. This juice is rich in natural meat flavor.

You may find the texture of canned ground beef to be a little finer than what you're used to, but the flavor is outstanding. Remember, you may have to use a spoon to remove the ground meat from the jars. No worries — once it's heated, the ground meat will return to the crumbly texture you know.

Canning Poultry

Poultry includes chicken, turkey, and other birds. To can fresh poultry (it hasn't been frozen), you use the cold pack method. To can poultry that has been previously frozen, you use the hot pack method.

This chapter refers to chicken for simplicity, but the instructions work the same for any poultry.

Canning is the perfect way to use roosters and older hens. (An older hen, known as a *stewing hen,* is one that is older than 1½ years.) These traditionally tougher birds are made tender and succulent through the canning process. The younger chickens tend to become too soft and are better if frozen.

Canning fresh poultry: Cold packing

Canned fresh chicken is probably the most superbly flavored way to cook poultry. It's canned in the simplest manner as well — cold packed into hot jars — making it a fast and efficient way to preserve poultry for your pantry. Once canned, the chicken falls off the bone, making cleaning a snap.

- ✔ **Preparing the carcass:** If you have whole chickens, remove the breasts to freeze separately and can the remaining parts of the bird. Separate the leg pieces at the joint so that you have a thigh and drumstick for each leg. Place the pieces of cold chicken in a large bowl, only preparing enough chickens for a full canner load.

  Make sure that the drumstick bone is not too tall for a lid to sit flush on the rim of the jar. If so, chop off the excess bone with a cleaver or refit.

- ✔ **Filling the jars:** When canning chicken, fit one chicken per quart. Cold-pack chicken pieces into each quart jar. Place the pieces close together, but not jammed in, fitting them like a puzzle, working around the jar until no more room is left (see Figure 3-1). Add one bouillon cube into each jar before hand-tightening the lid. Don't add any additional liquid to cold pack chicken because the canning process yields a surprising amount of liquid.

The natural gelatin in the chicken bones gives the cooled liquid a jellylike consistency. Once heated, this jelly will liquefy and be full of flavor.

FITTING A WHOLE CHICKEN INTO A JAR

Figure 3-1:
Fit in the chicken pieces like a puzzle — but not too tightly.

Canning prefrozen chicken: Hot packing

You may also can prefrozen chickens. Say that you have a freezer full of chicken, and your freezer suddenly breaks down. Now you need to process a large amount of poultry, and fast. You can successfully can prefrozen poultry as long as it's not freezer damaged, and you thaw it slowly in a refrigerator. (Don't use this technique on old, forgotten chicken that you suddenly found at the bottom of your freezer.) A good general rule: Can chicken that's been frozen for 4 months or less.

To can prefrozen chicken, you use the hot pack method: Cut up the chicken and separate the pieces at all the joints so that you end up with thighs and drumsticks. Save the more desirable breast pieces for a separate meal. Remove the skin if you like. (Doing so reduces the amount of fat in the jar.) Then cook the pieces about two-thirds of the way through. The meat finishes cooking in the canner.

Fill hot jars with hot chicken pieces, fitting them together like puzzle pieces, until the jar is full, leaving 1-inch headspace.

Canning Fish and Seafood

Many people are surprised to know that they can successfully can both fish and seafood — a great option if you fish and often end up with bags of frozen fillets you don't know what to do with. You can add seasoned broth or tomato juice to the jars, and the resulting food is delicious as well as a unique addition to your pantry.

Both fish and seafood fall into the delicate category. Both should be cold packed, and you must follow the recipe closely and handle the food with care throughout the process. But because they make wonderful additions to savory pies and soups or stews, they're worth the extra effort and care it takes to make a healthy and delicious product.

Fish and seafood differ from other meats because they're extremely low in acidity, which means that you have an even greater chance of error if you don't follow the recipe carefully. Because of the increased chance of error, canning fish is not the best project for a beginner. Try canning some other foods first. When you feel proficient with canning easier items (like fruits and vegetables), move up to meats and then to fish and seafood.

Picking your fish

When canning fish, use a mild-flavored fish from clean waters. Because fishing is a sport that requires an inexpensive license and a worm on a pole, you may find that fishing can fill a pantry for little to no cost.

Check with your local health department for official warnings and recommendations about eating freshly caught fish in your area.

Preparing fish and seafood

To prepare fish, you clean and scale it, but you don't remove the skin. You don't have to remove the tiny bones, either. (They'll become soft and edible when canned.) Then you cut the fish into pieces long enough to fill the jar and leave 1-inch headspace. If cutting chunks is desired, simply cut into pieces roughly the same size, again leaving 1-inch headspace.

To measure how long to cut your fish pieces, place the size jar you are using alongside a fillet of fish.

For seafood such as shrimp or clams, you just fill your jars with pieces of the seafood.

Filling the jar

Place the fish pieces into pint jars, skin side facing out (for a prettier finished jar), and leave 1-inch headspace. (Fish is not suitable for quart canning.)

Fish and seafood need to be canned as quickly as possible — preferably the day they're caught. If you want to can either of these foods, make a plan that includes the actual trip out to catch them. That way, your supplies are organized and ready to use when you return to the kitchen. When you have a basket of fish waiting to be canned, you don't want to be looking for your canning tongs.

Don't worry if you see crystals when canning. As a home canner, you can't prevent them from forming, and they usually dissolve when heated.

Chopped or Cubed Meat

Prep time: 1 hr • **Process time:** 1 hr, 30 min (quarts); 1 hr, 15 min (pints) • **Yield:** About 4 quarts or 8 pints

Ingredients	*Directions*
6 pounds lean meat **Water, tomato juice, or broth** **Canning salt or beef bouillon (optional)**	*1* Cut meat into cubes and brown lightly in dry skillet until the meat is about halfway done. (The canning process finishes the cooking.) While the meat is browning, heat up your choice of liquid until boiling.
	2 Ladle the cooked meat and your choice of boiling liquid into hot jars, leaving 1-inch headspace. Add a bouillon cube or ½ teaspoon salt to each quart jar or ¼ teaspoon salt to each pint jar, if desired.
	3 Process your filled jars in a pressure canner at 10 pounds pressure for 1 hour, 30 minutes (quarts) or 1 hour, 15 minutes (pints).
	4 After processing, if you find jars that haven't sealed, immediately refrigerate them and use them within 1 week. Boil the contents of each jar for 15 minutes before tasting or eating.

Per 4-ounce serving: Calories 266 (From Fat 115); Fat 13g (Saturated 5g); Cholesterol 115mg; Sodium 76mg; Carbohydrates 0g (Dietary Fiber 0g); Protein 35g.

Note: Serve this meat over biscuits in wintertime for a stick-to-your-ribs meal that really tastes great.

Wild Game in Gravy

Prep time: 1 hr, 30 min • **Process time:** 1 hr, 30 min (qts); 1 hr, 15 min (pts) • **Yield:** About 2 qts or 4 pts

Ingredients	Directions
3 pounds game	**1** Cut your meat into 1-inch chunks. In a large, nonreactive bowl, cover the meat with a brine solution made up of 1 tablespoon of salt per quart of water. Leave the meat in the brine for 1 hour. Then rinse thoroughly.
Canning salt	
Water	
3 cups beef broth or tomato juice	**2** In an 8-quart pot, brown the game over medium or medium-high heat until it is about two-thirds done. While meat is browning, bring your choice of liquid to a boil.
	3 Fill your prepared jars with pieces of game and boiling hot liquid (broth or tomato juice), leaving 1-inch headspace.
	4 Process your filled jars in a pressure canner at 10 pounds pressure for 1 hour, 30 minutes (quarts) or 1 hour, 15 minutes (pints).
	5 After processing, if you find jars that haven't sealed, immediately refrigerate them and use them within 1 week. Boil the contents of each jar for 15 minutes before tasting or eating.

Per 4-ounce serving of venison: Calories 126 (From Fat 51); Fat 6g (Saturated 2g); Cholesterol 63mg; Sodium 251mg; Carbohydrates 0g (Dietary Fiber 0g); Protein 18g.

Per 4-ounce serving of rabbit: Calories 126 (From Fat 46); Fat 5g (Saturated 2g); Cholesterol 50mg; Sodium 341mg; Carbohydrates 0g (Dietary Fiber 0g); Protein 19g.

Note: You can use this recipe for venison and rabbit, as well as any goat that might have a stronger flavor.

Canned Freshwater Fish

Prep time: 1 hr • **Process time:** 1 hr, 40 min • **Yield:** 12 pints

Ingredients	Directions
25 pounds fresh fish **Canning salt**	*1* Clean the fish, removing the entrails, scales, head, tail, and fins. Leave the skin intact. Cut the pieces of cleaned fish to fit the jars minus 1 inch for the required headspace.
	2 Fill the hot jars with fish, skin side out (refer to Figure 3-2) and add 1 teaspoon salt to each jar.
	3 Process the filled jars in a pressure canner at 10 pounds pressure for 1 hour, 40 minutes.
	4 After processing, if you find jars that haven't sealed, immediately refrigerate them and use them within 1 week. Boil the contents of each jar for 15 minutes before tasting or eating.

Per 4-ounce serving: Calories 212 (From Fat 85); Fat 9g (Saturated 2g); Cholesterol 83mg; Sodium 788mg; Carbohydrates 0g (Dietary Fiber 0g); Protein 30g.

Note: Use this as a base for a quick fish chowder. On a cold night, it tastes wonderful with crusty bread and a canned fruit on the side.

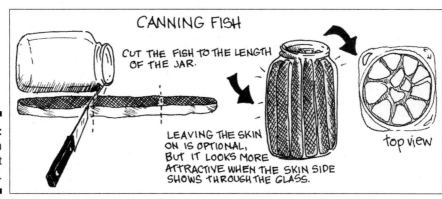

Figure 3-2: Place fish skin side out in jar.

CANNING FISH

CUT THE FISH TO THE LENGTH OF THE JAR.

LEAVING THE SKIN ON IS OPTIONAL, BUT IT LOOKS MORE ATTRACTIVE WHEN THE SKIN SIDE SHOWS THROUGH THE GLASS.

top view

Never-Fail Canned Chicken

Prep time: 30 min • **Process time:** 1 hr, 15 min • **Yield:** 7 quarts

Ingredients	*Directions*
Seven 3-pound chickens **Canning salt or bouillon cubes (optional)**	*1* Cut each chicken into parts, separating legs into thigh and drumstick pieces. Place the pieces in a large bowl, keeping them cold as you continue to cut. Remove the skin, if desired. Remove the breasts and use or freeze them separately.
	2 Fill the prepared jars with the chicken pieces until full, leaving 1-inch headspace. Add 1 bouillon cube or ½ teaspoon canning salt to each jar, if desired. (***Note:*** Due to each chicken being a little different, you may find that you fit different numbers of pieces into each jar.)
	3 Process your filled jars in a pressure canner at 10 pounds pressure for 1 hour, 15 minutes.
	4 After processing, if you find jars that haven't sealed, immediately refrigerate them and use them within 1 week. Boil the contents of each jar for 5 minutes before tasting or eating.

Per 4-ounce serving: Calories 214 (From Fat 88); Fat 10g (Saturated 3g); Cholesterol 97mg; Sodium 85mg; Carbohydrates 0g (Dietary Fiber 0g); Protein 29g.

Note: This chicken is perfect for any recipe calling for cooked or shredded chicken.

Vary It! If you're canning chicken that has been previously frozen and then thawed, cook it two-thirds of the way before filling the canning jars.

Canned Ground Beef

Prep time: 1 hr • **Process time:** 1 hr, 30 min (quarts); 1 hr, 15 min (pints) • **Yield:** 4 quarts or 8 pints

Ingredients	*Directions*
8 pounds lean ground beef **Water, tomato juice, or beef broth** **Canning salt (optional)**	*1* Lightly brown the ground beef in a dry skillet. While the beef is browning, bring your water, tomato juice, or beef broth to a boil.
	2 Ladle the ground beef into each prepared jar and cover with boiling liquid, leaving 1-inch headspace. Add ½ teaspoon salt to each quart jar or ¼ teaspoon salt to each pint jar, if desired.
	3 Process your filled jars in the pressure canner at 10 pounds pressure for 1 hour, 30 minutes (quarts) or 1 hour, 15 minutes (pints).
	4 After processing, if you find jars that haven't sealed, immediately refrigerate them and use them within 1 week. Boil the contents of each jar for 15 minutes before tasting or eating.

Per 4-ounce serving: Calories 261 (From Fat 123); Fat 14g (Saturated 10g); Cholesterol 101mg; Sodium 99mg; Carbohydrates 0g (Dietary Fiber 0g); Protein 32g.

Tip: Use this tasty food in any recipe that calls for ground beef.

Vary It! Add a single bouillon cube per quart in place of the salt for a slightly different flavor.

Canned Sausage in Casing

Prep time: 20 min • **Process time:** 1 hr, 30 min (quarts); 1 hr, 15 min (pints) • **Yield:** 5 quarts or 10 pints

Ingredients	Directions
5 pounds sausage in casing Broth or hot water	**1** Cut the sausage links into 3- to 4-inch pieces. Brown the sausage links lightly. Remove from heat, draining any fat. Pack the links into hot jars, leaving 1-inch head space.
	2 Process the filled jars in a pressure canner at 10 pounds pressure for 1 hour, 30 minutes (quarts) or 1 hour, 15 minutes (pints).
	3 After processing, if you find jars that haven't sealed, refrigerate them and use them within 2 weeks. Prior to eating or tasting, boil the food for 15 minutes.

Per 3-ounce serving: Calories 205 (From Fat 124); Fat 14g (Saturated 5g); Cholesterol 62mg; Sodium 523mg; Carbohydrates 2g (Dietary Fiber 1g); Protein 17g.

Canned Meatballs in Tomato Juice

Prep time: 20 min • **Process time:** 1 hour, 15 min (pts); 1 hour, 30 min (qts) • **Yield:** 5 qts or 10 pts

Ingredients	Directions
5 pounds ground meat **Tomato juice**	**1** Form the ground meat into 1-inch balls. Over medium-low heat, brown the meatballs lightly on all sides. Drain any fat.
	2 Pack the meatballs into hot jars, leaving 1-inch headspace. Pour hot tomato juice over the meatballs, leaving 1-inch headspace.
	3 Process the filled jars in a pressure canner at 11 pounds pressure for 1 hour, 30 minutes (quarts) or 1 hour, 15 minutes (pints).
	4 After processing, if you find jars that haven't sealed, refrigerate them and use them within 2 weeks. Prior to eating or tasting, boil the food for 15 minutes.

Per 3-ounce serving: Calories 112 (From Fat 61); Fat 7g (Saturated 3g); Cholesterol 34mg; Sodium 24mg; Carbohydrates 2g (Dietary Fiber 1g); Protein 10g.

Canned Shrimp

Prep time: 20 min • **Process time:** 45 min • **Yield:** 10 pints

Ingredients	Directions
5 pounds fresh shrimp 1 gallon water ½ cup salt 1 cup white vinegar	*1* Remove the heads of the shrimp. Discard the heads or save them for broth. Wash and drain the shrimp.
	2 Combine the water, salt, and vinegar in a large stockpot. Stir until the salt is dissolved. Add the shrimp and simmer for 10 minutes.
	3 Remove the shrimp from the brine and rinse. Peel the shrimp. Pack the shrimp into hot jars, leaving 1-inch headspace. Ladle hot brine over the shrimp.
	4 Process the filled pint jars in a pressure canner at 11 pounds pressure for 45 minutes.
	5 After processing, if you find jars that haven't sealed, refrigerate them and use them within 2 weeks. Prior to eating or tasting, boil the food for 15 minutes.

Per 3-ounce serving: Calories 84 (From Fat 8); Fat 1g (Saturated 0g); Cholesterol 165mg; Sodium 462mg; Carbohydrates 0g (Dietary Fiber 0g); Protein 18g.

Barbeque Chicken

Prep time: 20 min • **Process time:** 1 hr, 30 min (quarts); 1 hr, 15 min (pints) • **Yield:** 5 quarts or 10 pints

Ingredients	Directions
5 pounds cooked chicken **Barbeque sauce**	*1* In an 8-quart stock pot, add the cooked chicken and enough barbeque sauce to cover the meat. Bring the ingredients to a simmer over medium heat. Stir often to prevent sticking.
	2 Pack the mixture into hot jars, leaving 1-inch head-space. Process the filled jars in a pressure canner at 11 pounds pressure for 1 hour, 30 minutes (quarts) or 1 hour, 15 minutes (pints).
	3 After processing, if you find jars that haven't sealed, refrigerate them and use them within 2 weeks. Prior to eating or tasting, boil the food for 15 minutes.

Per 3-ounce serving: Calories 99 (From Fat 30); Fat 3g (Saturated 1g); Cholesterol 38mg; Sodium 96mg; Carbohydrates 4g (Dietary Fiber 1g); Protein 13g.

Canned Bulk Sausage

Prep time: 20 min • **Process time:** 1 hr, 30 min (quarts); 1 hr, 15 min (pints) • **Yield:** 5 quarts or 10 pints

Ingredients	*Directions*
5 pounds bulk sausage **Hot water or broth**	**1** In a 10-inch skillet, lightly brown the sausage. Drain any fat from the browned meat. Pack the sausage into hot jars. Pour hot water or broth over the packed meat, leaving 1-inch headspace.
	2 Process the filled jars in a pressure canner at 11 pounds pressure for 1 hour, 30 minutes (quarts) or 1 hour, 15 minutes (pints).
	3 After processing, if you find jars that haven't sealed, refrigerate them and use them within 2 weeks. Prior to eating or tasting, boil the food for 15 minutes.

Per 3-ounce serving: Calories 275 (From Fat 197); Fat 22g (Saturated 8g); Cholesterol 66mg; Sodium 784mg; Carbohydrates 1g (Dietary Fiber 0g); Protein 17g.

Note: When making your own bulk sausage for canning, leave out the sage because it creates a bitter flavor during the processing. Add powdered sage when reheating canned sausage, and you'll never know the difference.

Chapter 4

Mixing It Up: Soups, Beans, and Combos

*N*ot all canned foods are simply one ingredient. Canning combinations of foods gives you meals that are as fast and easy as store-bought heat-and-eat varieties. With a little bit of planning during the growing season, you'll keep your shelves stocked with a variety of meals for people on the go.

In this chapter, you get tips for combining high- and low-acid foods into savory soups, delectable sauces, or hearty one-pot meals. After your family gets a whiff of the aroma coming out of the kitchen, they'll think you've been slaving over the stove all day!

Canning Combined Foods: Method Matters

Pressure canning soups, sauces, and one-pot meals is the answer for healthy, quick meals without filling up your freezer. Pressure canning is a major timesaver in the long run: If you spend one day (or even a weekend) preparing soups, sauces, and other hearty meals, you can get a hot meal on the table in a flash and keep your freezer for ice cream and other treats!

But you have to think about more than which food combos go well together: You also have to know which processing method to use to safely preserve combined foods, which may contain both high- and low-acid foods.

Mixing low-acid foods and high-acid foods

Knowing that a pot of chili or spaghetti sauce contains both high-acid and low-acid foods (the chili contains tomatoes and vegetables, and the spaghetti sauce contains meat, tomatoes, and vegetables), how do you determine which method is right while still ensuring a safe product? Whenever you combine low- and high-acid foods, process the food as though it were low-acid: Use the pressure-canning method. For the same reason, whenever you include meat, fish, poultry, or seafood in your canned product, use pressure canning. Pressure canning, explained in detail in Book V, Chapter 1, is the *only* safe processing method to use when combining low-acid and high-acid foods. (For detailed instructions for pressure canning meat, fish, poultry, or seafood, refer to Book V, Chapter 3.)

Quite simply, adding low-acid foods to high-acids foods raises the acidity level of the food being processed above 4.6 pH (see Book II, Chapter 1), and the higher the acidity number, the less acidic a food is.

Mixing like foods with like

When you mix like foods with like (high-acid foods with other high-acid foods, for example, or low-acid foods with other low-acid foods), you process them in the manner suggested for their acidity level. You can process two high-acid fruits in a water-bath canner and two low-acid foods in a pressure canner. Always follow a recipe and make no changes.

Creating a Successful Meal

Obviously, the most important thing to know about processing combined products is to use the right processing method (see the preceding section). Beyond that, you can take other measures to ensure a successful product and a delicious (and easy) meal:

✔ **Cut all ingredients uniformly to ensure even heating.** Make sure that all your fruits, vegetables, and meat pieces are as even in size as possible, the same as you would for regular stove cooking.

✔ **Use the longest processing time given when combining foods.** For example, the processing time for corn alone in a 1-quart jar is 1 hour, 25 minutes. The processing time for lima beans alone in a 1-quart jar is 50 minutes. Therefore, the correct processing time for combining corn and lima beans in a 1-quart jar is 1 hour, 25 minutes.

✔ **Follow the recipe exactly.** Don't be tempted to add or adjust the ingredients in your recipe. Any variation changes the acidity level as well as the processing time (and sometimes the processing method) needed to destroy the microorganisms that cause botulism, the most serious form of food poisoning (refer to Book I, Chapter 1).

✔ **Always use the jar size recommended in your recipe.** Some combination foods may be canned in either pints or quarts; other foods may be suited only for pints.

✔ **Don't add uncooked pasta or rice to your food before canning your jars.** While these ingredients are wonderful additions to soups, the intense heat of pressure canning disintegrates your pasta or rice. For example, if your pasta cooking time in boiling water is 8 to 10 minutes and you extended the period to 30 minutes or longer at a temperature higher than boiling water (as occurs in the pressure canner), you end up with something that doesn't resemble pasta or rice.

Taking It from the Pantry to the Table

After selecting a jar from your pantry, follow these simple steps for quick, timesaving meals:

1. **Bring your canned food to a boil in a large pot, boiling the food for 15 minutes.**

   Don't be tempted to taste your food until after the boiling period has elapsed.

2. **Add your seasonings, such as salt, pepper, and fresh herbs.**

3. **Add pasta or rice, if desired.**

   Cook for the time recommended on the package, and test for doneness.

4. **Serve and enjoy!**

Whenever you pressure-can, you *must* boil the contents of the jar for 15 minutes before tasting or eating. Refer to Book V, Chapter 1 for safety information.

Stocking Up on Soups and Combos

Everyone loves to have a quick meal available when the day is hectic. Canning extra meals ahead of time allows you to pull together a fast, healthy meal for the family. Because you prepare the ingredients, you know that your family is eating the best possible food. Change your vocabulary from leftovers to opportunity!

When you're doubling a recipe, season lightly. Your canned portion will taste fresher if you re-season just before serving.

Making your own stock

Soup is the ultimate comfort food. The road to great soup starts with a flavorful *stock,* which is water infused with the flavors of vegetables and/or the bones from beef, poultry, or fish. A *reduced stock* is boiled rapidly, thus reducing the amount of liquid by evaporation and producing an intense flavor.

You can either purchase chicken and reserve the meat for another use or use the parts you may not normally eat, such as the neck, the back, the wings, or the less often used heart, liver, and gizzards. These pieces are packed with flavor; whether or not you use them is up to you.

Teaming up with tomatoes

Although tomatoes alone can be water-bath canned (see Book II, Chapter 3), if you combine them with low-acid vegetables, it changes the pH (acidity level). These combined foods must be treated and processed as low-acid foods — that means using a pressure canner.

Always time your mixed ingredients based on the longest processing time needed. The worst that will happen is your tomatoes will break down even smaller with a longer cook time. This breakage is rarely a concern for most recipes.

Including Meats in Canned Mixes

When thinking about your pantry contents, don't forget to add a few canned dishes that contain both vegetables and meats. These complete meals in a jar not only taste better than convenience food you can buy in a store, but they're also fresher and definitely healthier.

Canning a soup or stew gives you a little more breathing room for experimentation. Because you're canning based on the meat — the item that needs to be pressurized the longest — any other vegetable will be safely canned right along with it. When you're designing these soups and stews for your family, you can easily substitute vegetables or add more of another veggie that your family especially enjoys.

Following are some pointers:

- **When using strongly flavored vegetables, remember a little goes a long way.** Strongly flavored veggies, like those in the Brassica family (cabbage, Brussels sprouts, broccoli, and cauliflower, for example), tend to have an even more pronounced flavor after canning. If you're adding any of these vegetables, use a light touch. You can add cabbage to any soup you make, for example, but add only about half the amount you add of the other vegetables.

- **Don't worry about changes in consistency.** When you open a can of homemade soup or stew, you may find that it's thicker (in the case of the stew) or that the vegetables have gathered together at the bottom of the jar. This settling of ingredients is harmless. After warming, the food will thin and combine into the soup or stew you started out with.

Introducing Beans to Your Pantry

Beans are high in protein, calcium, phosphorus, and iron and are a good source of fiber. The more your family eats beans in their regular diet, the less they will suffer from any gassiness. You can use very effective over-the-counter remedies in the meantime.

Knowing the power of protein

It's not news that you require protein for good health. Protein is also what fills you up and keeps you feeling satisfied long after the meal is over. Protein is also the most expensive portion of a meal and takes the longest time to prepare. These are all great reasons to have protein canned and waiting to eat in the pantry!

Canning can help by allowing you the freedom to buy in bulk, buy meat when it's on sale, and be able to store it in any cool, dry place.

Save yourself the thawing and cooking time by having premade meals, including the protein component, ready to heat and serve.

Speeding up dinner using beans

Beans are definitely an underappreciated part of a well-stocked pantry. Beans offer the important protein addition. Beans mixed with rice are as complete a protein as a piece of meat, for much less cost. In fact, beans are extremely inexpensive to buy, come in a wide variety of textures and flavors, and are a great way to build up a filling recipe, for less money.

The drawback to using beans for some people is the prep time. You can minimize prep time by preparing a large batch of beans ahead of time and canning them! You can then use canned beans at a moment's notice, and all you'll need to do is heat them up.

Add premade beans to soups and sides and even heat them up and eat them plain. We like to eat a simple side dish of warmed beans, topped with a sprinkle of balsamic vinegar.

Chicken Stock

Prep time: 2 hrs • **Process time:** 25 min (quarts); 20 min (pints) • **Yield:** About 4 quarts or 8 pints

Ingredients	*Directions*
3 to 4 pounds chicken pieces	*1* Combine the chicken and water in a 6- to 8-quart pot; bring the mixture to a boil over high heat. Add the celery, onions, peppercorns, bay leaves, and salt. Reduce the heat; simmer, covered, about 2 hours or until the chicken is tender.
4 quarts water	
2 stalks celery, leaves attached, cut into 1-inch pieces	
2 medium onions, quartered	*2* Remove from the heat; skim off any foam. Remove the chicken pieces, reserving the chicken for another use.
15 peppercorns	
3 bay leaves	*3* Strain the stock through a mesh strainer or several layers of cheesecloth into a large bowl. Once the stock has cooled enough to place it in the refrigerator, chill the stock until you can easily remove the fat. Once the fat is removed, return the stock to the pot and bring it to a boil.
Salt to taste	
	4 Ladle the boiling hot stock into your prepared jars, leaving 1-inch headspace.
	5 Process your filled jars in a pressure canner at 10 pounds pressure for 25 minutes (quarts) or 20 minutes (pints).
	6 After processing, if you find jars that haven't sealed, immediately refrigerate them and use them within 1 week.

Per 1-cup serving: Calories 6 (From Fat 2); Fat 0g (Saturated 0g); Cholesterol 3mg; Sodium 39mg; Carbohydrates 0g (Dietary Fiber 0g); Protein 1g.

Turkey Stock with Vegetables

Prep time: 4 hr, 30 min • **Process time:** 1 hr, 25 min (qts); 1 hr (pts) • **Yield:** About 7 qts or 14 pts

Ingredients	*Directions*
3 quarts water	**1** Combine the water and turkey carcass in a 10- to 12-quart pot. Bring the mixture to a boil over high heat. Reduce the heat; simmer, covered, for 2 hours. Remove the lid and continue cooking for 2 hours more.
Carcass from a 12- to 15-pound turkey	
1 quart Beans with Salt Pork (recipe later in this chapter)	**2** Strain and remove the bones from the stock. Check the broth for seasoning, taking note that you may see salt and seasoning in the broth from the previous roasting of the turkey. Add seasonings to taste.
2 quarts Canned Tomatoes (recipe in Book II, Chapter 3)	
4 cups sweet corn	**3** Add the beans, tomatoes, corn, cabbage, onions, carrots, and celery to the strained stock and return to a boil. Boil for 5 minutes. (Your goal is simply to heat the soup to a boil so that it's as hot as possible for canning. You don't want to completely cook your vegetables.)
2 cups chopped cabbage	
2 cups chopped onions	
2 cups sliced carrots	
2 cups sliced celery	**4** Ladle the hot soup into your prepared jars, leaving 1-inch headspace.
	5 Process your filled jars in a pressure canner at 10 pounds pressure for 1 hour, 25 minutes (quarts) or 1 hour (pints).
	6 After processing, if you find jars that haven't sealed, immediately refrigerate them and use them within 1 week.

Per 1-cup serving: Calories 120 (From Fat 34); Fat 4g (Saturated 1g); Cholesterol 10mg; Sodium 62mg; Carbohydrates 17g (Dietary Fiber 4g); Protein 7g.

Note: This is a great recipe to make after a holiday meal when you have leftover turkey that is mostly picked clean of meat.

Stewed Tomatoes with Celery

Prep time: 30 min • **Process time:** 20 min (quarts); 15 min (pints) • **Yield:** About 3 quarts or 6 pints

Ingredients	*Directions*
5 to 6 pounds of peeled tomatoes to measure 4 quarts, chopped and seeded, reserving all liquid	*1* Combine the tomatoes, celery, onions, bell pepper, sugar, and salt in a 5- to 6-quart pot. Bring the mixture to a boil over high heat. Reduce the heat to medium, cover, and simmer for 10 minutes, stirring to prevent sticking.
1 large stalk celery, chopped	
½ medium onion, chopped	*2* Ladle the hot tomatoes into the prepared jars, leaving 1-inch headspace.
¼ green pepper, chopped	
1 tablespoon granulated sugar	*3* Process your filled jars in a pressure canner at 10 pounds pressure for 20 minutes (quarts) or 15 minutes (pints).
2 teaspoons salt	
	4 After processing, if you find jars that haven't sealed, immediately refrigerate them and use them within 1 week.

Per 1-cup serving: Calories 40 (From Fat 0); Fat 0g (Saturated 0g); Cholesterol 0mg; Sodium 535mg; Carbohydrates 8g (Dietary Fiber 2g); Protein 3g.

Note: Homemade stewed tomatoes are perfect in soups or sauces, as a condiment on scrambled eggs, or spooned over steamed summer squash with a grating of cheddar cheese.

Italian-Style Tomatoes

Prep time: 10 min • **Process time:** 20 min (quarts); 15 min (pints) • **Yield:** 3 quarts or 6 pints

Ingredients	Directions
4 quarts chopped tomatoes	**1** Combine all ingredients in a heavy pot. Cover and cook for 10 minutes.
¾ cup chopped celery	
¾ cup chopped onion	**2** Ladle the hot mixture into your prepared jars, leaving 1-inch headspace.
½ cup green pepper	
1 tablespoon sugar	**3** Process the filled jars in a pressure canner at 10 pounds pressure for 20 minutes (quarts) or 15 minutes (pints).
2 teaspoons dried marjoram	
4 cups sugar	
	4 After processing, if you find jars that haven't sealed, refrigerate them and use them within 2 weeks.

Per ½-cup serving: Calories 159 (From Fat 4); Fat 0g (Saturated 0g); Cholesterol 0mg; Sodium 14mg; Carbohydrates 40g (Dietary Fiber 2g); Protein 1g.

Note: These seasoned tomatoes are the perfect addition to any Italian meal. Cook them down even further, and you have an amazing marinara sauce.

Spaghetti Sauce with Meat

Prep time: 2 to 2½ hrs • **Process time:** 1 hr, 5 min • **Yield:** About 5 pints

Ingredients	*Directions*
12 ounces Italian sausage, bulk or links, mild or hot	*1* Remove the sausage casings if you're using link sausage. Brown the sausage in a 5- or 6-quart pot over medium heat, stirring to break up the sausage. Add the ground meat and the onions; continue cooking until the meat is brown and the onions are translucent. Drain off any fat.
½ **pound ground beef or turkey**	
2 medium onions, chopped	
4 garlic cloves, minced	
2 carrots, peeled and finely chopped	*2* Add the garlic, carrots, celery, and mushrooms to the pan with the sausage and ground meat; cook an additional 2 to 3 minutes. Add the tomato paste, tomatoes, wine, basil, parsley, salt, and pepper.
2 stalks celery, finely chopped	
½ **pound mushrooms, sliced**	
Two 6-ounce cans tomato paste	*3* Bring the mixture to a boil over high heat; reduce the heat to medium-low and simmer covered for 1½ to 2 hours, stirring often, until the sauce has thickened.
2 quarts canned stewed tomatoes, including the liquid	
1 cup red wine	*4* Ladle the hot sauce into your prepared jars, leaving 1-inch headspace.
1 tablespoon fresh basil, chopped	
1 cup chopped Italian flat-leaf parsley	*5* Process your filled pint jars in a pressure canner at 10 pounds pressure for 1 hour, 5 minutes.
1 teaspoon salt (omit if salt was added to your canned tomatoes)	*6* After processing, if you find jars that haven't sealed, immediately refrigerate them and use them within 1 week.
Freshly ground pepper to taste	

Per 1-cup serving: Calories 164 (From Fat 66); Fat 7g (Saturated 3g); Cholesterol 28mg; Sodium 552mg; Carbohydrates 13g (Dietary Fiber 3g); Protein 12g.

Vary 1t! For a meatless sauce, follow all the recipe instructions, omitting the sausage and meat. Process your pints for 25 minutes at 10 pounds pressure.

Easy Vegetable Soup

Prep time: 30 min • **Yield:** 4 servings

Ingredients	*Directions*
1 pint jar each of corn, carrots, peas, and peppers	*1* Combine one jar each of corn, carrots, peas, and peppers (or your favorite vegetable mix) along with their canning liquids into a large soup pot. Add enough water to cover the ingredients by an inch. Bring the vegetables to a boil over medium-high heat and boil for 15 minutes.
1 cup dried pasta, any kind	
1 teaspoon Italian seasoning (optional)	
¼ cup Parmesan cheese, grated	*2* Add the dried pasta and Italian seasoning to the boiling vegetables. Continue boiling the soup until the pasta is tender, about 15 minutes longer.
	3 Ladle the soup into four large serving bowls and sprinkle each with 1 tablespoon Parmesan cheese.

Per serving: Calories 435 (From Fat 40); Fat 4g (Saturated 1g); Cholesterol 4mg; Sodium 1,713mg; Carbohydrates 90g (Dietary Fiber 18g); Protein 17g.

Vary 1t!: This recipe uses canned corn, carrots, peas, and bell peppers, but you can use any combination that strikes your fancy — or that you have on hand.

Tip: Serve this hearty soup with sourdough bread.

Baked Chicken with Peppers

Prep time: 1 hr • **Yield:** 4 servings

Ingredients	Directions
1 pint of canned peppers	*1* Preheat your oven to 350°. Boil 1 pint of canned peppers and the canning liquid in a 6-quart saucepan for 15 minutes.
4 to 6 boneless, skinless chicken breasts	
1 teaspoon Italian or Mexican Herb Mix (recipes in Book VII, Chapter 3) or any other seasoning mix	*2* While the peppers boil, arrange the chicken breasts in an ovenproof pan. Pour the bell peppers and their liquid over the chicken breasts. Season as desired.
4 cups cooked rice	*3* Tightly cover the pan with aluminum foil to seal in the moisture and bake the chicken at 350° for 30 to 45 minutes, or until the chicken is done.
	4 Serve over rice.

Per serving: *Calories 380 (From Fat 34); Fat 4g (Saturated 1g); Cholesterol 73mg; Sodium 649mg; Carbohydrates 52g (Dietary Fiber 4g); Protein 32g.*

Beans with Beef

Prep time: 40 min • **Yield:** 4 servings

Ingredients	*Directions*
1 quart Canned Ground Beef (recipe in Book V, Chapter 3), or any ground meat	*1* In a 10-inch frying pan, bring the ground meat to a simmer and heat for 15 minutes. Season with salt, pepper, and your favorite herbs or spice blend. (***Note:*** If you're not using canned ground beef, brown your meat over medium heat until done.)
1 quart canned beans, any variety	
4 ounces dried elbow noodles	*2* While the meat is reheating, bring the canned dried beans to a boil in a large pot. Boil the beans for 15 minutes.
½ teaspoon Italian or Mexican Herb Mix (Book VII, Chapter 3), or to taste	
Salt and pepper to taste	*3* Carefully add the heated meat to the beans. Simmer over medium heat for 10 minutes to combine the flavors.
	4 While the meat and beans are simmering, prepare the noodles according to the package instructions, keeping them warm until ready to use.
	5 To serve, divide the noodles evenly onto four plates and ladle the beans and beef mixture over the hot noodles.

Per serving: Calories 600 (From Fat 215); Fat 24g (Saturated 9g); Cholesterol 116mg; Sodium 655mg; Carbohydrates 47g (Dietary Fiber 9g); Protein 49g.

Baked Beans

Prep time: 4 hr, 15 min • **Process time:** 1 hr, 35 min (qts); 1 hr, 20 min (pts) • **Yield:** 3 qts or 6 pts

Ingredients	*Directions*
2 pounds dried navy beans	***1*** Place the beans in a 6- to 8-quart pot. Add 3 quarts water to cover the beans; allow them to soak, covered, for 12 to 18 hours. Drain the beans, but don't rinse.
6 quarts water	
½ pound bacon, cut into pieces	
3 large onions, sliced	***2*** Return the beans to the pot; cover with the remaining 3 quarts water; bring the mixture to a boil over high heat. Reduce the heat; cover and simmer until the bean skins begin to split. Drain the beans, reserving the liquid.
⅔ cup packed brown sugar	
4 teaspoons salt	
2 teaspoons powdered mustard	
⅔ cup molasses	***3*** Transfer the beans to a 4-quart or larger covered baking dish. Add the bacon and onions. Combine the brown sugar, salt, mustard, and molasses in a large mixing bowl. Add 4 cups of the reserved bean liquid (if needed, add water to make 4 cups). Pour the sauce mixture over the beans. Don't stir.
	4 Cover the beans and bake them in a preheated 350° oven for 3 to 3½ hours. The consistency should be like a thick soup. Add more liquid if the beans become too dry.
	5 Ladle the hot beans into your prepared jars, leaving 1-inch headspace.
	6 Process your filled jars in a pressure canner at 10 pounds pressure for 1 hour, 35 minutes (quarts) or 1 hour, 20 minutes (pints).
	7 After processing, if you find jars that haven't sealed, immediately refrigerate them and use them within 1 week.

Per 1-cup serving: Calories 390 (From Fat 39); Fat 4g (Saturated 1g); Cholesterol 5mg; Sodium 889mg; Carbohydrates 73g (Dietary Fiber 12g); Protein 17g.

Cowboy Beans

Prep time: 30 min • **Yield:** 8 servings

Ingredients	*Directions*
1 large onion	**1** Peel and chop the onion into ¼-inch pieces. In an 8-quart saucepan, brown the meat. Once it begins to brown, add the onions and cook thoroughly. Drain the fat from the meat.
1 pound ground meat	
2 quarts of home-canned pinto beans	
1 cup brown sugar	**2** Return the meat/onion mixture to the pan. Add the remaining ingredients and heat over medium until bubbly, 10 to 15 minutes. Serve immediately.
1 cup black coffee	
1 cup ketchup	
½ cup brown mustard	
½ teaspoon salt	
½ teaspoon pepper	

Per 1-cup serving: Calories 486 (From Fat 72); Fat 8g (Saturated 3g); Cholesterol 35mg; Sodium 1,534mg; Carbohydrates 76g (Dietary Fiber 14g); Protein 24g.

Variation: For a kick of spice, you can add a whole cayenne pepper and remove it before serving.

Beans with Salt Pork

Prep time: 30 min • **Process time:** 1 hr, 35 min (qts); 1 hr, 20 min (pts) • **Yield:** 3 qts or 6 pts

Ingredients	*Directions*
1 pound dried beans	*1* Cover the dried beans with cool water and let them sit for 12 hours or overnight. Drain the beans; then cover them with fresh water and bring them to a boil. Allow the beans to boil for 30 minutes.
3 quarts water	
4 ounces salt pork, cut into the number of jars you're using (optional)	*2* Place one piece of salt pork (if desired) into each prepared jar and ladle the hot beans and the resulting bean broth into the jars. If you're not adding salt pork, add 1 teaspoon salt to each quart jar or ½ teaspoon canning salt to each pint jar, leaving 1-inch headspace.
Canning salt (optional)	
	3 Process your filled jars in a pressure canner at 10 pounds pressure for 1 hour, 35 minutes (quarts) or 1 hour, 20 minutes (pints).
	4 After processing, if you find jars that haven't sealed, immediately refrigerate them and use them within 1 week.

Per 1-cup serving: *Calories 273 (From Fat 103); Fat 12g (Saturated 4g); Cholesterol 12mg; Sodium 184mg; Carbohydrates 31g (Dietary Fiber 9g); Protein 13g.*

Note: This basic staple item combines plain beans with the light taste of salt pork. You can use these beans as an add-in for any soups or stews.

Chili

Prep time: 30 min • **Cook time:** 30 min • **Process time:** 1½ hr (qts); 1 hr, 15 min (pts) • **Yield:** 6 qts or 12 pts

Ingredients	*Directions*
12 cups of cooked tomatoes	**1** Peel and chop the tomatoes. Chop the onions and mince the garlic. Brown the meat and add the onions and garlic. Cook on medium heat, until the onions are tender.
2 pounds lean ground beef	
4 cups chopped onions	
2 cloves garlic, minced	
¾ cup chili seasoning	**2** Drain any fat from the ground meat mixture and place the mixture in a 6-quart saucepan. Bring to a simmer and cook for 25 minutes.
3 teaspoons salt	
2 teaspoons cumin seed	**3** Ladle into the prepared jars, leaving ½-inch headspace. Process the filled jars in a pressure canner at 10 pounds pressure for 1½ hours (quarts) or 1 hour, 15 minutes (pints).
	4 When the processing time is done, allow the pressure to return to 0, wait an additional 10 minutes, and then carefully open the canner lid. Use any unsealed jars within 2 weeks. Prior to eating or tasting, boil the food for 15 minutes.

Per 1-cup serving: Calories 131 (From Fat 51); Fat 6g (Saturated 2g); Cholesterol 28mg; Sodium 368mg; Carbohydrates 12g (Dietary Fiber 3g); Protein 10g.

Book VI

Freezing

The 5th Wave

By Rich Tennant

That's very nice of you, dear. But I really don't think just one beetle in the garden will do much damage.

In this book . . .

Frozen food doesn't have to be limited to popsicles for the kids and leftovers you tossed in and forgot. With a little planning and a few easy-to-follow (and remember) instructions, you can fill your freezer with foods you not only recognize but actually look forward to eating.

This book includes a chapter on the basics of freezing, ways to freeze food correctly for optimum flavor, and ideas for getting the most out of your frozen foods. You also find directions for freezing everything from fruits to vegetables to meats. Your freezer will become an important part of your pantry when filled with delicious foods that your family loves.

Chapter 1

Getting into the Big Chill

*W*elcome to freezing, the simplest and least time-consuming method for preserving food. Freezing works well for almost any food. With a minimum of planning and equipment (you may already have most of it), proper storage containers, and basic freezing techniques, keeping food from spoiling and tasting as if you just took it out of the oven or brought it home from the store is a piece of cake.

This chapter gives you the basics of freezing. The remaining chapters in Book VI provide detailed instructions on freezing different types of foods.

How Freezing Works

Since the advent of home refrigeration, people have discovered the joys of prolonging the life of fresh food by freezing. Freezing food is easy, convenient, and relatively inexpensive. The results produced from freezing food are superior to canning or drying. When food is properly prepared, packaged, and quickly frozen, there's no better method for retaining its natural color, flavor, and nutritive value.

The process of freezing lowers the temperature of the food to 0° or colder. This low temperature halts microorganism activity by slowing the growth of enzymes. Freezing doesn't sterilize food or destroy the microorganisms; it only stops the negative changes in the quality of your frozen food. The goal with freezing is to preserve the fresh quality of your food.

Evaluating your freezer

Before you embark on a freezing frenzy, you need to make sure that your freezer is in good working order — that is, frostfree with a constant temperature of 0° or lower.

Fortunately, today, most freezers are *frostfree,* automatically defrosting any buildup of ice in the freezer. Freezers that don't automatically defrost require defrosting when the ice buildup is ¾ inch, or at least once a year. You need to empty your freezer before defrosting it. (Refer to your owner's manual for instructions for defrosting your freezer as well as for tips for proper care and maintenance.)

Adjust your freezer thermostat, as needed, to maintain a temperature of 0° or colder. Purchase a freezer thermometer to monitor the internal temperature of your freezer.

Add no more food to your freezer than can freeze solid in 24 hours, about 2 to 3 pounds of food for each cubic foot of freezer space. Adding a large quantity of food to your freezer at one time may raise the temperature in the freezer above 0°. This stops the quick-freezing process and may affect the quality of your frozen food.

Checking out the types of freezers

If you're in the market for a freezer, make sure that you select a freezer based on your needs, the size of your family, your available space, your budget, and the cost required for running the freezer.

Refrigerators with freezer compartments are the most common units in homes today. The preferred model has a separate door for the refrigerator and the freezer. Separate doors allow you to regulate the temperature in each compartment with individual built-in thermostats.

Upright freezers and chest freezers, on the other hand, are made for freezing only. Upright freezers have a door on the front with shelves inside, while a chest freezer opens from the top and you reach into it. Sizes vary from 6 cubic feet of storage to 32 cubic feet of storage. A chest freezer allows the cold air to stay in place each time you open the door. They're a little harder to get to the frozen food, however. Use whichever style you prefer.

Choosing to Freeze

In practice, you can freeze any food. In reality, not all foods freeze well because of their texture or composition. The key to being happy with the results of freezing is to make sure that you select foods that freeze well and then freeze them properly.

The whys and wherefores of freezing food

There are many benefits of freezing food purchased from your supermarket or foods prepared in your home:

✔ **Time savings:** Freezing food saves you time twice: First, when you plan to freeze a portion, you make extra. Making a double batch of something (like soup or spaghetti sauce, for example) takes less time than it takes to make the same recipe at two different times. Second, getting an already-made and previously frozen food on the table or in the cookie jar takes less time (and effort) than making the item from scratch.

If you make soup or a casserole, double your recipe and put one in the freezer. If you're baking cookies, freeze some for another day or freeze some raw dough and bake it later. (Use an ice cream scoop for perfectly sized dough balls.)

✔ **Cost savings:** By taking advantage of sale pricing and purchasing perishable food in large amounts, you can reduce your food costs. Watch your weekly food ads for specials, buy those items in bulk, and freeze them. Freezing is a great way to keep the foods you enjoy on hand *and* protect your budget at the same time.

✔ **Convenience:** You'll always have a quick meal or quick dessert at hand for reheating, partial cooking, or complete cooking, depending on your time allowance.

Book VI

Freezing

What freezes well—and what doesn't

There are almost too many categories of good foods for the freezer, but in general, you can freeze most fresh vegetables and fruits, meats and fish, breads and cakes, and clear soups and casseroles.

Here's a list of foods that don't freeze well:

✔ **Cooked frostings and frostings made with fluffy egg whites and whipped cream.** These types of frostings become soft and *weep* (emit a thick liquid). *Note:* Butter-based frostings freeze well. Store-bought frostings aren't recommended for freezing.

✔ **Cooked pasta:** Reheated cooked pasta is soft, mushy, and shapeless. To successfully freeze, cook only to *al dente* (semi cooked) to avoid the mush factor once reheated.

✔ **Custards and cream-pie fillings:** These foods turn watery and lumpy.

- **Egg whites and meringues:** These crack, toughen, and turn rubbery.

- **Mayonnaise:** This condiment breaks down and separates.

- **Raw fruits or vegetables with a high water content:** Foods with a high water content, such as lettuce, watermelon, citrus fruit, and cucumbers, break down when frozen and become mushy beyond recognition when thawed. Tomatoes are an exception to this rule when they're used in cooked dishes, like stews. Tomatoes also become soft and watery, but usually this texture is desired in a soup or other cooked dish.

  When freezing fresh tomatoes, cut them into quarters. Package them in 1-cup portions for quick freezing and easy measuring.

- **Sauces and gravy:** Thickened sauces and milk gravies separate when they're frozen. Freeze your *pan drippings* — the juices produced from cooking a roast or turkey freeze without adding a thickener. Remove the fat as it solidifies, and you have a lowfat, flavorful start to your next gravy.

- **Yogurt, cream cheese, and sour cream:** These items tend to separate.

- **Soft cheeses, ricotta, and cottage cheese:** These dairy products tend to break down and separate when frozen.

- **Potatoes:** Potatoes become watery and grey when thawed. You can use them in a cooked dish, but even then the texture is mealy. If the recipe you want to freeze contains potatoes, leave them out of the initial recipe and add them as your reheat the dish.

Following a frozen path to success

Whether food is fresh from your garden or fresh from a store, your selection has an effect on the quality of your food after it's thawed. Of course, packaging materials, packaging procedures, and thawing methods play an important role in your frozen-food quality, as well.

Follow these tips for best freezing results:

- **Prepare your food quickly.** Be ready to freeze your foods the same day you pick them or purchase them. Have your supplies ready and the time set aside to freeze at the peak of freshness.

- **Package your food in moisture- and vapor-proof wrappings.** These products don't permit the penetration of air or moisture, two common spoilers. (To find out about other spoilers, head to "Avoiding Freezer Spoilage," later in this chapter.)

- **Keep your freezer at 0° or colder.** Frozen food stored at 15° to 20° may appear as solid as food stored at 0° or colder, but the quality of your thawed food stored at the warmer temperature is lower than food stored at 0° or colder.

✔ **Properly thaw your food to preserve its quality and eliminate bacteria growth.** For thawing instructions, head to the later section "Thawing: Getting It Right"

Avoiding Freezer Spoilage

Before getting started, you need to recognize the spoilers of frozen food. These spoilers reduce the quality, flavor, and freezer life of frozen foods. One or more of these issues may occur before, during, or after freezing. For more information on spoilers, refer to Book I, Chapter 1.

Bacteria, molds, and yeast

All fresh food contains microorganisms or bacteria. When active microorganisms are present in food, they multiply quickly and destroy the quality of your food, sometimes right before your eyes. The best example of a microorganism at work is a loaf of bread that becomes covered with green mold.

Bacteria are microorganisms that have no chlorophyll. Some bacteria may cause disease; other bacteria are actually good and are required for the fermentation process, such as that used for making beer.

You can prevent the growth of bacteria, mold, or yeast in your food by following these guidelines:

✔ Select food of the highest quality.

✔ Freeze your food at a temperature of 0° or colder.

✔ Use sanitary conditions when handling and preparing your food.

Enzymes

Enzymes speed up the ripening process and change the color and flavor of your food. Use these methods to retain the colors and the flavors in fresh fruits and vegetables before the freezing process:

✔ **Add sugar and antioxidants.** *Antioxidants* are a commercial antidarkening agent (see Book II, Chapter 2). Sugar and antioxidants keep fruit from darkening in color.

✔ **Blanch your veggies.** Briefly plunge them into boiling water and then into cold water to stop the cooking process.

Not all enzyme reactions are bad: When beef is *aged,* it sits in a chilled room for about one week. The enzymes naturally tenderize the meat, making it more desirable to consume. Fermenting foods — that is, allowing good enzymes to change a food's basic makeup — creates healthy and delicious new foods. For more on fermenting, check out Book IV.

Freezer burn and oxidation

Freezer burn and oxidation result from air coming in contact with your frozen food. *Freezer burn* is a change in color, texture, and flavor in the food during the freezing period because the air in the freezer removes moisture from the food and dries it out.

Oxidation is a chemical change in your frozen food. The technical term is *lipid oxidation,* which occurs on an atomic level and has to do with hydrogen atoms and free radicals. What is important to know is that enzymes have a lot to do with oxidation. By blanching foods (most commonly vegetables) before freezing, you stop or at least slow down the enzymes' actions and delay oxidation. Other steps you take to prevent oxidation are to properly wrap foods, use suitable containers, and follow correct storage times. (Check out the upcoming section "Packaging and Packing Your Bounty.") Oxidized foods have a funny, off-taste and color.

Ice crystals

When you think of ice crystals, you probably think of winter and snowflakes. But in the world of freezing, ice crystals aren't charming at all. They cause your frozen food to lose liquid and darken. Because the freezing process essentially turns the water in food to ice, the way to eliminate destructive ice crystals is to keep them as small as possible. Avoid ice crystals by a fast freeze and keeping foods as cold as possible at a temperature of 0° or lower, and using an airtight seal.

Packaging and Packing Your Bounty

Proper packaging is important for preserving the quality of your frozen food both during the freezing process and after it's thawed. Any excess air in your container may compromise the quality of your thawed food. Remove as much air as possible in bags and wraps and allow the recommended headspace in rigid freezer containers.

Similarly, how you fill your freezer is also important. Put too much unfrozen food in at once, and the temperature may rise above 0°. Fail to rotate your food, and you're more likely to use newer food before older food. The following sections explain how to package your food, pack your freezer, and keep everything organized.

Choosing a container

Protecting foods during the storage period requires containers that are easy to seal, suitable for low temperatures, and, most importantly, moisture and vapor proof. Three types of packaging materials meet the criteria for properly freezing food: rigid containers, freezer bags, and freezer paper and wrap.

Book VI

Freezing

Rigid containers

Rigid containers are the perfect solution for freezing any soft or liquid food, such as casseroles and soups, and they're reusable. The most desirable material for rigid containers is plastic, although some glass jars are made for freezing. Container sizes range from ¼ cup to 1 quart with a variety of sizes in between. Purchase container sizes that fit your freezing needs.

Choose square- or rectangular-shaped containers. They save space and fit better in your freezer than round containers.

Rigid containers approved for freezing prevent the spoilers from attacking your food as well as stopping moisture and vapors from penetrating your food. When you use them, be sure to allow the proper headspace so that your food or liquid can expand without forcing the top off. (You can find a table listing headspace guidelines in Book VI, Chapter 2.) A good rule: Allow ½ inch of headspace for shallow containers and 1 inch for tall containers.

Freezer bags

Freezer bags are readily available and reasonably inexpensive, require a minimum amount of storage space, and come in a variety of sizes. When using freezer bags, purchase bags labeled for freezing, because the thickness is moisture proof and protects the flavor of your food. We also prefer the locking zipper variety.

After placing your food in the bag, force out as much air as possible by folding the filled part of the bag against the nonfilled portion of the bag, pressing the air out while sealing the bag.

Freezer paper and wraps

Freezer paper comes coated or laminated and protects your wrapped food from air and freezer burn. Other freezer papers include heavy-duty foil, clear plastic wrap, waxed paper, and polyethylene (plastic) sheets.

Vacuum-sealing machines

A vacuum-sealing machine is a handy appliance that's great for packaging foods for the freezer. Air is almost completely removed from the package through a suction process, the trademark of this appliance. Most vacuum-sealing machines use materials that are freezer-safe or even microwavable and boil-proof. Vacuum-sealed foods are convenient for single-serving meals for home or at work.

Consider these additional items when you're purchasing a vacuum-sealing machine:

✔ **Cost:** Electric plug-in types range from a low of $50 to upward of $300. New battery or hand-powered vacuum sealers are available for as little as $10. Although relatively new to the market, the reviews look promising.

✔ **Replacement bags:** Most machines include bags to get you started. Consider the cost of replacement bags and the reputation of the manufacturer. Investing in a vacuum sealer that is limited by a certain make of bags may limit use of your machine in years to come.

✔ **Storage requirements:** Depending on the size of your kitchen, storing a vacuum-sealing machine may or may not be an issue. The ideal location for a vacuum sealer is usually on a counter, where you can use it at a moment's notice.

To extend the life of your vacuum-sealing bags, cut them larger than necessary and reseal them each time you remove some of the food inside. This technique works well for dry products. You can also refill and reseal the bags if the item inside was dry and fresh. This technique is not recommended for juicy foods or meats.

These papers and wraps are especially useful when packaging irregularly shaped foods, such as steaks and roasts. Freezer paper is primarily used for meat, because tight wrapping forces out excess air.

To freezer-wrap food, follow these steps (see Figure 1-1):

1. **Tear off a piece of freezer paper about double the size of your food.**

   You want to ensure that no areas are exposed.

2. **Place the food on the paper as close to a corner as you can get it without overlapping the paper.**

3. **Fold the corner tightly over the meat.**

4. **Fold the sides tightly over the center, one at a time.**

5. **Roll the package over until you reach the end of your freezer paper.**

6. **Securely tape the ends with *freezer tape*, a tape suited for cold temperatures.**

Alternatively, you can use drugstore wrap, shown in Figure 1-1.

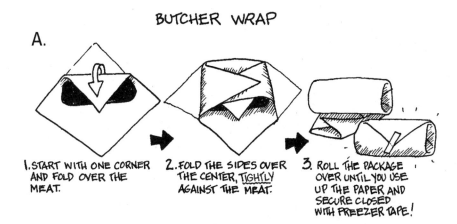

Figure 1-1:
Freezer-
paper
wrapping
techniques.

Tracking your frozen food trail

How many times have you looked in your freezer in astonishment that it's full and yet you have no idea what's taking up so much space? Have you ever defrosted what you thought was soup, only to discover you're now having stewed tomatoes for dinner? Solve the dilemma of freezer mystery food by following these simple tips:

- **Label each package with the item and the date before placing your food in the freezer.** Also include the weight of a roast, the quantity of cut-up tomatoes, your preparation method, or the number of servings. Use an indelible marker or a waterproof pen, which won't rub off.

- **Keep an up-to-date written record of food in your freezer to help with your meal planning.** Any sheet of paper works well. Make columns with the following headings: date, item (roast, spaghetti sauce, and so on), quantity or weight (1 cup or 3 pounds, for example), and any recipe or preparation ideas. Keep the list on your freezer door, crossing off items as you use them.

Packing your freezer

How you pack your freezer has an impact on the quality of your frozen foods. Follow these guidelines:

- ✔ **Cool your food to room temperature or chill it slightly before putting it in the freezer.** Cooling down your food speeds up the freezing process (the freezer doesn't have to work so hard to get the prechilled food down to 0° or lower), and it uses less energy.

- ✔ **When you first place your foods in the freezer, pack them loosely.** Once they're frozen solid, you can pack them tightly. The extra space initially lets the cold air circulate and freeze the foods more quickly.

- ✔ **Rotate your food.** To rotate your food, simply add new frozen foods to the back of the freezer and bring the older foods up front. That way, you can reach for the front of the group and get the oldest frozen food. Remember this acronym: FIFO (First In, First Out).

- ✔ **Use your frozen food within one year of freezing.** Table 1-1 lists approximately how long you can keep food in the freezer.

Table 1-1	Recommended Length of Time in the Freezer
Food	*Length of Storage at 0°F (–18°C)*
Fruits and vegetables, excluding citrus	12 months
Poultry	12 months
Fish	2 to 3 months
Ground meat	3 to 4 months
Cured or processed meat	1 to 2 months

Thawing: Getting It Right

Following the guidelines for freezing won't guarantee a great product without practicing proper thawing methods. So what's the big deal about thawing? Freezing only halts the growth of microorganisms. After thawing, bacteria and enzymes in your food are free to multiply as if they hadn't been frozen. Keep this growth at a standstill by thawing your food at a low temperature, preferably in a refrigerator, in its freezer container or packaging.

Thaw only what you need, using your food immediately upon thawing. If your food tastes funny or smells odd, harmful microorganisms may be present. Don't hesitate to dispose of any questionable food.

You don't need to thaw vegetables before adding them to a dish you're cooking. Instead, you can add them directly to the dish in the last 10 minutes of cooking. You can also place frozen unbaked goods directly into the oven to bake. You can place many previously prepared foods directly into the oven to reheat and bake, too.

Choices for thawing

Heat makes the spoilers grow faster, so the lower the temperature during the thawing period, the better for you and the quality of your food. Here are your best options for safely thawing and maintaining the quality of your food:

- ✔ **Thawing in your refrigerator:** This process is the best and safest way to thaw your food because of the low temperature. Plan your meal the night before and place your choice in your refrigerator to thaw; thawing larger pieces of meat, such as roasts, can take up to 24 hours.

- ✔ **Thawing at room temperature:** Leave your frozen food at room temperature for 2 hours. Then immediately place it in the refrigerator for the remainder of the thawing process. This option is great if you forget to take your food out of the freezer the night before.

- ✔ **Thawing in the microwave:** Use this method only if your microwave has a defrost cycle. This setting is important because you want the food to defrost evenly, not be cooked in one portion and frozen in another part.

- ✔ **Thawing in water:** Immerse your packaged food in cold water, never hot or warm water. By maintaining the lowest temperature possible when thawing your food, you'll inhibit bacteria and enzyme activity. Change the water every 30 minutes to ensure the coldest temperature possible.

Coping with an unexpected thaw

No matter how good technology is, everyone experiences a power failure at one time or another. This outage may be for a few minutes, a few hours, or, in the worst-case scenario, a few days. Don't panic, keep the freezer door closed, and resist the temptation to open the door to check the temperature.

A fully loaded freezer at 0° or colder usually stays cold enough to keep your food frozen for up to two days. A freezer that's half-full may not keep your food frozen for more than a day because air space doesn't maintain a constant temperature as efficiently as a piece of solidly frozen food.

If you do have a power outage, follow these tips for saving the contents of your freezer:

- ✔ **Check with your electric company to estimate the length of your power outage.** If you find that your freezer is the only electric appliance that isn't operating, check the electrical cord and plug for a good connection. If the plug isn't the problem, check your electrical panel for a blown fuse.

- ✔ **If you receive advance warning that your electricity will be off, set your freezer temperature to its coldest setting.** The colder temperature delays thawing during the time the electricity is off.

- ✔ **In the worst-case scenario, your freezer may be out long enough for your food to defrost.** Locate a supplier of dry ice and pack your food in the dry ice before it defrosts completely. (Ask your dry-ice supplier for safe packing and handling instructions.)

Dry ice is a refrigerant of solid carbon dioxide. Handle dry ice with care and never touch it with your bare hands. Even a short exposure to dry ice may cause frostbite.

To refreeze or not to refreeze thawed food

From time to time, even the best-laid plans change, and your defrosted food doesn't get used when you planned. If your food is only partially defrosted, indicated by the presence of ice crystals, it may be refrozen.

We don't suggest refreezing food as a regular practice, but if you're considering it for any reason, keep these things in mind:

- ✔ Don't refreeze completely defrosted low-acid foods, such as vegetables or meat sauces, after they reach room temperature. These foods may not be safe to eat.

- ✔ You can refreeze high-acid foods and most fruits and fruit products if they're still cold.

- ✔ You can safely refreeze partially thawed foods containing ice crystals if the food was thawing in your refrigerator.

Refrozen foods have a shorter shelf life than when first frozen. They may also taste different. If you refreeze an item, make a note on the package including the refreezing date. Use refrozen food as soon as possible. Follow this simple rule when evaluating refrozen, thawed food: When in doubt, throw it out! Eating spoiled food can be quite dangerous.

Chapter 2

Freezing Fruits

In This Chapter

▶ Readying fresh fruits for your freezer

▶ Exploring dry-packing and wet-packing methods

▶ Using syrups for packing your fruits in liquid

*F*reezing fruits is the second-best preserving method after canning. Preparing and processing fresh fruits for the freezer takes about one-third of the time of water-bath or pressure canning.

The equipment required for freezing fruits is more than likely already in your kitchen: a freezer, packaging materials (check out Book VI, Chapter 1), pots, a colander, measuring cups, measuring spoons, and a food scale. After your equipment and food is in order, you're ready to start freezing!

Choosing Your Fruits for Freezing

The key to a great frozen product starts with perfect, ripe fruit. Choose only perfect fruit, free of bruises and not overly ripe. In addition, be prepared to process your fruit the day it's picked or immediately after bringing it home from the store.

Don't feel like you have to grow your own fruits and vegetables to get the best produce. Local farmers' markets, food producers, and your supermarket can assist you with selecting your food, telling you when it was harvested or how long it has been on the shelf.

Packing Your Fruit

Fresh fruits require a minimum of preparation before packaging them for the freezer. First you need to wash them and then choose a packing method.

Not all packing methods are suitable for all fruits. Only methods recommended for each fruit are supplied in the recipes in this chapter.

Going the dry route for packing

This method works best with small, whole fruits like berries that you'll be thawing and eating as-is. If you would like the simplest method for freezing that summer bounty, *dry pack* is the easiest way to get the job done.

Simply packing fruit into freezer containers is fast and easy. You have two methods to consider:

- **Dry or unsweetened pack:** When you'll be eating the fruit or using it for pies, jams, or jellies, use this method. No sugar or liquid is added. There may be minor changes in the color, flavor, or texture of your fruit. If you want to keep fruit separate after being frozen, freeze it in a single layer on a cookie sheet and then place the frozen pieces into the container.

- **Dry sugar pack:** This method is preferred for most berries unless you're making pies, jams, or jellies (see the preceding bullet). Place your washed fruit on a shallow tray or a baking sheet. Evenly sift granulated sugar over the fruit. (A mesh strainer works well.) Then transfer the berries to a bowl and allow them to sit. The longer the berries sit, the more juice is drawn out. (You don't need to dissolve the sugar as in the wet-pack-with-sugar method — see the next section.) When your berries are as juicy as you want them, transfer the berries, including the juice, to a rigid freezer container, allowing the recommended headspace. (See the section "Following headspace guidelines," later in this chapter.)

Using the wet packing method

Wet pack can mean adding sugar, unsweetened with water added, or adding sugar and allowing the natural juices to become the moisture. Wet pack is best for uncooked dessert purposes and for unsweetened frozen fruits that are used for cooking.

If you're faced with less than perfect fruits that aren't suitable for freezing in their whole form, try pureeing them! Place the fruit in a small saucepan, add your choice of sugar, and cook until soft. Cool, puree, and then freeze.

Choose from the following methods for wet packing:

- ✔ **Wet pack with sugar:** Place your fruit in a bowl and sprinkle it with granulated sugar. Allow the fruit to stand until the natural fruit juices drain from the fruit and the sugar dissolves. Transfer your fruit and the juice to a rigid freezer container, allowing the recommended headspace. (See the section "Following headspace guidelines," later in this chapter.)

- ✔ **Wet pack with syrup:** Place your fruit in a rigid freezer container, adding syrup to completely cover the fruit and allowing the recommended headspace. Your fruit needs to be fully submerged in the syrup before sealing the containers. (For more on syrups and headspace, see the upcoming sections "Getting the lowdown on syrup" and "Following headspace guidelines.") Wet pack with syrup is best for firm fruits or fruits that have been pitted and sliced.

To solve the problem of *floating fruit,* or fruit rising to the top of the liquid in the jar, wad a piece of moisture-proof paper (foil works well) into a ball. Place it on top of the fruit to force the fruit to stay completely submerged when the container is sealed. Remove the paper after thawing your fruit.

Book VI

Freezing

Mastering the Frozen Fruit Process

Fruits may be frozen raw, with added sugar, or with added *syrup* (a mixture of sugar and water). Although adding sugar to your fruit isn't necessary, it's preferred. Occasionally, you'll add an *antioxidant* (an antidarkening agent) to the liquid to keep your fruit from discoloring.

When freezing fruit, follow these steps:

1. **Select fruit that is free from bruising and not overly ripe.**

2. **Work with small, manageable quantities, about 8 to 12 cups of fruit, which yield about 2 to 3 quarts frozen.**

   Note: Most of the recipes in this chapter use about 2 cups of fruit, which yield 1 pint. You can easily do multiple batches at a time to get the yield you want.

3. **Wash your fruit and allow it to drain thoroughly before packing it for freezing, to avoid it becoming a solid lump when frozen.**

4. **Prepare your fruit for freezing based on your final use: dry pack with sugar for pies, jams, and jellies or wet pack for uncooked desserts.**

5. **If called for in your recipe, add an antioxidant.**

   You do this step with a fruit that will oxidize when exposed to the air. Refer to Book II, Chapter 2.

6. **Fill your container, allowing the proper headspace.**

    Choose your storage container size and fruit-packing method based on how you intend to use your final product. The best choices for fruit packaging materials are rigid freezer containers and freezer bags (see Book VI, Chapter 1). Use rigid freezer containers when you add liquid to the fruit, like wet packing. Use freezer bags when no liquid is added to your fruit, like dry packing.

    For more on headspace, see the upcoming section "Following headspace guidelines."

7. **Label the package and let your freezer do the rest!**

Getting the lowdown on syrup

Adding syrups before freezing fruits allows you to manage the sugar content. If you're trying to control your sugar intake, use an extra-light or light syrup. For decadent dessert sweets, try the heavy syrup recipe.

Syrup is a sugar-and-water combination that you can make yourself. Table 2-1 lists the different types of syrups. To make the syrup, you simply dissolve the appropriate amount of sugar into water. You can use either cold or hot water. If using hot water, let the sugar syrup cool to room temperature before adding it to the fruit.

The concentration of sugar syrup is up to you, but usually you want a thin syrup to prevent a loss of flavor, especially if the fruit is naturally sweet or mild flavored. A medium to heavy syrup is used for sour fruits, such as sour cherries or grapes. Different recipes may call the syrup concentrations different things. Simply follow the concentrations as specified in the recipe you're using.

Table 2-1	Syrup for Freezing Fruit			
Type of Syrup	Sugar Concentration	Sugar	Water	Syrup Yield
Extra-light	20	1¼ cups	5½ cups	6 cups
Light	30	2¼ cups	5¼ cups	6½ cups
Medium	40	3¼ cups	5 cups	7 cups
Heavy	50	4¼ cups	4¼ cups	7 cups

Use these syrup estimates for planning the amount of syrup to make for filling your storage containers:

- **Sliced fruit or berries:** ⅓ to ½ cup of syrup for 1½ cups of fruit in a 1-pint container

- **Halved fruit:** ¾ to 1 cup of syrup for 1½ cups of fruit in a 1-pint container

Following headspace guidelines

Headspace is very important when freezing foods. Food expands when frozen, and you need the extra space to allow for this. In addition, if you're using glass jars and don't have enough headspace to accommodate the expanding food, the jars can break. To avoid this problem, use the headspace recommendation for the size containers you have (see Table 2-2).

Book VI

Freezing

Table 2-2	Headspace Guidelines for a Dry or Wet Pack		
Packing Method	**Container Opening Size**	**Pints**	**Quarts**
Dry pack	Narrow mouth	½ inch	½ inch
Dry pack	Wide mouth	½ inch	½ inch
Wet pack	Narrow mouth	¾ inch	1½ inches
Wet pack	Wide mouth	½ inch	1 inch

Thawing and Using Frozen Fruits

For retaining the best quality of your fruit after freezing, refer to Book VI, Chapter 1 and follow these guidelines:

- Open your container when a few ice crystals remain in your fruit.

- Use your fruit immediately after thawing; in fact, serving the fruit in a slightly frozen state will prevent the fruit from becoming too soft.

- When cooking with sweetened, thawed fruits, you may need to reduce the amount of sugar your recipe calls for.

- Avoid refreezing fruit by freezing in smaller packages and taking out only what you need. A good general rule is to freeze no more than 2 cups per container. This amount is commonly used in recipes and fits well in ziplock bags.

- Use your frozen fruit within one year.

Frozen Apples Packed in Sugar

Prep time: 25 min • **Yield:** 1 pint

Ingredients	Directions
1¼ to 1½ pounds apples **1½ tablespoons lemon juice** **8 cups water** **½ cup granulated sugar**	**1** Peel, core, and slice your apples into 12 or 16 pieces, dropping the slices into mixture of 1½ tablespoons lemon juice to 8 cups water to keep them from turning brown as you finish them all. (If you prefer, you can use an ascorbic or citric acid solution instead of the lemon juice and water.)
	2 Remove the apples from the antioxidant solution and place them in a shallow dish or on a baking sheet. Sprinkle the apple slices with granulated sugar or 1 part sugar to 4 parts apples. Let your apples be the guide here: Taste a slice with sugar to see whether the degree of sweetness is to your liking.
	3 Fill your container, allowing the proper headspace (refer to Table 2-2), and freeze.

Per ½-cup serving: *Calories 168 (From Fat 3); Fat 0g (Saturated 0g); Cholesterol 0mg; Sodium 0mg; Carbohydrates 44g (Dietary Fiber 2g); Protein 0g.*

Tip: Use crisp apples with a firm texture like Pippin or Golden Delicious. Because apples tend to get a little mushy when you defrost them, these apples are ideal for use in baked goods.

Vary 1t! You can also pack your apples in syrup. To do so, place your drained apple slices in rigid freezer containers, filling them with a cold heavy syrup (refer to Table 2-1), adding ½ teaspoon of an antioxidant solution to each container, and allowing the proper headspace (refer to Table 2-2).

Frozen Peaches Packed in Syrup

Prep time: 30 min • **Yield:** 1 pint

Ingredients	Directions
1 to 1½ pounds peaches **½ cup medium syrup** **¼ teaspoon antioxidant**	**1** Blanch the peaches by dipping them into boiling water for 30 seconds and then immediately into ice water, to remove the skin. (Don't leave the fruit in the boiling water for more than 1 minute.)
	2 Place ½ cup cold medium syrup (refer to Table 2-1) and an antioxidant into each rigid freezer container. Slice or halve the fruit directly into the pint container, discarding the fruit pits.
	3 Fill the container with additional syrup, allowing the proper headspace (refer to Table 2-2), and freeze.

Per ½-cup serving: *Calories 65 (From Fat 1); Fat 0g (Saturated 0g); Cholesterol 0mg; Sodium 0mg; Carbohydrates 17g (Dietary Fiber 2g); Protein 1g.*

Tip: Use freestone peaches to make removing the pit much easier. You can also freeze nectarines and apricots the same way!

Frozen Lemon Juice

Prep time: 10 min • **Yield:** 4 cups

Ingredients	Directions
8 lemons	**1** Squeeze the juice from the lemons into a measuring cup. Pour the juice into 1-ounce freezer containers or ice-cube trays.
	2 After the cubes freeze, remove them from the ice-cube trays and store them in freezer bags.

Per 1-tablespoon serving: Calories 4 (From Fat 0); Fat 0g (Saturated 0g); Cholesterol 0mg; Sodium 0mg; Carbohydrates 1g (Dietary Fiber 0g); Protein 0g.

Tip: If you prefer juice without pulp, place a small mesh strainer over the edge of your measuring cup; juice your fruit over the strainer.

Vary It! You can freeze lime juice the same way, so consider this recipe a two-fer.

Quick-Frozen Blueberries

Prep time: 15 min • **Yield:** 1 pint

Ingredients	Directions
1 to 1½ pounds blueberries	**1** Gently wash the berries, removing any stems. Spread the washed berries onto a towel-lined cookie sheet and allow them to air dry (about 15 to 20 minutes) to prevent them from sticking together while freezing.
	2 Place the baking sheet in your freezer. (This process is known as *quick-freezing* or *flash-freezing*.) When the berries are frozen, transfer them to freezer bags or rigid freezer containers.

Per ½-cup serving: Calories 64 (From Fat 4); Fat 0g (Saturated 0g); Cholesterol 0mg; Sodium 7mg; Carbohydrates 16g (Dietary Fiber 3g); Protein 1g.

Tip: This recipe uses blueberries, but you can use any type of berry (except strawberries); they all freeze well with this method. Whatever berries you choose, make sure they're firm.

Vary It! To pack your berries in syrup, place the berries into rigid freezer containers, covering them with cold medium syrup (refer to Table 2-1), allowing the proper headspace (refer to Table 2-2). If the berries float, add a ball of moisture-proof paper to keep the berries submerged.

Frozen Strawberries Packed in Sugar

Prep time: 60 min • **Yield:** 1½ pints

Ingredients	Directions
¾ to 1½ pounds fresh strawberries ½ cup sugar	**1** Wash your strawberries in water, being careful not to bruise them. Remove the hulls (stems). **2** Slice the strawberries lengthwise into a bowl. Add ¾ cup granulated sugar for each quart of strawberries, stirring the berries to dissolve the sugar. Let the strawberries and sugar sit for 30 minutes for the juice to develop. **3** Transfer your strawberries to rigid freezer containers, allowing the proper headspace (refer to Table 2-2).

Per ½-cup serving: Calories 121 (From Fat 3); Fat 0g (Saturated 0g); Cholesterol 0mg; Sodium 1mg; Carbohydrates 31g (Dietary Fiber 2g); Protein 1g.

Vary It! To pack your strawberries in syrup, place the sliced strawberries into rigid freezer containers. Fill the containers with a cold medium syrup (refer to Table 2-1), allowing the proper headspace (refer to Table 2-2).

Frozen Strawberry Puree

Prep time: 30 min • **Cook time:** 20 min • **Yield:** 1½ pints

Ingredients	*Directions*
2 to 4 cups strawberries **¼ cup water** **2 tablespoons granulated sugar (or to taste)** **1 tablespoon lemon juice (or to taste)**	*1* Wash, hull, and slice the strawberries. Place them in a 2-quart saucepan. Add the water to prevent the berries from sticking. Cook the berries on medium heat until soft (about 20 minutes). Remove the pan from the heat and let the fruit cool.
	2 Process the cooled fruit in a food processor fitted with a metal blade until pureed, or run it through a food mill. Add the granulated sugar and lemon juice to taste.
	3 Return the mixture to the saucepan and bring it to a boil over medium-high heat, stirring constantly. Remove immediately from the heat.
	4 Ladle the puree into 1-cup or smaller rigid freezer containers, allowing the proper headspace (refer to Table 2-2). Alternatively, freeze small amounts of fruit puree in ice-cube trays. Remove the frozen cubes from the trays and transfer them to a freezer-storage bag.

Per 2-tablespoon serving: *Calories 16 (From Fat 1); Fat 0 (Saturated 0g); Cholesterol 0mg; Sodium 0mg; Carbohydrates 4g (Dietary Fiber 1g); Protein 0g.*

Tip: Use frozen fruit purees for making fruit leathers, fruit sauces (by adding water, fruit juice, or a teaspoon of your favorite liqueur), as a concentrated flavor in fruit smoothies, or as a topping for your favorite ice cream.

Vary It! This recipe makes a strawberry puree, but you can make any kind of puree. Just use any amount of fruit you have on hand — 2 to 4 cups raw fruit is a good working quantity — and then add sugar to taste.

Frozen Mangoes Packed in Syrup

Prep time: 20 min • **Yield:** 1 pint

Ingredients	*Directions*
2 to 3 medium mangoes **½ cup cold light syrup**	*1* Peel the skin from the fruit, slicing the flesh away from the seed (see Figure 2-1).
	2 Measure ½ cup cold light syrup (refer to Table 2-1) into a rigid pint container. Slice the fruit directly into the container. Press the slices to the bottom of the container, adding more syrup to achieve the proper headspace (refer to Table 2-2).
	3 Add a ball of moisture-proof paper to keep the fruit submerged, secure the lid, and freeze.

Per 1-cup serving: *Calories 101 (From Fat 3); Fat 0g (Saturated 0g); Cholesterol 0mg; Sodium 0mg; Carbohydrates 26g (Dietary Fiber 2g); Protein 1g.*

Figure 2-1:
Peeling and
cutting a
mango.

Frozen Pineapple Packed in Syrup

Prep time: 20 min • **Yield:** 1 pint

Ingredients	Directions
1 pound pineapple 1 cup cold light syrup	**1** If using whole fruit, peel and core the pineapple (see Figure 2-2), cutting it into wedges or cubes.
	2 Pack your fruit into a rigid freezer container. Fill the container with the cold light syrup (refer to Table 2-1), allowing the proper headspace (refer to Table 2-2). Then seal and freeze.

Per ½-cup serving: Calories 96 (From Fat 0); Fat 0g (Saturated 0g); Cholesterol 0mg; Sodium 1mg; Carbohydrates 25g (Dietary Fiber 1g); Protein 0g.

Tip: Getting the ripest pineapple is essential for a sweet, juicy flavor. The stem end develops sugar first, so check for yellow eyes around the base.

TRIM AND CUT PINEAPPLE

Figure 2-2: Removing the rind and the core from a pineapple.

1.
LAY THE PINEAPPLE ON ITS SIDE. CUT OFF THE TOP FRONDS AND A SLICE OFF THE BOTTOM.

2.
WITH THE PINEAPPLE UPRIGHT, CUT OFF THE EYES WITH A KNIFE.

3.
CUT IN HALF

4.
CUT AGAIN INTO WEDGES OR SLICES.

Chapter 3

Freezing Veggies Like a Pro

In This Chapter

▶ Prepping veggies for your freezer

▶ Discovering perfect blanching

▶ Defrosting for beginners

Like fresh fruit, fresh vegetables are quick and easy to freeze. Freezing ensures that the freshest produce is available for your meals, and your budget will benefit from buying what is in season, when it's the most economical. Freezing is also a great way to stock up on the vegetables that you use most often.

If freezing mixed vegetables is desired, prepare each vegetable separately and then combine them before freezing. That way, each individual vegetable will remain at its peak flavor and nutrition.

Preparing to Freeze Vegetables

Follow these steps for freezing vegetables:

1. **Choose only perfect vegetables, free of bruises and imperfections, and not overly ripe.**

2. **Work with small, manageable quantities, about 2 pounds at a time.**

3. **Wash and drain your vegetables and prepare them according to your recipe (which usually specifies blanching the vegetables).**

   Be sure to allow the vegetables to dry thoroughly before freezing to prevent them from sticking together when frozen.

4. **Chill your vegetables before packing them for freezing.**

5. **Fill your container.**

   Allow the proper headspace, if you're using rigid containers (refer to Book VI, Chapter 2), or remove all excess air from freezer bags.

6. **Label your package, adding it to your freezer.**

Focusing on fresh

Knowing what is in season is the key to buying the freshest produce. When in season, the vegetable prices will be at their lowest, with an abundant variety to choose from. Farmers' markets and roadside vegetable stands are a great way to find large quantities of in-season veggies.

If buying directly from a producer, let them know that you're buying enough for freezing. They may assemble a bag or box of their freshest produce just for you.

Setting up for success

Regardless of the garden zone you're in, the growing cycle is the same for all produce. In the early season, leafy greens and fast growing vegetables are ready to harvest. Later in the season, the variety increases, and most of the produce will be ripening all at once. Finally, toward the end of the season, the root vegetables, pumpkins, and squashes are ready to harvest.

No matter what time of the growing season it is, these basic tips will make sure that you're ready for any produce that becomes ripe:

- ✔ Keep a supply of your favorite storage containers on hand for spur-of-the-moment storage.

- ✔ Have labeling supplies ready, including a permanent marker, freezer tape, paper, and a pen to make a list of what you have frozen.

- ✔ Make sure that you have enough space in the freezer to move the older containers to the front and place newest produce in the back.

- ✔ Have a preparation plan. Know how to prepare each vegetable for storage.

- ✔ Have any kitchen equipment ready and in good shape before heading out to buy your vegetables for storing.

Buy only what you have time to freeze within 24 hours from purchase. Produce starts to break down and decay from the moment it's picked. Stopping this process as fast as possible is crucial. Because of the time investment, be sure you set aside some time in your schedule for food preservation.

Freezing Vegetables to Perfection

The key to great frozen vegetables is a process called *blanching*. Blanching scalds the vegetables in boiling water, slows down the enzymes and the spoiling process, and preserves the color, flavor, texture, and nutritive value.

Blanching isn't necessary if you're using your frozen vegetables, like onions, in foods where you're concerned only with flavor and not color.

Book VI

Freezing

Blanching makes frozen veggies better

Blanching requires 100 percent of your attention. Vegetables blanched for too short of a time won't stop the enzymes in the vegetables, and microorganisms start where they were stopped after the vegetables thaw. Vegetables left in the boiling water too long start cooking and may become limp.

Follow these steps for successful blanching:

1. **Wash and drain your vegetables; then remove any peel or skin, if needed.**

   If you're not freezing your vegetables whole, cut them now.

2. **Bring a 5- to 6-quart pot of water to a boil and fill a large mixing bowl with ice water.**

   Add ice cubes to the mixing bowl because the hot vegetables increase the temperature of the ice bath. Cold stops the cooking process. Remember to have extra ice ready, to keep up with this step.

3. **Add your prepared vegetables to the boiling water for the amount of time specified in the recipe.**

   Begin timing your vegetables as soon as they're in the boiling water; don't wait for the water to return to a boil.

Blanch your vegetables in batches, no more than 1 pound vegetables in 1 gallon water.

4. **Remove your vegetables from the boiling water and plunge them into the ice-water bath, stirring the vegetables and circulating the ice water to stop the cooking process as quickly as possible.**

Don't leave your vegetables in the ice-water bath longer than they were in the boiling water.

5. **After the vegetables are chilled all the way through, remove them from the ice-water bath and drain them in a colander.**

6. **If you're dry-packing your vegetables, roll them in or lay them on clean, dry kitchen towels to remove excess moisture.**

Packing essentials

Pack your vegetables immediately after preparing them. Moisture-proof, vapor-proof freezer bags are the best choice for your vegetables. Don't season them before freezing them.

Removing all excess air is important to avoid the spoilers, such as freezer burn (refer to Book VI, Chapter 1). To remove air from your containers, follow these guidelines:

✓ **Freezer bags:** Package your vegetable pieces as close together as possible at the bottom of the bag, without bruising or squashing the vegetables. Fold the unfilled upper portion of the bag over the vegetables, gently pushing any air out of the bag. Seal the bag.

✓ **Rigid containers:** Use reusable containers when you're adding liquid to the vegetables. Allowing the proper headspace exhausts the air because the liquid in the container expands when it freezes. For headspace allowances, refer to Book VI, Chapter 2.

After filling your bags, place them in a single layer in your freezer. Quick freezing is important to the thawed quality of your vegetables. After the packages are frozen solid, you may stack them on top of each other.

Thawing and Using Frozen Vegetables

Properly thawing your vegetables completes the cycle of preserving your fresh vegetables by freezing. Thawed vegetable results are best when thawed in your refrigerator rather than on your kitchen counter. A package of vegetables containing a single serving size takes less time to thaw than a package containing 1 pound of vegetables.

Avoiding spoilage

You don't actually have to thaw your vegetables. You can always add them directly to hot water or a recipe and allow them to thaw and cook with the rest of the ingredients. If you freeze leftover vegetables for longer storage, this is a great way to use up the smaller packages of frozen veggies that are not enough to serve the entire family on their own. Think of them as nearly instant vegetable soup ingredients.

If you do need to thaw out your vegetables, use the same care as you would for any other frozen food. Do not thaw directly on the counter and avoid eating any thawed vegetables with an off flavor.

Coping with texture issues

When freezing vegetables, remember that freezing changes the texture of some of them. Although some vegetables will lose their crispness, they still remain tasty and nutritionally sound. If a particular vegetable becomes too soft to look attractive as a side dish, simply use it as an added ingredient in a recipe. Soups and sauces are wonderful places to include frozen vegetables that soften when frozen.

High-water content is the reason that some vegetables become soft when thawed. If individual pieces are needed, freeze blanched vegetables on a cookie sheet until hard and then place in containers for storage.

Frozen Asparagus

Prep time: 20 min • **Cook time:** 4 min • **Yield:** 1½ quarts

Ingredients	*Directions*
1 to 1½ pounds fresh asparagus	**1** Trim the tough ends from the asparagus spears, wash, and drain. Leave the spears whole or cut them into 1-inch pieces.
	2 Blanch the spears or pieces for 1 to 4 minutes, depending on size. (Thinner spears take less time.) Take the time to test your spears after each minute to check for a slightly crisp texture. Cool the asparagus immediately in an ice bath.
	3 Place the cooled asparagus into a colander to drain. Place the cooled asparagus in quart-sized freezer bags — 1 pound of asparagus fits nicely into a quart bag — removing all excess air before sealing the bag and placing it in the freezer.

Per ½-cup serving: *Calories 25 (From Fat 3); Fat 0g (Saturated 0g); Cholesterol 0mg; Sodium 12mg; Carbohydrates 5g (Dietary Fiber 2g); Protein 3g.*

Frozen Wax Beans

Prep time: 20 min • **Cook time:** 3 min • **Yield:** 1 pint

Ingredients	Directions
⅔ to 1 pound fresh wax beans	**1** Wash and drain the beans. Remove the ends and strings and cut them into 1-inch pieces.
	2 Blanch the beans for 2 to 3 minutes; cool immediately in an ice bath. Spread beans on a dry kitchen towel to dry thoroughly before freezing.
	3 Place the cooled beans in quart-sized freezer bags, removing all excess air before sealing and placing the bag in the freezer.

Per ½-cup serving: Calories 26 (From Fat 0); Fat 0g (Saturated 0g); Cholesterol 0mg; Sodium 8mg; Carbohydrates 6g (Dietary Fiber 3g); Protein 1g.

Frozen Shell Beans

Prep time: 20 min • **Cook time:** 4 min • **Yield:** 1½ pints

Ingredients	Directions
2 to 2½ pounds shell beans	**1** Wash and drain the beans.
	2 Blanch the beans for 2 to 4 minutes; cool immediately in an ice bath. Spread beans on a clean kitchen towel to absorb all excess moisture.
	3 Place the cooled beans in freezer bags, removing all excess air before placing the bag in the freezer.

Per ½-cup serving: Calories 158 (From Fat 12); Fat 1g (Saturated 0g); Cholesterol 0mg; Sodium 110mg; Carbohydrates 25g (Dietary Fiber 9g); Protein 12 g.

Frozen Bell Peppers

Prep time: 15 min • **Yield:** 2 pints

Ingredients	Directions
1 to 3 pounds fresh peppers	**1** Wash and drain the peppers. Remove the stems and seeds and slice the peppers into uniform pieces. (**Note:** You do not blanch peppers before freezing.)
	2 Place the bell peppers into a rigid container, leaving the appropriate amount of headspace. (Refer to Book VI, Chapter 2.) Seal and freeze.

Per ½-cup serving: Calories 15 (From Fat 1); Fat 0g (Saturated 0g); Cholesterol 0mg; Sodium 1mg; Carbohydrates 4g (Dietary Fiber 1g); Protein 1g.

Frozen Broccoli

Prep time: 20 min • **Cook time:** 4 min • **Yield:** 1 pint

Ingredients	Directions
1 pound fresh broccoli	**1** Wash and drain the broccoli, removing leaves and damaged spots. Cut the broccoli spears into ½-inch pieces.
	2 Blanch the broccoli for 3 to 4 minutes; cool immediately in an ice bath.
	3 Place the cooled broccoli pieces in freezer bags, removing all excess air before sealing the bag and placing it in the freezer.

Per ½-cup serving: Calories 30 (From Fat 0); Fat 0g (Saturated 0g); Cholesterol 0mg; Sodium 29mg; Carbohydrates 6g (Dietary Fiber 3g); Protein 3g.

Frozen Brussels Sprouts

Prep time: 20 min • **Cook time:** 3–5 min • **Yield:** 1½ pints

Ingredients	Directions
1 pound fresh Brussels sprouts	*1* Wash and drain the Brussels sprouts, removing any damaged outer leaves and sorting by size for blanching. (The smaller-sized sprouts use the shorter blanching time.) Trim the bottoms.
	2 Blanch the smaller Brussels sprouts for 3 minutes and the larger ones for 5 minutes; cool immediately in an ice bath. Spread the blanched Brussels sprouts on a clean kitchen towel to remove all excess moisture before freezing.
	3 Place the cooled Brussels sprouts in freezer bags, removing all excess air before sealing the bag and placing it in the freezer.

Per ½-cup serving: Calories 32 (From Fat 4); Fat 0g (Saturated 0g); Cholesterol 0mg; Sodium 17mg; Carbohydrates 7g (Dietary Fiber 2g); Protein 2g.

Frozen Onions

Prep time: 10 min • **Yield:** 1 pint

Ingredients	Directions
1 large or 3 small whole onions	*1* Peel and chop the onions. Do not blanch.
	2 Place the chopped onion in freezer bags, removing all excess air before sealing the bag and placing it in the freezer.

Per ½-cup serving: Calories 14 (From Fat 1); Fat 0g (Saturated 0g); Cholesterol 0mg; Sodium 0mg; Carbohydrates 3g (Dietary Fiber 0g); Protein 0g.

Frozen Carrots

Prep time: 20 min **Cook time:** 2 min • **Yield:** 1 pint

Ingredients	Directions
1 pound carrots	*1* Wash and drain the carrots, removing the tops and peeling the skin. Leave the carrots whole or slice (or dice) them into uniform-sized pieces.
	2 Blanch the carrots for 2 minutes (sliced or diced carrots) or 5 minutes (whole carrots); cool immediately in an ice bath. Dry the blanched carrots on a clean kitchen towel to remove all of the moisture.
	3 Place the cooled carrots in freezer bags, removing all excess air before sealing the bag and placing it in the freezer.

Per ½-cup serving: Calories 51 (From Fat 0); Fat 0g (Saturated 0g); Cholesterol 0mg; Sodium 58mg; Carbohydrates 12g (Dietary Fiber 3g); Protein 2g.

Frozen Corn

Prep time: 20 min • **Cook time:** 4 min • **Yield:** 3 pints

Ingredients	Directions
4 pounds corn (about 12 ears)	*1* Remove the husks and the silk from the corn. Wash the ears.
	2 Blanch the ears whole for 4 minutes; cool immediately in an ice bath. Cut the kernels from the corn after cooling.
	3 Place the corn in freezer bags, removing all excess air before sealing the bag and placing it in the freezer.

Per ½-cup serving: Calories 47 (From Fat 6); Fat 1g (Saturated 0g); Cholesterol 0mg; Sodium 8mg; Carbohydrates 10g (Dietary Fiber 2g); Protein 2g.

Tip: Add frozen corn to a soup or stew during the last 5 minutes of cooking.

Frozen Cauliflower

Prep time: 20 min • **Cook time:** 3 min • **Yield:** 1 quart

Ingredients	Directions
1¼ **pounds cauliflower** **Water** **White vinegar**	**1** Wash and drain the cauliflower, removing the leaves and core and cutting into 1-inch pieces.
	2 Blanch the cauliflower in a water-vinegar mixture (1 tablespoon of vinegar to 1 gallon of water) for 3 minutes; cool immediately in an ice bath.
	3 Place the cauliflower pieces in freezer bags, removing all excess air before sealing the bag and placing it in the freezer.

Per ½-cup serving: *Calories 7 (From Fat 1); Fat 0g (Saturated 0g); Cholesterol 0mg; Sodium 8mg; Carbohydrates 2g (Dietary Fiber 1g); Protein 1g.*

Tip: Presoaking cauliflower in a salt water solution of 4 teaspoons salt per gallon of water can help remove any worms or insects that may be hiding within. This is not a sign of spoilage, it simply means that the vegetable is organic.

Frozen Shelled Peas

Prep time: 20 min • **Cook time:** 1½ min • **Yield:** 1 pint to 1 quart

Ingredients	Directions
2 to 4 cups shelled peas	**1** Rinse the peas in cold running water.
	2 Blanch the loose peas for 1½ minutes; cool immediately in an ice bath.
	3 Place the cooled peas in freezer bags, removing all excess air before sealing the bag and placing it in the freezer.

Per ½-cup serving: *Calories 29 (From Fat 1); Fat 0g (Saturated 0g); Cholesterol 0mg; Sodium 1mg; Carbohydrates 5g (Dietary Fiber 2g); Protein 2g.*

Frozen Greens

Prep time: 20 min • **Cook time:** 1½ min • **Yield:** 1 pint

Ingredients	Directions
1 to 1½ pounds greens (beet, spinach, or Swiss chard)	**1** Wash the greens well, removing any thick stems.
	2 Blanch the greens for 1½ minutes, stirring constantly to separate the leaves; cool immediately in an ice bath. Drain blanched greens in a colander.
	3 Place the cooled greens in freezer bags, removing all excess air before sealing the bag and placing it in the freezer.

Per ½-cup serving: *Calories 36 (From Fat 2); Fat 0g (Saturated 0g); Cholesterol 0mg; Sodium 320mg; Carbohydrates 7g (Dietary Fiber 4g); Protein 3g.*

Tip: Your actual yield will vary depending on the type of greens you use. Spinach, for example, wilts much more than kale does and produces a smaller yield.

Frozen Okra

Prep time: 20 min • **Cook time:** 3–4 min • **Yield:** 1 pint

Ingredients	*Directions*
1 to 1½ pounds fresh okra	**1** Wash the okra well, removing stems. Do not cut (you leave okra whole for blanching). (***Note:*** Because larger pods can be tough, use only pods that are 2 to 3 inches in diameter.)
	2 Blanch the okra pods for 3 to 4 minutes and cool them immediately in an ice bath. You can pack the okra whole or in slices. If you prefer sliced okra, slice it after it has cooled.
	3 Place the cooled okra in freezer bags, removing all excess air before sealing the bag and placing it in the freezer.

Per ½-cup serving: Calories 40 (From Fat 2); Fat 0g (Saturated 0g); Cholesterol 0mg; Sodium 6mg; Carbohydrates 9g (Dietary Fiber 3g); Protein 2g.

Frozen Winter Squash

Prep time: 10 min • **Cook time:** 10–30 min • **Yield:** 1 pint

Ingredients	Directions
1 to 1½ pounds winter squash	**1** Peel the outer skin of the winter squash, scrape out the seeds, and cut the flesh into chunks.
	2 Place the squash in a 3-quart saucepan and add enough water to cover the bottom of the pan. Cook the squash over medium-low heat until the flesh is soft, about 10 to 30 minutes, or until a chunk slides off a fork. Remove the squash from the pan and mash it until smooth.
	3 Place the mashed squash in a rigid container, leaving the appropriate amount of headspace (refer to Book VI, Chapter 2). Seal and freeze.

Per ½-cup serving: Calories 43 (From Fat 1); Fat 0g (Saturated 0g); Cholesterol 0mg; Sodium 3mg; Carbohydrates 11g (Dietary Fiber 3g); Protein 1g.

Vary It! You can follow this same recipe to freeze pumpkin.

Frozen Summer Squash

Prep time: 15 min • **Cook time:** 3 min • **Yield:** 1 pint

Ingredients	*Directions*
1 to 1¼ pounds summer squash	*1* Wash the squash, remove the stems, and slice it into ½-inch rounds.
	2 Blanch the squash for 3 minutes; cool it immediately in an ice bath. (See the earlier section "Blanching makes frozen veggies better" for complete blanching instructions.) Drain the squash in a colander.
	3 Place the cooled squash in a rigid container, leaving the appropriate amount of headspace. Seal and freeze. You can also freeze squash flat in freezer bags.

Per ½-cup serving: Calories 22 (From Fat 0); Fat 0g (Saturated 0g); Cholesterol 0mg; Sodium 2mg; Carbohydrates 5g (Dietary Fiber 2g); Protein 1g.

Frozen Snow Peas

Prep time: 20 min • **Cook time:** 1 min • **Yield:** 3½ cups

Ingredients	Directions
⅔ **to 1 pound snow peas**	**1** Wash the snow peas, removing the stems and blossom ends.
	2 Blanch the whole peas for 30 seconds; cool immediately in an ice bath.
	3 Place the snow peas in freezer bags, removing all excess air before sealing the bag and placing it in the freezer.

Per ½-cup serving: Calories 18 (From Fat 1); Fat 0g (Saturated 0g); Cholesterol 0mg; Sodium 2mg; Carbohydrates 3g (Dietary Fiber 1g); Protein 1g.

Chapter 4

Freezing Fresh Herbs

In This Chapter

▶ Making a chill choice of herbs

▶ Deciding to roll, flatten, or cube

▶ Testing alternative techniques

T he flavors fresh herbs impart in just about any dish are truly a gift from nature, but frozen herbs are a great compromise when fresh herbs aren't available. Freezing is also an option for preserving delicate culinary herbs that tend to go all to pieces when they're dried. Some herbs seem to retain their fresh flavor better with this method, but your experience may differ.

Choosing the Right Herbs

Depending on who's talking, freezing may be as good as or better than drying for some herbs. Basil, chervil, chives, cilantro, dillweed, fennel, garlic greens, lovage, marjoram, mint, oregano, parsley, sage, sorrel, sweet Cicely, tarragon, and thyme all freeze well, and their flavor remains at its strongest. Drying these same herbs, if not done carefully, can result in pale, tasteless plants, worthless for flavoring.

If you're unsure whether an herb will freeze well, consider the moisture content. If the herb is juicy with tender leaves, it may be a good candidate for freezing instead of drying. Other herbs do well being stored either way. Try both ways and see which results you like better!

Thawed herbs are great in cooked dishes, but they aren't suitable as a garnish because they're limp after freezing and thawing.

Some herbs that freeze well with nothing more than a cleaning include chervil, chives, cilantro, comfrey, dill, lovage, mint, parsley, savory, sweet fennel, and thyme.

Some herbs, such as basil, mint, parsley, and cilantro, turn black if you freeze the leaves directly. Puree these herbs in just enough olive oil to make a slurry and then freeze them in ice cube trays. Using this technique helps to maintain their fresh flavor and color.

Preparing Herbs for the Freezer

To prepare fresh herbs for the freezer, follow these steps (see Figure 4-1):

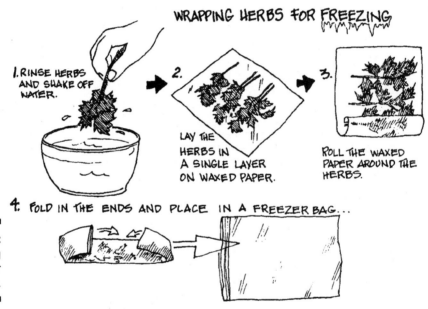

WRAPPING HERBS FOR FREEZING

1. RINSE HERBS AND SHAKE OFF WATER.

2. LAY THE HERBS IN A SINGLE LAYER ON WAXED PAPER.

3. ROLL THE WAXED PAPER AROUND THE HERBS.

4. FOLD IN THE ENDS AND PLACE IN A FREEZER BAG...

Figure 4-1:
Wrapping herbs for freezing.

1. **Clean the herbs.**

   Hold the bottom of the stems (don't remove the leaves from the stems) and swish the herbs in a bowl of cool water.

2. **Drain and dry the herbs, gently shaking off any excess water.**

3. **Lay the herb sprigs flat, not touching each other, on a piece of wax paper.**

4. **Starting at one end, roll the wax paper snugly over the herbs.**

   This step keeps the herbs separate and makes it easy to use one sprig at a time.

5. **Place the rolled herbs in a freezer bag, label the package, and freeze.**

You don't need to thaw the herbs before using them. Frozen herbs keep for six to eight months, but don't refreeze them. When you use frozen herbs in recipes, treat them as if they were fresh. Remove the frozen leaves from the stems and measure, snip, or crush them as you normally would.

If you grow your own herbs, harvest them early in the day before the sun wilts the leaves.

One of the nicest things about freezing is that you can harvest all season long and build a supply of delicious herbs for the time of year when you have no garden. As you freeze small quantities of herbs, you can add them to a previously frozen supply, as long as everything remains cold.

Sampling Frozen Herb Techniques

Just as people disagree about the wisdom of freezing herbs at all, people also disagree about whether to blanch herbs before freezing them. *Blanching* means to plunge the herb into boiling water for no more than a second or two. Gardeners who freeze vegetables usually believe that blanching keeps herbs firm, colorful, and fresh tasting. But others disagree. (Anti-blanchers often make an exception for basil, which blackens if frozen unblanched.)

Like any food storage method, preparing herbs for freezing requires some organization. Being organized doesn't mean you must find a single method that works and stick with it. Freeze some herbs in oil, others whole, to have a variety of flavor at your fingertips.

Freezing flat

A large blob of herbs stuffed into a bag can freeze unevenly, retaining moisture that changes the flavor and makes pieces stick together.

To freeze quantities, spread herbs in a single layer on a baking sheet. Place the baking sheet in the freezer for a couple of hours or until the herbs are frozen, transfer the herbs to freezer bags, pressing out as much air as possible, and then return them to the freezer.

Cubing the flavor

If you use herbs to flavor soups and stews, try freezing them in ice cube trays, as shown in Figure 4-2. After washing the herbs, remove the leaves from the stem and cut them into pieces. Place 1 teaspoon to 1 tablespoon of herbs in each opening of an ice-cube tray. Pour boiling water into the tray and freeze the herb cubes. After the cubes are frozen solid (usually 24 hours) pop them out of the tray and into a plastic freezer bag. When your recipe calls for 1 teaspoon or 1 tablespoon of an herb, add the ice cube to the dish and continue cooking! (Remember to use slightly less liquid in your recipes.)

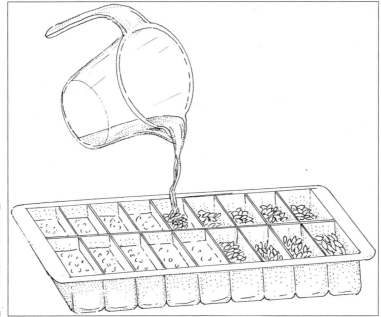

Figure 4-2:
Ice cube trays. They're not just for ice anymore.

If you're thinking of adding a frozen herb to a sauce, you can puree the herb in a blender or food processor with enough oil or water to make a paste and fill your ice cube tray with the mixture. If you often use a certain herb combination, such as basil and oregano, freeze the premeasured herbs together in cubes or freezer bags.

If you're still stumped for more ways you can freeze fresh herbs, try the following:

- **Herbed butter:** Add chopped fresh herbs to one cube of softened, unsalted butter. For a mild herb flavor, start with ¼ cup herbs, adjusting the amount to your personal taste. Transfer the flavored butter to an ice-cube tray sprayed with nonstick cooking spray and freeze the butter. After the butter is frozen (about 24 hours), remove the butter cubes, placing them in a labeled freezer bag. Serve the flavored butter with bread or add one to a casserole.

- **Herbed butter logs:** Flavor the butter as stated in the previous paragraph. Form the flavored butter into a log in a sheet of wax or parchment paper. Twist the ends, place the log in a freezer bag, and freeze it. Slice off what you need and return the log to the freezer.

Herbal Pesto

Prep time: 10 min • **Yield:** 1 cup

Ingredients	Directions
6 cubes frozen herb/oil cubes **2 cloves garlic** **¼ cup pine, cashew, or walnuts** **⅓ cup parmesan cheese** **Olive oil as needed**	*1* Remove herb/oil cubes from the freezer to thaw. Meanwhile, in a blender place the garlic, nuts, and cheese. Pulse the ingredients until finely textured. *2* Start blending, adding cubes of herb/oil through the top. Blend until thoroughly mixed. *3* Freeze pesto in ice cube trays and store in freezer bags for later use.

Per ¼-cup serving: Calories 201 (From Fat 178); Fat 20g (Saturated 4g); Cholesterol 5mg; Sodium 124mg; Carbohydrates 2g (Dietary Fiber 1g); Protein 5g.

Vary It! Pesto isn't just for basil. Use other herbs to create your own unique blend. Some herbs to try include flavored basils, catnip, and mints.

Garlic Broth

Prep time: 10 min • **Cook time:** 30 min • **Yield:** 2 quarts

Ingredients	Directions
2 quarts water **16 cloves frozen garlic, minced fine** **1 onion, chopped** **1 bay leaf** **Salt and pepper to taste**	*1* In a large saucepan, combine all ingredients. Simmer for 30 minutes. Strain for clear broth, if desired. *2* Freeze the cooled broth in 1-pint containers.

Per 1-cup serving: Calories 17 (From Fat 1); Fat 0g (Saturated 0g); Cholesterol 0mg; Sodium 74mg; Carbohydrates 4g (Dietary Fiber 1g); Protein 1g.

Vary It! Try adding dehydrated powdered vegetables for a rich, savory broth.

Tip: This recipe doubles or triples with ease.

Herb and Cheddar Muffins

Prep time: 15 min • **Bake time:** 20 min • **Yield:** 12 muffins

Ingredients

2 cubes frozen herbs, such as dill

1¾ cups flour

2 teaspoons baking powder

½ teaspoon salt

¼ cup sharp cheddar cheese

1 tablespoon brown sugar

⅓ cup crisp bacon pieces

1 cup milk

1 egg

4 tablespoons butter, melted

Directions

1 Thaw herb cubes. Preheat the oven to 400°.

2 Combine the flour, baking powder, and salt in a mixing bowl. Stir the thawed herbs, cheese, sugar, and bacon into the dry mix.

3 In a separate bowl, combine the milk, egg, and melted butter. Add the wet ingredients to the dry ones and mix gently. The batter will remain lumpy.

4 Fill lined muffin tins two-thirds full. Bake 20 minutes.

5 Cool the muffins completely.

6 Wrap each muffin in plastic wrap and place all wrapped muffins into a gallon freezer bag to freeze.

Per muffin: Calories 148 (From Fat 64); Fat 7g (Saturated 4g); Cholesterol 35mg; Sodium 234mg; Carbohydrates 16g (Dietary Fiber 1g); Protein 5g.

Vary It! Leave out the sugar and add Italian herbs for delicious dinner muffins.

Fried Sage Leaves

Prep time: 20 min • **Cook time:** 2–3 min • **Yield:** 8 servings

Ingredients	Directions
⅔ cup flour	**1** Mix the flour, beer, and salt and pepper. Let rest 15 minutes. Heat the oil in a deep-fat fryer. Dry the thawed sage leaves.
1 cup dark lager beer	
Salt and pepper to taste	
Oil for frying	**2** Beat the egg whites until soft peaks form. Fold the egg whites into the batter. Dip the sage leaves into the batter until well coated. Fry until golden brown and crispy.
40 frozen sage leaves	
1 egg white	

Per 5-leave serving: Calories 113 (From Fat 70); Fat 8g (Saturated 1g); Cholesterol 27mg; Sodium 81mg; Carbohydrates 9g (Dietary Fiber 0g); Protein 2g.

Herbal Mayonnaise

Prep time: 10 min • **Yield:** 1 cup

Ingredients	Directions
1 cube frozen herbs, thawed	**1** Place the egg yolk in a food processor and start blending. While the processor is blending, slowly add the oil in a fine stream. After the mixture thickens, add the vinegar.
1 raw, pasteurized egg yolk	
1 cup salad oil or olive oil	
1 tablespoon vinegar	**2** Scrape the finished mayonnaise into a small bowl and stir in the thawed herbs. Add salt and pepper as desired.
Salt and pepper to taste	

Per 1-tablespoon serving: Calories 123 (From Fat 123); Fat 14g (Saturated 2g); Cholesterol 13mg; Sodium 37mg; Carbohydrates 0g (Dietary Fiber 0g); Protein 0g.

Vary It! Make Greek aioli, or garlic mayonnaise, by substituting 4 cloves of frozen garlic, minced, for herbs.

Herbal Salad Dressing

Prep time: 10 min • **Yield:** ⅔ cup

Ingredients	Directions
2 cubes frozen herb/oil 1 clove frozen garlic ½ cup cider vinegar Salt and pepper to taste Additional oil as needed	**1** Remove the herb/oil cubes from your freezer to thaw. Meanwhile, in a blender, pulse the garlic and vinegar until blended.
	2 As you're blending, add the herb/oil cubes through the top and blend until thoroughly mixed.
	3 Add up to 2 tablespoons additional oil, if needed. Taste and add salt and pepper, if desired.
	4 To store, freeze in ice cube trays and then place frozen cubes into freezer bags until needed.

Per 2-tablespoon serving: Calories 49 (From Fat 46); Fat 5g (Saturated 1g); Cholesterol 0mg; Sodium 110mg; Carbohydrates 2g (Dietary Fiber 0g); Protein 0g.

Vary It! Try different herbs for your own flavors. Some herbs that taste great are basil, dill, fennel, rosemary, tarragon, and thyme.

Herbal Ice Cream

Prep time: 5 min • **Process time:** 15 min • **Yield:** 1 pint

Ingredients	*Directions*
2 cups milk **⅔ cup cream** **4 cubes frozen mint** **3 egg yolks** **¾ cup sugar**	*1* Combine the milk, cream, and mint cubes in a heavy saucepan. Heat the milk mixture on medium heat, until foamy.
	2 In a separate bowl, beat the egg yolks until thick. Add the sugar to the beaten eggs and stir well.
	3 Strain the milk mixture to remove the herbs. Add ½ cup of the warm milk mixture to the eggs; blend thoroughly. Add the blended egg/milk mixture to the remaining milk mixture in the pan.
	4 Pour into a bowl and chill completely in the refrigerator. Process in your favorite ice-cream maker. Ice cream will remain fresh for up to 4 weeks in the freezer.

Per ½-cup serving: Calories 402 (From Fat 204); Fat 23g (Saturated 13g); Cholesterol 231mg; Sodium 81mg; Carbohydrates 45g (Dietary Fiber 0g); Protein 7g.

Vary It! Surprise your guests by adding different herbs. Some tasty variations include lavender, lemon balm, and other flavored mints.

Herbal Sorbet

Prep time: 10 min, plus freezing time • **Cook time:** 30 min • **Yield:** 4 servings

Ingredients	Directions
½ **cup sugar**	**1** Combine the sugar, water, and herbs in a heavy saucepan. Bring to a boil. Remove from heat and cover.
1 cup water	
4 tablespoons frozen herbs	**2** Steep the mixture for 30 minutes. Strain to remove the herbs. Add the lemon juice and pour the mixture into an ice cube tray. Freeze for 2 hours.
2 tablespoons lemon juice	
1 egg white, beaten	
	3 In a blender, blend the frozen cubes with 1 beaten egg white. Return the mixture to the freezer in a small bowl and freeze for an additional 1 to 2 hours, or until frozen. Sorbet will remain fresh for up to 4 weeks in freezer.

Per ½-cup serving: Calories 105 (From Fat 0); Fat 0g (Saturated 0g); Cholesterol 0mg; Sodium 16mg; Carbohydrates 26g (Dietary Fiber 0g); Protein 1g.

Vary It! Some herbs that work well for this dairy-free dessert are rosemary, lemon balm, and lavender.

Herbal Marinade

Prep time: 10 min, plus marinating time • **Yield:** 1½ cups

Ingredients	Directions
4 frozen cubes of herb/oil 1 cup vinegar ½ cup water	*1* Thaw the frozen cubes of herb/oil. Combine the herb/oil, vinegar, and water in a gallon freezer bag. Add the meat to the bag and turn to coat all sides.
	2 Leave the meat in the marinade for 30 minutes for poultry to 1 hour for tougher pieces of meat. You can freeze marinade in ice cube trays and then store in freezer bags for up to 6 months.

Per 2-tablespoon serving: Calories 10 (From Fat 9); Fat 1g (Saturated 0g); Cholesterol 0mg; Sodium 0mg; Carbohydrates 0g (Dietary Fiber 0g); Protein 0g.

Vary It! For chicken marinade, try a blend of chives, fennel, marjoram, savory, or thyme. For red meat, try basil, marjoram, parsley, or thyme.

Herbal Syrup

Prep time: 10 min • **Cook time:** 45 min • **Yield:** ⅔ cup

Ingredients	Directions
6 cubes frozen mint 1 cup water 2 cups sugar Green food coloring (optional)	**1** Combine the mint cubes and water in a heavy saucepan. Bring to a simmer for 30 minutes. Strain to remove the mint leaves.
	2 Return the liquid to the saucepan, add the sugar, and return to a simmer. Continue heating for 15 minutes.
	3 Add food coloring, if desired. Freeze in ice cube trays and then place in freezer bags for up to 6 months.

Per 1-tablespoon serving: Calories 168 (From Fat 3); Fat 0g (Saturated 0g); Cholesterol 0mg; Sodium 16mg; Carbohydrates 42g (Dietary Fiber 4g); Protein 2g.

Tip: This herbal syrup is great as a topper for ice cream or cake.

Chapter 5

Freezing Poultry, Meat, and Seafood

*F*reezing meat, poultry, and seafood makes sense. The most expensive (and, perhaps, satisfying) portion of the meal, meats are more economical if purchased in bulk. If they're frozen in the portion sizes that your family needs, you can see at a glance what you have available.

Preparing for the Deep Freeze

Purchase meat, poultry, and fish from stores that practice sanitary handling procedures. If you're buying at a butcher store or fish market, ask them to wrap it for the freezer. If your food is prepackaged, repackage it for the freezer. (See the section "Packing Your Meat Properly," later in this chapter.)

When packaging, trim off undesirable bits of fat and bone to ensure that you're freezing just what you want to keep.

Timing is everything

Because meats are going to be the most expensive part of your food budget, timing is everything in order to keep within your budget. Watch fliers and store sales to know when meats will be going on sale. Once you have a supply of proteins in the freezer, you have the luxury of being able to wait for the best time to buy.

Look for sale prices and stock up with confidence. Your meats will remain tasty and nutritious when packaged correctly.

Buy your meats marked with the Use By date as far in the future as possible. This date is insurance that your meat is the freshest it can be when you purchase it. Meats that are at their Use By date will still be safe to freeze, however. Just know that they won't remain at their best, even frozen. Thaw and use these meats right away. They aren't suitable for refreezing.

Focusing on meal planning

When organizing your meats into how many meals you plan on making, you need a plan. Even the most organized pantry can become boring if the same meals are served repeatedly. Vary the meat throughout the week, rotating them to keep dishes interesting. Plan on using leftovers from one meal as the starter for the next dinner. Stretching your food dollar is easier if you know where the food is going to be used. Your freezer is the first step to having a food plan.

To keep your meal ideas fresh and appealing for the family, offer a variety of different dishes. Package different meats with meal ideas in mind. If you cook family dinners five nights a week, plan on having one night for poultry, one night for fish, and so on. Avoid getting stuck in the same old dinner rut by having a variety of meats and cuts of meats ready to go from the freezer.

Leftover meat from one dinner also makes a ready-made starter for lunch the next day. Save money and time by packaging into lunch portions as you clean up from the meal. Lunch is ready for the next day, with little extra effort!

Freezing for a small table

Freezing ahead is not just for large families. Freezing for one or two people is just as important. Often, remaining inspired is hard when you're cooking for just one or two people. It makes sense to have a variety of things at your fingertips to take the guesswork out of what's for dinner.

For smaller-sized dining, wrap just what you need for each meal. You can easily become disorganized with so many smaller packages in the freezer, so wrap each one separately and then bag into a larger freezer bag to keep them all neat.

Just because you're only cooking for a small number, don't pass up the deals you can get from family packaging. The price cut is considerable, and with your freezing techniques, savings can add up.

Packing Your Meat Properly

Divide your meat into meal-sized portions, always packaging steaks, chops, and chicken parts individually. Even though you may use more than one piece at a time, freezing and thawing time is less because you're working with a smaller mass. Freezer bags or freezer wrap are your best packaging materials for these foods.

Although it may seem counterintuitive, the packaging that meats come in from the meat section of the grocery store isn't suitable for freezing. Always repackage in your own freezer-suitable packaging, like a freezer bag, before adding to your own freezer.

In some cases, freezing a whole roast or chicken may make sense, perhaps for a special event or large dinner. But never freeze a whole stuffed bird because freezing time is increased, and microorganisms may be passed from the poultry to the stuffing. If the stuffing doesn't reach a high enough temperature during cooking to kill the bacteria, it may be passed to your family or guests, making them ill.

Choosing the perfect packaging

The most common packaging for putting meat in the freezer is the plastic freezer bag. Be sure to choose the proper bags. (See Book VI, Chapter 1 for more on freezer supplies.) Get bags just big enough to hold the portions you want to freeze. For a whole chicken, you'll probably need a 2-gallon bag. For steaks, you'll need quart- or gallon-size bags, depending on how many you plan to store in each bag. Check out Table 5-1, which offers a handy guide to packaging.

A few people still like to freeze meat in butcher's paper. *Butcher's paper* is heavy, plastic-coated, white or brown paper. Butcher's paper works quite well for parts, but the shape of a whole roast or chicken can be hard to wrap. The paper packages are either tied with string or sealed with special freezer tape. Duct tape or regular tape comes loose under freezer conditions.

Table 5-1	Freezing Various Meats		
Meat/Cut	*Best Packaging*	*Helpful Tips*	*Storage Life*
Beef, ground	Freezer bags or vacuum-sealed bags	Place two layers of wax paper between patties	3–4 months
Beef, steaks	Freezer paper or vacuum-sealed bags	Two layers of wax paper between steaks, if stacked	6–12 months

(continued)

Table 5-1 *(continued)*

Meat/Cut	Best Packaging	Helpful Tips	Storage Life
Beef, roast	Freezer paper or vacuum-sealed bags	Apply dry rub before freezing	6–12 months
Pork, chops	Freezer paper or vacuum-sealed bags	Apply dry rub or add marinade before sealing	3–6 months
Pork, roast	Freezer paper or vacuum-sealed bags	Apply dry rub before sealing	3–6 months
Pork, sausage	Freezer bag	Freeze in bulk or make patties	2 months
Chicken, whole	Freezer paper or vacuum-sealed bags	Apply dry rub before sealing	6–12 months
Chicken, boneless	Freezer bag	Pre-cut into strips for tenders	6–7 months
Chicken, cooked	Freezer bag	Package and label for soups, stir-fry	2–3 months
Fish	Freezer bag or vacuum-sealed bag	Do not add marinade, but dry rub is fine.	3–6 months; then flavor deteriorates
Seafood	Freezer bag or vacuum-sealed bag	Cook from frozen or semi frozen state	2–4 months

Freezing your pieces and parts

If you like to take a few pork chops out to cook at a time or if you want to save space in the freezer by packing chicken pieces in large bags, you can freeze pieces separately and then combine them in a bag after they're frozen. To do so, spread your pieces on a cookie sheet so that they don't touch each other, cover the meat with some plastic wrap, and freeze. When the pieces are frozen firm, you can combine them in one bag, and they'll be easy to separate.

Some people prefer to separate parts of a chicken with breasts in one package, legs in another, and so on. Others cut up a chicken and store all the parts from one chicken in one package. How you like to cook your chicken dictates how you package the parts. The number of parts per package is also something you need to consider.

Packing for success

Place your selected parts or whole chicken in the bag. Fill the bag as full as you can without making it hard to seal. The less air space in the bag, the better the meat will keep. If you're using a zipper-type closing bag, try to keep the seal area clean so that it will seal well.

Lay the bag on the table and partially seal it; then use your hands to push as much air out as possible. You want your bags to look flat and molded to the meat, not puffed with air. I (Amy) try to freeze in a single layer in the bag, so pieces are easy to remove one at a time.

As with any frozen food, label your packages with permanent marker. Mark what's in each package — three chicken breasts, for example — and the date you packed it.

Book VI

Freezing

Making Your Freezer Work for You

Home freezers aren't meant for freezing huge quantities of meat at a time. Don't start with an empty freezer, stuff it, and expect it to freeze your meat correctly. Chicken, for example, should be chilled to 40° or lower before you attempt to freeze it.

If you have empty spaces in your freezer, fill plastic milk bottles or 2-liter pop bottles with water and place them in the empty spaces after all the meat is frozen. Freezers that are full work more efficiently, and if the power goes out, your ice bottles will help keep the freezer cold.

From time to time, rotate the meat in the freezer so that you always use the oldest meat first. After six months, frozen chicken may still be safe to eat, but the quality starts going down. After a year in the freezer, frozen chicken should be cooked and fed to pets or discarded.

Thawing 101

Thaw your food in its freezer packaging in the refrigerator. For meat, allow 5 hours for each pound; for poultry, allow 2 hours for each pound; and for fish, allow 8 hours for each pound.

If your time is limited, thawing meat in cold water will decrease the time needed by about half. Here is how to thaw meat safely:

1. **Remove the meat from the freezer, but leave it in the sealed freezer bag.**

   If food has been wrapped in paper or other material that may not keep out water, place it in a freezer bag before continuing.

2. **Fill the sink or a pot large enough to hold the freezer bag containing the meat, with cold water.**

3. **Allow the meat to sit in the cold water, changing the water every 30 minutes until the meat becomes thawed.**

   The meat will be thawed and flexible enough to cook, but may still contain some ice crystals.

Don't allow the meat to completely thaw and the water to come to room temperature. This method promotes bacteria, and serious illness may result.

Following safety guidelines

Packaging for the freezer can seem simple, and it is. The main thing to remember is that you need to follow the same safety guidelines that the butcher uses. You can follow a few simple rules no matter what type of meat, poultry, or seafood you're preparing for the freezer.

- ✓ **Keep the meat cold.** Don't allow any type of meat to reach room temperature. Be prepared for dividing and packaging before you remove the meat from the refrigerator.

- ✓ **Keep all meats in the refrigerator, unless you're actually working on them.** Time passes quickly, and before you know it, the waiting product becomes too warm.

Wash all surfaces and utensils that come into contact with raw meat of any kind. Do not reuse freezer bags after they've contained raw meats. Even with thorough cleaning, bacteria can remain.

Chicken Tenders

Prep time: 40 min • **Cook time:** 30 min • **Yield:** 4 servings

Ingredients	Directions
4 frozen chicken breasts **½ teaspoon salt** **2 teaspoons poultry seasoning** **2 teaspoons garlic powder** **1 cup breadcrumbs** **2 tablespoons Parmesan cheese** **1 egg, beaten**	*1* Thaw the chicken until it's partially thawed, 30 to 40 minutes. Slice each chicken breast into three pieces lengthwise. *2* Combine the seasonings, breadcrumbs, and cheese in a flat dish. In a bowl, beat the egg until blended. Dip each chicken tender into egg and roll in bread crumb mixture. *3* Place each coated chicken tender on a cookie sheet. Bake at 400° for 45 minutes, or until golden brown and chicken is cooked through.

Per 3-ounce serving: Calories 232 (From Fat 53); Fat 6g (Saturated 2g); Cholesterol 128mg; Sodium 534mg; Carbohydrates 12g (Dietary Fiber 1g); Protein 31g.

Scalloped Oysters

Prep time: 10 min • **Cook time:** 30 min • **Yield:** 4 servings

Ingredients	Directions
20 frozen oysters **1½ cup panko breadcrumbs** **Salt and pepper to taste** **4 tablespoons butter (do not substitute)** **½ cup oyster liquid (add water, if needed)** **½ cup milk**	*1* Thaw oysters, reserving liquid. Grease an 8-x-8 baking dish. *2* Place a layer of breadcrumbs in the bottom of the dish. Add a layer of oysters and sprinkle with salt and pepper. Dot with butter. *3* Repeat with breadcrumbs, oysters, salt, pepper, and butter until all oysters have been used. Pour oyster liquid and milk over all. Bake at 350° for 30 minutes.

Per 3-ounce serving: Calories 243 (From Fat 127); Fat 14g (Saturated 8g); Cholesterol 73mg; Sodium 408mg; Carbohydrates 20g (Dietary Fiber 1g); Protein 8g.

Marinated Pork Chops

Prep time: Thawing and marinating time • **Cook time:** 20 min • **Yield:** 4 servings

Ingredients	Directions
2 cubes frozen herb/oil cubes (see Book VI, Chapter 4)	**1** Remove herb/oil cubes and pork chops from the freezer to thaw.
4 frozen pork chops	
2 cloves frozen garlic, minced	**2** Combine the thawed herb/oil cubes, garlic, water, and vinegar. Place the thawed chops in a gallon freezer bag and add marinade. Marinate for 3 hours.
¼ cup water	
¼ cup vinegar	**3** Drain the pork and reserve the marinade.
	4 In a dry, hot frying pan, sear the pork on both sides, and reduce the heat. Cook until the chops reach 145° in the center. Remove the finished chops, cover, and let rest for 3 minutes.
	5 Continue to heat the marinade until reduced by half. Pour over chops just before serving.

Per 3-ounce serving: Calories 161 (From Fat 59); Fat 7g (Saturated 2g); Cholesterol 67mg; Sodium 49mg; Carbohydrates 1g (Dietary Fiber 0g); Protein 23g.

Tip: Herbs that work well with pork include fennel, rosemary, sage, and thyme.

The Best Fried Fish

Prep time: 40 min • **Cook time:** 6 min • **Yield:** 4 servings

Ingredients	Directions
2 pounds frozen fish fillets	*1* Thaw wrapped fish in a bowl of cold water for 30 minutes and cut into equal-sized pieces. Pat fish dry. Mix flour and salt in a small bowl.
⅔ cup flour	
½ teaspoon salt	
½ teaspoon baking soda	*2* In a separate bowl, mix the baking soda and vinegar and then add the water. Add the vinegar mixture to the flour mixture. Beat until smooth.
1 tablespoon cider vinegar	
⅔ cup water	
	3 Dip fish into the batter and fry in a deep fryer until brown. Drain well before serving.

Per 3-ounce serving: *Calories 300 (From Fat 92); Fat 10g (Saturated 3g); Cholesterol 121mg; Sodium 546mg; Carbohydrates 8g (Dietary Fiber 0g); Protein 41g.*

Vary It! Serve fish European-style, with malt vinegar and salt.

Prepping fish and shellfish

You must keep fish and shellfish chilled from the time they're caught. Ideally, clean and freeze them immediately if you aren't using them within 24 hours.

Prepare your fish for your freezer based on its size:

✔ If it's less than 2 pounds, remove the tail, head, fins, and internal organs. Freeze it whole.

✔ If it's over 2 pounds, clean it the same way as you do a smaller fish. Cut it into fillets or steaks and wrap each piece separately for freezing.

One-Step Marinated Venison

Prep time: 10 min • **Cook time:** 14 min • **Yield:** 4 servings

Ingredients	*Directions*
4 venison steaks frozen in marinade	**1** Thaw the venison steaks in cold water. Melt the butter in a cast-iron skillet over medium heat.
2 tablespoons butter	**2** Fry the venison steaks for 7 minutes per side. Be cautious not to overcook. Let the venison rest for 10 minutes, covered, before serving.

Per 3-ounce serving: Calories 205 (From Fat 79); Fat 9g (Saturated 5g); Cholesterol 125mg; Sodium 57mg; Carbohydrates 0g (Dietary Fiber 0g); Protein 30g.

Tip: When freezing venison, add a marinade of any complimentary herbs, such as rosemary, sage, bay, marjoram, and juniper.

Chapter 6

Freezing Prepared Foods: Meals and Snacks

Work, children, school, after-school activities, and more! If you're like most people, you may struggle to get everything done and get a nutritious meal on the table. Filling your freezer with already-prepared or prepackaged meals and snacks allows you plenty of nutritious choices. In this chapter, you get great tips on freezing food and hints for planning your meals.

Appreciating the Convenience Factor

Freezing is a great option for taking advantage of buying food in large quantities at bargain prices, making large quantities of food, or saving leftovers. Taking a few minutes to package your food in meal-sized portions gives you flexibility in the amount of food you thaw.

Going in with a plan

The best way to budget and be able to serve healthy foods is to plan your meals. No more coming home from a busy day to find something to throw together. With a meal plan, you'll never have to wonder what to fix, and everyone benefits from a home-cooked meal. Here are some tips for meal planning:

✔ **Review your schedule for the upcoming week to determine your time available for preparing meals.** Use prepared meals, like soups or stews, on busy days. Cook meat or bake casseroles on not-so-busy days.

✔ **Make a list of your planned meals, including snacks.** Keep a second list with a complete inventory of food in your freezer. Create a basic list of 14 meals that are sure hits for your family. As long as you can pull out one of these favorites, you'll always have a meal on hand.

✔ **Keep your lists (planned meals and freezer inventory) on the front of the refrigerator.** Cross off items as you use them and the meals as you make them.

✔ **Get your family involved in meal planning and meal-making.** Offer each person two or three choices for their meals. Once everyone chooses, I (Amy) have plenty of ideas to rotate through the week, and everyone feels like they have something special coming up.

A great way to get children involved with mealtime is to include reheating directions when you freeze your foods. Then all they have to do is follow the directions and cook!

Freezing quick meals

Meals of convenience include casseroles, soups, and sauces. Freezing them in family-sized portions or as single servings provides options for meals later. Always use masking tape or freezer tape, label the food, and write reheating instructions right on the container. Labeling makes it easy for you or anyone else to pull out a meal and know how to prepare it.

When you're making main dishes, prepare your recipe and transfer your food to rigid freezer containers. If you're making a casserole, prepare it in a baking dish (approved for the freezer) up to the point of baking. Wrap it in heavy-duty aluminum foil. Thaw the unbaked casserole in the refrigerator and bake it according to your recipe. These dishes stay fresh one to two months in the freezer.

Ladle hot soup, stew, or sauce into rigid freezer containers, based on the portion you'll be using. Allow headspace of ½ inch for your pints and 1 inch for your quarts. (See Book II, Chapter 1 for more information on headspace.) These items freeze well for three to four months.

Cooking once a month

The ultimate way to save time and utilize your freezer to its fullest potential is to have a food plan. Cooking less and enjoying premade meals takes the stress out of both deciding on meals and knowing what you have in your inventory. There are many ways to accomplish cooking once a month. Here are some ideas to get you started:

✔ **Choose a basic meat and build recipes around it.** For example, cook four or more meals that use ground beef, cooked chicken, or ham. Once the meat is ready to use, it's fast and easy to measure it into the separate dishes as you assemble them.

✔ **List your ingredients and combine amounts.** If you need ½ cup onions for three recipes,

chop 1½ cups at one time. Chopping everything at once streamlines actual assembly.

✔ **When actually freezing meals, attach last minute add-ins to the dish with freezer tape.** Write the directions right onto the package itself, in addition to having a recipe card in your box with them.

✔ **Cook more than one meal at a time.** Double your recipe and freeze one right away in a foil-lined pan. Once frozen, pop the foil package out and use your pan for something else. When you're ready to cook the frozen meal, pop it right back into the pan once again.

Here are some freezing tips for soups, stews, and sauces:

✔ **Soups:** Use freezer containers no larger than 1 quart for quickly freezing your soups and preventing loss of flavor in your thawed product. If your workplace has a breakroom with a stove or microwave, freeze portions in single-serving containers and enjoy a hot lunch.

Potatoes frozen in soup and stew may darken or become mushy or mealy after freezing. You can still use them if you don't mind this discoloration or mushiness or simply omit them and add them when you reheat.

✔ **Stocks:** Use rigid freezer containers to store larger portions of stock; use ice-cube trays to store smaller portions. (Each cube is roughly equivalent to 1 ounce.) Transfer the frozen stock cubes to a freezer bag for storing. Add one to a soup or sauce for added flavor. You can find delicious stock recipes in Book V, Chapter 4.

✔ **Sauces:** Package your sauces in rigid freezer containers in quantities suited to your family's usage.

Clear soups and unthickened sauces freeze better than milk-based and thickened gravy dishes because the milk or thickener may separate during thawing. Make a note to add thickener to gravies when you reheat them or any other ingredients (like milk or cream) that you need to add before the meal is finished.

Don't add cooked pasta to your spaghetti sauce before freezing or freeze liquids with cooked grains and rice; their flavor and texture will be lost.

Freezing Breads, Snacks, and Other Treats

Have you ever felt like you had to finish a birthday cake before it went bad or had a partial loaf of bread grow fuzzy, green mold? Well, here's the answer to these (and other) challenges: Freeze these foods to save them.

Muffins, breads, buns, and rolls

When making bread, prepare your loaves to the point of baking, including all of the rising periods. Place your dough into a baking container approved for the freezer; wrap it for freezing.

To bake your bread, remove the wrapping, place the container of frozen dough into a preheated 250° oven for 45 minutes and then bake your bread as stated in your recipe.

When you're making muffins at home, make two or three varieties at the same time, wrapping them individually.

Cakes

Cakes with or without frosting may be frozen, but fillings can make your cake soggy. Butter-based frostings freeze well. Cakes freeze well for two to three months.

Cheesecakes, whole or leftover, are a favorite for freezing. They keep about four months in your freezer. Thaw the wrapped, frozen cheesecake in your refrigerator for four to six hours and serve it chilled.

Freezing leftover cake in single-serving sizes keeps you from thawing more cake than you may want available to you at one time.

Cookies

Who can resist warm cookies fresh from the oven? You can freeze both home-baked cookies or raw dough to bake later. Use both types within three months:

- **Homemade cookies, baked:** Store cooled cookies in rigid freezer containers, placing layers of wax or parchment paper between the cookies. Thaw at room temperature or place on a baking sheet in a preheated 350° oven for two to three minutes to warm them.

- **Homemade cookies, raw dough:** Freeze raw dough in rigid freezer containers, freezer paper, or freezer bags. Label bags of frozen dough with the baking temperature and time.

Book VI

Freezing

For slice-and-bake cookies, form your cookie dough into a log, wrap the dough in freezer paper, and freeze it. Thaw your dough slightly for easy slicing. Bake according to your recipe instructions.

For drop cookies, drop your cookie dough onto a baking sheet, leaving 1 inch between each cookie. Place the baking sheet in your freezer and quick-freeze the dough. Place the frozen cookies in freezer bags for storage. To bake your cookies, place them (frozen is okay) on a baking sheet and bake them as your recipe states.

Pies

You may freeze pies — just not cream pies and meringue pies — at almost any stage in the preparation process. (Check out Book II, Chapter 4 for pie-filling recipes.)

Have frozen pies ready to go, to have on hand for surprise guests or as a last-minute dish to pass at your next potluck. Freezing pies is also a great way to get a head start on holiday baking!

Follow these tips for freezing whole pies and pie ingredients:

- **Whole baked pies:** Wrap your pie with freezer wrap or place it in a freezer bag. Thaw it, wrapped, at room temperature for two hours; serve.

- **Whole unbaked pies:** Prepare your pie in the pie pan you'll bake it in.

  To reduce sogginess in your crust: Brush the inside of the bottom crust with shortening, add your filling, and brush the top crust with shortening. Do not cut vents and glaze the top; then wrap it for freezing.

For baking: Remove the freezer wrap and place your frozen pie on a baking sheet in a preheated 450° oven for 15 to 20 minutes. Reduce the temperature to 375°; bake 20 to 30 more minutes or until the top is golden brown.

✔ **Pie fillings:** If you love homemade pies, you'll find having frozen filling on hand a real timesaver for assembling pies, especially when you have a pie shell in the freezer, too. Simply prepare your favorite pie filling and ladle the hot filling into rigid freezer containers, allowing ½-inch head-space. Allow the filled containers to cool on your kitchen counter up to two hours. Then seal and freeze.

✔ **Pie shells, baked or unbaked:** Place your bottom piecrust in a pie pan for baking. Wrap the dough-lined pan in freezer wrap or place it in a freezer bag, stacking multiple filled pie pans on top of each other.

✔ **Pie dough, unrolled:** Form your pie dough into a flat, round disc. Wrap it tightly in a piece of plastic wrap and place it in a freezer bag.

When making dough for a double-crusted pie, separate it into two rounds before wrapping and packaging them for freezing.

Nuts

Freezing is perfect for keeping nuts fresh and ready to use. Freeze any size of shelled nut, raw or toasted, in rigid freezer containers or freezer bags. The bags that nuts come in are usually not suitable for freezing. If toasted nuts are desired, toast them and let cool to room temperature before freezing.

Freezing Dairy Products

Buying dairy products when they're on sale can help you keep your food costs in line and leave you better prepared for when you'd rather not go to the store for that one missing ingredient.

Knowing the best choices

By following a few simple guidelines, you can freeze some dairy products. Begin by packaging in heavy-duty aluminum foil, freezer bags, or plastic freezer wrap; the product's store packaging won't be enough.

Here are your best choices for frozen dairy foods:

- ✔ **Butter:** Unsalted and salted butter freeze well. Use salted butter within three months because the salt flavor disappears during the freezing process.

- ✔ **Soft cheese:** Soft cheeses, like blue cheese and Camembert, freeze better than hard cheeses. Use soft cheeses within one month.

- ✔ **Hard cheese:** Freeze hard cheeses such as Swiss, Gouda, and cheddar as a last resort because they crumble after freezing. Use these cheeses within six months.

- ✔ **Heavy cream:** Cream containing at least 40 percent butterfat can be frozen, but it can't be whipped after being frozen. You can, however, freeze dollops of whipped cream for later use.

- ✔ **Milk:** Homogenized milk can be frozen in sealed cartons, providing you allow room for headspace. Use within a month. (Some shaking may be required to restore smoothness.) Be aware that your milk jugs will bulge out of shape, which is normal.

Skipping the freezer

Not all dairy products are suitable for freezing. Yogurt, buttermilk, sour cream, cream cheese, whipped butter, and store-bought cottage cheese all freeze with less than desirable results. Save yourself the time and effort and stick with fresh.

Frozen Pie Crust

Prep time: 15 min • **Yield:** 5 single crusts

Ingredients	Directions
4 cups flour	**1** Combine the flour, sugar, and salt in a large mixing bowl. Combine the egg, milk, and vinegar in a 1-cup measuring cup.
1 tablespoon sugar or honey	
2 teaspoon salt	
1 egg	**2** Cut the lard (or shortening) into the dry ingredients, until it resembles coarse crumbs. Add the wet ingredients to the dry mixture. Mix until evenly combined.
½ cup milk	
1 tablespoon vinegar	
1¾ cups lard or shortening	**3** Knead until smooth and divide into 5 even pieces. Wrap each piece separately in plastic wrap and freeze.

Per serving (⅛ of crust): Calories 131 (From Fat 84); Fat 9g (Saturated 4g); Cholesterol 14mg; Sodium 120mg; Carbohydrates 10g (Dietary Fiber 0g); Protein 2g.

Tip: To use, remove from freezer as needed. Allow to come to room temperature for 30 minutes before rolling.

Frozen Date Nut Bread

Prep time: 45 min • **Bake time:** 1 hr • **Yield:** 1 loaf

Ingredients	Directions
One 8-ounce package of chopped dates **1 cup boiling water** **1 teaspoon baking soda** **½ cup flour** **1 egg** **1 cup sugar** **1 tablespoon butter** **1 cup walnuts**	*1* Place the dates in a mixing bowl. Pour boiling water over them and let sit until cool, about 30 minutes. Add all other ingredients to the date mixture and mix well. *2* Spread into a greased and floured loaf pan. Bake at 350° for 1 hour. Cool on a wire rack before wrapping and freezing.

Per slice (⅛ of loaf): Calories 323 (From Fat 108); Fat 12g (Saturated 2g); Cholesterol 30mg; Sodium 167mg; Carbohydrates 54g (Dietary Fiber 3g); Protein 4g.

Frozen Zucchini Cake

Prep time: 15 min • **Bake time:** 1 hr, 30 min • **Yield:** 1 Bundt cake

Ingredients	Directions
2 cups grated zucchini	**1** In a large mixing bowl, combine the zucchini, sugar, oil, and eggs.
3 cups sugar	
1½ cups vegetable oil	**2** In a second mixing bowl, combine the dry ingredients and add them to the wet ingredients. Add the nuts.
4 eggs	
3 cups flour	
2 teaspoons baking powder	**3** Pour into a greased and floured Bundt pan. Bake in the oven at 300° for 1 hour, 30 minutes. Cool and wrap tightly before freezing.
½ teaspoon salt	
1½ teaspoons cinnamon	
1 teaspoon baking soda	
1 cup chopped nuts	

Per slice (¹⁄₁₆ of cake): Calories 350 (From Fat 247); Fat 27g (Saturated 2g); Cholesterol 53mg; Sodium 216mg; Carbohydrates 22g (Dietary Fiber 1g); Protein 5g.

Book VII

Drying and Root Cellaring

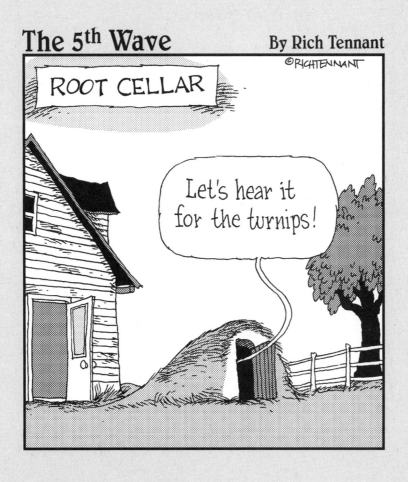

In this book . . .

Food preservation is not only all about canning and freezing. Book VII shows you all about preserving your foods by drying them.

In this part, you discover the art of drying foods, the different methods that work, as well as those that are no longer recommended.

This part also includes plenty of recipes for drying fruits and vegetables for delicious snacking or to speed up a quick dinner, and instructions for drying assorted common herbs for teas and seasoning. You also find out alternative ways to store your foods without losing quality and flavor.

Chapter 1

Getting a Big-Picture Look at Drying Foods

*I*n the world of food preservation, sun-drying is the oldest method known. Unlike canning and freezing, which require exact applications of processing procedures, drying food isn't exact or precise. Don't be surprised if you find yourself working by trial and error when trying to figure out how long it takes for your food to reach its degree of doneness. Just follow the general guidelines provided in that food's particular recipe and make adjustments. Remember, drying isn't exact an exact science.

In this chapter, you can find basic techniques for drying food and the best drying methods. You also discover how drying food prevents spoilage. Drying is easy to do in your home. Most of the equipment and tools you need, except an electric dehydrator, are probably just waiting for you in your kitchen.

Understanding How Dehydration Works

Drying food is also referred to as *dehydrating*. The goal of this technique is to remove moisture from your food. Achieving a successfully dried product requires removing 80 to 95 percent of the food's moisture. Removing moisture inactivates the growth of bacteria and other microorganisms but doesn't kill them.

Harnessing the heat

The following factors affect your finished product:

 ✔ **Heat:** The correct temperature is important in drying food. It must be high enough to force out moisture but not so high that it cooks the food. If your temperature is too high, your food exterior cooks or hardens before the interior of the food dries, trapping moisture in your food — known as *case hardening.* If your temperature is too low or the humidity too high, your food dries too slowly. Both of these dilemmas may cause your food to spoil before you consume it.

 The temperature guidelines for drying food are as follows: Fan only, or 95° for herbs, 125° for vegetables, 135° for fruit, and 145° for meat. Always follow the instructions for the correct drying temperature for your food in your recipe or the owner's manual for your dehydrator.

 ✔ **Dry air:** Dry air absorbs moisture leaving the food in the drying process. The higher the humidity, the longer foods take to dry because of the additional moisture in the air.

 ✔ **Air circulation:** Circulating air carries away moisture absorbed by dry air. Circulation keeps the humidity level constant in the drying chamber.

 ✔ **Uniform size:** Pieces of food uniform in size and thickness contain about the same amount of moisture and therefore dry in the same general time, preventing some pieces from not being completely dried and spoiling the entire batch when stored.

Gathering the tools for dehydration

After you decide which drying method you want to use, assemble your basic tools to aid you in completing the drying process. In addition to the basics that every kitchen should have (knives, cutting board, vegetable peeler, grater, and so on; go to Chapter 3 of Book I for a whole list of basic supplies), consider the following, which are particularly useful when you're drying food:

 ✔ **Blender:** Use this appliance to puree fruit. For a great fruit puree recipe, head to Chapter 2 of Book II.

 ✔ **Food processor:** You'll make uniform slices in a blink of the eye.

 ✔ **Oven thermometer:** For safely drying food in your oven, it's critical to know the exact temperature of your oven chamber.

✔ **Racks and tray:** Your electric dehydrator provides the correct size of trays for your unit. For oven- or sun-drying, you can use oven racks, net-covered racks, or baking sheets. Racks with mesh bottoms or oven racks work well and provide air circulation. To prevent food from falling off the racks, tightly stretch and pin layers of cheesecloth or nylon netting over the racks. If you use baking sheets, you need to rotate the sheets and turn the food over for even drying.

Considering other tips for successful drying

Drying is one of the easiest ways to preserve food. Still, following a few suggestions can ensure your success:

✔ **Pick quality food.** Food of high quality that's ripe, mature, and in top condition is the best for drying. If you dry food during the peak of its season, you get high-quality food at a lower price because the food is more abundant.

✔ **Wash and eliminate blemishes.** Always wash your food to remove dust, dirt, grime, or insects. When you clean your food, start with a clean sink and clean utensils. Any residue from previous use may cross-contaminate your food. (For detailed information on bacteria and safe food handling, check out Chapter 1 of Book I.)

✔ **Strive for uniform size.** It's important to prepare your food in uniform size and thickness for the food to be done at about the same time. If you have two different-size pieces of the same fruit, spread like sizes on one tray. Because one tray of food with smaller or thinner pieces will finish drying before the other tray with larger pieces, you won't spend time sorting through the food and disrupting the drying process.

✔ **Place your food carefully on the drying trays.** Whether you're using an electric dehydrator, a conventional oven, or Mother Nature, make sure you arrange the food in a single layer and leave spaces between the pieces of food so they're not touching each other or the edge of the tray.

Book VII

Drying and Root Cellaring

Taking the technical approach to drying

Drying is a simple concept that requires few tools. These tools, however, have to work the way you expect them to, or you'll end up with an unsatisfactory final product. Know your choice of equipment and how it works properly. Review the technique before starting a new food, especially if some time has passed since you last used it.

✔ **Watch for spoilage while the food's drying.** The shorter the drying period, the less opportunity there is for mold to develop on your food. If mold does develop, remove the moldy pieces and then clean the area with a cloth moistened with distilled white vinegar with an acidity level of 5 percent to kill mold spores.

✔ **Test your food for doneness.** The length of time required for drying your food varies with the quality of your food, whether you're using a pretreating method, your climate and humidity, the size of the food pieces, the moisture content of the food, and the drying temperature. This all means you can't blindly follow the recommended drying time. Instead, you have to test your food for doneness. Here's how: Remove a piece from the tray and allow it to cool completely. Then check to see whether it matches the recipe's description of how the food should look and feel when properly dried.

The easiest method for checking your dried food for doneness is touching and tasting it. It may sound overly simplified, but there's nothing like using your senses.

✔ **Store your cooled food in plastic bags, glass containers, or rigid plastic containers with airtight seals.** Make sure to label the container with contents and date. For more on storage containers and how to make your dried food last, head to the later section "Keeping Dried Food Longer."

Choosing a Dehydration Method

The three approved methods for drying food are using an electric dehydrator, using a conventional oven, and drying in the sun. All three methods work well when you follow basic food-drying procedures, use high-quality fresh food, and practice good sanitation for food preparation.

Electric dehydrators

If you dry a lot of food, an electric dehydrator is a great investment (see Figure 1-1). It's the most reliable method for achieving the most consistent results each time you dry food. This method dries your food evenly and quickly, doesn't tie up your oven, and produces great results in any weather.

A food dehydrator is your best bet because a controlled, clean heat combined with constantly moving air results in a completely dried product. To use a dehydrator, you simply layer your fruits and vegetables onto stacked trays and turn on the unit. Some dehydrators have fans that blow the warmed air over the drying food. Other units have a heating element at the bottom, and as the warm air rises, it filters through all the trays, drying the food in the process. If you're serious about drying, look for a dehydrator that has both a fan and heating element, as well as a thermostat that you can set at just the right temperature. After you place your food in your dehydrator, it needs little or no attention.

Figure 1-1:
Two examples of electric dehydrators.

To use an electric dehydrator, follow these steps:

1. **Prepare your food according to the recipe and arrange it carefully on the drying trays.**

2. **Following the instructions for using your dehydrator, allow the food to dry for the specified period of time.**

   Turn the pieces of food and rotate the trays from bottom to top to ensure even drying of all the food in the dehydrator.

3. **Test your food for doneness and then label and store it in an airtight container.**

Each time you use your dehydrator, review the operating instructions, including preheating the unit, filling the trays, setting the temperature, and the time recommended for drying your food. If you have any questions regarding the use or operation of your unit, contact the manufacturer. You can find this information in your owner's manual or check with the store you purchased it from. If you are Internet-savvy, most product manuals are also available online in PDF form.

If you're purchasing a dehydrator, carefully assess your needs. Then consider the following factors when making your final decision:

- ✔ **Overall construction:** Purchase a unit that's approved for safe home use by the Underwriters Laboratory (UL). If the unit isn't UL approved, don't buy it — it may not be safe for use in your home. Choose one with insulated walls that's easy to clean and drying trays that you can move easily in and out of the dehydrator without disturbing the food.

- ✔ **Capacity:** Purchase a dehydrator big enough to hold the amount of food you'll dry at one time. Typically, the most common-sized food dehydrator has four trays. Each tray holds about ¾ to 1 square foot of food. Some dehydrators expand to utilize 30 trays at one time. Snack-size dehydrators with two trays are also available.

- ✔ **Heat source:** Select one with an enclosed heating element. Wattage needs to accommodate about 70 watts for each tray the unit holds.

- ✔ **Fan:** The fan circulates the heated air around your food. Purchase a dehydrator with a quiet fan, because it runs for long periods of time. If your unit isn't equipped with a fan, you need to rearrange the trays more often during the drying period for an even drying.

When buying a dehydrator secondhand, always plug it in to hear how it sounds when running. The level of noise isn't an indicator of quality, but a loud dehydrator needs an out-of-the-way place to run, or it'll be too inconvenient to use.

- ✔ **Thermostat:** Purchase a dehydrator with an adjustable thermostat. Your temperature options need to range from 95° to 160°.

- ✔ **Drying trays:** Check for trays that are sturdy and lightweight; made from a food-safe product like stainless steel, nylon, or plastic; and easy to clean. Some manufacturers offer dehydrator accessories like extra drying trays and trays for drying fruit leather and herbs.

- ✔ **Cost:** Dehydrator prices may start as low as $65 and go up to $200 or more.

- ✔ **Warranty:** Check out the warranty term (one year is a good average) and any restrictions the manufacturer has for your dehydrator.

Conventional ovens

If you have an oven — gas or electric — that maintains a temperature between 130° and 150° with the door propped open, you can use your oven to dry food.

Your oven must maintain a temperature of 130° to 150° for 1 hour to safely dry food; maintaining these acceptable temperatures is difficult unless your oven can be set at less than the standard 200° as the lowest temp. The problem with higher temperatures is that they cook — they don't dry — the food. To test your oven's temperature, put an oven thermometer in the center of your oven with the door propped open and remember to check the temperature every once in a while to ensure that the heat is still on track.

Oven-drying takes longer than using a dehydrator and costs more because the oven uses a greater amount of electricity than an electric dehydrator does. In addition, if you use your oven for drying, it isn't available for any other use during that time.

To dry food in a conventional oven, follow these steps:

1. **Preheat your oven to the temperature setting in your recipe.**

   Use a separate oven thermometer to check for accuracy. Check the oven frequently to be sure food isn't over- or underdried.

2. **Wash and prepare your food as directed in your recipe.**

3. **Place your filled trays in the oven and leave the door propped open to allow moisture to escape during the specified drying time.**

   If you use baking sheets or other trays without holes or openings in the bottom, you must turn your fruit to achieve an evenly dried product. After the first side of the fruit has absorbed all the liquid on the top of the food, turn it over and repeat this for the other side. After this has been done on both sides, turn the food occasionally until it's done.

4. **Test your food for doneness and then label and store it in an airtight container.**

Sun- and air-drying

Sun-drying is the oldest and least expensive of the three methods and it lets you dry large quantities of food at one time. But — and these are big buts — it's dependent on perfect weather conditions to produce a safely dried product, and it can take days compared to hours in a dehydrator or a conventional oven.

Weather conditions must be perfect for sun-drying, making only a few climates suitable for this method. In general, you can find this climate only in the warm, dry Southwest and some Plains states. The ideal temperature for sun-drying fruit is 85° or hotter for many consecutive days, with the humidity level low to moderate. If your temperature drops more than 20° below your highest temperature during the drying period, your conditions are *not* suitable for this method. You also need good air circulation, a minimum of air pollution, and insect control around the food. Sun-drying is even less attractive for drying vegetables because the temperature needs to be at 100° or above for a number of days with the lowest evening temperature never dropping below 80° (even at night) *and* the humidity level needs to be low.

Sun-drying isn't safe for meats and fish because the low acidity level of the food, the low drying temperature, and the long drying period (taking many days) don't destroy the bacteria that cause your food to spoil.

Book VII

Drying and Root Cellaring

If you're willing to deal with the variances in weather conditions and the lengthy drying time, follow these step-by-step instructions:

1. **Wash and prepare your food as specified in your recipe.**

2. **Line your drying trays or racks with a double layer of cheesecloth or nylon netting.**

3. **Place your food on the tray and cover your trays with a single layer of cheesecloth or nylon netting to protect your food from insects and dust.**

   Stretch the cover tightly over the trays, but don't let it touch the food.

4. **Place your filled trays on benches or tables in full sunlight and check them regularly.**

   Check your trays at different times of the day, keeping them in full sun at all times. If your nighttime temperature varies more than 20° from the temperature at the hottest part of the day, move your trays to a warmer area (indoors or an enclosed patio area) for the evening, returning them outside when they can be in full sunlight. Relocate the trays if it rains, regardless of the temperature.

   If you use baking sheets or other trays without holes or openings in the bottom, you must turn your produce to achieve an evenly dried product. After the first side has absorbed all the liquid on the top of the food, turn it over and repeat this for the other side. After this has been done on both sides, turn the food daily until it's done.

5. **Check your fruit daily for evidence of mold.**

   Refer to "Considering other tips for successful drying" earlier in this chapter.

6. **Test your food for doneness and then label and store it in an airtight container.**

If one day is hot and sunny, yet the next is cloudy, you have a problem because mold can develop on partially dried foods before the weather turns back to hot and sunny again. In this situation, you need to use an alternative to sun-drying to finish the foods.

Keeping Dried Food Longer

You'll receive many months of rewarding flavor from your dried foods when they're protected from air, moisture, light, and insects. Generally speaking, food dried and stored properly can be kept from six months to one year.

Cooler air provides a longer shelf life for your food. The best storage temperature is 60° or colder. This temperature will hold your food for at least one year. Temperatures between 80° and 90° preserve the quality of your dried food for only about three to four months.

Check your unused dried food from time to time for any visible moisture or spoilage. If the food has signs of moisture, such as droplets of liquid in the containers, your food isn't completely dried. Use it immediately or repeat the dehydrating process and repackage it.

Packing your product

Suitable storage containers include the following:

- **Glass:** Home-canning jars with two-piece caps (see Chapter 3 of Book I) are a perfect choice for storing dried food. Wash them with hot soapy water and rinse them well, or wash them in a dishwasher. Dry and cool your jars completely before filling them and adding the two-piece caps. Reusing glass jars with lids also works well. Remove the cardboard liner that sometimes lines the underside of the plastic lid before washing and filling with herbs.

- **Plastic:** Heavy-duty (freezer) plastic bags with locking zipper-style seals work well. After placing your dried food in the bag, roll the bag to remove any extra air and press the seal together, making the bag airtight.

- **Metal:** If you buy coffee in cans, line the inside of a clean can with heavy plastic wrap, place your food inside, and add the tight-fitting lid.

- **Vacuum sealers:** If you own one of these units, now's the time to use it. Check your owner's manual for operating instructions and start packaging your dried food.

Book VII

Drying and Root Cellaring

Storage solutions

Always label your container with the type of food it contains, the date of processing, and, if you measure your food before placing it into the storage container or bag, the amount.

Because some pieces of fruit contain more moisture than others, be sure all your fruit is dried the same for storage. Try this tip from the Oregon State Extension Office: Fill a plastic or glass container with cooled, dried fruit about two-thirds full. Cover or seal tightly. Shake the container daily for two to four days. The excess moisture in some of the fruit will be absorbed by the drier pieces. Vegetables dry almost completely, so you don't have to do this with them.

Chapter 2

Drying Fruits and Vegetables

In This Chapter

▶ Choosing the best vegetables for drying

▶ Preserving the bright colors of your fruit

▶ Creating tasty snacks with dried produce

T his chapter discusses the rewarding process of drying fruits and vegetables. If you're short on pantry space or challenged by a small freezer in the kitchen, drying may be the perfect storage solution for you. Find out how to choose the best fruits and vegetables for drying, the guidelines for drying various kinds of produce, and how the fruits and veggies appear when fully dried.

Note: The per-serving nutritional analyses in this chapter represent the nutrition information for the food *before* it's been rehydrated. After rehydration, the vegetables plump up again and the quantity at least doubles.

Your Drying-At-a-Glance Guide

Traditionally, drying meant using the sun's warmth and a lot of time. Food would dry outside on screen-covered trays during the day, and you'd bring in the trays at night, before the cool night air could cause condensation. Flies and other wildlife were a cause for concern, and you had no way to know whether airborne bacteria were present until you ate the food and got sick because of it. Of course, you can still dry foods that way, but easier ways are also available thanks to ovens and dehydrators. (Refer to Chapter 1 of this book for a basic explanation of these drying methods.)

Knowing the best fruits and vegetables to dry

Most fruit is suited for drying, with a few exceptions. Fruits *not* recommended for drying include avocados, citrus fruits (except for the peel), crab apples, guavas, melons, olives, pomegranates, and quinces.

Vegetables that dry well include beans, beets, cabbage, carrots, corn, greens, onions, peas, sweet and hot peppers, potatoes, pumpkins, tomatoes, and zucchini.

Drying know-how

Although drying seems pretty, well, cut and dried (pick the freshest produce you can find, prepare it as necessary, and put it in a food dehydrator for the required time and temperature), you can ensure that you'll end up with a tasty, edible product by following some basic rules:

- ✔ Many of the best fruits for drying oxidize and brown easily when their flesh is exposed to air. See the section "Pretreating your fruit," later in this chapter.

- ✔ Not all fruits and vegetables need to be peeled before drying. Leaving on clean, washed skin increases the final nutritional content. Peels often contain fiber and other nutrients that only add to the overall benefit of the produce.

- ✔ Rotate the trays around to ensure they all get even heat. For best results, cut all the food into evenly sized pieces and spread the pieces in a thin layer on the drying trays.

- ✔ Dry one type of produce at a time, to avoid mixing of flavors.

- ✔ Make sure the fruits and vegetables are completely dried before sealing. To know that, you need to know what a properly dried fruit or vegetable looks and feels like. Not all are crispy when dried. Often, a vegetable is dried properly yet remains pliable.

The drying process involves many factors: moisture in the food that you're drying, the accuracy of the thermostat in the dehydrator, how full the trays are, and the humidity on the day you're drying. You may have to experiment a bit to figure out what works best. The drying process isn't as accurate as other methods in this book, like canning and freezing. The final goal is to remove enough moisture so that organisms that spoil food can't grow.

Prepping Your Produce

Using the best, perfectly ripe fruits and vegetables for drying is important for a dried product that's worthy of high marks and rave reviews. Any blemish or decay will only prevent a sanitary, healthy result in your produce.

Sizing up your preparation options

Drying time is partly determined by the size of your fruit and veggie pieces. For example, larger pieces of fruit take longer to dry than smaller pieces of the same fruit. So the smaller you cut your peaches or the thinner you slice your carrots, the less time you need to produce a safely preserved dried product, within reason. Cutting your food pieces too thin will result in overdrying, and, many times, the super-thin pieces will stick and actually become impossible to remove.

Pretreating your fruit

Pretreating makes your fruit look good by preventing *oxidation* and *discoloration,* the darkening of the fruit flesh after it's exposed to air.

Using a pretreating method before drying your fruit isn't as important as it is when you're canning fresh fruit. In fact, it's not necessary at all, but it does assist you with the drying process by shortening the drying time. The following sections explain your pretreating choices.

At one time, sulfuring fruit was popular for preserving color and vitamins in dried fruit. Sulfur is unsafe for any drying method other than sun-drying because it produces dangerous sulfur dioxide fumes when heated, which occurs when you dry fruit in an oven or dehydrator.

Water blanching

Water blanching is the best for maintaining the bright fruit color. Immerse the fruit in boiling water for a short period of time and then immediately plunge it into ice water to stop the cooking process started by the boiling water. Drain the fruit well.

Steam blanching

Steam blanching is the most common method used for fruit. In fact, fruit retains more of its water-soluble vitamins and minerals from steam blanching than water blanching. To steam blanch, hang a colander on the inside edge of a pot of boiling water, making sure the colander doesn't touch the water. Place your fruit in the colander and heat it as directed in your recipe. Cool your fruit quickly in a bowl of ice water. Drain the fruit well.

Dipping in a solution

With this method, you immerse your fruit into a liquid or a solution (such as lemon juice or Ever-Fresh) to control darkening. Dipping the fruit helps it retain vitamins A and C that are lost during the oxidation process. Check out Chapter 2 of Book II for details on these solutions.

Drying Fruits and Vegetables Step by Step

Properly dried fruits and vegetables are a treasure to use at a later time. After you dry, label, and store your fruits and veggies, you'll have delicious and healthful snacks at your fingertips all year round.

Fruits and vegetables contain a lot of water, and you may be surprised at just how much volume you lose when you dry them. So don't be put off by the amount of produce you start with, wondering where you're going to store it all. Four pounds of fresh blueberries, for example, makes 1¼ cups dried blueberries. And the best news? All the taste and nutrition is still there. The only thing missing is the water.

If you're using an electric dehydrator, verify the correct drying temperature for your fruit in your owner's manual. If it differs from the guidelines given in your recipe or this section, use the temperature in your manual.

This procedure is simple and is detailed in Book VII, Chapter 1 for the three drying methods. Here's a summary for drying fruits and vegetables in a dehydrator or an oven:

1. **Preheat your oven or dehydrator and prepare your trays.**

2. **Prepare your produce as directed in your recipe.**

3. **Place your prepared pieces on your prepared trays or racks.**

4. **Place the filled trays in your dehydrator or oven and begin the drying process.**

5. **Check and rotate the trays periodically to ensure even drying of the entire batch.**

6. **At the end of your drying time, check for the proper degree of doneness.**

7. **Package your dried product in temporary containers, like plastic bags, and allow them to *condition* or *mellow*.**

   This process distributes any moisture left in the fruit pieces to other, drier pieces, reduces the chance of spoiled fruit, and may take up to one week.

8. **Package and label your product for storage.**

Don't add fresh fruit or vegetables to partially dried trays. The fresh product increases the humidity in the drying chamber and adds moisture back to what has been drying. This adjustment in the humidity level affects drying and increases the drying time for the entire batch.

When you take the fruits and vegetables from the dehydrator, they're ready to be stored in an airtight container in a cool, dry place out of direct sunlight. Because they're both very dry, fruits and veggies will absorb moisture from the air and can deteriorate in both quality and taste.

For best results, store batches together, but keep them in separate containers. For example, keep all dried tomatoes in a gallon jar, but inside the jar, divide them into separate storage bags, with each bag holding tomatoes dried on different days. This way, if something isn't quite right about a particular batch of vegetables, your entire season's storage isn't ruined.

You can store dried fruits and vegetables for up to a year as long as you keep them dry and out of sunlight.

Book VII

Drying and Root Cellaring

Enjoying the Final Product

Most dried produce is used just as it's stored after the drying process. Dried fruit is great added to hot or cold cereal or baking batters. You can use dried vegetables for snacking and add them to soups and stews in the last few minutes of cooking.

When chopping dried fruit, spraying your knife with no-stick cooking spray keeps the pieces from sticking to your knife.

Rehydrating your dried produce

If you prefer your dried fruit or veggie a bit chewier, soften or rehydrate it. *Rehydrating* is the process of adding moisture back to the produce. Your rehydrating options for fruit are

- ✔ **Boiling water:** Place the desired amount of fruit in a bowl. Cover the fruit with boiling water, allowing it to stand for 5 to 10 minutes to plump, or add moisture, to your fruit. Use this method when adding fruit to jams, chutney, or baked goods. Substitute fruit juice or wine for water.

- ✔ **Steaming:** Place your fruit in a steamer or a colander over a pot of boiling water. (Refer to the section "Steam blanching," earlier in this chapter.) Steam your fruit for 3 to 5 minutes or until plump.

- ✔ **Sprinkling:** Put your fruit in a shallow bowl and sprinkle with water or fruit juice. Allow it to soak in the moisture. Repeat until the fruit reaches the level of moistness you desire.

To rehydrate your dried vegetables, add 1½ cups boiling water to 1 cup dried vegetables. Let the veggies stand for 20 to 30 minutes to absorb the water. If they absorb all the water and they're not as plump as you'd like, add about 2 cups water and let them stand until most of the water is absorbed. Use the vegetables as you would raw ones; cook them or add them to a soup or stew. A good general rule is 1 cup dried vegetables equals 2 cups reconstituted vegetables.

Avoid pouring vegetables over a steaming pot, straight from the storage container. Doing so can cause the moisture from the steam to condense in the container and promote mold. Always pour dried vegetables into a separate dish or your hand before adding to your recipe.

Spotting signs of trouble: Good produce gone bad

Although it doesn't happen often — especially if you follow instructions — sometimes your fruits and vegetables don't dry properly. Or maybe they dried all right, but something happened during storage. Here are the warning signs that dried vegetables aren't safe to eat:

- ✔ **Black or brown specks suddenly showing up on food.** This is mildew on the surface, and it can make you sick.

- ✔ **Moisture building up inside the storage container.** Whether you store your dried produce in a bag or glass jar, no moisture should *ever* be inside the container.

- ✔ **An off odor to the vegetables.** You can usually detect this odor when you first open the storage container. This scent is a sign of mildew, due to moisture being present.

- ✔ **Vegetables sticking together after being stored.** Vegetable pieces shouldn't have any stickiness when stored; they should remain loose and easily separated.

Dried Apples

Prep time: 20 min • **Dry time:** 6–8 hr • **Yield:** 1½ cups

Ingredients	*Directions*
4 pounds firm apples	*1* Wash, peel, and core your apples. Slice the apples into ¼- to ½-inch thick rings (see Figure 2-1). Dip the apple slices in your choice of dipping solution, if desired.
	2 Arrange the apple slices on your trays and dry in a conventional oven or dehydrator for 6 to 8 hours at 130° to 135°, rotating the trays occasionally to facilitate even drying. (Sun-dry for 2 to 3 days.)
	3 Test for doneness: The apples should be soft, pliable, and leathery.

Per ¼-cup serving: Calories 147 (From Fat 7); Fat 1g (Saturated 0g); Cholesterol 0mg; Sodium 0mg; Carbohydrates 38g (Dietary Fiber 5g); Protein 0g.

Tip: Apples with a tart flavor and firm texture dry best. Some good choices are Pippin, Granny Smith, Jonathan, and Rome Beauty.

Figure 2-1:
Cutting
apple rings.

Dried Apricots

Prep time: 20 min • **Dry time:** 18–20 hr • **Yield:** 2 cups

Ingredients	*Directions*
6 pounds fresh apricots	*1* Wash the apricots and then cut in half, discarding the pits. Dip the apricot halves in your choice of dipping solution, if desired.
	2 Arrange the apricot halves on your trays, skin side down, cut side up. Dry them in a conventional oven or dehydrator for 18 to 20 hours at 130° to 135°, rotating the trays occasionally to facilitate even drying. (Sun-dry for 2 to 3 days.)
	3 Test for doneness: The apricots should be pliable and leathery with no moisture pockets.

Per ¼-cup serving: *Calories 152 (From Fat 11); Fat 1g (Saturated 0g); Cholesterol 0mg; Sodium 3mg; Carbohydrates 35g (Dietary Fiber 8g); Protein 4g.*

Drying produce in a convection oven

If you happen to have a convection oven, try using it for drying before investing in an electric dehydrator. *Remember:* Your oven will be out of commission for cooking until your produce is dry.

Set your oven at 140° to 150° and leave the door open about ½ inch. Rotate the trays or racks every few hours for even drying. Cool a piece before testing it for doneness.

Dried Bananas

Prep time: 20 min • **Dry time:** 10–12 hr • **Yield:** ¾–1 cup

Ingredients	Directions
2 pounds fresh bananas	**1** Peel and slice the bananas to ¼-inch thickness. Dip the banana slices in your choice of dipping solution, if desired.
	2 Arrange the slices on your trays and dry in a conventional oven or dehydrator for 10 to 12 hours at 130° to 135°, rotating the trays occasionally to facilitate even drying. (Sun-dry for 2 days.)
	3 Test for doneness: The bananas should be pliable and crisp, almost brittle.

Per ¼-cup serving: Calories 134 (From Fat 6); Fat 1g (Saturated 0g); Cholesterol 0mg; Sodium 2mg; Carbohydrates 34g (Dietary Fiber 4g); Protein 2g.

Tip: Use ripe, yellow-skinned fruit with a few brown speckles.

Dried Blueberries

Prep time: 20 min • **Dry time:** 24 hr • **Yield:** 1¼ cups

Ingredients	Directions
4 pounds fresh blueberries	**1** Drop the blueberries into boiling water for 30 seconds. Remove them from the water and drain. Place the drained berries on paper towels to remove any excess water.
	2 Place the blueberries on your trays and dry in a conventional oven or dehydrator for about 24 hours at 130° to 135°, rotating the trays occasionally to facilitate even drying. (Sun-dry for 2 to 4 days.)
	3 Test for doneness: The blueberries should be leathery and hard, but shriveled like raisins.

Per ¼-cup serving: Calories 203 (From Fat 12); Fat 1g (Saturated 0g); Cholesterol 0mg; Sodium 22mg; Carbohydrates 51g (Dietary Fiber 10g); Protein 2g.

Tip: Use plump berries that aren't bruised.

Dried Cherries

Prep time: 20 min • **Dry time:** 14–28 hr • **Yield:** 2 cups

Ingredients	*Directions*
6 to 8 pounds fresh cherries	**1** Wash the cherries in cold water. Then cut them in half and remove the pits.
	2 Place the cherry halves on your trays skin side down, cut side up. Dry them in a conventional oven or dehydrator for 2 to 3 hours at 165°, or until you see a slightly leathery appearance to the skin and cut surface. Then reduce the heat to 135° and dry for an additional 12 to 25 hours. (Sun-dry for 2 to 4 days.) Rotate the trays occasionally to facilitate even drying.
	3 Test for doneness: The cherries should be leathery, hard, and slightly sticky.

Per ¼-cup serving: Calories 220 (From Fat 27); Fat 3g (Saturated 1g); Cholesterol 0mg; Sodium 0mg; Carbohydrates 51g (Dietary Fiber 7g); Protein 4g.

Tip: Drying cherries only enhances their rich taste. They taste great out of hand or in your next muffin recipe. Any sweet or sour cherries work well.

Dried Citrus Peel

Prep time: 20 min • **Dry time:** 1–2 hr • **Yield:** ⅛ cup

Ingredients	*Directions*
1 pound fresh oranges	*1* Wash the citrus fruit and remove a thin layer of peel with a vegetable peeler. Be careful not to get any of the white, bitter pith. If you do, don't use that part of the peel.
	2 Arrange the peel on your trays and dry in a conventional oven or dehydrator for 1 to 2 hours at 135°, rotating the trays occasionally to facilitate even drying. (Sun-drying is not recommended.)
	3 Test for doneness: The peels should be crisp, but not brittle.

Per 1-teaspoon serving: *Calories 2 (From Fat 0); Fat 0g (Saturated 0g); Cholesterol 0mg; Sodium 0mg; Carbohydrates 1g (Dietary Fiber 0g); Protein 0g.*

Tip: Dried citrus peel makes a great addition to your tea. It gives a fruity zip to desserts and sweetbread recipes. Try citrus peel in muffins and cakes. Use only organic fruits, to avoid any toxins on the skin.

Dried Peaches

Prep time: 20 min • **Dry time:** 24–36 hr (halves); 14–16 hr (slices) • **Yield:** ½ cup

Ingredients	Directions
2 to 2 ½ fresh peaches	**1** To prepare peaches, remove the peel, cut the fruit in half, and remove and discard the pits. Leave the fruit in halves or slice them into ¼-inch pieces. Dip the fruit in your choice of dipping solution, if desired.
	2 Arrange the fruit on your trays (if you're drying halves, place them skin side down, cut side up). Dry in a conventional oven or dehydrator 24 to 36 hours (halves) or 14 to 16 hours (slices) at 130° to 135°, rotating the trays occasionally to facilitate even drying. (Sun-dry for 2 to 6 days.)
	3 Test for doneness: The fruit should be leathery, pliable, and shriveled with no moisture pockets.

Per ¼-cup serving: Calories 42 (From Fat 1); Fat 0g (Saturated 0g); Cholesterol 0mg; Sodium 0mg; Carbohydrates 11g (Dietary Fiber 2g); Protein 1g.

Vary It! Although this recipe uses peaches, you follow the same steps to dry nectarines. The only difference is that you leave the peel on in Step 1.

Dried Pears

Prep time: 20 min • **Dry time:** 12–18 hr • **Yield:** 1½ cups

Ingredients	Directions
4 pounds fresh pears	**1** Wash, peel, and core the pears. Cut them into halves, quarters, or ¼-inch slices. Dip the pear pieces in your choice of dipping solution, if desired.
	2 Arrange the fruit on your trays and dry in a conventional oven or dehydrator for 12 to 18 hours at 130° to 135°, rotating the trays occasionally to facilitate even drying. (Sun-dry for 2 to 3 days.)
	3 Test for doneness: The pear pieces should be leathery with no moisture pockets.

Per ¼-cup serving: Calories 164 (From Fat 10); Fat 1g (Saturated 0g); Cholesterol 0mg; Sodium 0mg; Carbohydrates 42g (Dietary Fiber 7g); Protein 1g.

Tip: Use dried pears in any recipe calling for dried apples.

Dried Pineapple

Prep time: 20 min • **Dry time:** 12–18 hr • **Yield:** 1½ cups

Ingredients	Directions
6 pounds fresh pineapple	**1** Cut away the peel and the eyes from the pineapple and remove the core. Cut the flesh into ¼-inch-thick rings.
	2 Arrange the pineapple rings on your trays and dry in a conventional oven or dehydrator for 12 to 18 hours at 130° to 135°, rotating the trays occasionally to facilitate even drying. (Sun-dry for 4 to 5 days.)
	3 Test for doneness: The pineapple rings should be leathery and not sticky.

Per ¼-cup serving: Calories 116 (From Fat 9); Fat 1g (Saturated 0g); Cholesterol 0mg; Sodium 2mg; Carbohydrates 29g (Dietary Fiber 3g); Protein 1g.

Drying nuts and seeds

If you're lucky enough to have access to a nut tree, you can easily dry and store this delicious food. Because they have such a high fat content, nuts need to be stored properly in order to remain fresh and good tasting. Here's an overview of how to get nuts from tree to freezer:

1. With few exceptions, nuts fall from the tree when ripe. Pick off the ground daily to prevent bug infestation.

2. After picking, nuts need to be hulled. This process removes the inedible outer coating so the kernel can dry out.

3. Hulled nuts then need to be dried, or *cured*. In this case, curing means left to dry out naturally for a length of time, to let the kernel season, or become tasty. Place your hulled nuts into a basket and keep them out of the way near a furnace or attic.

4. Drying times vary with nut variety. Most nuts need several weeks of drying time. After they're dry, nuts can be stored for up to a year.

Seeds are another unique and easy-to-grow product for storage. Simply grow a few sunflower seeds that are labeled for eating (many are now ornamental) and cut the flower head off after the seeds have fully formed. Hang the heads upside down to dry in a clean place, out of direct sunlight, for two weeks until fully dried. Remove the seeds and store them in a cool, dry place. Stir them once a week to check for decay.

Fruit Leather

Prep time: 20 min • **Dry time:** 6–8 hr (dehydrator); 18 hr (oven) • **Yield:** 8–12 servings

Ingredients

One of any of the following fresh fruits:

   2 to 3 pounds apples (about 8 to 12)

   3 to 4 pounds apricots (about 24)

   3 to 4 pounds peaches (about 8 to 12)

   4 pints strawberries

Water or fruit juice (optional)

Corn syrup or honey (optional)

⅛ teaspoon ground spices (optional): choose from allspice, cinnamon, cloves, ginger, mace, nutmeg, or pumpkin pie spice

¼ to ½ teaspoon pure extract flavors (optional): choose from almond, lemon, orange, or vanilla

Directions

1 Cover your drying trays or baking sheets with a heavy-duty, food-grade plastic wrap. If your dehydrator comes with special sheets for your trays, use those.

2 Wash your fruit and remove any blemishes. Prepare your fruit as directed earlier in this chapter.

3 Puree the fruit in a blender until smooth. Strain out any small seeds, if desired, with a mesh strainer or a food mill. If your puree is too thick, add water or fruit juice, 1 tablespoon or less at a time. If your puree is too tart, add corn syrup or honey, 1 teaspoon at a time. Add spices or extract flavors, if desired.

4 Spread the puree onto the prepared trays to a thickness of ⅛-inch in the center and ¼-inch-thick around the edges. (You want the edges thicker than the center because the edges dry faster.) If you use cooked fruit, it must be completely cool before spreading it on the trays (see Figure 2-2).

5 Dry your fruit leather at a temperature of 135° in a dehydrator or 140° in a conventional oven. Dry the fruit until it's pliable and leatherlike with no stickiness in the center.

6 Roll the warm fruit leather, still attached to the plastic, into a roll. Leave the rolls whole or cut them into pieces with scissors. Store the rolls in a plastic bag or an airtight container.

Per ½-cup serving of apple puree: *Calories 55 (From Fat 3); Fat 0g (Saturated 0g); Cholesterol 0mg; Sodium 0mg; Carbohydrates 14g (Dietary Fiber 2g); Protein 0g.*

Per ½-cup serving of apricot puree: *Calories 76 (From Fat 6); Fat 1g (Saturated 0g); Cholesterol 0mg; Sodium 2mg; Carbohydrates 18g (Dietary Fiber 4g); Protein 2g.*

Per ½-cup serving of peach puree: *Calories 64 (From Fat 1); Fat 0g (Saturated 0g); Cholesterol 0mg; Sodium 0mg; Carbohydrates 16g (Dietary Fiber 3g); Protein 1g.*

Per ½-cup serving of strawberry puree: *Calories 43 (From Fat 5); Fat 1g (Saturated 0g); Cholesterol 0mg; Sodium 1mg; Carbohydrates 10g (Dietary Fiber 3g); Protein 1g.*

Note: The spice flavoring will intensify as the fruit leather dries. Use a light hand and no more than ⅛ teaspoon total in each batch.

Note: Sun-drying isn't recommended for this recipe.

ROLLING FRUIT LEATHER

1. AFTER YOU REMOVE THE PEEL, STEMS OR CORES, BLEND THE FRUIT TO A SMOOTH PASTE.

2. SPREAD THE PUREE EVENLY ON A LINED BAKING SHEET WITH TURNED UP SIDES.

3. DRY THE PUREE UNTIL IT FEELS LEATHER-LIKE AND PLIABLE. REMOVE IT FROM THE TRAY WHILE IT'S STILL WARM. ROLL IT!

4. CUT EACH ROLL INTO 4 TO 6 PIECES. WRAP EACH PIECE IN PLASTIC WRAP OR WRAP EACH WHOLE ROLL IN PLASTIC WRAP.

Figure 2-2: Preparing and rolling fruit leather.

Dried Fruit Medley

Prep time: 15 min • **Yield:** 4½ cups

Ingredients	Directions
½ cup toasted almonds	**1** Place all the ingredients in a large bowl; stir to combine and distribute the fruit and nuts evenly.
½ cup sunflower seeds	
½ cup dried apples, cut into ½-inch pieces	**2** Store your mix in home-canning jars or other airtight containers.
½ cup dried apricots, cut into ½-inch pieces	
½ cup dried banana slices	
½ cup dried pears, cut into ½-inch pieces	
½ cup dried pineapple, cut into ½-inch pieces	
½ cup raisins	

Per ½-cup serving: Calories 267 (From Fat 83); Fat 9g (Saturated 1g); Cholesterol 0mg; Sodium 5mg; Carbohydrates 47g (Dietary Fiber 6g); Protein 6g.

Tip: This dried fruit medley is a great blend for a quick and nutritious snack. Make up small packages to grab and go.

Vary It! Mix in a little bit of chocolate candies.

Dried Shell Beans

Prep time: 10 min • **Dry time:** 6–8 hr • **Yield:** 1½ cups

Ingredients	Directions
1 pound of shell beans of your choice	**1** Remove the pods and collect the beans. Place the beans on the dehydrator tray(s) in a single layer, adding enough to fill, but be sure that the beans are in a single layer on the trays.
	2 Set your dehydrator temperature to 120° and dry the beans for 6 to 8 hours, or until you can break a bean in half by hitting it with a hammer or other heavy object. Rotate the trays occasionally to facilitate even drying.
	3 Remove your dried beans from the trays, place them in a tightly sealed container, and freeze them over-night to kill any tiny bug eggs that may be hiding in them. Store your dried beans for up to 1 year.

Per ½-cup serving: Calories 129 (From Fat 10); Fat 1g (Saturated 0g); Cholesterol 0mg; Sodium 37mg; Carbohydrates 26g (Dietary Fiber 6g); Protein 12g.

Tip: Leave these beans on the vine until the pods are dry and shriveled. When you can hear the beans rattling inside the dry pods, it's time to pick them. Many times, dried beans in the pod are available at your local farmers' market, where you can buy them inexpensively by the pound.

Dried Beets

Prep time: 10 min • **Dry time:** 8–10 hr • **Yield:** 2 cups

Ingredients	Directions
2 pounds of beets	**1** Cut off the leaf and root ends of your beets and cook the beets in boiling water until tender, about 20 minutes. Thinly slice the beets and arrange them in a single layer on your dehydrator trays.
	2 Set your dehydrator temperature to 120° and dry the beets for 8 to 10 hours, or until the slices are hard. Rotate the trays occasionally to facilitate even drying.
	3 Place the dried beets in an airtight container and store for 6 months in a cool dry place, out of direct sunlight.

Per ½-cup serving: Calories 65 (From Fat 2); Fat 0g (Saturated 0g); Cholesterol 0mg; Sodium 119mg; Carbohydrates 15g (Dietary Fiber 4g); Protein 2g.

Tip: An easy way to get the skin off a beet is to drop each boiled beet into ice water for a few seconds before pulling off the skins.

Note: To use dried slices, eat them as-is or boil for 30 minutes in plain water, until soft once again.

Dried Cabbage

Prep time: 10 min • **Dry time:** 6–10 hr • **Yield:** 2 cups

Ingredients	Directions
1½ **pounds fresh cabbage**	**1** Remove any tough outer leaves; then core and shred the cabbage. Blanch the shredded cabbage for 2 minutes in boiling water and cool immediately in ice water. Drain well. Place the cabbage shreds in a thin layer on the dehydrator trays.
	2 Set your dehydrator temperature to 120° and dry the cabbage shreds for 6 to 10 hours, stirring every few hours to keep them from sticking together and rotating the trays occasionally to facilitate even drying. Start checking for doneness after 4 hours. Completely dried cabbage will shrink quite a bit and feel brittle.
	3 Store the dried cabbage in glass jars or plastic bags, in a cool, dry place.

Per ½-cup serving: Calories 43 (From Fat 4); Fat 0g (Saturated 0g); Cholesterol 0mg; Sodium 31mg; Carbohydrates 9g (Dietary Fiber 4g); Protein 2g.

Tip: To use the dried cabbage, measure out the amount desired and sprinkle it directly into boiling soups or stews.

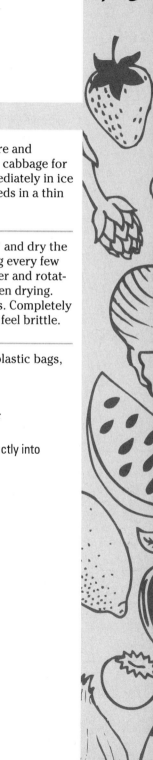

Dried Carrots

Prep time: 10 min • **Dry time:** 8–10 hr • **Yield:** 1 cup

Ingredients	Directions
1 pound fresh carrots	**1** Scrub the carrot skin with a vegetable brush to remove any trace of dirt. Cut off the tops and about ¼ inch of the carrot itself to remove any of the green, bitter part of the carrot. Then cut the carrots into ⅛-inch slices or shred finely.
	2 Blanch the slices or shreds for 2 minutes in boiling water and then cool immediately in ice water. Drain well. Layer carrot slices or shreds in a single layer on your dehydrator trays.
	3 Set the temperature on your dehydrator to 120° and dry the carrots for 8 to 10 hours, or until they're tough and leathery, stirring at least once to ensure that the pieces don't stick. Rotate the trays periodically to facilitate even drying.
	4 Store the dried carrots for up to 1 year in a tightly sealed container.

Per ½-cup serving: Calories 102 (From Fat 0); Fat 0g (Saturated 0g); Cholesterol 0mg; Sodium 116mg; Carbohydrates 23g (Dietary Fiber 6g); Protein 3g.

Tip: To remove as much water as possible from the blanched carrots, especially for shreds, use paper towels.

Tip: You can add dried, shredded carrots as-is to sweetbreads and cakes for added fiber and natural sweetness; they'll absorb moisture and become delicious during the cooking process.

Dried Greens

Prep time: 10 min • **Dry time:** 4–6 hr • **Yield:** ¼ cup

Ingredients	Directions
1 pound fresh greens	**1** Trim and wash the greens thoroughly to remove any fine grit. Blanch the greens until they're limp, about 2 minutes. Spread them in a thin layer onto your drying trays.
	2 Set the temperature on your dehydrator to 120° and dry the greens for 4 to 6 hours, or until the greens are crispy, stirring once to keep them from sticking together and rotating the trays occasionally to facilitate even drying.
	3 Store your dried greens for up to 1 year in a tightly sealed container.

Per ¼-cup serving: *Calories 227 (From Fat 29); Fat 3g (Saturated 0g); Cholesterol 0mg; Sodium 195mg; Carbohydrates 45g (Dietary Fiber 9g); Protein 15g.*

Note: Check drying greens carefully to ensure they're layered loosely enough to fully dry. Greens that are stuck together may hold moisture and develop mold.

Vary It! You can create a powder to add as-is to any sauce or baked good. Simply pulverize the dried greens in a food processor.

Dried Onions

Prep time: 10 min • **Dry time:** 12 hr • **Yield:** ¼ cup

Ingredients	Directions
1 pound fresh onions (3 large or 4 to 5 medium)	**1** Thinly slice your onions or chop them evenly so that the pieces are of uniform size to facilitate even drying times. Arrange the onion slices or chunks in a thin layer on your drying trays.
	2 Set the temperature on your dehydrator to 120° and dry until brittle, about 12 hours, rotating the trays every 4 hours or so to ensure even drying.
	3 Store your dried onions for up to 1 year in a tightly sealed container.

Per ¼-cup serving: *Calories 172 (From Fat 6); Fat 1g (Saturated 0g); Cholesterol 0mg; Sodium 14mg; Carbohydrates 39g (Dietary Fiber 8g); Protein 5g.*

Tip: You can add dried onions to any dish that you normally use onions in. If needed, simply add hot water to dried onion, soaking for 15 minutes, before adding to your dish.

Dried Peas

Prep time: 5 min • **Dry time:** 9–12 hr • **Yield:** ¼ cup

Ingredients	Directions
1 pound fresh peas	*1* Shell and blanch your peas for 2 minutes in boiling water; then chill in ice water and drain. Arrange the peas in a thin layer on your drying trays.
	2 Set the temperature on your dehydrator to 120° and dry until the peas are shriveled and hard, about 9 to 12 hours, stirring at least once to prevent sticking. Rotate the trays periodically to facilitate even drying.
	3 Store your dried peas for up to 1 year in a tightly sealed container.

Per ¼-cup serving: Calories 367 (From Fat 16); Fat 2g (Saturated 0g); Cholesterol 0mg; Sodium 23mg; Carbohydrates 66g (Dietary Fiber 23g); Protein 25g.

Tip: Peas shrivel up quite a bit when dried but plump up nicely when added back to water or broth. Add dried peas to broth or stew and simmer for 30 minutes.

Dried Potatoes

Prep time: 10 min • **Dry time:** 10–12 hr • **Yield:** ¾ cup

Ingredients	*Directions*
1 pound potatoes (about 4 to 5 medium)	**1** Wash and peel the potatoes. Cut them into ½-inch strips for shoestring potatoes, or ⅛-inch slices, making sure all pieces are of uniform size for even drying.
	2 Blanch the potatoes for 5 minutes and drain. Arrange them in a single layer on your drying trays.
	3 Set the temperature on your dehydrator to 120° and dry the potatoes until they're hard and brittle, at least 10 to 12 hours, stirring after the first 4 hours to prevent sticking. Rotate the trays occasionally to facilitate even drying.
	4 Store the dried potatoes for up to 1 year in a tightly sealed container or in plastic freezer bags.

Per ¼-cup serving: *Calories 108 (From Fat 1); Fat 0g (Saturated 0g); Cholesterol 0mg; Sodium 6mg; Carbohydrates 25g (Dietary Fiber 2g); Protein 2g.*

Tip: To prevent your potatoes from turning brown during drying, dip them in a mixture of 2 tablespoons lemon juice to 1 quart water prior to drying.

Note: When you dry potatoes, make sure that they're completely dry; otherwise, they'll mildew during storage.

Sweet Potato Crunch Sticks

Prep time: 10 min • **Dry time:** 12 hr • **Yield:** 8 servings

Ingredients	*Directions*
1 pound sweet potatoes, washed, peeled, and sliced into shoestrings **1 tablespoon olive oil** **½ teaspoon sea salt**	*1* Blanch the shoestring sweet potatoes in boiling water for 5 minutes and dip in ice cold water. Drain well. Dry the potatoes on paper towels to remove any outside moisture.
	2 Place the sweet potatoes in an 8-quart bowl and add olive oil. Toss well to coat. Spread the shoestring pieces in a single layer on your drying trays. Sprinkle with salt.
	3 Set the temperature on your dehydrator to 120° and dehydrate the shoestring potatoes until they're crispy, at least 12 hours. Rotate the trays occasionally to facilitate even drying.
	4 Store (if you can!) in a cool, dry place.

Per serving: Calories 50 (From Fat 16); Fat 2g (Saturated 0g); Cholesterol 0mg; Sodium 291mg; Carbohydrates 8g (Dietary Fiber 1g); Protein 1g.

Vary It! For a slightly different flavor, add any seasoning you like during Step 2.

Dried Tomatoes

Prep time: 5 min • **Dry time:** 12–16 hr • **Yield:** ⅛ cup

Ingredients	Directions
2 pounds fresh Roma or paste-style tomatoes (about 10 to 12)	**1** Dip tomatoes in boiling water for 1 minute and then plunge them into icy water for 30 seconds. Slip off the skins and core. (**Note:** If you're using slicing tomatoes, remove the seeds.)
	2 Cut the tomatoes into ⅛-inch slices or ¼-inch cubes. Take care to cut uniform pieces. Place slices or cubes onto trays, in a single layer.
	3 Set the temperature on your dehydrator to 120° and start checking for dryness after 6 to 8 hours. Remove the trays, flip all slices over or stir the cubes well, and dry for another 6 to 8 hours or until brittle. Rotate the trays occasionally to facilitate even drying.
	4 Store for up to 1 year in a tightly sealed container.

Per ⅛-cup serving: Calories 191 (From Fat 27); Fat 3g (Saturated 0g); Cholesterol 0mg; Sodium 82mg; Carbohydrates 42g (Dietary Fiber 10g); Protein 8g.

Note: This recipe works with both paste-style and slicing tomatoes, but the drying times are much shorter for paste style.

Zucchini Chips

Prep time: 10 min, plus marinating time • **Dry time:** 12 hr • **Yield:** 4 servings

Ingredients	*Directions*
1 pound zucchini (about 3 medium) **¼ cup Italian-style salad dressing**	*1* Wash and slice the zucchini into ⅛-inch thin slices. Place the slices in a large bowl or gallon-size plastic, sealable storage bag. Pour the Italian-style dressing over the slices and toss to coat.
	2 Marinate the zucchini in the dressing for 15 minutes. Place marinated slices in a single layer on your drying trays.
	3 Set the temperature on your dehydrator to 120° and dry the zucchini slices for 12 hours (or until crisp), turning at least once. Rotate the trays occasionally to facilitate even drying.
	4 Store the zucchini chips for up to 3 months in a 1-gallon, sealable plastic storage bag.

Per serving: Calories 91 (From Fat 66); Fat 7g (Saturated 1g); Cholesterol 0mg; Sodium 118mg; Carbohydrates 6g (Dietary Fiber 2g); Protein 11g.

Tip: These crispy chips absorb moisture from the air quickly. After you open them, use them as quickly as possible to avoid them becoming soft.

Soup and Stew Mix

Prep time: 10 min • **Yield:** 4 cups

Ingredients	Directions
1 cup dried potatoes	**1** Combine the dried potatoes, carrots, peas, and onions in a large bowl.
1 cup dried carrot slices	
1 cup dried peas	**2** Store the stew mix in a moisture-proof container in a dark, cool place.
1 cup dried onions	
	3 To use, measure out the amount of vegetables you want and then simply add them to your broth and simmer until tender, about 30 to 40 minutes.

Per ½-cup serving: *Calories 188 (From Fat 6); Fat 1g (Saturated 0g); Cholesterol 0mg; Sodium 40mg; Carbohydrates 38g (Dietary Fiber 10g); Protein 9g.*

Note: If you don't have dried potatoes, dried carrots, dried peas, or dried onions on hand, use the instructions in the earlier recipes to dry each vegetable and then proceed with this recipe.

Chapter 3

Drying Herbs

Herbs are one of the most important and expensive ingredients in any dish. Drying them can save you a lot of money and give you a much fresher and fuller flavor than any found on a store shelf. Drying herbs is also an easy way to create your own signature blends for cooking and herbal tea. You'll always have your favorites on hand if you dry them yourself.

This chapter shares the most common herbs that dry well and some recipes for making herbal blends that everyone can enjoy.

Harvesting Herbs

The best herbs for drying are those you grow in your own garden. If you don't have a green thumb, the next best thing is to buy your herbs from a farmers' market that sells produce grown without chemical sprays and picked as recently as the day you buy it.

Picking the best herbs for drying

The best herbs for drying are those that are *resinous,* or contain the most oils. The oils are where the scents and flavor come from. Herbs that have very juicy stems and overly thick leaves don't dry well.

If you find that your herb of choice seems to become tasteless or dries to a black mess, try freezing that herb instead. Two common cooking herbs that don't dry well are chives and basil. Blend a little olive oil with these fussy herbs and freeze them instead. (Go to Book VI, Chapter 4 for details.)

Timing the harvest

Your herb-drying success relies on more than which herbs you pick and how you dry them. Take note of these helpful harvesting suggestions:

✔ Harvest your herbs just after the morning dew dries but before the hot, noonday sun hits them. The heat from the sun drives the fragrant oils out of the leaves and blossoms, so the herbs have less flavor.

✔ Harvest only what you can reasonably deal with right away, whether you're bagging it up to refrigerate or hanging it up to dry.

✔ Harvest seeds such as caraway, dill, and coriander by shaking ripe flowerheads into a paper bag. Seeds, which begin forming after the flower is pollinated and the petals fall off, are ripe and ready for collecting when they turn from green to brown or black.

✔ If you choose herbs from a farmers' market, look for fresh, vibrant leaves, a strong smell, and clean, healthy-looking plants. Avoid buying wilted or shriveled herbs, because they've been picked too long ago.

Hanging Around: Proper Drying

Hanging is a relatively easy way to dry herbs — as long as you remember a few basics. The goal is to dry your herbs quickly in order to retain as much of their fresh flavor as possible.

Herbs are dry when they crumble easily. Remove the leaves from the stems. Crush soft leaves (like basil, sage, and oregano) by hand. Store harder leaves (like rosemary, tarragon, and thyme) whole, crushing them with a rolling pin before using them.

Store your dried herbs in small containers. Glass jars with tight-fitting lids work best. For your herbs to maintain the best flavor during storage, keep them away from heat, light, and your refrigerator.

Harnessing the power of air

The best herbs for hanging in bundles are those that have long stems, such as lavender. Other good candidates to suspend, batlike, in a cool, dark, dry location are anise, borage, caraway, chamomile, marjoram, mint, oregano, parsley, rosemary, sage, savory, tarragon, and thyme.

Follow these steps to air-dry herbs (and check out Figure 3-1 as well):

1. **If you're harvesting herbs from a garden, cut the stems (don't pick them), leaving an extra inch or two for tying them in bunches.**

2. **Rinse your herbs quickly by dipping them in a bowl of cool water and shaking off the excess water.**

3. **Pat them dry with a paper towel, making sure that they're completely dry to prevent mildew.**

   This step is necessary only if herbs are particularly dusty.

4. **Tie the herb stalks near the cut part of the stem in small bunches (no more than five or six stems) with cotton string or thread.**

   Don't mix your herb bunches because flavors transfer during the drying process.

5. **Either hang the herbs upside down in a good location (see Figure 3-1) or place the tied herb bundle in a paper bag with holes or slits cut in it for air circulation before hanging the bag in a warm room.**

   The bag protects the herbs from light and catches any loose seeds that you can use to replant your herbs.

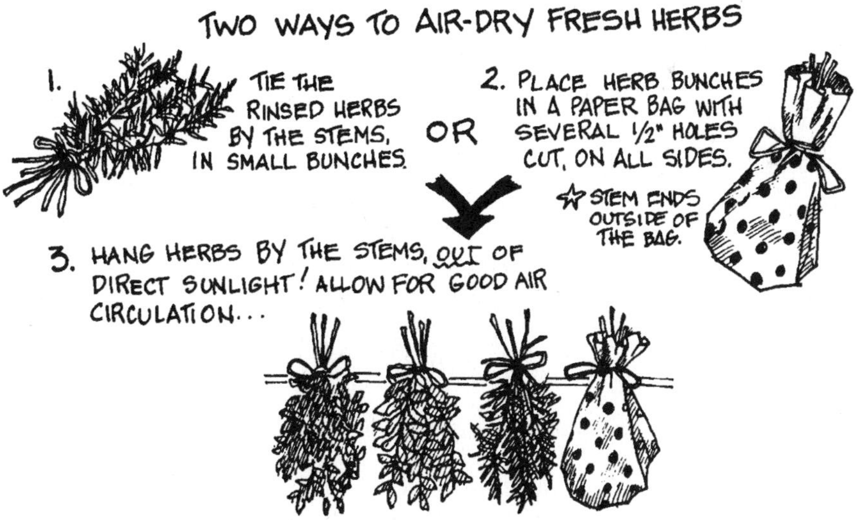

Figure 3-1:
Two ways to air-dry fresh herbs.

Keeping an eye on location

The key to hanging herbs to dry is location. The perfect place to hang your herbs must be

- ✔ **Dark:** The sun bleaches and discolors herbs, stealing their precious oils. You may need to block sun coming in windows.

- ✔ **Dry:** It seems silly to say that a place for drying herbs should be dry, but keep in mind how humid a kitchen can get. Attics are often good, but if you live in a humid climate, you need a dehumidifier there as well.

- ✔ **Warm:** Herbs dry best where the temperature stays between 80° and 85°. Keep an eye on sunny room temperatures, as they can fluctuate quite a bit during the hot summer days.

- ✔ **Clean:** Steer clear of sheds or rooms where you fill your lawnmower or use other chemicals, or any areas where mice may play periodically. To keep culinary herbs sanitary, some people loosely wrap them in cheesecloth or in paper bags punched full of holes.

- ✔ **Well ventilated:** Cross-ventilation from open doors and windows is the most natural solution to keeping air moving. If all else fails, a fan set on low helps to stir the air. And avoid overcrowding; aim to have a minimum of 6 inches between bunches and walls.

Drying with Ovens and Dehydrators

You can speed the process of drying herbs by using equipment that you probably already own:

- ✔ **Conventional ovens:** Some experts are adamantly opposed to using a conventional oven to dry herbs because getting an oven to stay at the ideal 80° to 90° is so difficult. Some people with gas stoves say the pilot light emits just enough heat. An oven thermometer can tell you whether your oven can heat in the right range.

  To dry in the oven, spread leaves and flowers in a single layer on a baking sheet and place them in an oven set as low as possible. Leave the oven door partially open to let moisture and excess heat escape. Keep a close eye on the temperature, opening the door more or turning off the oven as necessary to keep the temperature between 80° and 90°. Drying can take from 10 minutes to several hours. Check the herbs often and turn them periodically.

  Be sure to allow herbs to cool before you bottle them; store them as you would air-dried herbs.

- ✔ **Microwave ovens:** Most culinary herbs dry in a microwave in a minute or less. The downside to this convenience is that you have to watch like a hawk to make sure that your herbs don't become too hot, which gives them a burned flavor.

  Begin by spreading a single layer of herbs on a paper towel and then cover them with a second towel. If you have washed the herbs, be sure they're completely dry before you place them in the microwave. Set the temperature to high and microwave the herbs for 45 seconds. If the herbs haven't dried completely, give them another microblast of 10 or 20 seconds. Continue blasting away until all moisture is gone. Allow the herbs to cool and then store them as you would air-dried herbs, in airtight containers set in a cool, dark place.

- ✔ **Dehydrators:** These gizmos are sold primarily for drying fruit and making beef jerky. They're also good for drying herbs; they operate like low-level toaster ovens that rotate their contents on racks. In terms of drying speed, dehydrators fall between the microwave and air drying. Herb foliage dries in three to ten hours. Follow the manufacturer's instructions for the recommended setting to dry herbs properly.

Drying Common Herbs

Book VII

Drying and Root Cellaring

The following sections outline several herbs that are easy to dry. Each of the following sections tells you how to dry herbs in ovens or dehydrators. If you want to air-dry these herbs, simply follow the instructions in the earlier section "Hanging Around: Proper Drying."

When selecting your herbs, choose those you're familiar with first.

Chamomile

Chamomile is a delicate flower that's as lovely as it is useful. Harvesting chamomile, however, is difficult in a major scale, making it loved by home gardeners but expensive as an herb farm crop.

To harvest chamomile for drying, pick the individual chamomile flowers as they bloom and just after the dew dries in the morning. These instructions are very important because chamomile's delicate scent is easily lost if you're not careful. Some leaves are fine to include because they also have some chamomile flavor.

To dry chamomile, follow these steps:

1. **Lay the flowers in a single layer on trays.**

2. **Set your oven or dehydrator temperature between 115° and 125° and dry for 3 to 5 hours, checking carefully after 4 hours and rotating the trays periodically to facilitate even drying.**

   You don't want to overdry the flowers. They're fully dry when the tiny petals curl inward, and the center of the blossom is totally dry.

3. **Store in an airtight container, out of sunlight.**

To use your dried chamomile, pour 1 cup boiling water over 1 tablespoon dried flowers; then cover and steep for 3 minutes. (Don't steep chamomile too long; it can produce a bitter taste.)

Dill

Dill, an herb that grows anywhere, has tiny leaves and a large, flowering seed head. Harvest the leaves any time you want. Use dill leaves in dressings and pickle mixes. This herb makes a refreshing dip for vegetables and tastes great added to your summer salads.

Drying dill is super easy. Follow these steps:

1. **Lay the dill leaves in a single, loose layer on trays.**

2. **Set your oven or dehydrator temperature between 100° and 115° and dry 3 to 5 hours, rotating the trays periodically to facilitate even drying.**

   Properly dried dill leaves are crispy.

3. **Store dried dill in airtight containers, out of light.**

   This herb loses its delicate flavor quickly if left in sunlight for too long.

Mint

Mint is arguably the herb most people are familiar with and also the easiest herb to grow. It requires only sunlight and water to thrive. Yes, you can grow mint on a counter in a glass of water — forever!

To dry mint, follow these steps:

1. **Cut the stems that seem to want to straggle and lay them on a drying tray.**

   After the mint has dried, it's easier to pull off the leaves without damaging them.

2. **Set your dehydrator or oven temperature between 115° and 125° and dry for 3 to 5 hours, rotating the trays periodically to facilitate even drying.**

   Properly dried mint leaves easily crumble in your hand.

3. **Store mint in airtight containers.**

Try making dried mint into tea or adding a few leaves, crumbled, to boiled potatoes.

Oregano

Oregano is another easy-to-dry herb. Use it in any tomato-based dish, and oregano adds a distinct flavor to your meals. By drying oregano, you ensure that you have plenty of this popular flavoring available throughout the winter months. Use only young leaves because older oregano has a tendency to taste bitter.

To dry oregano, pick the young leaves after the dew dries in the morning and then follow these steps:

1. **Remove any leaves that have insect damage or have been crushed while harvesting.**

   These leaves sometimes turn an unappealing black when drying.

2. **Arrange the leaves in a single layer on trays, but don't fill them too full; you want air to flow around them.**

3. **Set the temperature on your dehydrator between 115° and 125° and dry the oregano for 3 to 5 hours, rotating the trays periodically to facilitate even drying.**

   Properly dried oregano is dry and crumbly.

4. **Store dried oregano in its whole form until ready to use.**

To use dried oregano, crush the leaves in your hand just before adding them to a dish. Add oregano to a dish in the last 10 minutes of cooking to preserve the flavor.

Book VII

Drying and Root Cellaring

Rosemary

Rosemary is a centerpiece to any herb garden. Its scent is recognizable by nearly everyone, and its lovely bluish flowers are truly special. You can harvest rosemary throughout the season. To dry, cut the smaller, side stems where they branch off from the main stem and then follow these steps:

1. **Lay the cut pieces onto the drying trays.**

2. **Dry the herb for 6 to 8 hours at a temperature between 110° and 115°, rotating the trays periodically to facilitate even drying.**

   Rosemary is done when the leaves slightly shrivel and release from the stem easily.

3. **Remove the leaves by holding the stem over a dish or container and running your fingers along the stem.**

   The leaves come off with a gentle touch, and you're left with a clean stem.

   Save the dried rosemary stems for making kabobs. They contain plenty of the rosemary flavor, and they make a unique presentation. Use the stems as you would skewers.

4. **Store rosemary leaves whole and only break them up right before adding to your recipe.**

   Waiting to break the leaves keeps most of the flavor inside until needed.

Sage

Sage is an easy-to-grow herb that's available as seeds or plants that quickly grow into small, lovely bushes. You can use any variety of garden sage for drying. Some offer a stronger flavor than others, so be sure to taste it before purchasing to find your favorite. To dry sage leaves, harvest them as they become large enough (½ inch or more in length) and then follow these steps:

1. **Lay out your sage leaves in a single layer on your drying trays.**

   Be sure to leave room between the leaves for even drying.

2. **Dry the herb for 6 to 8 hours at a temperature between 115° and 125°, rotating the trays periodically to facilitate even drying.**

   It's dry enough if a leaf crumbles in your fingers.

   Be careful to dry these leaves thoroughly; they're slightly thicker than many other herbs and require careful attention.

3. **Store the dried leaves in their whole form until needed.**

If you find that you use rubbed sage often, dry the whole leaves and rub them through a mesh strainer to create a fluffy sage powder perfect for cooking.

Stevia

Stevia may not be as widely known as some of the other herbs in this chapter, but it's a very useful herb. It has been used for hundreds of years in other parts of the world as a replacement for sugar. Stevia users have found that it has a slight licorice aftertaste. You may find that your family enjoys stevia as much as sugar!

To dry, pick the stevia leaves as needed throughout the growing season and then follow these steps:

1. **Lay the leaves on your drying trays in a single layer.**

   Be careful to not overlap, as they can mold quickly if left in a warm place without adequate circulation.

2. **Set your oven or dehydrator temperature between 115° and 125° and dry for 4 to 6 hours, rotating the trays periodically to facilitate even drying.**

   Properly dried stevia leaves crumble easily in your hand.

3. **Store in an airtight container, away from direct sunlight.**

To make stevia sweetener, steep the dry leaves in boiling water and leave them to cool. You can then measure the resulting "tea" by the drop into any drink that requires a sweet taste. Be warned that it's extremely sweet — 300 times sweeter than table sugar, in fact — so start with a drop at a time.

If you find that you always sweeten a particular herbal tea, try adding ½ teaspoon dried stevia to the original recipe. Taste the sweetness of the tea and adjust the dried herb as needed.

Thyme

Thyme has many uses: It tastes great mixed with other herbs for flavoring Italian dishes, and it can hold its own when paired with poultry. Thyme comes in many varieties, but the drying technique is the same. Follow these steps:

1. **Snip off stems as soon as your plants are large enough for drying and lay them whole, in a single layer, on your drying tray.**

2. **Set your oven or dehydrator temperature between 110° and 115° and dry the thyme for 4 to 6 hours, rotating the trays periodically to facilitate even drying.**

   Properly dried thyme leaves are dry and crisp.

3. **Store dried thyme, stems and all, in a cool, dry place away from sunlight.**

   Thyme loses its flavor quickly when left in sunlight.

When you're ready to use your dried thyme, crush the tiny stems right along with the leaves. If the stems are too woody, strip the leaves off right before use.

Getting Creative with Herb Blends

Creating herbal blends for cooking is a matter of using your senses to choose what smells and looks best. If you match the types of foods you eat most often with herbs that complement these foods, you'll be able to create your own signature blends. In addition to the cooking blends in this section, you'll also get a taste of how you can mix herbs to create lovely teas.

Dry each herb separately as explained in the preceding sections before combining. After your herbs are dry, you can experiment with different combinations to see what tastes the best.

Going the rack route

For some herbs, hanging isn't good enough. Their stems are too short, too soft, too skinny, or too wiry to make bunching them an easy process. For these guys — as well as for individual leaves, flowers, seeds, and roots — you need a drying rack.

You can buy a rack, but you can also repurpose an old window screen. Or, if you have only a few leaves or petals to dry, you can spread them in the bottom of a basket or on a paper towel laid on a cake rack or wooden dish rack.

Spread your herbs in a single layer on the drying surface. Stir or turn them every day or two to avoid excessive curling and to discourage mold from developing.

How long does drying this way take? As always, it depends on what you're drying and where you live, but plan on five days to two weeks.

Italian Herb Mix

Prep time: 10 min • **Yield:** 1 cup

Ingredients	*Directions*
¼ cup dried marjoram, crumbled	*1* Combine all ingredients in a medium bowl and mix well.
¼ cup dried oregano, crushed	
¼ cup dried rosemary leaves, crushed	*2* Transfer the herb mix to an airtight container and store in a cool, dry place.
¼ cup dried thyme leaves, crushed	

Per 1-tablespoon serving: Calories 11 (From Fat 3); Fat 0g (Saturated 0g); Cholesterol 0mg; Sodium 2mg; Carbohydrates 2g (Dietary Fiber 1g); Protein 0g.

Tip: Blend this mix with olive oil and baste onto grilled chicken. Sprinkle it on any Italian foods or add it to your favorite soups.

Mexican Herb Mix

Prep time: 10 min • **Yield:** 1 cup

Ingredients	Directions
½ tablespoon chili powder (adjust for desired heat)	**1** Combine all ingredients in a medium bowl and mix well.
⅛ cup dried epazote leaves, crushed	
⅛ cup dried basil leaves, crushed	**2** Transfer the herb mix into an airtight container and store in a cool, dry place.
¼ cup dried oregano leaves, crushed	
¼ cup cumin seeds, ground just before use	
¼ cup dried coriander seeds, ground just before use	

Per 1-tablespoon serving: Calories 16 (From Fat 7); Fat 1g (Saturated 0g); Cholesterol 0mg; Sodium 6mg; Carbohydrates 3g (Dietary Fiber 2g); Protein 1g.

Note: Add this herb mix to ground meat for tacos, burritos, and Mexican-themed soups and dips.

Tip: You can find epazote leaves at large grocery stores in the ethnic foods section or online from most herb suppliers.

Rice Mix

Prep time: 10 min • **Yield:** 1¼ cups

Ingredients	*Directions*
1 cup long-grain rice	*1* Combine all the ingredients in a medium bowl.
2 teaspoons chicken bouillon granules	
2 to 3 teaspoons dried herbs of your choice	*2* Transfer the mix to a glass container or clear food-safe bag. Seal the jar or tie the bag closed.
¼ teaspoon kosher salt	

Per ½ cup serving of prepared mix: Calories 139 (From Fat 3); Fat 0g (Saturated 0g); Cholesterol 0mg; Sodium 490mg; Carbohydrates 30g (Dietary Fiber 1g); Protein 3g.

Vary It! Instead of chicken bouillon, use beef or vegetable bouillon for a slightly different taste.

Tip: Make up a cooking instruction card and keep it with the mix. To prepare the rice, add the rice mix to 2 cups water in a 2- to 3-quart saucepan. Bring the rice to a boil over high heat, stir, cover, and reduce the heat to medium-low. Cook for about 30 minutes. (Don't lift that lid to peek.) Remove the rice from the heat and let the rice stand for 30 minutes. Fluff the rice with a fork and serve immediately.

Lemon Lover's Tea Blend

Prep time: 10 min • **Yield:** 1 cup

Ingredients	*Directions*
¼ **cup dried lemon balm leaves**	*1* Combine all the ingredients in a medium bowl and mix well.
¼ **cup dried chamomile flowers**	
¼ **cup dried lemon verbena leaves**	*2* Transfer the tea blend to an airtight container and store it in a cool, dry place.
¼ **cup dried lemon thyme leaves**	

Per 1-tablespoon serving: *Calories 5 (From Fat 0); Fat 0g (Saturated 0g); Cholesterol 0mg; Sodium 2mg; Carbohydrates 1g (Dietary Fiber 1g); Protein 0g.*

Tip: To make a cup of tea, pour 1 cup boiling water over 1 tablespoon tea blend; then cover and steep for 3 to 5 minutes. This fruity, bright tea blend tastes great hot or iced.

Vary It! Love mint? Try a mint tea blend by combining ¼-cup measures of dried peppermint leaves, dried spearmint leaves, dried catnip leaves, and dried (crushed) lemon balm.

Dried and chilled: Using refrigerators to dry herbs

The "cool" approach to preservation is becoming increasingly popular because drying herbs this way retains both their flavor and color. Spread a single layer of leaves or flower petals on a baking sheet covered with paper towels and place it in the main section of the refrigerator (not the crisper). Drying usually takes two to four days, depending on the herb and the refrigerator. This technique works especially well for herbs that can be challenging to dry in other ways — parsley, dill, and chives, for example.

Chapter 4

Drying Meats

Drying meat is one of the most delicious techniques out there for meat storage. Drying a piece of meat properly only enhances the flavor and creates a uniquely flavored product that truly satisfies.

Jerky is a well-known type of dried meat. The flavoring you add becomes concentrated as the meat dries. This process results in a chewy, delicious snack that packs a protein punch. From sweet to spicy, you'll find a never ending array of flavor profiles for jerky, something sure to please everyone in the family.

This chapter shares how to decide on what meats to dry, the equipment you need for different types of drying, and various types of dried meats.

Snacking on Meats

Probably the most recognizable type of dried meat is jerky. You can find it in most grocery and convenience stores, for a shockingly high price! The availability of jerky reflects the fact that it comes in a range of flavors that appeal to everyone.

People make jerky from many types of lean meats. Beef, poultry, and wild game all make a delicious product. You can make resealable bags and sticks of dried meat at home for a fraction of the cost you'd pay at the store. Plus, by making it yourself, you can control the ingredients and find just the right balance of flavors that your whole family will enjoy.

Tasting the nutrition

With the exception of seasoned jerky, dried meats usually mean salty meats, particularly if they aren't properly prepared. Dried meats are meant to be soaked in water for a time to remove excess salt before cooking. Salted fish and country hams are both examples of meat that has been dried and then refreshed for eating.

Traditionally, dried meat was shaved off and eaten because it was used by hunters and other people who didn't remain in one place for very long; they needed to carry their food with them. These folks ate a different product than the one you see today; it was tough, leathery, and nowhere near the finely tuned snack that you see in the modern pantry.

Planning the perfect quantity

Dried meats are approximately one-fourth the weight of fresh meats. You can prepare dried meats and then store them in larger quantities, easily removing the amount you need. When using a meat dryer at home, you dry the meat in strips, place the dried strips in freezer bags, label them, and then store them in the freezer until needed.

Many people eat dried meat as part of a snack platter or carry it along with them as a treat. Because you have to chew on it for an extended period, it makes a great portable snack that provides energy for a rigorous day of hiking or exercise.

Using different drying techniques

You can dry in a number of ways:

- **Electric dehydrator:** The most common method for modern meat drying, an electric dehydrator is a device with a fan that blows a gentle current of air up and over trays of drying meat. A good dehydrator needs to reach 160°, and a fan is highly recommended.

- **Oven-drying:** You can try your hand at drying meat by using your oven. Place meat on specially made drying racks or a cookie rack placed on a cookie sheet (to collect any drippings). The temperature is 145°.

- **Sun-drying:** Although sun-drying has historically been a technique used to dry meats, it isn't considered safe today. Dry your meats indoors to avoid any issues that can result in a spoiled product and serious illness.

Selecting and Preparing Meat

You can dry many meats. The main concerns are having too much fat or unappetizing parts that won't dry properly or will cause spoilage. A bit of fat may seem appealing on a juicy steak, but "juicy" isn't a word you want to associate with meats that are going to be dried.

Dried meats require nothing more than trimming, slicing, and drying. However, seasoning is what makes your dried meats fun. Try to dry meats using different flavors to see which you like best.

The qualities you look for in a prime piece of meat for dinner are the qualities you want to avoid for a piece of meat for drying. Fat goes rancid, and it's difficult to get out of meat for drying. Look for meat that you may deem tough for a dinner plate, and you more than likely have the perfect cut for drying.

Choosing the right cuts

Meats that work best for drying are lean and mean. Use cuts of meats that are considered tough, with long muscle fibers. These guidelines are especially true for beef. Wild game tends to be extremely lean, so choosing a cut that works is less of a problem. Avoid fatty fish for the same reason. Look for these cuts of meat:

Book VII

Drying and Root Cellaring

- ✔ **Beef:** Sirloin, top round, and ribeye. You can certainly use others, but they'll require more preparation before drying.

- ✔ **Wild game and goat:** Most cuts are suitable for drying. Remove any visible membrane that covers the meat, and, of course, any fat. Venison, elk, and moose all make great jerky.

- ✔ **Poultry:** Breast, legs, and thighs are all suitable for drying, but be sure to remove all traces of skin and fat. Freeze the cleaned poultry pieces before cutting to make slicing easy and more uniform.

- ✔ **Fish:** Drying fish at home isn't recommended because it's difficult to get the conditions just right. Drying fish involves a long salting process to draw off the majority of moisture and then careful drying, with plenty of stacking, pressing, and rearranging.

Equipment and timesaving tips

Drying equipment for meats is the same as it is for fruits and vegetables. A properly working dehydrator, with a thermostat and a fan, is recommended. Meats need to be kept at the proper temperature for the entire time you're drying them, and the key to doing that is a thermostat and a fan.

You can also use an oven for drying if you can set it at a low enough temperature to dry — and not cook — the meat inside. If possible, you want to avoid ovens that heat from the top, no matter what temperature. If your oven's top heating element comes on at any temperature, place a cookie sheet on the top rack and then place the drying meats on the next rack down. This trick will protect the meat from the direct heat.

An electric oven may not have the necessary ventilation to dry meats properly. If you have an electric oven, prop open the door just a little to allow heat and moisture to escape. Most oven doors allow for propping open an inch or so and will hold themselves that way.

Racks and trays are other necessary equipment. Meats have to be suspended to allow airflow on all sides. You can accomplish this meat-suspension by using special racks or metal cookie cooling racks placed on trays or cookie sheets to collect any drippings that fall off the meat.

Whether you use an oven or a dehydrator, don't overload the trays. You should have room for airflow between each piece of meat and between each tray. You may have to make smaller-sized batches than anticipated. Immediately refrigerate any remaining meat that won't fit in the dryer. You can use it in your next batch.

Packing and Storing Meats

Because people usually eat dried meats in small quantities, package them in containers that can be reopened numerous times and then tightly resealed. You should also store dried meats in the refrigerator or freezer for long-term storage.

One of the best containers for storing dried meats is a freezer bag. These bags can be filled and the excess air removed many times. The seals are recloseable, and, even when frozen, the bags remain flexible enough to manipulate.

Another handy way to store dried meats is to use a vacuum sealer. They're a little less convenient to reseal, so freeze them in smaller serving sizes and then place these small bags into a larger freezer bag for easy access.

Place a small quantity of dried meat in the refrigerator for your family to use. A two-week supply of meat for snacking is a good quantity. Keep the rest of the dried meat in the freezer so that you can refill the smaller supply in the fridge. This ensures that the meat stays fresh for as long as possible in the freezer.

Using your freezer

When drying and storing dried meats, think of your freezer as a tool. It's a pantry, although a cold one. Storing is best done with a firm hand on organization and rotating. Check out these ideas for organizing a freezer:

- **Use the FIFO (First In First Out) system.** When you put a food into the freezer, place it behind the other containers of the same food. That way, you use up the oldest foods first. Think of the way grocery stores stock their shelves.

- **Use larger boxes or hard-sided containers, racks, and baskets to keep small bags of dried products organized.** Your packages of dried meats may not lie completely flat, yet they will stand up in a small box with ease. This also makes keeping track of what you have left much easier.

- **Keep packages on the smaller side.** When divvying up dried meats, remember that most people eat them as a snack. Resist the urge to pack a freezer bag to the brim in order to use less packaging. It makes more sense to package what your family will use in a short period of time and remove that amount as needed. This tip reduces spoilage from forgotten food as well.

- **Replace and add to the freezer's contents before you run out.** If you're using up one type of dried food faster than another, make a note of it and add more before the first selection is gone.

Book VII

Drying and Root Cellaring

Remembering to label

Labeling is key to proper dried meat storage. After meats are dry, they tend to look a lot like one another. Nothing is worse than thawing a package of dried meat for kids' lunches and finding that it's the smoking hot variety your husband likes but the kids can't eat.

Label everything with the date you made it, the flavoring, a rough idea of quantity or serving, and even uses. This may seem like a lot of information, but you waste your good storage intentions if you forget what you have on hand.

Labeling extends to another important part of freezer storage: your inventory list. Post the inventory list either on the door of the freezer or in another area that you must pass by or look at when preparing food. List types of dried meats, quantity, and the date you placed them in the freezer. This list will be invaluable when you start making your own flavorings and playing around with types of meat for drying. If a package tastes particularly good, you'll have an accurate way to find out what you did. And if a batch of meat doesn't taste good or is slightly off, you can easily remove it at once.

Label bags according to meats inside by using different colored markers. If you have only one type of marker, try a simple symbol for each type of dried meat. For example, a small star for beef, a flame for spicy marinated jerky, and a circle for poultry give you an accurate representation of what's inside the bag at a glance. These labels may be useful if you have a picky child who likes the taste of something but may not be open to trying it if he knows the ingredients.

Avoiding spoilage

The biggest problem of drying and keeping foods at home is spoilage. Taking care to bring the meats up to the proper temperature (and keeping them there for the entire drying process) is important. So is using clean containers, clean surfaces, and clean racks in your drying equipment.

Because drying meats often means drips and splatters, thoroughly clean all your equipment before putting it back into storage. When taking equipment out for a new use, look it over for any missed food spills that may harbor bacteria.

Once frozen or refrigerated, meats need to remain at that temperature. For example, allowing dried meats to sit on a counter and then putting them back into the freezer for a later date is unsafe. Consider the freezer the first place for storage, the fridge the second, and then take the food out to be eaten.

Keeping it dry

Not much can damage properly dried and frozen meats. The one thing that can be a problem, however, is moisture. Because dried meat contains far less moisture than the air around it, it naturally reabsorbs some of that moisture anytime you leave it out. This reabsorbing of moisture can promote rancidity and decay. Minimize this potential problem by storing your dried meat in tightly wrapped and sealed containers.

Consider these tips for preventing dried meats from spoilage due to high moisture:

✔ **Wrap an airtight seal around the meat.** Use clinging wraps like plastic wrap for a layer right next to the meat. Then continue as you normally would with a container for freezing.

✔ **Open packaging only when you need to.** If you wrap and rewrap dried meats, each time the packaging is opened, the meat will be exposed to moist air. If you find that you need to get into your dried meat packages often, make a note of the quantities that you're using and wrap that size the next time.

Making Jerky

Jerky is the ultimate protein treat. It's fast to make and fun to eat, and you can flavor it from sweet to super spicy. *Jerky,* in the simplest definition, is strips of meat allowed to dry and become chewy. Add to that the step of marinating, and you're on your way to fantastically flavored meat.

Jerky is meant to be dried, but it should still remain pliable. Check out the level of flexibility by removing a piece of finished jerky and allowing it to cool. Warm jerky is pliable, even if it's overcooked. You can cut through a cooled piece of jerky fairly easy, and it should have a uniform color throughout. Pieces should bend easily, like leather.

Traditionally, jerky was made by hanging meat over the cooler smoke of a campfire and allowing it to dry. The smoke kept the insects from bothering the meat (too much) and added flavor as a bonus. As you can imagine, this method wasn't very precise.

Jerky is dried at cooler temperatures, not cooked. You must use low heat and take care that the outside of the pieces doesn't dry too fast, creating a shiny, impervious layer that won't evaporate moisture properly. To prevent this from happening, consider the following tips:

✔ **When the dryer is preheated and ready to load, work quickly to get the job done and the door back on.**

✔ **Load all trays with fresh meat at the same time.** Don't add fresh meat to a batch of jerky that's already started to dry. This mistake can bring the overall temperature of the meat down far enough to promote bacterial growth.

✔ **Keep track of the temperature of a batch at the lowest tray, and remember to rotate full trays.** This ensures even drying, with no areas that may not be getting enough airflow.

✔ **Don't dry at too high a temperature.** Start with a temperature of 10° to 20° lower than your desired temperature, and after the first 30 minutes, increase by 10°. Increase by 10° again after 1 hour. This tip reduces the chance of the outside layer of your jerky becoming dry and keeping the juices locked inside.

Book VII

Drying and Root Cellaring

Cutting and slicing

After you choose your meats for jerky making, the next step is to cut them properly. Jerky needs to be cut to a thin, uniform size to allow the marinade to penetrate the meat more completely. Here are some tips for the best results:

- ✔ **Always cut meat across the grain.** The result is pliable jerky, which is easier to bite off and chew. To be sure, examine the piece of meat to see the directions of the meat fibers, which should not be visible in a properly cut piece.

- ✔ **Whether you use a knife or a slicer, the basics are the same: Cleanliness is the first line of defense against decay.** Wash all work surfaces, equipment, and your hands before handling meat for cutting. Plastic gloves are inexpensive, and you can quickly strip them off in case you need to do something else during the process. Gloves are considered sanitary unless you handle something else that may not be clean enough. Keep a box on hand and change them often.

- ✔ **Partially freeze (or thaw) meat before cutting.** This technique allows you to get a cleaner, finer cut. Meat that's partially frozen is somewhat bendable. Don't freeze meat until it's rock solid because trying to cut hard, frozen meat is dangerous.

- ✔ **Don't slice too thinly, even if you think it will hurry the drying process.** Jerky that has been sliced too thinly will dry too quickly or even scorch, resulting in an inedible product and wasting a lot of meat. Slice meat any way you want, but keep slices at ¼ inch and roughly 6 to 8 inches long. There are no hard and fast rules, but these guidelines give you a conveniently sized piece of jerky.

Going with ground

With jerky going mainstream, more equipment has been showing up in retail stores. A jerky gun or shooter makes jerky making fun and accessible. These shooters look just like a caulking gun, but you load or fill the tube with seasoned, ground meat! By pressing the trigger, you press out sticks (think Slim Jim–style) or flat, evenly laid pieces of jerky.

Before you buy a jerky shooter, make sure that it's easy to take apart and clean. Clean the assorted tips after each use; any meat you miss can cause contamination of future batches of jerky.

When making ground meat jerky, remember the following:

- ✔ **Seasoning becomes much more concentrated after the meat is dried.** If you add too much seasoning, you may not be able to eat the jerky. Flavor ground meat with a light hand.

- ✔ **Don't overhandle the ground meat.** After mixing seasonings into ground meat, cover the mixture and chill. This process gives you a cleaner piece of jerky that will hold together.

- ✔ **Use a lean ground meat.** Although the texture is ground, you still want to avoid fat. This rule is important to remember when you're buying ground poultry. Check the label to make sure fat and skin aren't blended into the meat, making the fat content too high.

- ✔ **Don't marinate ground meat.** Add dry seasonings directly to the meat and mix well.

Try mixing wild game and beef together when making ground jerky. This is a good way to use wild game that may have a stronger flavor. After you combine it with a mild beef, the taste of the jerky flavoring is the only one people will notice.

Book VII

Drying and Root Cellaring

Basic Jerky Marinade

Prep time: 3 hr • **Yield:** Marinade for 2 pounds meat

Ingredients	Directions
⅔ **cup soy sauce**	*1* Combine all ingredients.
⅓ **Worcestershire sauce**	
2 tablespoons honey	*2* Pour over sliced meat in a freezer bag or flat dish.
3 teaspoons coarse ground pepper	*3* Marinate for a minimum of 3 hours or overnight.
1 teaspoon liquid smoke	

Per 1-tablespoon serving: Calories 17 (From Fat 0); Fat 0g (Saturated 0g); Cholesterol 0mg; Sodium 597mg; Carbohydrates 3g (Dietary Fiber 0g); Protein 1g.

Vary It! This is a basic recipe. Add heat by adding red pepper flakes. You can substitute maple syrup for the honey.

Marinade for Poultry Jerky

Prep time: 3 hr • **Yield:** Marinade for 1 pound meat

Ingredients	Directions
¼ cup soy sauce	**1** Combine all ingredients.
1 tablespoon liquid smoke	
⅓ cup Worcestershire sauce	**2** Pour over sliced meat in a freezer bag or flat dish.
1 tablespoon brown sugar	**3** Marinate for a maximum of 3 hours.
2 teaspoons garlic powder	
2 teaspoons onion powder	

Per 1-tablespoon serving: Calories 19 (From Fat 0); Fat 0g (Saturated 0g); Cholesterol 0mg; Sodium 457mg; Carbohydrates 4g (Dietary Fiber 0g); Protein 1g.

Vary It! Sprinkle coarse ground pepper onto marinated poultry just before drying.

Citrus Jerky Marinade

Prep time: 3 hr • **Yield:** Marinade for 2 pounds meat

Ingredients	*Directions*
¼ **cup pineapple or other citrus juice**	*1* Combine all ingredients.
⅔ **cup soy sauce**	*2* Pour over sliced meat in a freezer bag or flat dish.
⅔ **cup Worcestershire sauce**	
1½ **teaspoons white pepper**	*3* Marinate for a maximum of 3 hours for poultry and fish and overnight for red meats.
1 **teaspoon garlic powder**	
1 **teaspoon onion powder**	

Per 1-tablespoon serving: Calories 18 (From Fat 0); Fat 0g (Saturated 0g); Cholesterol 0mg; Sodium 728mg; Carbohydrates 3g (Dietary Fiber 0g); Protein 1g.

Vary It! Add some heat by adding cayenne pepper to the mix, ½ teaspoon at a time.

Asian Jerky Marinade

Prep time: 3 hr • **Yield:** Marinade for 2 pounds jerky

Ingredients	*Directions*
1 cup soy sauce	*1* Combine all ingredients.
⅓ cup rice wine vinegar	
1 tablespoon sesame oil	*2* Pour over sliced meat in a freezer bag or flat dish.
1 teaspoon fresh shredded ginger	*3* Marinate for a maximum of 3 hours for poultry and fish and overnight for red meats.
1 teaspoon garlic powder	
1 tablespoon brown sugar	

Per 1-tablespoon serving: *Calories 16 (From Fat 6); Fat 1g (Saturated 0g); Cholesterol 0mg; Sodium 669mg; Carbohydrates 1g (Dietary Fiber 0g); Protein 2g.*

Vary It! Add heat by adding 1 teaspoon Asian chili sauce.

Sweet and Savory Jerky Marinade

Prep time: 3 hr • **Yield:** Marinade for 2 pounds jerky

Ingredients	Directions
¼ **cup dark brown sugar**	**1** Combine all ingredients.
½ **cup Tamari sauce**	
½ **cup Worcestershire sauce**	**2** Pour over sliced meat in a freezer bag or flat dish.
1 teaspoon garlic powder	
¼ **cup molasses**	**3** Marinate for a maximum of 3 hours for poultry and fish and overnight for red meats.
1 teaspoon pepper	

Per 1-tablespoon serving: Calories 25 (From Fat 0); Fat 0g (Saturated 0g); Cholesterol 0mg; Sodium 371mg; Carbohydrates 6g (Dietary Fiber 0g); Protein 1g.

Vary It! Add liquid smoke if you want a smoky flavor.

Dry Seasoning for Ground Jerky

Prep time: 40 min • **Yield:** Seasoning for 1 pound ground meat

Ingredients	Directions
2 teaspoons salt	**1** Combine all ingredients.
½ teaspoon white pepper	
1 teaspoon chili pepper	**2** Mix into 1 pound ground meat.
1 teaspoon garlic powder	**3** Chill for 30 minutes and fill jerky gun.
1 teaspoon onion powder	

Per 1-tablespoon serving: Calories 13 (From Fat 2); Fat 0g (Saturated 0g); Cholesterol 0mg; Sodium 2,327mg; Carbohydrates 3g (Dietary Fiber 1g); Protein 1g.

Vary It! Spice things up by adding cayenne, ½ teaspoon at a time.

Seasoning for Ground Poultry Jerky

Prep time: 40 min • **Yield:** Seasoning for 1 pound ground poultry

Ingredients	Directions
1 teaspoon salt	**1** Combine all ingredients.
2 teaspoons paprika	
1 teaspoon garlic powder	**2** Mix into 1 pound ground meat.
1 teaspoon ground thyme	
1½ teaspoons black pepper	**3** Chill for 30 minutes and fill jerky gun.

Per 1-tablespoon serving: Calories 17 (From Fat 4); Fat 0g (Saturated 0g); Cholesterol 0mg; Sodium 1,165mg; Carbohydrates 4g (Dietary Fiber 1g); Protein 1g.

Vary It! Substitute ground thyme for poultry seasoning.

Chapter 5

Planning Your Root Cellar

· ·

In This Chapter

▶ Exploring root cellars

▶ Making your own storage spaces

▶ Containing your cold storage crops

▶ Storing foods safely

· ·

An often overlooked food storage idea is underground storage. The traditional root cellar is an efficient way to keep many foods fresh throughout the winter months. Keeping your harvest at its best through cold storage is easier than you think! If you're not lucky enough to have a place for an actual root cellar, all sorts of other creative ways can help you keep foods at the proper temperature.

In this chapter, you discover creative ways to store your produce and find out how to select the best foods to keep in cold storage.

Finding Your Cold Storage

Before refrigeration and artificial preservatives, cold storage was the way to go if you needed to store produce over the winter. The basic idea behind cold storage is that you can prolong the shelf life of both fresh and canned produce by keeping them in a cool, dark place under just the right conditions.

By combining the perfect mix of temperature and humidity, you can expand your storage to a large variety of foods. Temperature and humidity aren't the only considerations, however. An area used for cold storage also needs to have proper ventilation to keep the food as fresh as possible. And ease of access is vital, too.

✔ **Temperature:** Cold storage temperatures range from 32° to 60°. The right temperature for any given food is one that slows the enzymes responsible for decay. Different foods require different storage temperatures. Beets, for example, need temps just above freezing; pumpkins and squashes, on the other hand, need temps in the 50° to 60° range.

✔ **Humidity:** Depending on the foods you want to store, your root cellar or alternative cold storage area needs a humidity range from 60 to 95 percent. Foods such as carrots, parsnips, and turnips store best at 90 to 95 percent humidity. Sweet potatoes and onions, on the other hand, do much better at a humidity of no more than 70 percent.

If you plan to store foods that require very different humidity and temperature levels, you need to use more than one storage area. It's not uncommon to have a dry cold storage area with lower humidity (like you get in an area that has a cement floor) and a higher humidity area (which you get in an area with a dirt or gravel floor).

To keep track of temperature and humidity level in the air, buy a simple thermometer unit, called a *hydrometer* (see Figure 5-1).

✔ **Ventilation:** No matter what type of storage area you choose, it must be able to let warm air out and cool air in.

✔ **Ease of access:** Because you have to regularly check your stored food, you need a place that you can get into easily and that allows you to easily move things around.

Figure 5-1:
A hydrometer for checking temperature and humidity.

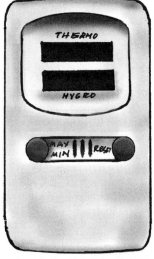

Read on to find out what your cold-storage options are and head to Book VII, Chapter 6 to discover the optimum humidity levels and temperatures required for specific foods.

Making use of the traditional root cellar

Root cellars have had a long and important place in the history of food storage. Root cellars were most often the actual cellar of old homes and farmhouses. These older houses had cellars with dirt floors, perfect for keeping foods cool and the humidity higher than average.

If you're lucky enough to have an actual dirt-floor root cellar, all you need to do to store your produce there is provide sturdy shelving and rodent-proof the area by covering any holes or potential rodent-friendly entryways with wire mesh. You can also place rodent bait in out-of-the-way areas and check often for rodent activity.

A preexisting root cellar usually contains some sort of air vent or pipe located at the top of the area to allow warm air to rise and escape. If you don't have a preexisting air vent, periodically open a window or door to the outside to allow warm air out and fresh air in.

In modern homes, cellars (or basements) often have concrete floors and are generally too warm and dry for food storage. Carefully measure your temperature and moisture content before placing your produce in a cellar that may not have optimum conditions.

Seeking DIY storage spaces

If you don't have a cellar with a dirt floor, you have alternatives. Take a look at your cellar layout and consider the areas suggested in the following sections.

Stairwells

Does a stairwell lead from your basement to the outside? If so, add an insulated door to separate the stairwell from the main room, and voilà, you have a cold storage space that has built-in shelves: the stairs! Just place bins of produce on each step and pans of water under the stairs for moisture, and you have an efficient storage area (see Figure 5-2).

A stairwell is particularly good because the stairs create areas with varying temperatures, allowing for a wide array of conditions that can benefit many different kinds of foods.

Figure 5-2:
A stairwell converted into a cold storage area.

Be sure to place a hydrometer in this area, as well as a few inexpensive thermometers on different steps, to gauge the best conditions for your stored foods. The temperature will vary quite a bit as you go up the stairs.

Storm shelters

Do you have a storm shelter (also called a storm cellar)? In the Midwest, storm shelters are often underground cellars separate from the house or basement. (Think of Dorothy in *The Wizard of Oz,* when she runs through the yard to get to the storm cellar during the tornado.) These shelters are perfect for adding some shelves and neat bins of produce. They're below the frost line, have adequate ventilation, and are weatherproof.

Whether your home had a storm shelter when you moved in or you decided to build one yourself, be certain to block any ventilation pipes with fine screen to keep rodents out.

You'll use up your stored foods long before the storm season approaches. Even so, keep your cold storage organized and neat.

Straw-bale storage

If you have a small area in your yard, you can construct a simple straw-bale storage area (see Figure 5-3) to hold your root crops, like potatoes, rutabagas, turnips, and parsnips.

The best location for straw-bale storage is one that tends to stay dry. Don't place these storage areas in high moisture areas (where you generally have a buildup of snowdrift, for example, or where water tends to puddle after storms). Also, don't build one close to buildings that protect the area from winter temperatures. You want the straw bales to be able to stay freezing cold on the outside and yet insulate the produce inside.

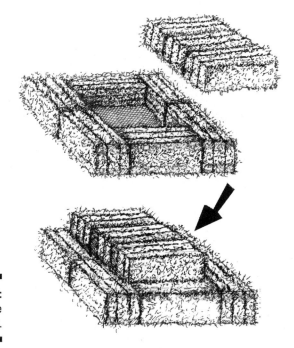

Figure 5-3:
Straw-bale
storage.

After you find a suitable location, follow these steps to build your straw-bale storage area:

1. **Place two bales of straw in a line, with the ends touching; about 16 inches away, place two more bales parallel to the first two.**

   This spacing is adequate for the bales you lay on top to cover the open space completely.

2. **Place one straw bale on each of the remaining ends to enclose a box shape in the center.**

   You've just made a large square in the center.

3. **Cover the ground in the center of the square with a screen.**

   You don't have to use the screen, but doing so helps keep your produce protected from critters that may be inclined to dig under the whole thing.

4. **Layer some soft straw on the bottom of the square to cushion the produce.**

   If you put a screen in the center, place the straw over the screen.

5. **Layer your root crops, very gently, into the bin.**

   Take care not to dump or toss your vegetables. Bruised food quickly turns to spoiled food.

6. **When the bin is full, layer another couple inches of straw onto the food.**

7. **Place bales of straw across the top of the now-filled bin.**

   Your food is now protected from winter in a breathable storage bin.

To check on or access the food inside, simply remove the top two bales. Replace the bales carefully and evenly to cover the hole each time. In the late spring or when the straw-bale storage area is empty, simply take the bin apart and use the straw as mulch for your garden.

Some people use hay bales for these storage bins, but we don't recommend it. Hay molds rather quickly, sometimes spoiling the produce inside. Hay bales also seem to absorb more moisture than straw bales. If you use hay, check periodically for moisture damage, and remove the offending produce immediately.

Storage tubs

You can bury food-safe, rubber tubs up to their rims in the ground, place your produce inside, put on the lid, and then cover the whole thing with a thick layer of straw for a simple cold storage arrangement. These bins are easy to wash and the tight lids keep the foods fresh and sanitary and keep rodents out.

Following Simple Storage Rules

Underground storage is the fastest and possibly easiest way to store foods. You do, however, have some rules to follow, no matter what variety of food you want to keep over the winter.

Selecting storage stars

Foods must be in perfect condition — not too ripe or picked too early. Overly ripe fruit is extremely fragile and in the last stage before naturally decaying. Food that's too green doesn't do particularly well either. These foods may change color or become agreeably soft in storage, but they won't truly ripen and develop their best flavor in these conditions.

Make sure you pick your food at just the right ripeness, as fresh as possible, and store it immediately. Don't allow it to sit at room temperature while you decide what you're going to do with it.

Choosing partners carefully

Be careful about how you pair foods. Some foods produce gases that make other foods spoil. For example, apples produce a gas that makes potatoes start to sprout. Put these two together, and you'll end up with potatoes that are soft and inedible. Cabbage is a very strongly scented food that's better stored in an outside area, away from more delicately flavored items.

Garlic, onions, turnips, and rutabagas can also give off strong enough odors to affect their neighbors. If possible, keep these types of produce away from the milder items.

When storing produce, consider organizing items by their temperature and humidity needs. A fruit that needs a high humidity will have a much shorter life when stored near items that need a drier location. Don't hesitate to rearrange the storage area as you use up the items.

Picking the right storage container

Choose containers that let you keep things neat and organized. Some ideas:

- **Rubbermaid-style tubs:** You can stack these tubs when they're not in use, their covers fit tightly, and you can easily fill them with damp sand for foods that need increased humidity. Use clear bins to avoid colors leaching into foods and so that you can easily see all the produce inside. Shop at restaurant-supply stores for food-safe bins.

- **Wooden bins or boxes:** Recycle these storage containers from thrift stores and some grocery stores. Even if you have to pay a few dollars for each, they'll give you years of service and allow for neat, tidy stacking. If you're stacking wooden boxes, place the first row in a line, place a couple of sticks across the boxes for air circulation, and then place the next boxes on top. You want to let the moisture and gases escape, which allows the food to last longer.

- **Five-gallon pails:** You can find these pails for next to nothing from bakers and other restaurants. You don't need to include the lid; in fact, for cold storage, it's best not to. Fill the clean, dry bucket with produce, layer a damp cloth on the top, and stack these buckets in a pyramid shape, allowing plenty of airflow between.

Book VII

Drying and Root Cellaring

- **Old dressers:** You can arrange these unconventional pieces against a wall and use the drawers to keep your produce in a dry and safe place. Line the drawers with newspaper for easy cleaning. Keep them slightly ajar for proper air circulation.

Choosing the best packing materials

After choosing the right location, the next most important thing to do is to choose what packing material you'll use to protect your produce. You can keep bins filled simply with pieces of fruit or vegetables, but the weight of the produce will eventually result in bruises, and you'll have to throw away some food. Wrapping or nestling produce into soft, dry material will help insulate and protect each piece. You may already have these packing materials:

- **Blankets:** Blankets make great liners for bins and boxes. If you're using something like dresser drawers for storage, a folded blanket will make that location soft enough for any type of produce to rest on. Blankets also have the benefit of being easy to wash. Use blankets to wrap large pieces of squash before setting them down. This helps protect the skin of the squash from nicks or bruises.

- **Newspaper:** If you have plenty of extra newspaper lying around, use it as packing material. Use sheets of it to wrap individual pieces of produce before packing them into their crate. I (Amy) use sheets of newspaper to rest my green tomatoes on, and then I add another layer on top of the tomatoes to help them ripen faster. If any tomato decides to decay instead, the absorbency of the newspaper helps make cleanup easy.

- **Sand or leaves:** Some produce likes to wait out the winter snuggled into damp sand or leaves. Containers filled with sand are extremely heavy, so place your container and then fill it with clean, damp sand. Look over leaves carefully for any unwanted insect inhabitants; the benefits to using leaves are that they're lightweight and, best of all, free.

Tending your stash

You must care for your cached foods, even while they're in storage. Weekly checking for bruising, decay, dryness, and mold is essential. (Damaged or ripening produce gives off *ethylene,* a gas that encourages other fruits and veggies to further ripen, so yes, one bad apple really can spoil the whole bunch.) As the winter progresses, remove any produce that has blemishes. Your remaining foods will continue to last longer.

Rearrange your produce carefully. After a month, you may discover that you've used enough of your stored produce to enable you to bring the bottom layer up to the top. Be careful of excess handling, though; gently place each food back in place to avoid bruising.

Chapter 6

Preparing and Cellaring Veggies and Fruit

. . . .

In This Chapter

▶ Unearthing the best candidates for cellaring

▶ Prepping produce for cold storage

▶ Giving fruit a shot in your root cellar

. . . .

*F*resh fruits and veggies are wonderful, but the bad news is that they pretty much grow only during warm weather, and they don't last forever. If you want to continue to extend the shelf life of many of your garden crops, go underground and give root cellaring a try.

Foods that store well are generally the less juicy and delicate things, like root vegetables and firm fruits. Many families enjoy these foods; they provide a fresh taste when bland winter fare abounds, and they extend your food pantry to include fresh, tasty choices. (**Note:** You may be able to extend the life of more tender foods, like eggplant or broccoli, but don't count on them lasting for months as the other foods will. You can keep these treats in storage about two weeks, but no longer.)

If you're ready to dig into the world of root cellaring, Book VII, Chapter 5 covers the basics of planning and setting up a root cellar or alternative cold storage space. (You may be surprised at some of the options you already have at your disposal.) This chapter discusses which veggies and fruits keep well in cold storage and how to prepare them, with valuable guidelines for maintaining optimum temperature and humidity.

Stashing Vegetables for a Cold Day

Vegetables need a little preparation before you put 'em in the cellar. Cut off leaves and stems, but don't cut into the flesh of the vegetable, which promotes spoiling.

Pick veggies at optimum maturity, not before they ripen or after their prime. Ripe vegetables have the best flavor and the highest nutritional content. Choose only those veggies in perfect shape and remove any items from storage if and when they do start to spoil because this spoiling is catching. (Damaged or ripening produce gives off *ethylene,* a gas that encourages other fruits and veggies to further ripen.)

As a general rule, harvest root crops as late as you can in the season and don't wash the dirt from the roots. Simply use your hand or a rag to remove some of the loose soil.

The following sections list some vegetables that keep very well in cold storage; also refer to Table 6-1 for a handy guide to the specific vegetables.

Table 6-1	Storing Various Veggies		
Vegetable	*Special Preparations*	*Optimal Temperature/ Humidity*	*Storage Life*
Brussels sprouts	Store only unblemished, fresh Brussels sprouts.	32°–40° 90–95% humidity	3–5 weeks
Cabbage	Wrap cabbage in newspaper or store away from other foods, which may absorb the strong odor of cabbage.	32°–40° 80–90% humidity	3–4 months
Carrots	Put them in cold storage as soon as they're harvested.	32°–40° 90–95% humidity	4–6 months
Onions	After clipping the tops off, keep them in the sun for a week before storage.	35°–40° 60–70% humidity	4–6 months
Peppers (sweet)	Store only unblemished, fresh peppers.	45°–55° 85–90% humidity	2–8 weeks
Peppers (hot)	Store only unblemished, fresh peppers.	50°–60° 60–70% humidity	2–8 weeks

Vegetable	Special Preparations	Optimal Temperature/ Humidity	Storage Life
Potatoes	Toughen the skins before storage by letting them sit in the open air (but not in the sun) for 2 weeks.	32°–40° 80–90% humidity	4–6 months
Radishes	Put them in cold storage as soon as they're harvested.	32°–40° 90–95% humidity	2–3 months
Squash	Leave the stem on and let the squash sit in the sun for about 2 weeks until the rind hardens.	50°–60° 60–70% humidity	4–6 months
Tomato (ripe)	Store only unblemished, fresh tomatoes.	45°–55° 85–90% humidity	1–2 months
Tomato (green)	Store only unblemished, fresh tomatoes.	50°–70° 60–70% humidity	4–6 weeks

Beets

Beets are prolific and inexpensive to grow, meaning you'll end up with plenty for storage if you plant a few rows. Harvest beets late in the season, after the nights become freezing cold. If you're buying beets at a farmers' market, fresh, crisp tops are the best indication that the beets were just picked.

To prepare the beets for storage, cut off the tops, leaving the beet itself intact. (Don't wash them.) Then place the beets in your coldest storage — temperatures just above freezing, 32° to 40°, with 90 to 95 percent humidity. To increase humidity naturally, place the beets on moist sand.

Some gardeners recommend leaving beets in the ground, covered with a thick layer of straw. They say beets and other root crops can be harvested directly from the ground in the coldest part of the winter. Be aware, though, that rodents may destroy root crops before you get a chance to harvest them. So before you follow the advice of the "leave 'em in the ground" crowd, make sure that you — and not rodents — will be the benefactor.

Book VII

Drying and Root Cellaring

Cabbage

Cabbage adds bulk and crunch to many winter dishes. Keeping cabbage in storage requires a few extra precautions, however, to ensure that it remains useable throughout the winter and doesn't ruin other food nearby.

First, cabbage gives off a strong odor while in storage, which is normal. (Don't confuse this smell with spoilage.) The problem with the smell is that apples and other fruits can absorb the flavor of cabbage. The key is to make sure that you don't store cabbage too closely to these other types of foods. If you must store cabbage close to other foods, wrap individual heads with newspaper to contain the odor.

The longer cabbage remains in storage, the stronger its taste when you cook it. If your family doesn't like the stronger taste, plan on using up cabbage early in the storage season.

Cabbage needs to be stored in a damp area. If you store cabbage in a place that's too dry, the heads dry out, and the dry, wilted leaves are wasted. Fortunately, you can take care of this tendency with a simple pan of water.

To prepare cabbage for storage, choose unblemished cabbage that hasn't been picked for long. Remove the tough outer leaves. Wrap each head in newspaper and store it where temperatures are just above freezing, 32° to 40°, and the humidity levels are between 80 and 90 percent. Place a pan of water near the cabbage to provide enough moisture during storage.

Carrots

Carrots are another root vegetable that stores well and tastes sweet and crisp throughout the winter months. Just as you do with beets, pick carrots as late as possible in the season. Avoid any that have grown too large and pithy, however, because these carrots have used up their natural sweetness and will taste bitter.

To prepare carrots for storage, trim off the tops, leaving the carrot itself intact. Don't wash them; simply brush off excess soil if you want to. Place carrots with beets in coldest storage of 32° to 40° with high humidity of 90 to 95 percent. Carrots do especially well in moist sand.

Garlic

You can never have enough garlic, especially since garlic is so easy to store. If you're growing your own garlic, simply pull the bulbs after the tops dry and fall over. Allow the garlic bulbs to dry thoroughly out of direct sunlight until the outside of the bulbs have become dry and papery. Purchased garlic bulbs have already been dried. Look for the papery outer layer that you always see on a store-bought bulb.

Dry bulbs on newspaper outside during the warm summer days, but bring them in during the cool nights to prevent condensation. Repeat this process for a few days, until the garlic is completely dry.

When the garlic is thoroughly dry, tie bunches of tops together or braid in attractive garlic braids. Alternatively, trim tops from bulbs and place them in women's stockings, tying a knot between bulbs. You can hang this long chain of bulbs on a nail in a cool and slightly damp area. If you do keep them in cold storage, place them in an area that's 30° to 45° with a humidity level of 60 to 70 percent.

Onions

Most onions keep very well in cold storage. Some varieties, such as the extra sweet onions, however, don't last long. When planting, choose varieties that say they work well for storage. (You'll see the term "good keeper.") These onions last throughout the storage season.

Harvest onions the same as garlic. Pull them when the tops turn brown and fall over. After you pull them, you must also cure them, as you do garlic: Place them on newspaper to dry during the warm days, bringing them in during the cool night hours to avoid condensation buildup. When storing purchased onions, you don't have to worry about this step. They're already dried for you.

To store, gently place onions in a crate, loose mesh bag, or ladies' stockings, tying a knot between each onion. To prevent mildew on onion skins, air circulation is vital, so make sure that your cold storage has adequate ventilation. (See Book VII, Chapter 5 for more information on ventilation.) The ideal storage conditions are temperatures of 35° to 40° and humidity of 60 to 70 percent. If, throughout the season, you find onions with some mildew on them, simply use those onions first. Generally, the mildew is on the outer layers, leaving the inside of the onions fresh.

Potatoes

Potatoes are the easiest of all fruits and vegetables to store. To prepare for storage, harvest late in the season. Don't wash the potatoes; instead remove excess soil with your hand or a soft rag. Inspect them carefully for bruising or nicks in the skin. (Fresh potatoes have a more delicate skin than those that have been harvested for a few days.) If you find any bruising or nicks, keep these potatoes out of storage and use them within a few days.

Store potatoes in complete darkness at 32° to 40° and 80 to 90 percent humidity. Every week, check them for damage. At least once a month, turn and rearrange them. Finally, don't let them freeze. A frozen potato is a ruined potato; it can't be saved.

The most important rule for storing potatoes is to store them in complete darkness. First, the darkness signals dormancy for the potato, and it won't sprout. Second, potatoes subjected to light become bitter over time. Other than perfect darkness, potatoes really do well in almost all storage conditions.

Squashes

Rich in Vitamin A and other essential nutrients, squashes bring in some of that color you probably crave during the winter months.

Squashes store very well. Check them periodically for mildew on the skins, wiping off any mildew you find with a damp cloth. If you see a squash that's starting to get decay marks, consider taking it out of storage and using it right away.

To prepare squashes for storage, don't wash them; simply brush off any dirt. Store them in complete darkness at 32° to 40° and 80 to 90 percent humidity. Use pans of water to keep humidity high, if needed. Every week, check them for damage. At least once a month, turn and rearrange them.

Turnips

Turnips are an underappreciated root crop. They're easy to grow: You simply plant them early in the season, weed them a few times, and harvest them late in the season, after the nights become freezing cold.

To prepare turnips for storage, don't wash them. Simply brush off any excess soil with your hand or a rag, and trim off the turnip tops.

Store them in your coldest storage area; just above freezing is ideal (temperatures of 30° to 40°). The humidity should be high; between 90 and 95 percent is optimal. Turnips are another food that stores well in damp sand.

Consider turnips a crop that provides two separate foods: the greens and the root. So, after you trim the tops to prepare the root for cold storage, don't throw away the greens. You can dry them for use later. To see how to keep turnip tops, head to Book VII, Chapter 2 for info on drying greens and Book V, Chapter 2 for instructions for canning greens.

Tomatoes

You may be surprised to see tomatoes, which are both fragile and juicy, in this list of good cold-storage vegetables. Tomatoes can, however, be kept for a limited period of time in cold storage.

When you store tomatoes, you store the whole plant, not just the individual tomatoes. So at the end of the growing season, select any tomato plants that have fruit with the slightest hint of ripening (any color change, from slight yellow to orange) and follow these steps:

1. **Remove any fruits from the plant that are still fully green or too small to ever ripen.**

2. **Pull the entire plant out of the ground and hang it upside down in temperatures between 55° and 70°, with moderate humidity of 60 to 70 percent.**

   An unheated garage or cellar stairwell works great for this.

The tomatoes will ripen slowly over time, right on the vine. You'll be amazed at the vine-fresh flavor.

Setting Aside Fruit

Because of their juicy nature, not all fruits are suitable for storage. Choose fruits that are known to store well; sometimes even varieties of the same fruit can be stored, while others won't last a month.

Check fruits and handle them delicately. A bump or bruise will speed up the decay process, and if one piece starts to decay, its neighbor will soon join in.

Book VII

Drying and Root Cellaring

Fruits can also absorb odors from stronger scented vegetables like cabbage, onion, and garlic. Store these things as far apart as you have room for.

Apples

Apples store very well. Choose a variety that's known for storage. Kept well, apples can last throughout the entire winter — four to six months! Toward the end of that time, a perfectly good apple may become slightly shriveled. This is simply from the loss of moisture, not nutrition.

Choose apples that are unblemished and firm. (They shouldn't give at all when pressed.) Check in bright light for dents and soft spots.

To store, layer the apples carefully in very cold temperatures (between 30° and 35°), with a high humidity between 80 and 90 percent. (Place a pan of water in the area where they're stored.) Check apples every few weeks for any that may be starting to decay.

Try covering your bin of apples with a damp (not dripping) cloth, which remains damp for at least a day. And make it a habit to replace the cloth every couple of days when you check other stored produce.

Pears

Pears store very well and make a nice change from apples. In years when apples are affected by blight or scald and are too expensive, pears can be more available.

Pick pears you plan to store when they're just ripened. (Don't choose pears that are too ripe, or soft; simply leaning against each other can cause them to bruise.) To help protect the fruit, wrap each pear in a sheet of newspaper before storing. Keep temperatures cold, 30° to 35°, with high humidity (80 to 90 percent). Pears can keep for several months in this manner.

Book VIII
Smoking, Salting, and Curing

The 5th Wave   By Rich Tennant

"This is a wonderful rub. We use it on everything — fish, chicken, calluses..."

In this book . . .

The techniques of smoking, salting, and curing should no longer be shrouded in mystery. They're all easy to master for the home cook. The fun is in trying out your own flavorings along the way.

In this book, you discover the how and why of each form of preservation. Each ingredient plays a role in the outcome of the food, and you will know which way is best to preserve your food based on the taste profile you want.

With a large resource of recipes to choose from, you'll be off to a fast start, making your foods taste even better with any of these techniques.

Chapter 1

Keeping Meats

*B*efore the days of refrigerators, people had other ways to keep meat from spoiling. These methods are still being used today, although they're often just a hobby.

You can freeze, can, or dry meat for storage. You can also prolong the time before it spoils (as well as its quality and taste) with three other methods: smoking, curing, and salting. These methods aren't just for preservation, although they're successful at that. Each technique creates its own unique flavor that adds a new facet to everyday eating. In this chapter, I discuss smoking, curing, and salting meats.

A pantry can contain one kind of meat, preserved in a variety of ways, each resulting in different flavors. Eating from the pantry need never be boring again.

Understanding the Techniques

No matter which technique you choose, preserving meats means slowing the deterioration of the flesh by making it more difficult for dangerous bacteria, yeasts, and molds to grow. In this chapter, I focus on these three meat preservation techniques:

✔ **Smoking:** Infusing meat with a pleasant tasting smoke by smoldering specific woods and allowing the smoke to flow around the meat for a specific time.

✔ **Curing:** Applying a mixture of salt, pink salt (nitrates/nitrites), and seasonings to a piece of meat and allowing it to sit for an extended time. This process draws out the natural moisture within the meat. This drawing process can also be combined with the exchange of the meat's juices with flavored liquid. This technique is called pickling or brining. (See Chapter 3 of Book III for additional information on pickling meat.)

✔ **Salting:** A basic application of salt to a piece of meat. This process creates country style ham and prosciutto. To salt, you apply a layer of salt to the meat, keep it chilled for 60 days (this step coincides with the old-fashioned style of butchering hogs in the fall), and then smoke it for additional flavor.

Different meats react better to dry curing, like dry rubs and smoking, than to wet brining, like pickling, while other meats require a two-step wet/dry curing in order to taste their best.

Each of the preservation techniques has similarities. You can cure meat wet, dry, or a combination of the two. You smoke meat after the curing process has finished. The two basic methods for curing meats are smoking and curing, because salting requires an extended period of hanging and then smoking just right to be done correctly.

Smoking

The two types of smoking are hot and cold smoking. Each type has the same basic premise of allowing smoke to flavor meat, but that's where the similarity ends.

Hot smoking

Hot smoking is the process that most people are familiar with. It's the type of smoking you think of when you eat barbequed meat. The meat is cooked indirectly in hot temperatures and smoky conditions, flavoring and cooking the meat over the course of several hours. At the end of the smoking period, the meat is ready to be eaten. The smoke has imparted flavor to the outside and inside of the meat, creating an entirely new taste.

Hot smoking has as many variations as there are cooks. Many cooks keep their recipes secret, and no amount of persuasion will get them to give up the wood (or woods) they use, how long their meat smokes, or even what type of smoker they use.

After you have the basic technique down, experience is the best teacher. You'll soon discover what type of wood and length of smoking time you prefer. Poultry and fish are exceptionally delicious when they undergo the hot smoking method.

When smoking meats for the first time, use a tried and true recipe to find out how a properly smoked piece of meat is going to taste. You'll have plenty of time for experimenting after you work out the basic technique.

Cold smoking

Cold smoking also improves the flavor and dries the meat. Because the cold smoking method is used for preservation, it requires a clearer understanding of what the smoke actually does to the meat, and how to do it safely and properly.

The preserving ingredient when using the cold smoking method also comes from smoke, usually from burning hardwoods, such as hickory, oak, or mesquite. (You can make a homemade smokehouse from an old refrigerator or other large container.)

This method takes at least 24 hours in a smokehouse to accomplish, with three phases to the process:

1. **In the drying phase, heat the smokehouse to 125° for 8 hours.**

2. **Introduce the smoke and increase the temperature to 135° for another 8 hours.**

3. **In the final 8 hours, continue the smoke and increase the temperature to 180°.**

Curing

Curing meat is another option for preservation, and you achieve it by putting the meat in a solution of salt and other substances, such as nitrates and sugar. It can greatly improve a meat's flavor.

Although you can find many recipes, the two basic ways to cure meat are through brine curing (also known as pickling or corning) or dry curing. You can use *brine curing* without the added step of smoking or drying the meat. As the name suggests, you cover the meat with brine and allow it to soak in order to absorb flavor and become tenderized.

Dry curing is more successful for longer storage. The dry cure is rubbed directly onto the meat. This method is more forgiving for the beginner. You can find a wide variety of commercially prepared dry cures available; they're premeasured and mixed. They're often very salty by their nature, and after dry curing a few times, many enthusiasts begin mixing their own recipes. Here's a basic method for dry curing meat:

1. **Apply 1 ounce of dry cure mixture per pound of meat, rubbing it in well onto the entire surface of the meat.**

2. **Place meat in a dry, clean container that holds a rack that will allow the resulting brine to drip off the meat.**

3. **Cover the meat and allow it to cure in a cool dry place for the amount of time recommended on the packaging.**

4. **Remove the meat, dry it off with cheesecloth, and place it in a gunny sack (burlap bag) to keep the flies off.**

5. **Hang the meat in a cool place to dry.**

Dry cured meats still need to be cooked before eating.

Salting

When you think of curing meats, the technique you probably think of first is salting. Although the idea of meat hanging in the smokehouse may seem like a romantic notion, it's a little more involved than that.

People still eat salted meats today. Country-style hams and the decadent prosciutto are examples of salt-cured meats. They're sometimes smoked afterward to add to their flavor. To create a country style ham, take these steps:

1. **Trim a chilled, fresh ham of excess fat.**

2. **Combine 1 pound salt with 1 pound sugar.**

3. **Apply salt and sugar mixture to the outside of the ham.**

4. **Wrap paper around the ham tightly to keep the salt layer in place and place the ham in a muslin sack.**

5. **Place the wrapped ham on a shelf in a cool place to dry.**

6. **Allow the ham to cure for 2½ days per pound.**

7. **After curing, unwrap and hang for 30 to 40 days in temperatures that are less than 40°.**

Assembling Your Ingredients

When preserving meats by using any method, the key to developing the perfect flavor is gathering the correct ingredients. The basic ingredient list is the same, but the many variations of those ingredients can change your results.

- ✔ **Salt:** Flavors the meat, but also draws out moisture from within the meat, making it less inhabitable for bacteria that can cause illness. Salt also helps the cure to penetrate the meat, bringing the flavor throughout the entire thickness of the piece. Although you can use salt on its own, it would be unpalatable to eat, and the meat would take on an unsavory color.

- ✔ **Nitrates or nitrites:** This ingredient is used for flavor enhancement, provides the appealing pink-cured color, and helps prevent rancidity. A natural impurity found in salt, nitrites are essential to curing meat. Because this ingredient can be dangerous if used in too high a ratio, it's most often added as part of a purchased mixture.

- ✔ **Sugar:** To counteract the salty taste and add a new facet of flavor, sweetener is sometimes added to the curing process. Most commonly used in wet brine, sugars can include cane sugar, honey, or maple syrup.

- ✔ **Additives:** Herbs and spices are added to the brine to create a unique recipe.

Spicing up the meat palate

Spices are the single thing that can change a recipe from boring to taking center stage. Add these flavors to make a less palatable cut of meat taste appealing. Some ideas for flavorings are bay leaves, peppercorns, cloves, garlic, and onion. This is the perfect place to start playing with heat, too. The combination of salty and hot is a surefire hit for most people. Look for powdered hot peppers and make your meat as spicy as you dare.

Loving the sweeter side of meats

It may come as a surprise to you that an essential ingredient in most rubs and brines is sweetness! The sugar can be white, brown, maple syrup, honey, molasses, or any combination of sweeteners. These unexpected flavors add an additional flavor component, smoothing out the saltiness and helping to take the sting out of the spiciness factor.

Book VIII

Smoking, Salting, and Curing

Sugars will burn, so if you're adding them to a dry rub mixture, be aware that the outside of the meat may burn before the inside is finished cooking. To avoid this tendency, keep a careful eye on the food while it cooks. This problem isn't an issue when you smoke meats, so make your brines and rubs as sweet as you want for smoking recipes.

Gathering Your Gear

Simple, essential pieces of equipment will make your meat-curing hobby safe and efficient. Look for things that are clearly in good working order and labeled for use in the manner you expect them to be. Chapter 3 of Book I discusses some general preservation equipment; Chapters 2, 3, and 4 of this book detail more specific supplies for each method.

Many hobbyists get involved in tweaking their gear to better suit what they want it to do, but until you know what properly preserved meats look, smell, and taste like, follow directions and know your gear's limitations.

Don't forget to start building a library! Find old books from when preserving meats was commonplace. You can gather recipes and techniques from days gone by, when it was imperative to know how to fill the pantry.

After you have a library of information, check for updated safety and ingredient information. Modern science has figured out that the back shed may not be the best place to hang a winter's store of beef.

The old books are to get your creative juices flowing, and the updated information keeps you safe while you try out what you learn. Both kinds of books are important to have on your bookshelf.

Sizing up the equipment

When you first start exploring all the equipment that's available for smoking and preserving meats, you may be shocked at the prices! Looking more closely, you'll find that these things are designed to smoke a hundred or more pounds at a time — much more than a home-preserving enthusiast needs to begin with.

Look for the same quality in much smaller sizes for your own use. And follow these basic rules:

- ✔ **Look for clear instructions:** All equipment should come with clearly marked instructions for use. These instructions remove the guesswork, which can be dangerous when preserving meat.

- ✔ **Consider the quality:** The quality of the product is very important. You're working with heat, smoke, and raw meat. It's important that your unit has properly working thermometers and shelving, and that all parts will hold up under the conditions you'll be putting them in.

- ✔ **Check the availability of fuel and parts:** Many beginners become discouraged when they find that the required upgrades are available from only one source, or they run out of the fuel included in purchase and no one carries the correct sort of fuel. Be sure you can maintain and continue to use your gear for years to come.

- ✔ **Start with a kit:** If you have trouble finding all the equipment and supplies you need at first, try looking for a ready-made kit. This kit may seem like a shortcut, but it's truly the perfect way to start out right. You can usually find all the seasoning, curing products, essential tools, and clear-cut recipes included in one place. Take the guesswork out of your newfound hobby by purchasing everything in a foolproof kit.

Consulting with experts

Where do you go to buy what you need for proper ingredients, equipment, and recipes? Find other enthusiasts! Look for technique-specific websites and e-mail lists. You'll find more than anyone can read in a day, so choose the ones that clearly contain a lot of how-to articles and forums rather than just products to buy. Nothing is nicer than being able to ask someone directly about how a product works for them.

Sausage-making experts all over the world are just waiting to talk casing and spices. If you're trying to create an old-fashioned country ham, you can find forums to walk you through the process.

Attend events where other people are smoking their foods; outdoor contests and tailgate parties are a good place to start. Ask where they buy their equipment. Even if they're working on larger equipment than you think you'll ever need, the same supplier usually offers a smaller home version as well.

No matter where you start your search, after you find other people and stores that supply your preserving equipment, you'll soon be set up with the right equipment to get started on your meat preservation journey.

For real-life, expert advice, try your local extension office. Call and ask for anyone who has knowledge of the specific technique you're looking for. This office is the biggest hidden gem in every state in the United States. Extension offices are located all over the country, and they're staffed by experts in their field. Your local county extension office can help you navigate some of the lesser-known food preservation methods, with updated and safe advice, for free.

Start small and learn to perfect each step before you take on a more difficult task. Other than safe food handling rules, which must be followed, you'll be learning how to create the perfect product for your own pantry. Enjoy the process.

Book VIII

Smoking, Salting, and Curing

Chapter 2

Taking on Smoked Meats

Smoking meats is an age-old way to preserve them. At one time, it was the main way of storing meats. Smokehouses were commonplace, and there wasn't a lot of variety in taste or process.

Smoking does a number of things. The smoke colors and flavors the meat, and it also dehydrates the meat and slows the spoilage in any available fat. Smoking has become more of a flavoring technique than a stand-alone way to preserve food. The styles, flavors, and recipes are enough to keep a hobby smoker busy for years. A true smoking enthusiast is never completely satisfied with the end product and considers his smoking ability a work in progress.

Settling on a Smoker

The smoker is the central tool (other than meat) that you need. The smoker needs to provide a chamber to allow the food to be enveloped by smoke — without cooking the meat at too high a temperature. Several styles of smokers have their own fan base. Find a smoker that suits your needs and enjoy the process.

Choosing a type

When choosing your style of smoker, consider how much time you'll have to tend to it. Some types of smoking take days; if you don't have that kind of time to devote to watching over the meat, having some automation may be the way to go.

Charcoal smokers

You most often run into two varieties of charcoal smokers for home cooks on the commercial market:

- ✔ **Vertical smoker:** A vertical smoker (see Figure 2-1) is one of the all-time most popular smokers and not terribly hefty in size or cost. You use it by cooking a significant distance over the heat and with a water pan between the heat source and the cooking grate to keep the meat moist.

- ✔ **Offset horizontal smoker:** An offset horizontal smoker (see Figure 2-1) keeps the fire in a compartment separate from the meat. You have a large cooking surface and vents to control the heat and keep it moving through the cooking chamber.

Figure 2-1: On a vertical charcoal smoker (left), the meat cooks far above the heat. An offset horizontal smoker separates the fire and the cooking surface.

Electric or gas smokers

The term *electric* is a slight misnomer. Electric smokers do use electricity, but that electricity heats and then burns the wood (see Figure 2-2). Many electric smokers can keep a set temperature, and some even come with a remote control to allow truly laid-back smoking! Just set your temperature and go.

Figure 2-2:
You find electric and gas smokers in a range of styles.

Some say that a smoker without charcoal can't produce the same smoky flavor of a charcoal smoker. But if you like the exacting control of a self-regulating smoker, an electric smoker may be right for you.

Rigging a charcoal grill

Using a charcoal grill as a smoker is a good way to test the barbecue waters. If you find you enjoy smoking, you're likely to want to upgrade, but a large kettle grill with a lid is a reasonable starting point.

The main difference between grilling and barbecuing is that when you grill, you cook directly over the heat source. Barbecue cooking uses indirect heat. To make that happen in a grill, do the following:

1. **Prepare your heat source.**

   Use a chimney starter (see "Using a chimney starter," later in this chapter) to light your fuel.

2. **Place the fuel.**

   When the charcoal is hot, heap it onto only one side of the kettle's bottom grate, leaving the other side free for the meat.

3. **Add wood.**

   Put soaked wood chunks or an aluminum-foil packet of wood chips directly onto the coals.

Book VIII

Smoking, Salting, and Curing

4. **Get ready to cook.**

   Place the top grate onto the kettle and give it a few minutes to heat up.

5. **Carefully put your meat on the grate.**

   Place your meat on the side of the grill *opposite* the heat source. Figure 2-3 shows you how your setup should look.

Figure 2-3: Keep your meat out of the direct line of the heat source when you use your charcoal grill as a smoker.

6. **Close the lid to smoke the meat.**

   Leave the vents or intake partially open to keep oxygen moving over the smoldering wood, and to encourage good circulation of the heat throughout the grill. Adjust the upper vent or exhaust above the meat and opposite the fire to draw heat and smoke toward the meat.

Check the temperature intermittently by inserting a candy thermometer into the vent on the grill's lid. (Make sure the vent is positioned over the food that you're cooking so you know you're reading the temperature where you're most concerned about it.) Open the vents farther to increase heat, and narrow them to decrease it. Add more charcoal if you need to increase the heat by several degrees.

Because the heat is on only one side of the grill, you need to move your meat regularly so that each piece gets roughly the same amount of time next to the hottest area. Doing so helps you cook your food evenly.

Deciding on sizes

After choosing your type of smoker, you need to choose the proper size. Buy a larger smoker than you think you may need. Because so much time and technique are involved in smoking, you probably won't grab the smoker on a daily basis to smoke a pound of meat. When the smoker is filled, the process is more economical, so you should plan on smoking big batches of meat less often.

Be sure your smoker will fit the largest turkey that you've ever purchased! In my experience, this is an important consideration.

Playing with Fuel and Flavor

Think of smoke as seasoning, and you soon see that changing the flavor of the smoke results in delicious changes to the meat. Smoke flavor is developed by the different fuels you use. The sky is the limit when it comes to blending and creating flavored smokes.

Before choosing your fuel, see whether this decision has already been made for you. Most smokers recommend using a specific type of wood in their units.

You can add wood to your grill or smoker in a couple different forms:

✔ **Chips** are small pieces along the lines of mulch. Wrap them in heavy-duty aluminum foil and tear several holes in the foil to give the smoke a route out of the packet and onto your meat.

Fish easily picks up a metallic flavor from the foil, so if you're planning to smoke fish, you may want to use wood chunks instead.

- ✔ **Chunks** are good-sized pieces of wood that are 3 or 4 inches across. Before you use them, soak them in cold water for half an hour to an hour. Drain off the excess water and then place the chunks right on top of your charcoal.

Avoid using softwood to smoke meat. Pine trees and other conifers smell great, but they do terrible things to the taste of meat. Any seasoned hardwood is fair game. The next section gives you a rough idea of what different woods do for your barbecue.

Describing characteristics of woods

The type of wood you use to smoke meat affects the way it tastes. Varieties of wood and meats can be paired like wines and cheeses.

Here's a rundown of the characteristics you find in different types of wood:

- ✔ **Almond** or **pecan** wood imparts a mild, nutty (surprise!) taste.

- ✔ **Apple** and **cherry** woods do what their fruits would: They give a sweet, fruity flavor.

- ✔ **Hickory** provides an intense flavor; be careful not to use too much.

- ✔ **Maple** is mild and versatile, and its smoke is a little sweet.

- ✔ **Oak** is a finicky option because it has a distinct flavor that can easily come across too strong.

- ✔ **Walnut** comes off as bitter if you use too much of it. Better to use it restrainedly and with a milder choice, like one of the fruit woods.

Choosing charcoal

You can buy charcoal in two varieties, both of which have their enthusiasts:

- ✔ **Charcoal briquettes:** Made from charred hardwood and coal, charcoal briquettes are the most commonly used medium for backyard grilling. Briquettes are in many cases eschewed by serious barbecue cooks because of the additives that are compressed into them to keep the briquettes burning and hold them together.

- ✔ **Lump charcoal:** Made from charred hardwood and nothing else, lump charcoal doesn't have the additives you find in charcoal briquettes (nor does it have the smooth shape — hence, the name). Lump charcoal burns hotter and faster than briquettes. You pay more for it, but depending on the sensitivity of the meat you're cooking, lump charcoal may be worth the expense, because you won't have the chemical additives that may flavor the meat.

If you choose to use charcoal briquettes (and plenty of great barbecue cooks do), avoid the kind with the lighter fluid built right in. The chemicals that help you light it burn right off the briquettes and waft into your food, giving it an acrid taste. Using lighter fluid straight from the squeeze bottle is a bad idea as well and for the same reason. Check out the next section, "Using a chimney starter," to find out the best way to get charcoal burning without adding unwanted flavor.

Using a chimney starter

Through the magic of a chimney starter, you can light charcoal easily and quickly without pouring on the lousy-tasting chemicals you find in lighter fluid. You can buy a chimney starter (see Figure 2-4) at most hardware or home-supply stores.

Figure 2-4:
A chimney starter gets your coals ready for cooking without adding chemicals.

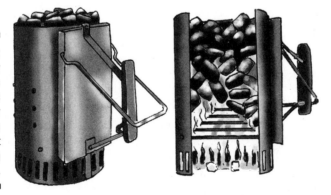

Book VIII

Smoking, Salting, and Curing

You use it by stuffing newspaper into the bottom section and filling the top section with charcoal. Set it in a safe place and light the newspaper. In 15 to 20 minutes, your coals are ready to go. Just dump them into the smoker.

Increasing heat is easier than reducing it, so proceed cautiously with charcoal. Start out with slightly less than you think you need and add more if necessary.

Testing Tips on Technique

After you figure out what fuel you want to use, turn your attention to technique. Because the rules to smoking have endless variations, the art of smoking meats remains interesting and ever changing.

Planking perfection

Using a plank to smoke on is a special technique that literally means placing a soaked wood in the smoker, with the meat placed on the moistened wood. Cedar is the most common, but cherry, maple, oak and alder planks are also available. Traditionally used to smoke fish, planks are also used for poultry and pork.

Saucing, rubbing, and mopping

Get used to these terms. They all refer to applying flavors to the outside of meats before and during the smoking process.

- **Saucing:** Sauces usually contain sweeteners that can cause them to burn. You most commonly add them at the end of the smoking process, and you use them on meats that will be ready to eat, like barbeque.

- **Rubbing:** Rubs are a mixture of flavorings that are quite literally rubbed onto the entire surface of the meat before smoking. You leave the meat to absorb the flavoring, and then you smoke it. Rubbed meats create a crust that's especially sought after by fans of this technique.

- **Mopping:** This refers to a wet application of flavoring, usually a very thin sauce that's wiped on over and over, to keep the meat moist. You can find an endless variety of recipes for mop sauces.

Building your own sauces

Concocting your own from-scratch barbecue sauce isn't as complicated as most people think.

The base you use makes up the largest part of your sauce, although it won't necessarily end up being the most notable flavor. Sauce bases set the tone and hold your other ingredients together in a harmonious mix.

Three bases serve as the starting block for most of the barbecue sauces that cooks in the United States stake their names on: mustard, tomato, and vinegar.

In addition to those bases, every sauce that works has a balance of sweet, sour, and seasonings. Many throw in heat, too, to keep things interesting. When you start dreaming up your own sauce, keep in mind that you want one element to do most of the work. A sauce needs an identity if it's to become a standout. If you prefer a sweet sauce, let an element like apricot preserves take the stage and give hot elements the role of backup singer. If you want a sour, vinegary sauce, heat and sweet do the doo-wop work.

The following sections run down the common ingredients that go into the various elements of great sauces.

Sweet ideas

Standard granulated sugar adds sweetness, sure, but so do a lot of other ingredients, many of which add much more interesting combinations of flavors along with the sweet:

- ✔ Brown sugar
- ✔ Fruit juices (anything from apple to raspberry or pomegranate)
- ✔ Fruit preserves, jams, or jellies
- ✔ Honey
- ✔ Light corn syrup
- ✔ Pure maple syrup
- ✔ Molasses

Sour notions

If you're going to have a little sweet in your sauce, you need some sour, too, to keep the mix from becoming more of a dessert glaze than a suitable topper for meat. Here are the most-used options:

- ✔ Lemon or lime juice
- ✔ Prepared mustard
- ✔ Vinegar
- ✔ Worcestershire sauce

Book VIII

Smoking, Salting, and Curing

Seasonings

Pungent fresh vegetables like onions, garlic, and peppers add a lot of depth (and in some cases a little sweetness) to your sauce. Dried herbs and spices go even farther. Less usually is more when it comes to seasonings, so proceed carefully as you season your sauce.

Here are some of the seasonings that commonly make it into barbecue sauces:

- Allspice
- Celery seed
- Cinnamon
- Garlic powder
- Ginger
- Onion powder

Hot touches

Plenty of people pride themselves on cooking up the hottest of the hot sauces. Whether you're looking for your guests to gasp or just make their eyes water a bit, a number of spices can help you achieve your desired effect:

- Cayenne pepper
- Chili powder
- Crushed red pepper
- Horseradish
- Hot pepper sauce
- Minced fresh hot peppers

Perfecting the Process

Like any skill, learning to smoke meats to perfection takes practice. If you aren't satisfied with your finished product, try one of these simple solutions:

- If the meat is **too chewy,** it was overly cooked and/or at too high a temperature. Reduce the cook time and/or lower the temperature.
- If your meat has a **bitter flavor,** the meat was smoked too heavily. Reduce smoking time or switch to a lighter tasting wood.

✔ If the meat **doesn't have enough smoke flavor,** increase the smoking time or switch to a more pronounced flavored wood.

✔ If your meat includes **chemical flavors,** they're probably a result of lighter fluids or other combustibles you used when starting the fuel. Use resinous woods instead.

No matter how you decide to flavor your smoked meats, proper storage is essential for safe and delicious eating.

Hanging around

In your mind, you may envision smoked links of sausage and hams hanging in smokehouses, waiting to be eaten. The truth is, this is a risky way to store meats.

Most smoked meats will be eaten right away, but if you have any left over, or if you have too much smoked for immediate use, refrigerate the extra for up to three days. If you want to store them longer than three days, wrap and freeze the meat. Always refrigerate fish immediately after smoking. Freeze any extra fish after wrapping tightly in freezer paper.

Cold smoked foods are merely flavored. They need to be thoroughly cooked before eating.

Packaging tips

Smoked meats have such unique flavors, and you must package them properly if they're going to remain tasty and not impart that smoky flavoring on everything in the storage area around them.

Take any meat that you won't cook and eat right away and wrap it in airtight packaging and freeze it.

Simple Cedar Planked Salmon

Prep time: 1 hr • **Cook time:** 20 min • **Yield:** 6 servings

Ingredients	Directions
3 cedar planks	**1** Soak cedar planks for 1 hour. Combine all ingredients except salmon in a flat dish. Add salmon to dish and marinate for 20 minutes, turning pieces after 10 minutes.
⅓ cup vegetable oil	
⅓ cup tamari	
1 tablespoon rice wine vinegar	**2** Preheat grill to a medium high heat. Place planks on preheated grill and heat them until they smoke slightly. Place marinated salmon on heated planks. Close grill and cook salmon for 20 minutes.
1½ teaspoon sesame oil	
1 teaspoon chopped garlic	
2 pounds salmon fillets	

Per 3-ounce serving: *Calories 224 (From Fat 81); Fat 9g (Saturated 1g); Cholesterol 86mg; Sodium 317mg; Carbohydrates 0g (Dietary Fiber 0g); Protein 33g.*

Vary It! Change it up by using an olive oil and Italian herb mix.

Dry Rub for Ribs

Prep time: 10 min • **Yield:** 1 cup

Ingredients	Directions
¼ cup salt	**1** Combine all ingredients. Rub over every inch of meat, working the rub in well with your hands.
¼ cup pepper	
¼ cup paprika	**2** Allow meat to sit for 6 to 12 hours before smoking.
¼ cup garlic powder	

Per 1-tablespoon serving: *Calories 16 (From Fat 2); Fat 0g (Saturated 0g); Cholesterol 0mg; Sodium 1,746mg; Carbohydrates 3g (Dietary Fiber 1g); Protein 1g.*

Tip: Great for brisket, too!

Smoked Pork Loin

Prep time: 15 min, plus marinating • **Cook time:** 20 min per lb • **Yield:** Seasoning for 2 pork loins

Ingredients	Directions
¾ **cup Tender Quick**	**1** Combine all ingredients except the pork loin in a large baking dish. Rub the mixture over the entire surface of the pork tenderloins.
1¾ **cups brown sugar**	
2 tablespoons black pepper	
3 tablespoons garlic powder	**2** Place the pork in a pan and cover with water. Place in the refrigerator for 3 days. On the fourth day, smoke the pork, using apple wood, until the interior of the tenderloins reach 165°.
2 tablespoons onion powder	
2 pork tenderloins	

Per 3-ounce serving: *Calories 154 (From Fat 43); Fat 5g (Saturated 2g); Cholesterol 62mg; Sodium 814mg; Carbohydrates 5g (Dietary Fiber 0g); Protein 22g.*

Smoked Chicken Wings

Prep time: 20 min, plus marinating time • **Cook time:** 2 hr • **Yield:** Dry rub for 3 pounds wings

Ingredients	Directions
1 teaspoon salt	*1* Mix the salt, paprika, garlic powder, thyme, and black pepper well. Rub the chicken wings with olive oil. Sprinkle the herb mixture on all sides of the wings.
2 teaspoons paprika	
1 teaspoon garlic powder	
1 teaspoon ground thyme	*2* Seal the wings in a zippered plastic bag, or cover tightly with plastic wrap, and refrigerate 4 hours. Smoke the wings for 2 hours at 250°.
1 teaspoon black pepper	
3 pounds chicken wings	
¼ cup olive oil	

Per 3-ounce serving: Calories 290 (From Fat 202); Fat 22g (Saturated 5g); Cholesterol 1mg; Sodium 395mg; Carbohydrates 1g (Dietary Fiber 0g); Protein 20g.

Mop Sauce

Prep time: 5 min • **Yield:** Sauce for 2 pounds meat

Ingredients	Directions
2 tablespoons of your favorite dry rub	*1* Combine all ingredients.
½ cup apple cider vinegar	*2* Apply to your red meats with a barbeque mop.
½ cup beer	

Per 2-tablespoon serving: Calories 12 (From Fat 1); Fat 0g (Saturated 0g); Cholesterol 0mg; Sodium 437mg; Carbohydrates 2g (Dietary Fiber 0g); Protein 0g.

Vary It! Substitute plain water for the beer, if desired.

Pulled Pork Marinade

Prep time: 10 min, plus marinating time • **Yield:** Marinade for 2 pounds meat

Ingredients	*Directions*
⅔ **cup soy sauce**	**1** Combine all ingredients. Pour over sliced meat in a freezer bag or on a flat dish.
⅓ **Worcestershire sauce**	
2 tablespoons honey	**2** Marinate for a minimum of 3 hours.
3 teaspoons coarse ground pepper	
1 teaspoon liquid smoke	
2 pounds your choice of fresh pork	

Per 2-tablespoon serving: *Calories 35 (From Fat 0); Fat 0g (Saturated 0g); Cholesterol 0mg; Sodium 819mg; Carbohydrates 7g (Dietary Fiber 0g); Protein 1g.*

Vary It! Add heat by adding red pepper flakes. Or substitute maple syrup for the honey.

Smoke in a bottle

Liquid smoke is made from the condensed smoke coming off popular barbecue woods, like hickory and mesquite, as they're heated. The liquid is collected, filtered, and then bottled and shipped to the shelves of a grocery store near you. (Look for it among the condiments.)

In most cases, nothing goes into the bottle but the condensed smoke. Still, most liquid smoke products on the market have a distinct flavor that makes them easily discernable from the flavor that slow-smoking provides. Using liquid smoke is a shortcut, and shortcuts tend not to come off as well as the real thing.

Still, if you're short on time or live in an apartment or anywhere else that keeps you from doing actual smoking (or if you just have no interest in the smoking process), liquid smoke is a viable alternative. Its flavor is super-concentrated, so you need only a few drops to give smoke flavor to a sauce.

Dry Rub for Smoked Pork

Prep time: 10 min, plus refrigeration time • **Yield:** Dry rub for 2 pounds pork chops

Ingredients	*Directions*
¼ **cup brown sugar**	**1** Combine all ingredients. Rub the mixture into the surface of the pork chops.
¼ **cup paprika**	
2 tablespoons salt	
2 tablespoons black pepper	**2** Wrap tightly and refrigerate for 3 to 12 hours before smoking.
½ **tablespoon cayenne pepper**	
2 teaspoons dry mustard	
3 teaspoons garlic powder	
2 teaspoons ground thyme	
2 teaspoons ground sage	
1 tablespoon ground cumin	

Per 1-tablespoon serving: Calories 30 (From Fat 5); Fat 1g (Saturated 0g); Cholesterol 0mg; Sodium 1,000mg; Carbohydrates 6g (Dietary Fiber 1g); Protein 1g.

Dry Rub for Fish

Prep time: 10 min, plus refrigeration time • **Yield:** Dry rub for 2 pounds fish

Ingredients	Directions
1 cup maple sugar (not syrup) ½ cup salt	**1** Combine all ingredients. Rub the mixture over all sides of the fish.
1 tablespoon coarse ground pepper 2 tablespoons dried dill leaves 2 teaspoons powdered mustard	**2** Wrap tightly or place in a sealed dish and refrigerate for 2 hours before smoking.

Per 1-tablespoon serving: Calories 21 (From Fat 1); Fat 0g (Saturated 0g); Cholesterol 0mg; Sodium 2,068mg; Carbohydrates 5g (Dietary Fiber 0g); Protein 0g.

Vary It! If you can't find maple sugar, substitute brown sugar.

Chapter 3

Curing and Salting

In This Chapter

▶ Curing tips

▶ Choosing wet and dry rubs

▶ Experimenting with salts

Curing and salting meats are ways to preserve them. Curing indicates that a flavoring (containing salt) has been applied to the meat surface for a time, before cooking. Salting meats is another descriptive term for removing fluids from meat in order to store them.

Considering Curing

Curing meat is a preserving method that has a rich history. If you've ever tasted bacon, dried (chipped) beef, or real country ham, you've tasted the main ingredient in the curing process: salt. There's more to curing, however, than just salt. Adding other ingredients to the salt mixture helps to cut the strong salty taste and imparts a flavorful addition to the preserved meat.

Although popular for many years, plain salt curing successfully preserved meat but gave it a harsh flavor. Meats that are preserved country-style are sometimes plain salt cured, but they must be soaked before cooking to remove the excess salt and make the meat palatable.

No matter what type of meat you're preserving, you'll get the tastiest results if you use the best method for that meat. Table 3-1 lists some common meats and the best methods for preserving them.

Table 3-1	Meats and Methods of Preservation	
Meat	**Best Method(s) of Preservation**	**Additional Information**
Ham	Brining or dry curing. The choice depends on your personal preference.	Country-cured, or salt-cured, hams are often popular in the southern United States. Brine cured hams are injected with the flavored brine and then additionally submerged into more brine to be certain that the cure comes in contact with the entire piece of meat.
Bacon	Curing and then smoking. It's generally dry cured.	Bacon doesn't freeze well for more than a few months because of its high salt content, so take that into consideration when planning quantities to preserve. It may be better to cure smaller amounts more often.
Corned beef	Curing in a brine.	It takes 5 days or more of brining to create this succulent meat, but after you make the brine, nothing but time is necessary for the corning to happen.
Pastrami	Curing in a brine (corning) and then smoking.	Smoking the meat heightens the flavors infused by the corning process and turns ordinary beef into something spectacular.
Poultry	Curing.	Choices for poultry usually contain a lower amount of salt because the flavor is so delicate. Curing poultry imparts a lovely taste and pink color to the meat.
Fish	Curing.	Because of its delicate flesh, fish gives the best results if it's dry cured and not brined. If you choose to use wet brine, don't allow the fish to remain in the mixture for more than an hour, or it may become mushy.

Choosing dry or wet curing

The two types of cures are dry and wet (or brine) cures. Both types of cures are used for the same reason: to tenderize and preserve meat that will then be dried or smoked.

✔ **Dry cures** are applied directly to the meat. A dry cure transfers the flavor faster than a wet cure because it isn't diluted by any liquids. Dry cures are a good choice for beginners because they require no equipment other than the meat, the cure, and the container that holds the coated meat.

Dry cures are available premixed, containing the sugar, the seasonings, and the actual ingredient that does the curing. Dry cures help season the meat, adding an appealing color and characteristic flavor.

Any dry rub includes the same basic ingredients: salt, sugar, and nitrate and/or nitrite.

✔ **Wet curing,** also known as pickling or corning, is the art of creating a seasoned brine that covers the piece of meat, allowing flavoring and moisture to be absorbed over time. Wet cures are as individual as the location from which they originated.

Wet cures can also be injected directly into the meat. This step speeds up the curing process and increases juiciness of the end product. Injection is a common technique used in today's meat preservation.

Salting and sugaring

Salting and *sugaring* refer to mixtures of ingredients that are single steps to the overall process of preserving. Salt is the primary ingredient used to cure meat. When it was first used alone, it preserved the meat by dehydration and osmosis, which inhibited bad bacteria from flourishing. (*Osmosis* is a natural process by which moisture moves out of a cell because of the higher concentration of salt outside the cell's wall.) When a meat is said to be cured country style, it means that the salt curing process was used.

Sugaring is another way to add to a preserved meat's overall flavor profile. Sugaring is a misnomer because the process also includes salt. Sugaring is sometimes called a sweet pickle cure because the brine used is sweetened with brown sugar and/or molasses. Sugar curing is most often done to pork products. Meats that are sugared need to be cooked before eating.

Knowing nitrates and nitrites

People eventually realized that meats were more flavorful and more visually appealing with the addition of *potassium nitrate*. This chemical, also known as saltpeter, kept the meat an attractive pink color and helped to inhibit the growth of bacteria. It gave preserved meats the tanginess you associate with these foods. Although people no longer use saltpeter, sodium nitrite, the modern version, is still used when curing.

There has been much controversy over the use of nitrates and food safety. The United States Department of Agriculture (USDA) has come to the conclusion that the amounts of nitrates in meat should be regulated, but under their guidelines, nitrates are considered safe.

Nitrates are used in such small amounts that they're mixed with salt in order to be accurately measured. For this reason, preserving mixes are often premade and sold with the nitrates included. Using a mix ensures that you don't use too much. This ingredient is sold in premixed form, under names like Morton's Sugar Cure, Tender Quick, or Bradley's Sugar Cure. You add it to meat based on weight. What could be easier?

Experimenting with Salting

What makes preserving meats so interesting is that after you get the basics down, you have limitless ways to create your own special flavors. Experimenting with salting meats is a great way to make just what your family enjoys eating. The difference in a food that's eaten and one that's passed up may just be the flavorings you add.

Choosing between brining or dry curing

How do you choose which technique to use? Although you can create your own recipes, the best results depend on the type of meat you're working with. Brining and dry curing both tenderize meats, and, arguably, brining also adds moisture. A good general rule is to use a brine for thick or heavy cuts of meat (a whole turkey, roasts, a whole carcass); the brine ensures that the flavoring gets into every portion of the meat. That doesn't mean that dry rubs won't work with these types of meat, but it will take much longer for the moisture/flavor exchange to happen.

Testing the techniques

Testing is a matter of changing up the meats you use, the addition of seasonings and brining times, letting a rub sit before smoking, and more. Take notes on your recipe changes to be sure that you can re-create your successes and avoid making mistakes that result in anything less than brag worthy.

You have endless recipes waiting to be discovered as long as you remember the main ingredients to any successful meat cure: Salt, sugar, and nitrates or nitrites. Use a premade mix like Quick Cure and add your own flavorings, to keep things simple and successful.

Mixing up flavorings

After you decide on the process of curing, the fun begins. Creating new flavors is what makes meat preservation such an interesting hobby. Using only one kind of meat, you can create multiple finished flavors by simply changing up the curing seasonings.

The basic ingredients for a cure are salt, sugar, and nitrates or nitrites. Other than the nitrate/nitrite ingredient (sold as Pink Salt), which should be a purchased product, you can switch the other ingredients to suit your individual taste preference. If you're looking for inspiration, consider the following ideas:

- ✔ **Sugar:** Try substituting plain, white sugar for brown sugar, honey, maple syrup, or molasses. Or mix different sugars for a whole new taste.

- ✔ **Salt:** When adding salt to the cure, try some of the newer smoked salts. They come with a natural smoky flavor already in them, and they can add just the right amount of different taste.

    Don't use iodized salt. Iodine can impart unwanted flavor into your meat.

- ✔ **Spicy heat:** Every cure would benefit from adding a little bit of heat. Depending on your preference, this heat can be a pinch or more. Cayenne pepper is a simple way to increase the spice without going overboard. Many hot peppers are now available in powdered form if you're daring enough to try them.

- ✔ **Herbs:** When choosing herbs to include in the brine or dry rub, use the most fragrant ones you can find. Old herbs don't have much flavor left in them. Powder the herbs just before adding to the mix for the most flavor. Choose herbs that you'd normally use to season your meat on the plate; this tip ensures that the herbs will complement the finished product.

Always keep track of what you're adding by writing it down. Forgetting an ingredient is easy to do, and if it happens, you may not be able to replicate your favorite recipe again.

Book VIII

Smoking, Salting, and Curing

Troubleshooting and Storage

Anyone interested in preserving her own meats at home can feel a special connection to the days of old. This thread to the past is important and can give you many tried and true recipes for successful outcomes. Remember that science has discovered that many of the preservation techniques used in times of old actually aren't safe. You no longer have to take chances with bacterial growth and food-borne illnesses.

To avoid problems, remember these simple rules:

- **Smell:** Simply cutting off or overcooking meat that smells spoiled is no longer acceptable. It was once thought that rotten meat could still be eaten if it was cooked thoroughly. Discard any meat that has a foul, fishy, or simply off odor.

- **Mold:** Although there are beneficial molds that help ferment meats, avoid all mold unless you're experienced enough to know with 100-percent certainty that you're dealing with one of those beneficial molds. If your meat develops mold, it's recommended that you discard the entire piece. Be sure to write down the experience, temperature, and any other distinguishing issues with that batch of meat.

- **Temperature:** Temperature is essential to producing a healthy, edible piece of meat. Use a proper thermometer and don't rely on any other method to be sure that you're storing your meats at the correct temperature.

- **Cleanliness:** It may have been that in olden days, settlers would prepare and store meats in less than sanitary conditions. Doing so is no longer necessary in modern times. Be sure to clean all surfaces, utensils, and your own hands any time you're working with meats.

- **Avoiding nitrates:** Nitrates/nitrites are an important part of the meat curing process. The concern over nitrates in food has been tempered by the use of commercially premixed seasonings. Using a mix ensures that you use the smallest amount needed. They're toxic in larger doses.

Meeting the bad guys

Preserving meat properly depends on sticking with basic guidelines and knowing what problems look like. Careful observation is needed to evaluate the freshness and safety of your dried meats.

- **Molds:** Some varieties of mold are actually beneficial to the flavoring and fermenting of meats. Proper temperature, moisture, and air circulation are key to preventing dangerous mold growth. Be sure to closely follow the recipe for your particular cut of meat and adhere to the exact recommendations. If you find mold growing on your meat, it's safest to throw it away and start fresh.

- **Botulism:** *C. botulinum* spores are found naturally in soil and water. The spores can also sometimes be found in honey. The spores themselves aren't dangerous until they germinate. Once they do, botulism is produced. Although extremely rare, botulism is also dangerous. Botulism is tasteless and odorless, so it's important to prevent botulism from the start. Nitrites prevent the formation of the botulism toxins.

- **Listeria:** *Listeria monocytogenes* is a type of bacteria that's found naturally in water and soil. Listeria has been found in home-cured meats. Listeria causes flu-like symptoms, muscle aches, stiff neck, and even convulsions. Dangerous for anyone, listeria can cause miscarriage or premature birth in pregnant women and should be avoided by everyone. The USDA recommends heating all home-cured meats and deli meats to steaming hot before eating. Listeria is even found in vacuum-sealed meats, so be safe and heat before eating.

Storage solutions

Many people start preserving meats because they have a large amount of product at once and they need to store it properly. Back in the day, people successfully hung meats in smokehouses or even in the rafters, and they cut off portions as needed. Modern day storage enthusiasts no longer store meat in potentially unsafe ways.

Hanging meat

Hanging meats is a normal step to some preservation methods. The hanging process is done in a heat- and moisture-controlled area that allows the beneficial bacteria to develop and flavor (ferment) the meat. This technique is common in sausage making. (See Book VIII, Chapter 4 for more on sausage making.)

Hanging meat before cutting is still used today at many small-town meat processors. A fresh carcass is hung for ten days or more, until it's cut and wrapped. We hang our beef carcasses for 18 days before processing, and they're delicious.

Book VIII

Smoking, Salting, and Curing

When hanging meat for storage, the temperature of the area is very important. The meat must remain at a low enough temperature and humidity to inhibit unwanted mold and bacterial growth. The ideal temperature is between 50° and 60°. Humidity also plays a part in the drying and storing process. Proper humidity is between 65 and 80 percent. A digital hygrometer is a small unit that accurately measures both of these things at the same time.

When hanging meat for curing, the most accurate way to gauge whether meat is finished curing is to weigh it. The texture changes as the moisture evaporates, and it's a matter of personal taste when that's finished.

Wrapping meat

Wrapping meat correctly is the final step to keeping all your hard work tasting fresh. Before hanging, meats are often wrapped in paper or cloth. This step keeps off dust and contaminants, and it provides that extra measure of protection to your dried product.

Salting herbs

In the days when folks' home freezers were smaller than their radios, Grandma would salt down her tender herbs. If you have some space in your own pantry or root cellar, you may want to experiment with this method, which leaves herbs tasting surprisingly fresh.

Cover the bottom of a glass or ceramic container (which has an airtight lid) with a layer of noniodized or kosher salt and then add a single layer of herbs. Barely cover the herbs with salt and add another layer of herbs. Continue alternate layering, ending with a salt layer.

You can leave dill or flat-leaf parsley on its stems, but strip the leaves of other herbs to make sure that they lie flat. Seal and store in a cool, dark place. Rinse the salt off the herbs as you use them.

Corned Beef

Prep time: 20 min, plus brining time • **Cook time:** 2½ hr • **Yield:** Brine for up to 5 pounds beef brisket

Ingredients	*Directions*
1 gallon water 2 cups kosher salt ½ cup sugar 4 teaspoons Pink Salt 4 tablespoons pickling spice 5 pounds brisket 2 medium onions 2 medium carrots 2 celery stalks 6 cloves of garlic	*1* Combine the water, salt, sugar, Pink Salt, and 2 tablespoons pickling spice in a large pot. Bring to a boil, stirring often, until the salt and sugar are dissolved. *2* Remove from heat and cool to room temperature. Refrigerate until cold. *3* Place the brisket in a large stockpot and cover with the cold brine. Refrigerate for at least 5 days. *4* Remove the meat from the brine and rinse. Place the meat in a large pot. Add just enough water to cover the meat and add the 2 remaining tablespoons pickling spice. *5* Chop the onions, carrots, celery, and garlic and add them to the pot. Bring to a boil. Reduce heat and simmer 2½ hours or until meat is tender.

Per 1-ounce serving: Calories 92 (From Fat 61); Fat 7g (Saturated 3g); Cholesterol 26mg; Sodium 234mg; Carbohydrates 0g (Dietary Fiber 0g); Protein 7g.

Vary It! Leave out the garlic if desired.

Brined Turkey

Prep time: 20 min, plus brining • **Cook time:** 4–4½ hr • **Yield:** Brine for up to 20-lb turkey

Ingredients	*Directions*
2 quarts water	*1* Combine the water, salt, and brown sugar in a large pot. Stir until dissolved.
1 cup salt	
1 cup brown sugar	*2* Slice the lemon and orange. Place the sliced fruit into the pot of water and add the cinnamon sticks and cloves.
1 medium lemon	
1 medium orange	
2 cinnamon sticks	*3* Place the turkey into a large canning pot or stockpot. Pour the brine over the bird and add fresh water to cover. Refrigerate the brined bird overnight.
⅛ cup whole cloves	
One 20-pound turkey	
	4 The following day, remove the bird from the brine, and roast, covered, at 325° for 4 to 4½ hours, or until internal temperature reaches 165°.

Per 1-ounce serving: Calories 62 (From Fat 27); Fat 3g (Saturated 1g); Cholesterol 22mg; Sodium 155mg; Carbohydrates 0g (Dietary Fiber 0g); Protein 8g.

Pastrami

Prep time: 20 min • **Cook time:** 5 hr • **Yield:** 1½ pounds pastrami

Ingredients	Directions
1½ pounds corned beef	**1** Dry the corned beef completely.
¼ cup coriander seeds	
¼ cup peppercorns	**2** Coarsely grind the coriander and peppercorns together. Press the coriander/peppercorn coating into the entire surface of the meat.
	3 Smoke the coated meat at 225° for 1 hour per pound.

Per 1-ounce serving: *Calories 92 (From Fat 59); Fat 7g (Saturated 3g); Cholesterol 24mg; Sodium 222mg; Carbohydrates 1g (Dietary Fiber 1g); Protein 7g.*

Wet Rub for Fish

Prep time: 20 min, plus wrap time • **Cook time:** 1½ hr • **Yield:** 1 cup

Ingredients	Directions
1 cup real maple syrup	**1** Apply the maple syrup to the fish fillets on both sides. Sprinkle liberally with salt. Wrap tightly and refrigerate overnight.
1 tablespoon salt	
2 pounds fish	
	2 Smoke the fish for 1½ hours at 200°, or until the fish is opaque and flakes easily.

Per 1-ounce serving: *Calories 51 (From Fat 8); Fat 1g (Saturated 0g); Cholesterol 13mg; Sodium 196mg; Carbohydrates 6g (Dietary Fiber 0g); Protein 5g.*

Note: Use a fruity wood, such as apple or cherry, for the smoking process.

Yellow Mustard Wet Rub

Prep time: 20 min, plus wrap time • **Yield:** Rub for up to 3 pounds meat

Ingredients	*Directions*
1 tablespoon cracked peppercorns	*1* Combine the pepper, salt, garlic powder, Italian seasoning, and paprika in a bowl. Rub the yellow mustard over the entire piece of meat of your choice. Press the dry mixture over the surface of the mustard-coated meat.
4 tablespoons salt	
1 tablespoon garlic powder	
2 tablespoons Italian seasoning	*2* Wrap the meat tightly in plastic wrap for at least 1 hour or overnight if possible. Grill or smoke to desired doneness.
1 tablespoon paprika	
¼ cup yellow mustard	

Per 1-tablespoon serving: Calories 10 (From Fat 3); Fat 0g (Saturated 0g); Cholesterol 0mg; Sodium 2,382mg; Carbohydrates 2g (Dietary Fiber 1g); Protein 1g.

Chapter 4

Making Sausages

Making sausage is a simple concept. If you can mix a meatloaf, you have the basics of making a great sausage. The trick is figuring out how to combine the right seasonings to create the taste that you and your family will love.

Assembling Your Equipment

Making sausage requires simple equipment. If you're making sausage in patties or in bulk, you need only the seasonings and ground meat. Traditional sausage links require casings and a stuffer. No matter what equipment you have, making delicious sausage is worth the effort.

For simple sausage making, you need the following essentials:

- **Ground meat:** You can choose any meat, and it should be as fresh as possible. Buy only what you can prepare right away because the meat must stay as cold as possible throughout the process. If you have meat that isn't ground, you need a meat grinder.

- **Ground fat:** Fat is essential to the flavor and shape of good sausage. Many recipes suggest proper meat-to-fat ratios and types of meats that you can combine for further flavoring.

- **Seasoning:** The sky is the limit when it comes to seasonings. Start with recipes and work your way up to experimenting on your own. Seasonings make the difference between a so-so patty of ground meat and a fantastic sausage patty.

✔ **Casings:** This ingredient is actually optional. Casings create the links you're familiar with, but beginning sausage makers have an easier time starting with loose sausage or sausage patties.

Grinding and stuffing

Making sausage starts with the meat itself. Choose meat with no skin, gristle, bone, or blood clots. Because a tasty sausage means a juicy one, you usually add fat to the lean meat in a ratio of two parts meat to one part fat. Avoid adding too much fat, or your sausages will shrink too much when you heat them. Fat, however, is an essential part of the sausage-making process. Fat provides taste, of course, and also moisture. Leaving out this essential ingredient results in a dry, stringy product.

Pork shoulder and beef chuck have the perfect ratio of lean meat to fat. No additional fat is needed.

The meat must be ground in order to make the sausage. When grinding meat the more spiced the sausage, the coarser the grind you need. Most grinders come with blades (plates) that chop the meat into the recommended grind. Follow the recommendations in the recipe.

To get the right texture, you may need to grind the meat before changing the plate and regrinding the meat. Water and/or ice is often added to the meat because grinding causes heat, which melts the fat. Melted fat leads to an undesirable texture, so cooling the meat as you grind is necessary.

Both manual and electric grinders work very well for home sausage making. The electric variety often has additional attachments for stuffing the already ground meat. You don't, however, need a stuffing attachment to make sausage. You can create patties, leave sausage in bulk, and even create your own shaped sausage and wrap it by hand.

Casings and wrappings

For a professional look, casings are essential. Originally, using a casing meant using natural sheep or pig casings, and these options may still be available in your area. These casings are actually the cleaned and sanitized intestine from the animal. These animal intestines have been used for thousands of years, and they provide what's known as the bite, or snap, that some sausages have. Natural casings are completely edible, although they may be difficult and expensive for the home sausage maker.

Casings made from other substances are also available. Casings made from collagen are more readily available and less expensive. They come in both edible and inedible varieties, so note the difference on the packaging. They've been improved in recent years, providing a more flavorful bite than they're known for. Collagen casings are easier for the home sausage maker to manipulate, making them a good choice. Made from the natural collagen found in beef or pork hides, tendons, and bones, they are completely digestible.

Casings can be made from completely inedible ingredients, such as plastic or cellulose. Cellulose casings are designed to hold the sausage shape through the cooking and/or curing process and then are made to be cut or peeled away. Modern mass-produced hot dogs or skinless franks are made by using cellulose casings.

You can also use oven wrap–style plastic, parchment paper, and even foil in sausage making. For the home sausage maker, these materials may be the most useful way to experiment with sausage links. These DIY casings are perfect for some of the fancier sausages that you'll be making tiny batches of, when pulling out the stuffer is more work than it's worth. Making your own wrapping is also a great way to jump in and get started without investing much time or money.

Look for the recommended width of the casings that a recipe calls for. They come in various sizes, from ¾ inch to 20 inches in diameter!

Pulling Together Your Ingredients

The basis of all great sausage is the meat. Whether you want poultry, pork, beef, or wild game, use the best meat for the job. Some meats, such as goat or wild game and even some poultry, have fat that can taste bad when cooked into sausage. Because a clean-tasting fat is the second most important ingredient, adding good-tasting fat is essential. Flavorings like salts, herbs, and fillers all add to the dimension of taste that you find in the world of sausages. You'll find a wide variety of old-school ingredients to try, with plenty of new ideas for flavorings. Sausage-making ingredients offer endless possibilities.

Meeting the meats

No one meat makes the best sausage; each variety has its fans. Meat should be fresh and high quality. It should have the right lean meat to fat ratio and should be clean. The finished sausage won't improve the taste of lesser quality or old meat. If you follow this rule, you can make pretty much any meat into delicious sausages. But first consider these main players:

Book VIII

Smoking, Salting, and Curing

- **Pork:** Of all the meats, pork is the most common for sausage. Pork takes on a delicious tang when cured, and you can choose from a wide variety of recipes for this one type of meat. When choosing pork, use pork shoulder or pork trimmings with the ratio of fat to meat that the recipe calls for.

- **Beef:** Beef makes fantastic sausage, hot dogs, and dried summer sausage. It can, of course, be used for any sausage recipe you have. When using beef, be certain to have the correct ratio of meat to fat. Beef's mild flavor works well in combination with other meats as well.

- **Poultry:** Chicken, turkey, and even wild game birds all make great sausage. Their naturally mild-flavored meat picks up seasonings very well. If you're using poultry to avoid red meat, don't forget that casings can come from a red-meat animal. If this is an issue, use an alternative casing or create bulk sausage and make patties.

- **Wild game:** Venison is the most common meat in wild game sausage, and these sausages taste fabulous! They do require the addition of fat, and sometimes additional meat, to make the correct ratio.

- **Vegetarian:** You can make tasty sausage without using meat. Although nontraditional, you can make sausages by using mashed beans, TVP (textured vegetable protein), tofu, and bulgur wheat. These sausages are flavored with the same seasonings as regular sausage, but they're hand-formed into patties or link shapes and then unwrapped after cooking.

Filling with fillers

Fillers for sausage aren't just a meal stretcher. Although they do increase the recipe size, they're important for flavoring and texture. Fillers include items like bread, dry milk powder, flour, egg, bulgur wheat, onions, and garlic. You can even add vegetable bits if the flavors are complementary.

Sausage recipes with additional fillers can still be smoked and cured, but take care, because the addition of fillers means a shorter shelf life. Consider the alternative recipes for sausage to be used up quickly, like fresh sausage.

Processing with a Plan

Processing begins the fun part of sausage making. At this point, you prep your available ingredients and lay out a plan for creating your sausages. Are you making links or patties, simply putting up as much bulk Italian sausage as you can, or creating a whole new spice mixture? Now is the time to get your hands in the mix!

Prepping the ingredients

After you decide on the recipe, the next step is prep. Follow all basic food safety guidelines:

- ✔ Reduce the spread of bacteria by washing your hands before and during the sausage-making process.

- ✔ Start with a clean work area and clean meat. This means fresh meat, kept at the proper temperature.

- ✔ Marinate raw meat in the refrigerator only. Don't allow it to come to room temperature.

- ✔ Keep the meat as cold as possible during processing. This means adding ice to the meat as you grind and working quickly to get the product back into the refrigerator as soon as you can. Placing meat in the freezer for 30 minutes before grinding can also result in a better grind.

- ✔ Use a thermometer and not just the dial on a smoker and/or dehydrator to be certain that you're processing the meat at the correct temperature.

Choosing techniques

If you're a beginning sausage maker, get used to the technique by starting with easier products that have fewer steps. You can find hundreds of ways to make a simple sausage, using purchased ground meat and adding spices. Make your sausage into patties and fill your freezer. After you become savvy to the process, begin making links and wrapping them by hand. Stuffing with casings is the next logical step, and by then, you'll be familiar enough with the sausage-making process that it'll be easy. Smoking and curing sausages isn't difficult, but it may overwhelm the beginner. Try these techniques after simple sausage making comes easily.

Storing Sausages

Storing methods depend on the type of sausage you're making. The basic idea is the same for all types: Keep the meat as cold as possible and eat it as soon as you can. But some sausages have a longer shelf life that decreases dramatically after you open them. All sausage needs to be in the refrigerator, and most can withstand the freezer nicely. Check out Table 4-1 for details on how to store your final product.

Book VIII

Smoking, Salting, and Curing

Table 4-1   Best Storage Practices for a Variety of Sausages

Type of Sausage	Examples	Tips	Shelf Life
Fresh	Loose breakfast sausage, Italian style, etc.	Refrigerate immediately	Up to 3 days
Smoked, uncooked	Any homemade sausage that is simply smoked	Best eaten as soon as possible	Up to 7 days
Smoked, cooked	Bologna, hot dogs	Freeze for up to 3 months	Once opened, use within 7 days
Dry sausage	Pepperoni and Genoa salami	Open only when it will be used fairly quickly	Once opened, eat within 7 days
Semi-dry	Summer sausage	Keep cold; don't allow to warm to room temp and then re-chill	Unopened: 3 months Opened: 3 weeks
Specialty	Scrapple, head cheeses	Keep refrigerated; best used right away	Up to 3 days after opening

Smoking for flavor and preservation

Smoked sausage is heated in order to add a new facet of flavor and to pasteurize it. This process extends its shelf life, improves overall appearance, fixes the color, and, in the case of hand-wrapped links, causes the sausage to retain its shape.

Smoke sausages until they reach the correct internal temperature; check the temp by using a calibrated thermometer. You can't rely solely on the dials on the smoker itself.

Although smoking meat is an art, most smoked sausage recipes include temperature and time, taking the guesswork out of this technique.

Freezing for long-term storage

In the case of sausage making, the freezer is your friend. Because sausage is a ground product, often with additives and extensive handling, it has a shorter shelf life than a plain cut of meat. Freezing is the answer!

If you're making a larger quantity of sausage than you can consume within three to seven days, wrap it tightly and freeze it. Better yet, use a vacuum sealer and freeze small amounts that you'll use up in one meal.

Trying Some Troubleshooting Tips

All the traditional issues you have with raw meat come into play with sausage. Meat must remain as cold as possible. Don't allow it to come to room temperature and then cool it numerous times. Work quickly and efficiently to get your processing finished as soon as possible and to get the finished product back into the refrigerator or freezer.

Knowing the enemy

What's the worry with sausage? The truth is that the more a meat is handled and added to, the greater the chance of introducing bad bacteria. Working so much with raw meat just provides that much more opportunity to spread bacteria throughout the work area and contaminate surfaces that aren't even part of your sausage making equipment.

Food-borne illness is the sickness you get as a result of eating contaminated foods. Because meat is highly perishable, it's a good candidate for harboring this contamination. Food-borne illnesses include *E. coli* and botulism, and those are just the most talked about. The symptoms of eating bacteria-laden food include diarrhea, cramping, fever, and vomiting. Because these symptoms may not develop for up to two weeks after ingesting the offensive food, tracking the original problem can be difficult. When making sausage at home, it's imperative that you follow food safety guidelines and know the problems that you *can* see.

Book VIII

Smoking, Salting, and Curing

Spotting the problems

Some signs that your sausage may be in trouble include

✔ **Bulging casings:** This issue may be caused by air pockets that remain after the initial filling of the casings, so when you do the filling, poke air pockets out as you go and work carefully. If you see any new bulges, however, discard the sausage.

✔ **Off smells:** Distinguishing these odors in cold sausage may be difficult, but do smell the product carefully before eating. Sometimes you miss it in the cold product, but after it begins cooking, the off odor becomes very clear. Discard any sausage that you think even *might* smell bad.

✔ **Mold:** Molds are tricky. For the beginning sausage maker, mold should never be present. Some molds help create specific types of sausage (salami for example), but they're fuzzy white molds, and the experienced sausage maker will know to look for it during a specific time frame. At home, any mold is suspicious, especially if it's blue, green, or black in color. Discard any moldy meat.

✔ **Forgotten meat, or meat that's left out too long:** It happens. Everyone forgets a batch, or something gets pushed back to the rear of the fridge. If your sausage has been forgotten and come to room temperature, or if you discover it in the back of the refrigerator, discard it. Even a tiny amount of bad bacteria can make you seriously ill.

Cabrito Sausage

Prep time: 15 min • **Yield:** 2 pounds

Ingredients	Directions
2 teaspoons ground sage	*1* Combine the sage, salt, pepper, and chili powder. Combine the ground cabrito and the ground pork. Sprinkle over the meat mixture and combine thoroughly.
1½ teaspoons salt	
1½ teaspoons pepper	
½ teaspoon chili powder	
1 pound ground cabrito (goat meat)	*2* Form into several patties or keep in bulk as desired. Wrap tightly and refrigerate for 3 days to cure and allow flavor to develop. If storing for longer than 3 days, freeze for up to 1 month.
1 pound ground pork	

Per 3-ounce serving: Calories 183 (From Fat 88); Fat 10g (Saturated 4g); Cholesterol 70mg; Sodium 506mg; Carbohydrates 1g (Dietary Fiber 0g); Protein 22g.

Bulk Breakfast Sausage

Prep time: 10 min • **Yield:** 1 pound

Ingredients	Directions
¼ teaspoon ground thyme	*1* Combine the thyme, sage, pepper, and salt. Sprinkle over the meat and combine thoroughly.
¼ teaspoon ground sage	
¼ teaspoon ground black pepper	*2* Form into several patties or keep in bulk as desired. Wrap tightly and refrigerate for 3 days to cure and allow flavor to develop. If storing for longer than 3 days, freeze for up to 1 month.
1 teaspoon salt	
1 pound ground pork	

Per 2-ounce serving: Calories 165 (From Fat 104); Fat 12g (Saturated 4g); Cholesterol 52mg; Sodium 441mg; Carbohydrates 0g (Dietary Fiber 0g); Protein 14g.

Vary It! Add red pepper flakes for a spicier version of this sausage.

Bulk Italian Sausage

Prep time: 10 min • **Yield:** 1 pound

Ingredients	Directions
1 medium onion, minced	**1** Add the onion and garlic to the meat and combine thoroughly. Sprinkle the remaining seasonings over the meat mixture and mix again, until evenly dispersed throughout.
2 cloves garlic, minced	
½ teaspoon black pepper	
½ tablespoon salt	**2** Form into several patties or keep in bulk as desired. Wrap tightly and refrigerate for 3 days to cure and allow flavor to develop. If storing for longer than 3 days, freeze for up to 1 month.
½ teaspoon fennel seed	
¼ teaspoon thyme	
½ teaspoon paprika	
¼ teaspoon cayenne	
1 pound ground pork	

Per 3-ounce serving: Calories 205 (From Fat 124); Fat 14g (Saturated 5g); Cholesterol 62mg; Sodium 523mg; Carbohydrates 2g (Dietary Fiber 1g); Protein 17g.

Bulk Farm Sausage

Prep time: 15 min • **Yield:** 3 pounds

Ingredients	*Directions*
1½ teaspoons black pepper 1 tablespoon salt ⅛ teaspoon ground thyme ½ teaspoon marjoram 4 cloves minced garlic 2 pounds ground raw pork 1 pound ground bacon ½ cup ice water	*1* Combine the pepper, salt, thyme, marjoram, and garlic. Combine the pork and bacon and sprinkle the spice mixture over the meat evenly; mix well. *2* Pour ice water over the mixture and mix again. Form into several patties or keep in bulk as desired. If storing for longer than 3 days, freeze for up to 1 month.

Per 2-ounce serving: Calories 192 (From Fat 128); Fat 14g (Saturated 5g); Cholesterol 50mg; Sodium 674mg; Carbohydrates 1g (Dietary Fiber 0g); Protein 15g.

Vary It! Spice it up with up to 2 teaspoons ground cayenne pepper.

Venison Sausage

Prep time: 15 min • **Yield:** 10 pounds

Ingredients	*Directions*
6 pounds ground venison	*1* Combine the ground meats and mix well. Combine the red pepper, salt, sage, pepper, and garlic. Stir the spice mixture into the water.
4 pounds ground pork shoulder	
4 tablespoons crushed red pepper flakes	*2* Pour the spice and water mixture over the ground meat and mix well. Make patties and refrigerate for up to 3 days, or freeze for up to 3 months.
6 tablespoons kosher salt	
1½ tablespoons ground sage	
5 tablespoons black pepper	
3 tablespoons garlic powder	
1½ cups ice water	

Per 3-ounce serving: Calories 184 (From Fat 82); Fat 9g (Saturated 3g); Cholesterol 82mg; Sodium 557mg; Carbohydrates 2g (Dietary Fiber 1g); Protein 23g.

Tip: When adding sage, use a light hand if you plan on freezing. Sage becomes very pronounced after being frozen, and you may end up with too strong a flavor. Once thawed, add more sage while cooking if desired.

Fresh Chicken Sausage

Prep time: 15 min • **Cook time:** 10 min • **Yield:** 1½ pounds

Ingredients	*Directions*
1 egg 1 cup milk 1 small onion, finely minced ½ teaspoon ground sage 1 tablespoon finely chopped parsley 1 pound finely ground raw chicken, containing skin and both dark/light meat	*1* Beat the egg, milk, onion, sage, and parsley until combined. Add to the ground chicken and mix thoroughly. *2* Make small patties and cook in a frying pan with a small amount of water until golden brown.

Per 3-ounce serving: Calories 95 (From Fat 39); Fat 4g (Saturated 2g); Cholesterol 67mg; Sodium 56mg; Carbohydrates 3g (Dietary Fiber 0g); Protein 11g.

Vary It! Try substituting other fresh herbs that pair well with poultry, such as rosemary.

Meatless Sausage

Prep time: 15 min • **Cook time:** 6 min • **Yield:** 4–6 servings

Ingredients	*Directions*
2 cups cooked and mashed lentils	*1* Combine the mashed lentils, breadcrumbs, oil, eggs, salt, pepper, and sage. Form the mixture into patties.
1 cup breadcrumbs	
½ cup coconut oil or olive oil	*2* Dip the patties lightly in flour. Fry until golden brown.
2 eggs	
1 teaspoon salt	
1 teaspoon pepper	
2 teaspoons fresh sage or 1 teaspoon dried sage, or to taste	
⅓ cup flour	

Per 3-ounce serving: Calories 237 (From Fat 127); Fat 14g (Saturated 11g); Cholesterol 47mg; Sodium 378mg; Carbohydrates 21g (Dietary Fiber 4g); Protein 7g.

Vary It! Use whatever kind of beans you have in place of the lentils.

Fish Sausage

Prep time: 15 min • **Cook time:** 15–20 min • **Yield:** 2 pounds

Ingredients	Directions
2 pounds canned salmon	**1** Combine all ingredients.
1 egg	
½ teaspoon pepper	**2** Form into patties and fry in butter.
1 teaspoon salt	
¼ teaspoon ground bay leaf	
¼ teaspoon smoked paprika	
1 teaspoon lemon or lime juice	
2 tablespoons butter	

Per 3-ounce serving: *Calories 135 (From Fat 77); Fat 9g (Saturated 3g); Cholesterol 73mg; Sodium 536mg; Carbohydrates 0g (Dietary Fiber 0g); Protein 15g.*

Note: Fish sausage doesn't freeze well. Use it fresh.

Fresh Polish-Style Sausage

Prep time: 15 min • **Cook time:** 15 min • **Yield:** 2 pounds

Ingredients	Directions
3 cloves garlic, finely minced 1½ teaspoons white pepper	**1** Combine the garlic, white pepper, and marjoram. Add the spices to the ice water and mix well.
1 tablespoon fresh chopped marjoram 1 cup ice water	**2** Pour the spices and water over the ground meat and mix thoroughly. Form into patties.
2 pounds ground pork butt 3 bottles of dark beer	**3** Simmer the patties in beer until brown and no longer pink in middle.

Per 3-ounce serving: *Calories 178 (From Fat 90); Fat 10g (Saturated 4g); Cholesterol 67mg; Sodium 57mg; Carbohydrates 1g (Dietary Fiber 0g); Protein 19g.*

Vary It! This recipe may be stuffed into hog casings if desired. They taste wonderful grilled.

Note: Because this is a fresh sausage, you must freeze it if you don't use it within 3 days.

Summer Sausage

Prep time: 30 min, plus refrigeration time • **Cook time:** 1½ hr • **Yield:** Two 1-pound rolls

Ingredients	Directions
2 pounds ground beef	*1* Mix ingredients well and place in the refrigerator for 12 hours. Remove from the refrigerator and remix. Divide the cold mixture in half and shape into rolls.
2 tablespoons Tender Quick	
1 teaspoon liquid smoke	
½ teaspoon garlic powder	*2* Wrap each roll tightly with foil. Place the rolls in the refrigerator to cure for up to 4 days, if desired. Poke several holes in the foil to allow excess fat to drain away.
1 teaspoon black pepper	
½ cup cold water	
	3 Place in a broiler pan and bake at 325° for 1½ hours. You can eat this sausage cold or freeze it for up to 3 months.

Per 2-ounce serving: Calories 137 (From Fat 79); Fat 9g (Saturated 4g); Cholesterol 45mg; Sodium 885mg; Carbohydrates 0g (Dietary Fiber 0g); Protein 13g.

Book IX
Juicing

"Jane start drying fruit. Before that, we just eat cheetah. Too much fast food not good."

In this book . . .

*J*uicing is not only for athletes! In this book, you find out what is involved in adding juicing to your family's diet. The equipment is not especially difficult to find, but what you buy needs to fit the style of juicing you see yourself doing. We include a huge list of savory, sweet, cleansing, and filling juice recipes to get you started.

Chapter 1

Juicing for Better Health

• •

In This Chapter

▶ Fitting juicing into your life

▶ Creating your own blends

▶ Storing juice for optimum nutrition

• •

We all know how many servings of fruits and vegetables it takes to get our RDA of nutrition each day. And we also know that it is rare to succeed in following those guidelines.

Juicing is a perfect way to increase the fresh fruits and veggies you eat, in a portable package. In this chapter, we show you how easy it is to create delicious juices that your whole family will love to drink.

Appreciating the Power of Juicing

Juicing is simply a matter of breaking down foods, to release the juice within. Depending on the type of juicer you use, every part of the fruit or vegetable is liquefied, ensuring that you're getting all the vitamins, minerals, and fiber your body craves.

Which would you rather do: Eat a bowl containing 2 apples, 2 carrots, and a cup of spinach or drink a glass of sweet-tasting juice to start your day?

Getting in the nutrition

You may ask yourself how juicing can benefit you and your family. Juicing with a conventional juicer does remove the fiber that whole fruit contains, but the vitamins and minerals are still available. These are a few reasons to incorporate this tasty food into your everyday living. If you are

Finding the right combinations

How do you know what combinations to make? Start out with the basics and then get creative. Is there some fruit or vegetable juice you buy that you *know* you enjoy the taste of? Buy fruit in its whole form and juice it yourself. Have your family become enthusiastic with the idea of making their own juice from the things they drink already. Try to replicate the combinations that you already buy. It will be less expensive and much fresher if you do it yourself.

✔ **Too busy for a sit down meal?** Juicing can bring a healthy meal to your glass. It takes mere minutes to whip up a fruity blend of nutrition; you can drink it while you check your morning e-mail!

✔ **Have picky or fussy eaters?** Kids seem to fall under this moniker, but plenty of adults don't like to eat most vegetables and fruits whole. Make a glass of juice and disguise the flavors of the less-than-appreciated foods.

✔ **Have a low appetite or elderly?** For those who just don't seem to ever be hungry, every bite holds extra importance. Juicing will fill their glass with nutrition and is often more appealing.

Drinking it raw or cooked

Fresh juice is usually consumed right away, made from raw foods. Many juice enthusiasts believe that juice still contains healthy enzymes when it's raw, and that oxidation (foaming) is also detrimental to final product.

If you're like many people, you simply want healthy juice available, as much as possible. Juicing at home means you can have fresh, raw juice when the produce is in season, and you can can or freeze it for when it's not. Either way, juice is delicious and full of vitamins and minerals that we all need for a healthy diet.

Discovering the Types of Juicers

Juicing equipment can be as simple as a sharp paring knife and citrus juicer, for a glass of orange juice in the morning. If you're going to be making fabulous fruit and vegetable combinations, however, you'll need to get a juicing machine.

Before deciding on the type of juicer to purchase, think about how often you'll be making juice. Do you want to cut and core all the pieces of fruits and vegetables, or would you like to use the entire piece of fruit? Most notably, if you're going to be juicing leafy greens and/or wheatgrass, check that the juicer will handle these types of foods. Many juicers cannot. These answers will factor in your choice of juicer.

Some juicers include

- **Manual juicers:** These juicers are just what they sound like. Used mainly for citrus fruits, these manual juicers use the pressure of your hand to squeeze out what you can from juicy fruits like oranges and lemons. These juicers are good for the occasional breakfast glass of OJ.

- **Hand-cranked juicers:** These juicers are also manual, but you crank a handle to power this type. Good for larger amounts of juice, these juicers can be hard to clean, so find out how it comes apart before buying. You need to core fruits and vegetables in order to go through this type.

- **Blender juicers:** Some juicers are actually high-powered blender types. These juicers are more expensive, but they make short work of peels and seeds, along with any sort of fruit or vegetable you throw into them. Their warranty is usually excellent and will last a lifetime.

- **Centrifugal juicers:** These juicers grind up fruits and vegetables and then use *centrifugal* (the ground up food swirls around so quickly that it is pressed outward) force to remove the juice from the pulp. These juicers come in a wide variety of quality and styles (and prices). Read all reviews before making a choice.

- **Masticating juicers:** These juicers also grind up fruits and vegetables, but are more efficient at removing juice from the pulp. The most enthusiastic juicers believe that masticating juicers are the best way to juice because they create less heat than centrifugal juicers. Masticating juicers can also handle leafy greens and other difficult-to-juice items easier.

- **Twin-gear juicers:** These high-end juicers can handle anything. They produce the least foam and least amount of heat when making juice. Some people believe that the quality of juice is reduced when it's aerated and heated. Because of their price, twin-gear juicers aren't for the beginning juicer. They're an investment for the serious juicer.

Finding Your Ingredients

Just like most healthy diets, juicing requires the freshest ingredients. Of course, it would take monumental planning to drink only juices that were in season. Luckily, your technique for juicing changes based on the time of year your desired ingredients are purchased, keeping nutrition high and costs as low as possible.

Going organic

Of course, talking about juicing means talking about organics. When choosing your fruits and vegetables, keep in mind that you're going to be juicing every part of the produce. If your fruits are not organic, many of the chemicals and waxes applied to them will not wash off. Using nonorganic foods for juicing isn't necessarily a bad thing; it just means that you have to remember to wash items very well and peel them before pushing through the juicer.

As long as your juicer can handle it, if the fruit or veggie is organic, you don't need to peel it.

Growing or buying

If at all possible, growing your own produce is the least expensive way to begin juicing, but you don't have to, however. Buying your juicing items local is the next best thing to your own garden. In fact, because juicing requires a large quantity of fruits and veggies, sometimes buying from your local farmstand makes more sense.

When buying from a farmstand or farmers' market, ask some basic questions before buying your juicing foods:

- **Is it organic?** Either way, you can use the produce, but you do need to know if the skins need to be removed or can be eaten.

- **What is in season?** Buying seasonal items are usually the least expensive and freshest way to purchase them. Ask your farmer what is fresh today, what is going to be soon, and what he has growing. That way, you can plan and create juice blends that can incorporate things as they ripen.

Gathering Tips on Techniques

Juicing enthusiasts, from busy moms to raw foodists, seem to have their own specific technique that they think is best. Having some flexibility, however, makes sense when juicing.

In the spring and summer, you can buy fresh, inexpensive produce and juice like crazy. You can also start canning and freezing juices to drink during the winter months, when produce is at its highest price. That way, you enjoy healthy juice all year round.

Choosing your flavors

With an endless variety of flavors, you'll be sure to invent some favorite juice blends. Choose sweet things to balance tart or stronger flavored things. You will soon be throwing together mixes that even your pickiest tasters will love. If you're just starting out, here are some flavor profiles to look for:

- ✔ **Sweet tastes:** Sweet flavors include carrots, most fruits, beets, and red cabbage. Add to vegetable mixes to please the sweet lovers.

- ✔ **Juicy extenders:** These ingredients are fairly neutral in taste and give a lot of juice for their size. They're great to dilute stronger flavors and help fill the glass while saving you money. Try watermelon, honeydew, green grapes, cucumbers, or zucchini.

- ✔ **Rich flavors:** Add items like dark grapes, any stone fruits, papaya, and bananas when you want that rich, nectar–like flavor of an expensive juice blend.

- ✔ **Green flavors:** These flavors are wonderful for that cleansing, bright taste we often attribute to healthy living. The greens are full of chlorophyll and vitamins everyone needs. Try adding a handful at first and then increase the amount as you like. Some greens that add sparkle to your juice are wheatgrass, dandelion greens, spinach, and kale. Parsley and other herbs are also popular, but are a bit more strongly flavored, so start with a bit less of these greens.

Think about the flavor components you're adding. Are they mainly sweet? Strongly flavored? Balance them with extenders to create a full cup of perfectly flavored juice.

Timing your juicing

Timing your juice is important for the best flavors. No matter if you're juicing for the pantry or making fresh juice for immediate consumption, it's always best to be ready to either preserve or drink it right away.

Fresh produce makes fresh juice. Allowing juice to sit in the refrigerator or, worse, at room temperature results in the juice continuing to age or decay. Always plan on juicing to drink right away or juicing to preserve immediately.

Storing and Preserving

Juice is a wonderful keeper. It tastes just as fresh and good if previously frozen or canned, as it does when used immediately. The trick is to have your supplies at the ready, when the produce ripens, and then get the juice from the tree to the freezer or jar in record time.

Keeping your juice fresh

To get the best nutrition out of it, you must keep your juice fresh. To keep your juice fresh, buy ripe, clean fruits or vegetables and don't allow them to sit around for longer than a day or two, before turning them into juice.

If you're canning or freezing, have a plan of action before you bring home a bushel or go pick boxes of something. Be ready to store them in juice form. The produce will not only be healthier for you in the end, it will be less overwhelming when you end up with three bushels of apples that are ripened at the same time.

Storing tips

Store your juices in airtight freezer containers if frozen, and canning jars that fit the size juices your family will consume right away. If you're canning for one or two people, for example, you may need to preserve in pints instead of quarts.

Freeze juice right in glass jars if you have the room. Remember that juice will expand, so leave ½-inch headspace. And do handle the jars carefully. Using clean glass jars is a great way to recycle any you may be collecting.

When your juice is canned, store it in a cool, dark place. Light can fade your juice, and many people believe that some nutrients are lost in these juices. Remember to use the FIFO (First in First Out) method: Use the oldest juices first, adding fresh juice jars to the back of the row so that the easiest ones to access are the oldest ones.

Chapter 2

Juicing Fruits and Veggies

The idea of drinking your fruits and vegetables has become more and more popular in recent years, which is really no surprise. Juice recipes that incorporate fruits from apples to apricots and vegetables from carrots to kale can be quick, easy ways to give your diet a healthy boost.

One big bonus to adding fresh juicing to your family's diet is being able to get the important nutrients into everyone in a pleasing way. Juicing is like a multivitamin in a glass.

In this chapter, we show you how to incorporate all the fruits and vegetables you always wanted your family to eat into delicious juices that they'll be asking to drink!

Capturing Fruity Nutrition

Many people are surprised to discover that many vegetables actually produce a rich, sweet juice when put through a juicer. Juicing is a great way to get those veggies that the most stubborn family member refuses to eat off the plate and into them. Combining a vegetable with a fruit is a great way to do just that.

You can fit a full day's allowance of fruits and veggies into your routine easily, if you simply turn that bowl of produce into juice!

Avoiding sugar shock

When drinking juice, you're creating a food that is already broken down enough that it's absorbed into the bloodstream much faster than its whole equivalent. Sensitive people may feel the effects of the sugars in a negative way. Other people feel no negative effect when drinking juices, but find themselves tired soon after their body digests the juice, leaving them feeling hungry. Both of these issues are caused by the increase in natural sugars in the blood, also known as a *sugar spike*.

A simple way to reduce this sugar spike is to keep the skins on the fruits and add a protein component to the juice. Think smoothies! Add protein powders, tofu, milk, and nuts to give a little more complexity to the recipe and help you feel full longer. They'll also reduce the burst of sugars your body will have to deal with.

Deciding on skins and seeds

If possible, include the whole fruit when juicing. With the exception of banana skins, stone fruit seeds, mango seeds, and avocado seeds, your juicer will most likely make short work of these parts. Use common sense and always check your juicer manual to be certain that your type of juicer can handle the entire fruit.

Drinking Your Veggies

Even if you love most vegetables, getting your daily allowance of them every single day can be difficult. Juicing is a way to get a large quantity of those same veggies in a much smaller package.

Some vegetables, like cabbage and beets, are surprisingly sweet when juiced. If you're unsure how a veggie tastes when juiced, juice a little and actually taste it before committing to making a big batch of juice. Once you know how each vegetable tastes, you can sweeten it up if needed by adding a neutral fruit like apples or cucumbers, or you can add some additional flavor by choosing something that has a richer taste, like carrots or pineapple.

You don't need to drink an unpleasant-tasting juice simply to get the juice down. You can tone down every strong flavor with the right partner in the mix.

Just as a juice can end up too strongly flavored, some fruits and vegetables don't translate into juice with much of their own flavor. You can boost the taste by adding fruits, herbs, and green things. Most herbs can be added as they are, stems and all. The exception would be a particularly woody stemmed herb, like rosemary or thyme. These leaves would need to be stripped from the stem because the stem contains no juice and can add a bitter taste to the finished juice.

Good Morning Juice

Prep time: 5 min • **Yield:** 1 serving

Ingredients	*Directions*
2 apples **2 large carrots, tops removed**	*1* Wash the apples and carrots. Peel the apples, unless you're using organic. Halve or quarter the apples in order for them to fit into your juicer.
	2 Juice your prepared produce according to the manufacturer's directions. Drink immediately.

Per 1-cup serving: Calories 208 (From Fat 10); Fat 1g (Saturated 0g); Cholesterol 0mg; Sodium 50mg; Carbohydrates 53g (Dietary Fiber 9g); Protein 2g.

Sunny Juice

Prep time: 5 min • **Yield:** 1 serving

Ingredients	*Directions*
1 apple **1 grapefruit** **1 orange**	*1* Wash and peel your fruit, unless you're using organic. Halve or quarter the fruit in order to fit it into your juicer.
	2 Juice your prepared produce according to the manufacturer's directions. Drink immediately.

Per 1-cup serving: Calories 219 (From Fat 7); Fat 1g (Saturated 0g); Cholesterol 0mg; Sodium 1mg; Carbohydrates 56g (Dietary Fiber 9g); Protein 3g.

Watermelon Sparkle

Prep time: 5 min • **Yield:** 2 servings

Ingredients	Directions
1¼ **pounds of watermelon**	**1** Wash the watermelon rind before cutting into quarters. Peel the rind, if desired. Cut the melon into pieces to fit in your juicer.
	2 Juice your prepared produce according to the manufacturer's directions. Drink immediately.

Per 1-cup serving: Calories 47 (From Fat 0); Fat 0g (Saturated 0g); Cholesterol 0mg; Sodium 3mg; Carbohydrates 11g (Dietary Fiber 1g); Protein 1g.

Tip: If the watermelon is organic, juice the watermelon seeds and rind along with the flesh.

Spice Up Your Morning

Prep time: 5 min • **Yield:** 1 serving

Ingredients	Directions
1 orange **3 large carrots** **1½-inch piece gingeroot**	**1** Wash the produce and gingerroot. Peel the orange. Halve or quarter the produce in order to fit it into your juicer.
	2 Juice the prepared produce according to the manufacturer's directions. Drink immediately.

Per 1-cup serving: Calories 164 (From Fat 5); Fat 1g (Saturated 0g); Cholesterol 0mg; Sodium 78mg; Carbohydrates 40g (Dietary Fiber 10g); Protein 4g.

Smooth and Fruity

Prep time: 5 min • **Yield:** 1 serving

Ingredients	Directions
6 to 8 strawberries **2 small apples**	*1* Wash the fruit. Peel the apples (unless organic) and hull the berries. Halve or quarter the apples in order to fit them into your juicer.
	2 Juice your prepared produce according to the manufacturer's directions. Drink immediately.

Per 1-cup serving: Calories 142 (From Fat 9); Fat 1g (Saturated 0g); Cholesterol 0mg; Sodium 1mg; Carbohydrates 36g (Dietary Fiber 6g); Protein 1g.

Can't Beat Bananas

Prep time: 5 min • **Yield:** 1 serving

Ingredients	Directions
1 orange **1 banana**	*1* Wash and peel the orange and banana. Halve or quarter the fruit to fit in your juicer.
	2 Juice the prepared produce according to the manufacturer's directions. Drink immediately.

Per 1-cup serving: Calories 173 (From Fat 6); Fat 1g (Saturated 0g); Cholesterol 0mg; Sodium 3mg; Carbohydrates 44g (Dietary Fiber 6g); Protein 3g.

Vary It! This recipe is a super starter juice for someone new to juicing. This mild-tasting juice is also lovely when mixed in equal parts with your favorite milk.

Tropical Dream

Prep time: 5 min • **Yield:** 1 serving

Ingredients	Directions
¼ pineapple 1 orange 1 banana	**1** Wash and peel the orange. Peel and core the pineapple. Divide the pineapple into quarters. Peel the banana. Halve or quarter the fruit in order to fit it into your juicer.
	2 Juice your prepared produce according to the manufacturer's directions. Drink immediately.

Per 1-cup serving: Calories 231 (From Fat 11); Fat 1g (Saturated 0g); Cholesterol 0mg; Sodium 4mg; Carbohydrates 59g (Dietary Fiber 8g); Protein 3g.

Tip: This is a great dessert juice!

Juicy Berry

Prep time: 5 min • **Yield:** 1 serving

Ingredients	Directions
½ cup blueberries ½ cup strawberries 1 apple	**1** Wash the produce. Peel the apple, unless organic.
	2 Juice your prepared produce according to the manufacturer's directions. Drink immediately.

Per 1-cup serving: Calories 136 (From Fat 9); Fat 1g (Saturated 0g); Cholesterol 0mg; Sodium 5mg; Carbohydrates 35g (Dietary Fiber 6g); Protein 1g.

Sweetness and Light

Prep time: 5 min • **Yield:** 1 serving

Ingredients	Directions
1 pear **¼ pineapple** **¼-inch piece gingeroot**	**1** Wash the fruit and gingerroot. Peel the pineapple. Halve or quarter the fruit in order to fit it into your juicer.
	2 Juice your prepared produce according to the manufacturer's directions. Drink immediately.

Per 1-cup serving: *Calories 162 (From Fat 13); Fat 1g (Saturated 0g); Cholesterol 0mg; Sodium 2mg; Carbohydrates 41g (Dietary Fiber 6g); Protein 2g.*

Vary It! Check your owner's manual and leave the skin on the pineapple if your juicer has the power to juice it with the skin included.

Grape Juice

Prep time: 5 min • **Yield:** 1 serving

Ingredients	Directions
⅔ cup green grapes **⅔ cup black grapes** **1 celery stalk**	**1** Wash your produce. If your juicer requires it, remove the grapes from the stems before juicing.
	2 Juice your prepared produce according to the manufacturer's directions. Drink immediately.

Per 1-cup serving: *Calories 155 (From Fat 7); Fat 1g (Saturated 0g); Cholesterol 0mg; Sodium 57mg; Carbohydrates 39g (Dietary Fiber 3g); Protein 3g.*

Watermelon Lemon Drop

Prep time: 5 min • **Yield:** 2 servings

Ingredients	Directions
1¼ **pounds watermelon** **1 lemon**	**1** Wash the fruit. Peel the lemon. Remove rind from the watermelon. Halve or quarter the fruit in order to fit it into your juicer.
	2 Juice your prepared produce according to the manufacturer's directions. Drink immediately.

Per 1-cup serving: *Calories 53 (From Fat 0); Fat 0g (Saturated 0g); Cholesterol 0mg; Sodium 3mg; Carbohydrates 13g (Dietary Fiber 1g); Protein 1g.*

Vary It! Juice the watermelon peel and seeds.

All Kinds of Apple

Prep time: 5 min • **Yield:** 1 serving

Ingredients	Directions
1 apple ¼ **pineapple**	**1** Wash and peel the fruit, unless using organinc. Halve or quarter the fruit in order to fit it into your juicer.
	2 Juice your prepared produce according to the manufacturer's directions. Drink immediately.

Per 1-cup serving: *Calories 131 (From Fat 8); Fat 1g (Saturated 0g); Cholesterol 0mg; Sodium 1mg; Carbohydrates 34g (Dietary Fiber 4g); Protein 1g.*

Tip: Check your owner's manual and leave the skin on the pineapple if it has the power to juice the skin.

Veggie Blast

Prep time: 5 min • **Yield:** 2 servings

Ingredients	Directions
½ cucumber ½ cup spinach 2 carrots, tops trimmed 1 apple	**1** Wash the produce and peel the apple (unless organic) and the cucumber. Halve or quarter the produce as needed in order to fit it into your juicer.
	2 Juice your prepared produce according to the manufacturer's directions. Drink immediately.

Per 1-cup serving: Calories 79 (From Fat 3); Fat 0g (Saturated 0g); Cholesterol 0mg; Sodium 47mg; Carbohydrates 19g (Dietary Fiber 4g); Protein 2g.

Tip: You can juice the cucumber with the skin on, unless it has a wax coating.

Berry Smoothie

Prep time: 5 min • **Yield:** 1 serving

Ingredients	Directions
1 cup strawberries ½ cup blueberries ½ cup almond milk 4 ice cubes	**1** Wash the berries. Place the berries, almond milk, and ice in the juicer.
	2 Blend ingredients on high for 30 seconds, or until smooth. Drink immediately.

Per 1-cup serving: Calories 118 (From Fat 21); Fat 2g (Saturated 0g); Cholesterol 0mg; Sodium 82mg; Carbohydrates 25g (Dietary Fiber 6g); Protein 2g.

Vary It! Add a scoop of protein powder for even more nutrition.

Don't Tell Them Juice

Prep time: 5 min • **Yield:** 2 servings

Ingredients	Directions
¼ **head of cabbage**	*1* Wash the produce. Remove the outer leaves of the cabbage. Peel the orange and the apple (unless organic). Halve or quarter the produce in order to fit it into your juicer.
1 **orange**	
1 **apple**	
	2 Juice your prepared produce according to the manufacturer's directions. Drink Immediately.

Per 1-cup serving: Calories 101 (From Fat 6); Fat 1g (Saturated 0g); Cholesterol 0mg; Sodium 21mg; Carbohydrates 25g (Dietary Fiber 6g); Protein 3g.

Tip: If you don't tell them, no one will ever guess that this sweet juice contains cabbage!

Sweet Blueberry Carrot

Prep time: 5 min • **Yield:** 1 serving

Ingredients	Directions
1 **cup blueberries**	*1* Wash the blueberries. Peel the carrots. Add the parsley to your juicer first; the carrots will help press all the parsley through.
2 **large carrots, tops removed**	
1 **sprig parsley**	
	2 Juice your prepared produce according to the manufacturer's directions. Drink immediately.

Per 1-cup serving: Calories 144 (From Fat 8); Fat 1g (Saturated 0g); Cholesterol 0mg; Sodium 60mg; Carbohydrates 35g (Dietary Fiber 8g); Protein 3g.

Tip: If you're using organic produce, leave the skin on the carrots.

Tomato Juice

Prep time: 1 hr • **Process time:** 40 min (pints); 45 min (quarts) • **Yield:** 7 quarts or 11 pints

Ingredients	Directions
25 pounds tomatoes **Lemon juice or citric acid**	*1* Wash and core tomatoes. Roughly chop them into chunks.
	2 Place the tomatoes in a large pot and bring them to a simmer over medium heat, stirring frequently to prevent scorching. Cook the tomatoes until they're soft, about 25 to 30 minutes.
	3 Strain the tomatoes through a food mill to separate the juice from the skins and seeds. Return the juice to the pot and bring it to a simmer over medium heat. Simmer 5 minutes.
	4 Ladle the hot juice into your canning jars. To each quart jar, add 2 tablespoons lemon juice or ½ teaspoon citric acid. To each pint jar, add 1 tablespoon lemon juice or ¼ teaspoon citric acid. Leave ½-inch headspace.
	5 Process the filled jars in a water-bath canner for 40 minutes (pints) or 45 minutes (quarts) from the point of boiling. Use any unsealed jars within 2 weeks.

Per 1-cup serving: Calories 70 (From Fat 0); Fat 0g (Saturated 0g); Cholesterol 0mg; Sodium 32mg; Carbohydrates 14g (Dietary Fiber 4g); Protein 6g.

Vegetable Juice

Prep time: 30 min • **Cook time:** 1½ hr • **Process time:** 20 min • **Yield:** 10 quarts

Ingredients

8 quarts tomatoes

4 medium carrots, peeled and sliced

3 onions, chopped

4 stalks of celery, chopped

2 medium beets, peeled and chopped

3 green peppers, cored and chopped

Salt (optional)

10 tablespoons lemon juice

Directions

1 Core and chop the tomatoes and place them in a 6-quart pot. Add the remaining vegetables and bring to a boil over medium-high heat. Reduce heat and simmer until all vegetables are soft, about 20 minutes.

2 Strain the cooked vegetables through a food mill and return them to the pot. Return the juice to boiling.

3 Ladle the boiling juice into the prepared jars. Release any air, adding 1 tablespoon lemon juice to each quart jar.

4 Process the filled jars in a pressure canner at 10 pounds pressure for 20 minutes. When the processing time is done, allow the pressure to return to 0, wait an additional 10 minutes, and then carefully open the canner lid. Prior to drinking or tasting, boil the food for 15 minutes. Use any unsealed jars within 2 weeks.

Per 1-cup serving: *Calories 40 (From Fat 5); Fat 1g (Saturated 0g); Cholesterol 0mg; Sodium 25mg; Carbohydrates 9g (Dietary Fiber 2g); Protein 2g.*

Dairy-Free Smoothie

Prep time: 5 min • **Yield:** 1 serving

Ingredients	Directions
1 orange **1 banana**	**1** Wash and peel orange. Peel the banana. Halve or quarter the fruit in order to fit it into your juicer.
1 cup vanilla-flavored rice milk	**2** Juice your prepared produce according to the manufacturer's directions. Combine the fresh juice with the rice milk, stirring gently. Drink immediately.

Per 1-cup serving: *Calories 303 (From Fat 24); Fat 3g (Saturated 0g); Cholesterol 0mg; Sodium 93mg; Carbohydrates 72g (Dietary Fiber 6g); Protein 4g.*

Vary It! In place of vanilla, you can try other milks, such as almond or soy.

Chapter 3

Juicing for Health: Detoxification

The world around us is filled with toxins. To be honest, it can be a real challenge to get healthful, toxin-free food and to dodge all the toxins that exist in the environment. That's the bad news: So many toxins exist at such high levels that you simply can't escape their reach.

The good news is that you can fight back against the situation. You can make adjustments to your lifestyle — starting with your diet but reaching far beyond — to limit the amount of toxins you're exposed to. And you can make a concerted effort to detoxify the harmful substances that already exist in your body.

Part of that effort lies in the magic of juicing. So if you're looking for a practical addition to your kitchen that will give you some flexibility in the way you prepare your detox foods, look no further than a juicer.

Taking a Look at Toxins

A *toxin* is any substance that your body can't use in a purposeful way or that requires energy to be removed. Even substances that your body has to have to survive can be toxic if you get too much of them.

If you start looking around for toxins, you don't have to go very far. Start by looking under your kitchen sink. See those disinfectants and cleaners? They're almost certainly loaded with chemical toxins. Open your pantry. Do you have any processed foods in there? Be honest. If so, check the ingredients lists. If you see any words that you can't pronounce, those are probably toxins. Chances are your hair spray, deodorant, and other personal hygiene products contain toxic substances, too. Don't even go into your garage — you could spend all day in there discovering toxins.

To be fair, in many of these cases, the amount of toxins you're exposed to at one time is usually small. But toxins are very stubborn; they accumulate in your body and can add up pretty fast.

Identifying toxins

If you have a good grasp of what's out there in terms of toxins, you can more easily identify and avoid them:

- **Natural chemicals:** People often think of toxins as manmade chemicals, but Mother Nature provides plenty of toxins, too. You've experienced these toxins if you've ever brushed up against poison ivy or been bitten by a spider. The key to limiting the amount of damage that natural toxins do to your body is avoidance.

- **Living toxins:** In addition to the natural chemicals that act as toxins, plenty of living things can have toxic effects on your health. Bacteria, for example, are all around you. Some types of bacteria are helpful, like the kinds that live in your intestines and help digest your food, but many other types are extremely toxic and harmful. Yeasts, parasites, and viruses are other common living toxins.

- **Manmade chemicals:** In the past 100 years, man has been really busy creating new things that are supposed to make our lives easier and better. Unfortunately, many of these things contain toxic chemicals and/or are made using some sort of toxic process. The chemical creations include pesticides, petrochemicals, and food additives, to name just a few.

Finding out how toxins get in

You're surrounded by toxins. But how do these toxins end up in your body where they can cause harm? Here are the common routes:

- **Ingesting toxins orally:** It may seem crazy to stick toxins into your mouth, but most people do so every day. Food is the biggest source of toxins. Processed foods today contain more than 3,000 chemicals that aren't natural. These chemicals enhance flavor and can preserve food for months, if not years. Many food preservatives can have really harmful effects on the body. Even if toxins aren't *in* your food and water, you may have toxins *on* your food. At the top of this list are pesticides and chemical fertilizers that are meant to help grow food but end up in your body, assaulting your organs and tissues.

- ✔ **Inhaling toxins:** When it comes to airborne toxins, remember that anything you smell is getting into your body. If something has a chemical smell, parts of that chemical are entering your body through your mucous membranes and lungs. Even scarier is the fact that many chemicals have no smell, so you don't know that you're breathing them in.

- ✔ **Taking toxins in through your skin:** Your skin does a very good job at keeping out toxins, but it isn't perfect. Your skin is capable of absorbing chemicals that come in contact with it, and toxins are no exception.

Adding up over the long run

Anyone living in the developed world is exposed to chemicals and other toxic substances on a daily basis. These toxins are more varied and exist in much higher quantities than ever before. Scientists really don't know the long-term health effects of all these toxins, but we *can* see the health effects of the toxicity that people suffer from now. Small doses of toxins usually don't have an immediate effect, but the long-term accumulation can eventually cause entire organ systems to fail with no obvious cause. Thousands of people currently face chronic diseases that weren't even on the books a century ago, and the average child born today comes into the world with more than 200 different toxins already present in her body.

This information isn't meant to cause you to panic about the toxins that surround you, but you should at least realize what you're up against. You must also realize that you can take steps to avoid toxins and detoxify your body to counter the toxic trend.

Reaping the Benefits of Detoxification

Detoxification is any process that either removes a substance that is harming your body or changes a toxic substance so that it's no longer injurious. Dozens of different detoxification methods exist, but broadly speaking, you can split detoxification up into two categories:

- ✔ **Internal:** Human bodies have an extraordinarily complex array of systems that change, break down, attack and destroy, or eliminate threats to their internal environment and health. The primary internal systems for detoxification are the stomach, intestines, liver, immune system, kidneys, and lungs. For thousands of years, these systems have helped humans enjoy relatively good basic health, but for most of those years, the exposure to toxins was very low and rarely caused a problem. That's not so today.

✔ **External:** When it comes to external detoxification, your skin is second to none. Your skin serves as an important barrier that keeps many toxins from entering your body. Your sweat glands, which are extremely important sites for detoxification, are also housed in your skin.

When you think about toxins, you can consider them poisons. You don't want poisons floating around in your body, do you? Toxins can affect virtually every system and part of your body, causing a massive decrease in efficiency and function. Toxins also cause disease. Removing toxins — and avoiding them in the first place — can have some truly startling positive effects on your health:

✔ **Increased energy:** Many toxins directly affect the production of energy in your body, and when your toxic levels are high, you have far less energy than you would enjoy if your systems were toxin free (or close to it). The more toxins you can remove and keep out, the more energy you'll have.

✔ **Boosted immune function:** Your immune system plays a major part in detoxification. The more it has to work to get rid of toxins, the less work it can do on its normal tasks (such as preventing infections and killing cancer cells). Getting rid of toxins makes life easier for your immune system, allowing it to do its job effectively.

✔ **Managed stress:** Most people think of stress as an emotional response to an unwanted situation. That's definitely one cause of stress, but toxins can put even more stress on your body, which reacts the same to emotional stress and toxic stress. Stress harms your body in many different ways, including (but not limited to) organ damage and brain problems. Managing toxic and emotional stress can be a major contributor to good health.

✔ **Decreased fat:** Everyone needs a little stored energy, and fat is one of the ways you fulfill that need. Unfortunately, many people are storing enough energy (in the form of fat) for several people. That's a medical problem — a very serious one. In addition to the strain obesity puts on your cardiovascular system, obesity has a toxic element to it that many people don't understand. Fat-soluble toxins are stored in your fat cells, and these cells release toxins into your bloodstream on a regular basis. You have to get the toxins out of the fat cells before you can reduce the fat. Then, with less fat, the toxins have fewer places to hide.

Enhancing detoxification

What's the best way to get rid of toxins? Avoid them in the first place. An ounce of toxin prevention is worth far more than a pound of detoxification cure. But you can do only so much when it comes to dodging toxins. Lucky for you, you have a whole host of systems and natural mechanisms that will help you eliminate the toxic substances that course through your veins (and your arteries, and your tissues, and your organs . . .).

True, your body can take care of quite a bit of detoxification on its own, but today's elevated toxin levels demand that you give your body a hand. If you want to enjoy long-term good health, you must work hard to enhance and augment your body's detox efforts by taking these steps:

- **Choose your food wisely.** You can drastically cut down on your toxicity by making good food choices. If you can eliminate processed foods from your diet, dodge most genetically modified foods, and embrace all things organic, you'll be doing your health an enormous favor.

- **Fill in the gaps with supplements.** The quality of food has dropped dramatically in the last few decades. As if that weren't enough, your body needs even more essential nutrients than ever before if you expect it to fight off the ever-increasing amount of toxic threats that surrounds you. Because of these factors, the vast majority of people — particularly people living in the United States — need to take supplements to ensure the best possible intake of vitamins, minerals, essential fatty acids, and other key nutrients.

- **Cleanse through chelation.** Heavy metals are some of the most common toxins. If you think you may be suffering from dangerously high levels of heavy metals, such as lead and mercury, chelation could be a good choice for you. *Chelation* is a medical treatment that uses a medication to trap and remove heavy metals from your body's tissues.

- **Use a sauna.** Sweating is an outstanding way to use your body's natural systems to flush out toxins, particularly the fat-soluble ones that contribute to obesity and continually poison us. You should be sweating every chance you get! Exercise is a great way to work up a sweat, but if you really want to sweat it out, nothing beats a sauna.

Going organic

Organic foods are plants or animals that are grown or raised without toxins. That means they're not sprayed with toxic pesticides, injected with antibiotics or hormones, processed with toxic additives or processes, or packaged in toxic containers. Organic foods have become increasingly popular in recent years; sales of organic foods have increased by 20 percent in each of the last seven years.

Eat organic foods whenever possible, but you need to be a real label hawk when examining organic options. Here's the breakdown:

- **Specific Ingredients are Organically Produced:** This designation is nothing special because it can be used on a label for any product that has only one organic ingredient.

- **Made with Organic Ingredients:** Foods in this category have to contain only 70 percent organic ingredients. Needless to say, a lot of nasty stuff can exist in the remaining 30 percent. Don't make the mistake of thinking foods with the Made with Organic Ingredients label are toxin-free.

- **USDA Organic:** This categorization can be confusing. In order to qualify for a USDA Organic label, a food must be made of 95 percent organically produced ingredients. The obvious question: What's up with the other 5 percent? Therein lies the problem. The non-organic 5 percent can contain all sorts of materials that don't fit very well at all in a detox diet, including food colorings and animal intestines. Buying USDA Organic foods is generally a little better than buying foods that aren't organic in any way, but it's nothing to shout about.

- **100% Organic:** This is the best of the best. The 100% Organic label is reserved for products that are wholly and completely organic. This means that you don't have to worry about artificial fertilizers, pesticides, genetic modification, antibiotics, or sewer sludge fertilizer.

If you want to buy truly organic food, make sure that you look for 100% Organic on the label.

Eating the Detoxification Way

If you're not enjoying optimal health or if you're struggling with obesity, you need to take a good, hard look at the many benefits of a detox diet. Changing what you eat (and how you eat it) so that you're focusing on wholesome, healthy foods and cutting out toxic ingredients is the first and most important step toward ensuring good health and maintaining a healthy weight. The principles for detox dieting are relatively simple, but the changes they require can be pretty tough. (They're not as tough, however, as living an unhealthy and obese life.)

Not many people make the connection between toxins and obesity, but you need to be aware of clear, proven relationships if you want to stay at a healthy weight. Getting on (and sticking with) a detox diet will go a long way toward minimizing your toxicity. And if you can make detox dieting a part of your life *for life,* you'll lose the extra, harmful pounds that weigh you down and damage your health.

First of all, fat is a storehouse for toxins in your body. Fat-soluble toxins are tucked away in fat cells to prevent them from harming your organs and other vital tissues. When the toxins are more concentrated, the fat cells get bigger in an effort to keep them diluted. If you can avoid toxins and detoxify the toxins you're already carrying around with you, shedding fat becomes much easier.

In addition, body fat stresses your body's systems. For every pound of fat your body makes, it has to make about 4 miles of blood vessels. Carrying 25 extra pounds of fat means your heart has to pump blood through another 100 miles of vessels. That's bad news for the most important muscle in your body, and it's just the beginning. Fat wreaks havoc on your joints, contributes to diabetes, and causes too many other conditions to list here. Lose the toxins, lose the unhealthy foods from your diet, and you'll lose the fat. And then your health will flourish.

Honey Lemon Hot Juice

Prep time: 5 min • **Yield:** 1 serving

Ingredients	Directions
1 lemon, unpeeled	**1** Wash the lemon and gingerroot, but do *not* peel the lemon. Halve or quarter the fruit in order to fit it into your juicer and process.
1-inch piece of gingerroot	
2 tablespoons raw honey, or to taste	
1 cup hot water	**2** Pour into a large mug. Add the honey and stir. Fill the mug to the top with boiling hot water. Drink Immediately.

Per 1-cup serving: Calories 144 (From Fat 0); Fat 0g (Saturated 0g); Cholesterol 0mg; Sodium 3mg; Carbohydrates 40g (Dietary Fiber 0g); Protein 0g.

Note: This strong-tasting drink may not be palatable for young children.

Tip: Sip slowly during colds and flu.

Green Detox Juice

Prep time: 5 min • **Yield:** 1 serving

Ingredients	Directions
1 cup spinach	**1** Wash all ingredients. Peel the kiwi. Halve or quarter the fruit in order to fit it into your juicer and process.
3 kale leaves	
1 orange	**2** Drink immediately.
1 kiwi	

Per 1-cup serving: Calories 129 (From Fat 10); Fat 1g (Saturated 0g); Cholesterol 0mg; Sodium 39mg; Carbohydrates 29g (Dietary Fiber 1g); Protein 4g.

Clear Skin Berry Juice

Prep time: 5 min • **Yield:** 1 serving

Ingredients	Directions
2 cups blackberries 1 cup strawberries 1 cup raspberries	*1* Wash the berries, place them into your juicer, and process.
	2 Drink immediately.

Per 1-cup serving: Calories 256 (From Fat 21); Fat 2g (Saturated 0g); Cholesterol 0mg; Sodium 2mg; Carbohydrates 62g (Dietary Fiber 6g); Protein 4g.

Tip: This juice helps clear your skin.

Kiwi Berry Cleanse

Prep time: 5 min • **Yield:** 1 serving

Ingredients	Directions
2 kiwis 3 cups blackberries 1 cup blueberries	*1* Wash the kiwis and berries. Peel the kiwis.
	2 Halve or quarter the kiwis in order to fit them into your juicer and process.
	3 Drink immediately.

Per 1-cup serving: Calories 406 (From Fat 29); Fat 3g (Saturated 0g); Cholesterol 0mg; Sodium 9mg; Carbohydrates 100g (Dietary Fiber 7g); Protein 6g.

Vary It! Try different berries that are in season.

Nature's Broom Juice

Prep time: 5 min • **Yield:** 2 servings

Ingredients	Directions
3 apples 3 pears	**1** Wash the apples and pears. Peel the apples (unless they're organic).
	2 Halve or quarter the fruit in order to fit it into your juicer and process. Drink immediately.

Per 1-cup serving: Calories 256 (From Fat 14); Fat 2g (Saturated 0g); Cholesterol 0mg; Sodium 0mg; Carbohydrates 66g (Dietary Fiber 3g); Protein 1g.

Tip: This juice is a great way to get your bowels moving.

Bye, Bye Heartburn Juice

Prep time: 5 min • **Yield:** 2 servings

Ingredients	Directions
2 papaya 2 mangos	**1** Wash, peel, and pit the fruits.
	2 Halve or quarter the fruit in order to fit it into your juicer and process. Drink immediately.

Per 1-cup serving: Calories 253 (From Fat 9); Fat 1g (Saturated 0g); Cholesterol 0mg; Sodium 0mg; Carbohydrates 65g (Dietary Fiber 2g); Protein 3g.

Tip: This juice is a delicious heartburn-relief blend.

Cherry Berry Arthritis Juice

Prep time: 5 min • **Yield:** 2 servings

Ingredients	Directions
1 cup cherries ½ cup blackberries	*1* Wash all ingredients. Pit the cherries. If the cucumber isn't covered in wax, keep the skin intact.
2 carrots 1 cup spinach	*2* Halve or quarter the produce in order to fit it into your juicer and process.
1 medium cucumber	*3* Drink immediately.

Per 1-cup serving: *Calories 125 (From Fat 4); Fat 0g (Saturated 0g); Cholesterol 0mg; Sodium 52mg; Carbohydrates 29g (Dietary Fiber 1g); Protein 4g.*

Arthritis Relief Drink

Prep time: 5 min • **Yield:** 2 servings

Ingredients	Directions
3 kiwis 4 large carrots	*1* Wash all ingredients. Peel the kiwi and the apple (unless organic).
1 green apple	*2* Halve or quarter the produce in order fit it into your juicer and process, using the greens first.
	3 Drink immediately.

Per 1-cup serving: *Calories 168 (From Fat 9); Fat 1g (Saturated 0g); Cholesterol 0mg; Sodium 56mg; Carbohydrates 41g (Dietary Fiber 4g); Protein 3g.*

Give-Me-Energy Drink

Prep time: 5 min • **Yield:** 1 serving

Ingredients	Directions
1 sweet potato	**1** Wash all ingredients. Peel the lemon.
1 beet	
1 lemon	**2** Halve or quarter the produce in order to fit it into your juicer and process.
1 carrot	
	3 Drink immediately.

Per 1-cup serving: Calories 212 (From Fat 1); Fat 0g (Saturated 0g); Cholesterol 0mg; Sodium 149mg; Carbohydrates 53g (Dietary Fiber 1g); Protein 5g.

Tip: Try this fun blend before your morning commute.

Spring Jumping Juice

Prep time: 5 min • **Yield:** 1 serving

Ingredients	Directions
½ cup dandelion leaves	**1** Rinse the dandelion leaves. Wash the carrot and oranges. Peel the orange.
1 large carrot	
2 oranges	**2** Halve or quarter the produce in order to fit it into your juicer and process.
	3 Drink immediately.

Per 1-cup serving: Calories 155 (From Fat 7); Fat 1g (Saturated 0g); Cholesterol 0mg; Sodium 49mg; Carbohydrates 36g (Dietary Fiber 2g); Protein 3g.

Wheatgrass Breeze Drink

Prep time: 5 min • **Yield:** 1 serving

Ingredients	Directions
1 orange 1 small apple 2-inch bunch of wheatgrass	**1** Wash the fruit. Peel the orange and the apple (unless organic).
	2 Process the wheatgrass through your juicer. Halve or quarter the fruit in order to fit it into your juicer and process.
	3 Drink immediately.

Per 1-cup serving: *Calories 125 (From Fat 5); Fat 1g (Saturated 0g); Cholesterol 0mg; Sodium 0mg; Carbohydrates 31g (Dietary Fiber 1g); Protein 2g.*

Note: Not all juicers can handle wheatgrass. Check your owner's manual before attempting this recipe.

Cilantro Sweet Juice

Prep time: 5 min • **Yield:** 1 serving

Ingredients	Directions
5 cups cilantro 2 green apples 1 carrot	**1** Wash all ingredients. Peel the apple (unless organinc). Remove the top of the carrot, if it's still attached.
	2 Halve or quarter the produce in order to fit it into your juicer and process.
	3 Drink immediately.

Per 1-cup serving: *Calories 199 (From Fat 11); Fat 1g (Saturated 0g); Cholesterol 0mg; Sodium 77mg; Carbohydrates 49g (Dietary Fiber 2g); Protein 3g.*

Note: This juice is for grownups only, because detoxing isn't recommended for children unless it's done under a doctor's care, and cilantro is a serious detox herb.

Perfect Start Juice

Prep time: 5 min • **Yield:** 1 serving

Ingredients	Directions
3 carrots 1 cucumber	**1** Wash the carrots and cucumber. Trim tops of carrots, if desired.
	2 Halve or quarter the produce in order to fit it into your juicer and process.
	3 Drink immediately.

Per 1-cup serving: Calories 129 (From Fat 3); Fat 0g (Saturated 0g); Cholesterol 0mg; Sodium 124mg; Carbohydrates 29g (Dietary Fiber 2g); Protein 4g.

Super-Charged Juice

Prep time: 5 min • **Yield:** 1 serving

Ingredients	Directions
1 lemon 1 apple ¼ head red cabbage ½ large fennel bulb	**1** Wash all ingredients. Peel the lemon and the apple (unless organic).
	2 Halve or quarter the fruit in order to fit it into your juicer and process.
	3 Drink immediately.

Per 1-cup serving: Calories 159 (From Fat 9); Fat 1g (Saturated 0g); Cholesterol 0mg; Sodium 77mg; Carbohydrates 40g (Dietary Fiber 2g); Protein 4g.

Vary It! Keep the peel on the lemon, if desired.

Best Spring Juice

Prep time: 5 min • **Yield:** 1 serving

Ingredients	*Directions*
8 stalks of asparagus **2 apples**	*1* Wash all ingredients. Peel the orange and the apples (unless organic).
1-inch bunch of wheatgrass **1 orange**	*2* Halve or quarter the produce in order to fit it into your juicer and process.
	3 Drink immediately.

Per 1-cup serving: *Calories 236 (From Fat 13); Fat 1g (Saturated 0g); Cholesterol 0mg; Sodium 14mg; Carbohydrates 57g (Dietary Fiber 3g); Protein 5g.*

Note: Not all juicers can handle wheatgrass. Check your owner's manual before attempting this recipe.

Tip: Drink this juice in spring, when the asparagus is in season.

Index

Notes